TERRITORIAL URBANISM NOW

TERRITORIAL URBANISM NOW!
CALL FOR A SOCIAL AND ECOLOGICAL
URBAN PLANNING AND DESIGN

INSTITUTE OF URBANISM: AGLAÉE DEGROS / EVA SCHWAB /
ANNA BAGARIĆ / SABINE BAUER / JENNIFER FAUSTER /
RADOSTINA RADULOVA-STAHMER /
MARIO STEFAN / ALICE STEINER (EDS.)

jovis

Territorial Urbanism Now!

Aglaée Degros

August 2023, With help of the notes taken during the symposium by Rahel Győrffy

"The world is on fire" (The Straits Time, 2020, 0:19). These were the words with which Gary Hildebrand opened the 2022 academic year at the Harvard Graduate School of Design. Global warming, melting ice caps, forest fires, floods and droughts, the migratory crisis, the energy crisis—what can we urban designers and planners do about it?

It's time to face up to our responsibilities and to question our planning routines and how they contribute to the combustion of the world through our current practices of transforming the environment.

Anthropocene urbanism is based on the spatialization of built growth, which goes hand in hand with an enormous consumption of resources (materials, energy, water, soil, etcetera). But these resources are finite and the impact of our influence on planet Earth is becoming more evident, with observable effects. In 2022, the International Architecture Biennale Rotterdam hosted an urbanism event entitled IT'S ABOUT TIME, celebrating the 50th anniversary of the publication of *The Limits to Growth* in 1972. In this report, the Club of Rome—a diverse assembly of academics, scientists, politicians, diplomats, and industrialists—outlined the potential outcomes of a steep rise in population, agricultural production, resource extraction, industrial output, pollution, and biodiversity decline. The publication sparked global attention, heralding the beginning of a heightened environmental consciousness (IABR, 2022).

And yet built growth is still occurring at the expense of our natural environment. In Austria, a total of 5,368 hectares of fields, meadows, pastures, and vineyards were built on in 2022, a space equivalent to the entire province of Burgenland (Greenpeace, 2023). In Germany, around 45% of residential and traffic areas are currently "sealed," i.e., built on, concreted, or paved over. Important soil functions, such as water permeability and soil fertility, are thus lost as a result of our excessive spatial consumption (Umweltbundesamt, 2023). Paradoxically, since these natural capabilities have the potential to mitigate many of the consequences of anthropogenic climate change, reducing them is twice as disastrous.

Many appeals to curb climate change have been made that we cannot ignore: from the scientific community (IPCC, 2022), from activist groups (Fridays For Future, Last Generation, Extinction Rebellion, etcetera) as well as committed citizens. On 9 April, 2024, the European Court of Human Rights ruled in favor of a complaint a group of elderly Swiss women had lodged (KlimaSeniorinnen Schweiz, 2024). The Climate Seniors consider that the risk taken by the Swiss Confederation in not currently pursuing the objective of limiting the rise in temperature to 2°C is inadmissible. In their view, the Confederation is not doing enough to fulfil its duty to protect its citizens. "We are complaining because everything we hold dear is at stake. Global warming is making people sick. We, the elderly, are among them. What's more, we must act today to protect our descendants from even more serious consequences." (KlimaSeniorinnen Schweiz, 2023) Also, in a ground-breaking legal decision, a Montana judge ruled in favor of young people who had accused state officials of violating their constitutional rights by promoting fossil fuels. In a court order, Judge Kathy Seeley of the 1st District Court, affirmed the plaintiffs' claim that a stable climate is included in a right to a "clean and healthful environment," guaranteed in the state's constitution (Noor, 2023).

We cannot ignore those calls. It's time, time to change now, the way we think about, organize, and develop our environment!

TERRITORIAL SHIFT

This disciplinary shift in urban planning and design is being instigated in the most innovative and radical way. This transformation has been galvanized not by spatial design but by a popular legislative initiative launched by Teresa Vicente, professor of Philosophy of Law at the University of Murcia. Targeting the Mar Menor, a site that has been under continual pressure from both residential building and agricultural production, this legislation represents a last chance for this ecosystem's recovery. The Spanish lagoon in southeastern Spain became a legal entity in 2022. Its new status, recognized by a vote in Parliament, should enable anyone to take legal action on its behalf.

Thus, the Mar Menor—a 170 square kilometer saltwater lagoon, situated in the autonomous region of Murcia in southeast Spain—etched its place in the Spanish and European legal framework on September 21, 2022. Consequently, it becomes a legal entity in the same way as an individual or corporation, enabling anyone to pursue legal recourse in its name (Ruiz, 2022).

By virtue of its new legal status, the lagoon and its surrounding territory has shifted from being an object to becoming a subject. This shift within our discipline has been advocated by Paola Viganò, who stands for a movement towards different values and ethics. Talking about turning points and redefining territory requires a clear understanding of the concept itself. Viganò refers to its use in a Latin American context.

In the 1990s, "territorial" primarily referred to the reclaiming of land by populations previously deprived of their territory, particularly in Latin America. Geographers used the term to support practices aimed at returning land to specific communities. So it was, in a sense, a process of privatization, an aspect it also faced criticism for (Viganò, 2022).

Bruno Latour, meanwhile, provides a renewed definition of territory as a set of elements that allow us to subsist, distinguishing it from the previously used definition of geo-political entity: "what it needs for its subsistence, and consequently, what it is prepared to defend, if necessary with its own life. This applies to a wolf as much as to a bacterium, to a company as much as to a forest, to a deity as much as to a family. What needs to be documented are the properties of a land—in every sense of the word property—by which it is possessed and on which it depends" (Latour, 2021).

As he elaborates, territory, as interpreted here, doesn't denote an administrative or geographical entity. Instead, it signifies a dynamic network comprising agents and activities, encompassing configurations that traverse all spatial and temporal scales (Latour, 2021). Territorial Urbanism is thus a movement (as it takes the *-ism* form) grounded in this notion of territory—the substantive is transformed, in this case, into an adjective. In other words, the elements or systems that sustain the living qualify the movement.

COLLECTIVE RESPONSIBILITY

Territorial Urbanism is becoming a kind of urbanism in reverse, where priority is given to what has been neglected by Anthropocene urbanism. It gives priority to systems and elements: green and blue ecological continuities, watersheds, soil valorization, active and collective mobility, etcetera. Previously housed in residual spaces, these systems are becoming structuring elements. The *Ruimte voor de rivier* [Room for the River] program in the Netherlands is an illustration of this current mindset. While the tradition in the Netherlands since modern times has been to reclaim land from the sea, this huge project returns space to the Maas River, in order to prevent flooding by ensuring that the river's fluctuations follow a more natural course. In Nijmegen, for example, the space given over to the river is so wide that the different arms have made it possible to create a partly inhabited island. The new watershed is both the result of careful planning and the return of space to the vegetal world. It's the XXL version of Gilles Clément's *The Garden in Movement*: long before ecological concerns became omnipresent, this landscape architect defended the idea that we should let plants transform space, identifying microclimates and spaces in order to see how they work. "If we start from the principle that diversity is at risk, we need to protect it. Perhaps we can amplify it in a garden" (Clément, 2017). Unlike the garden, this rivershed, which is not manmade, is left to the species that inhabit it.

Territorial Urbanism requires a different mindset, with an emphasis on natural space and ecological continuity. Today, it is no longer a question of safeguarding the wilderness, as Henry Thoreau did in America in reaction to the Industrial Revolution. Instead, as the geographer Estienne Rodary (2016) advocates, we need to develop "a policy of connectivity." He argues that the temptation to preserve "enclaves of nature" is ecologically and socially incompatible with our times. In short, Territorial Urbanism does not act *on* nature, but *with* it: it's not a question of protecting it from a distance but of being responsible in our day-to-day actions (Vincent, 2020).

This approach requires not only collaboration with different disciplines, as seen in Clément's *Garden* (design, agronomy, horticulture, etcetera), but also collaboration between many operational instances of decision-making and action (since the scale of a river crosses all those levels), as well as the close involvement of citizens whose relationship with the environment has been profoundly transformed. Living behind the defense of certainty (a relative certainty that is underestimated in the light of climate change) provided by a dyke is entirely different from living along a flexible and unpredictable zone that is subject to the flux of the weather, sometimes wet, sometimes dry. A collective goal (involving different disciplines, actors, decision makers and citizens) is being pursued. The climate challenge cannot be met at plot level by the individual, only at the level of the common space by the community if we aim for inclusivity. This approach to the climate challenge is similar to the spirit of Paris's new *plan local d'urbanisme* (PLU). The plan aims to symbolically ban air-condition-ing units and considers that the fight against rising temperatures is a collective problem that must be resolved on a city-wide scale. It also devotes a great deal of attention to planting the city. By 2040, there should be around 10 square meters of green space for every Parisian, as recommended by the World Health Organization (currently 5.8 square meters). Green continuities are planned: a 25-hectare urban park will be created in the north of Paris. Ten new parks will be spread across the city. Massive trees will be planted along the ring road (Mairie de Paris, 2023).

BUILT HABITAT

What does it mean for the built environment if it is no longer a structuring element? It becomes subordinate to the continuity resulting from the ecological logic of the territory. Developing the city therefore no longer means building growth, but rather improving the quality of the space between the city's existing stock of buildings. If the growth of the built environment is dissociated from wider urban transformation, then the built environment is, in a sense, freed from its role as the driving force behind urban transformation. In response to Rodary, who considers the national parks inherited from the colonial period to be "wild spaces inhabited by social spaces," Territorial Urbanism considers cities to be "social spaces inhabited by wild spaces." At the same time, it aims to mitigate the dualism between the human and the non-human. It is not necessary to create a new district to improve the city, but rather to create missing green links, to develop collective and active mobility that frees up collective space, and enhance the watersheds. We need to look at the urban soil: where the tree roots communicate with each other, the microclimate of wasteland. These are seemingly trivial gestures whose multiplication could in fact change our mindset.

In this approach to urbanism, there is a shift in the way the built environment is considered. The strategy of maintaining the natural habitat begins by rejecting new buildings as object of speculation, instead reusing existing buildings or developing new buildings in a frugal way. This refusal to build is taken up by Stefan Rettich, who questions the link between urban development and growth (Rettich, 2022). In addition, he introduces the notion of urban obsolescence, which shapes urbanization and development or, more precisely, transformation. In this model of thinking about urban vacancies, typological obsolescence has always been influential in the transformation of cities, since vacancies can be understood as the release of free urban space with immensely high reuse potential. Urban obsolescence could prove to be a remedy for the issue of land consumption, since a new circularity could be established through adaptive reuse. This obviously requires the development of new sustainable functions for entire typologies, and not just the sporadic adaptive reuse of individual buildings (hence the terminology of typological obsolescence as a potential for urban renewal). An illustration of this approach can be found in the work of Magic Sun, a landscape design student at Harvard GSD, who proposed that a former steelworks site in Luxembourg should not be transformed into a new housing disctrict. Instead, her project proposed transforming an industrial wasteland into a manufacturing site for renovation products made from recycled materials. These products will be used for the necessary (energy) renovation and downsizing of the existing building stock surrounding the site. Rather than constructing new buildings, the project proposes a renovation and reallocation carried out in cocreation with local residents. Meanwhile the site itself will become an industrial landscape combining pastoral industrial condition and ecology (see studio on Decarb Lux, 2022).

Another avenue in the new relationship between urban development and the built environment, which concerns construction rather than reuse, is to approach through a much less dualistic relationship between nature and buildings. In a way, this marks a return to the original concept of territorialism used in Latin America in the 1990s, where anthropocentrism is replaced by ecocentrism—it is less a question of protecting but of limiting the use of resources through ethical and legal limits (Viganó, 2022).

Elsewhere, the architect Susanne Eliasson proposes the Garden Metropolis as a take on the built environment, which allows new buildings but calls for a greater awareness of our environment's limited resources. The Garden Metropolis recognizes and emphasizes the urgency of the climate situation but believes that the idea of simply stopping construction is counterproductive. In Eliasson's view, doing so simplifies a complex issue and breeds confusion: according to human nature, there must always be a certain degree of development. So, rather than stop building, we should stop all building on undeveloped sites and slow down new construction completely.

She proposes a vision of building that accommodates frugal growth, and invites us to reconsider the balance between nature, mutualization, and the individual. This is a concept which, although it generally refers to urban models based on horizontality (often linked to sprawl), addresses the issue of the spatialization of density (Eliasson, 2022). It is also a counter proposal since it seems that the buildings developed as part of this green continuity are often borrowed from the high-density slab typology. It is as if the architecture generated by green continuity could only translate density into modern forms—advantageous for their vertical standardization, but far removed from current ways of living. In this case, the question for architects to consider is how to densify without building towers or slabs. Instead, we need to look towards alternative models of densification that respond to the need for housing but also enhance ecological connectivity (unlike the indefinite green space of modern public development). In the course of history, such models have of course been developed (Lyppens, 2022). Perhaps all we need to do is rediscover these experiments, like the fifty-nine apartments in three buildings by the architect Alfred Beadle in Phoenix—to which Eliasson refers—or, as [Glen] Lyppens proposes, the Beacon Hill district in Boston, the only topography that is respected in the city. These examples have their roots in the fringes of urbanism but are also instances of how private property can be combined with mutualization and not confused with the exclusive right to express individual freedom. Density calculations reflect a balance between land use, quality of life, and the natural environment rather than being a calculation of the property value of a plot of land.The time for visionless market-led architecture and urbanism is over—it is essential to not confuse growth with quality of life and to no longer respond to the market but to anticipate changes within it (Meyer, Wagner, 2022). The built environment must be much more an inhabited territory than a speculative one.

If we want to survive the post-fossil energy society and avoid capitulating to techno-solutionism, then now is the time to enhance an urbanism based on natural continuity, mutualization, and the prioritization of frugal use of resources... The window for action is small but full of opportunity! (Smets, 2022).

CHARTIER, D. and RODARY, E. (2016) *Manifeste pour une géographie environnementale*. Paris: Presses de Sciences Po.

CLÉMENT, G. (2017) *Le jardin en mouvement*. Paris: Sens et Tonka.

ELIASSON, S. (2022) 'How to design the Territory? Garden Metropolis [Keynote],' Territorial Turn: Towards just, ecological and collaborative urbanism. University of Technology Graz, September 15th.

GREENPEACE (2022) *Bodenversiegelung in Österreich*. Available at: https://greenpeace.at/hintergrund/bodenversiegelung-in-oesterreich/

INTERNATIONAL ARCHITECTURE BIENNALE ROTTERDAM (2022) *About*. Available at: https://www.architecturebiennalerotterdam2022.nl/en/about/theme

KLIMASENIORINNEN SCHWEIZ (2024) Climate action. Available at: https://en.klimaseniorinnen.ch/

LATOUR, B. (2021) *Où suis-je? Leçons du confinement à l'usage des terrestres*. Paris: Empecheurs.

LYPPENS, G. (2022) *Robuuste Collectieve Tussenruimte: En onderzoek naar de relatie tussen architectonische en territorial ruimte in stedelijke woningclusters*. Antwerp: Universiteit Antwerpen.

MAIRIE DE PARIS (2023) 'Le Plan local d'urbanisme.' Available at: http:// pluenligne.paris.fr/plu/sites-plu/site_statique_55/pages/page_1175.html

MEYER, H. and WAGNER, A. (2022) 'How to deal with transformation.' Discussion with Radostina Radulova-Stahmer, Stefan Rettich, Maik Novotny and Anna-Maria Jäger, *Territorial Turn: Towards just, ecological and collaborative urbanism*. University of Technology Graz, 15 September.

NOOR, D. (2023) 'Montana's landmark climate ruling: three key takeaways,' *The Guardian*, 20 August. Available at: https://www.theguardian.com/us-news/2023/aug/20/what-happened-montana-climate-trial-decision

RETTICH, S. (2022) 'Green Sofa Stefan Rettich.' Interview with Institute of Urbanism, University of Technology Graz, 15 September.

RUIZ, M. (2022) 'Teresa Vicente: "Aprobar la ILP del Mar Menor ha sido como subir el Everst"' *La Verdad*, 29 September. Available at: https://www.laverdad.es/lospiesenlatierra/noticias/teresa-vicente-aprobar-20220921185226-nt.html

SMETS, M. (2022) 'Closing Plenary.' Discussion with Aglaée Degros, Paola Viganó, Han Meyer, Judith Schwentner, Christine Braunersreuther, Bertram Werle, and Günter Riegler, *Territorial Turn: Towards just, ecological and collaborative urbanism*. University of Technology Graz, 16 September.

THE STRAITS TIME (2020) '"The world is on fire," Greta Thunberg tells British climate rally.' 29 February. Available at: https://www.youtube.com/watch?v=6I5MafKxqHg

UMWELTBUNDESAMT (2023) *Bodenversiegelung*. Available at: https://www.umweltbundesamt.de/daten/flaeche-boden-land-oekosysteme/boden/bodenversiegelung#was-ist-bodenversiegelung

VIGANÓ, P. (2022) 'How to shift to a territorial vision?' [Keynote], *Territorial Turn: Towards just, ecological and collaborative urbanism*. University of Technology Graz, 16 September.

VINCENT, P. (2020) 'Cohabiter avec tous les vivants,' *Le Monde*, 25 July. Available at: https://www.lemonde.fr/series-d-ete/article/2020/07/25/cohabiter-avec-tous-les-vivants_6047239_3451060.html

Space, Life, and Design

Paola Viganò

This text is a light revision of the keynote lecture delivered at the Territorial Turn Symposium in Graz.

How is it possible to adapt the complex discipline of urban and territorial design at both the conceptual and ethical level? My sense is that the socio-ecological transition has at least two implications for territorial and urban design. The first implication concerns the epistemological dimension of design, its capacity to produce new and original knowledge; the second heads towards the ontological dimension. Between these two stands the complex relationship between the current building culture forged in modern times and an emerging "culture of transition," based on the rarefaction of resources and the adaptation of what is already there. My hypothesis is twofold: that we need to construct a new gaze in order to cope with the extensive conceptual redefinitions this transition demands; and that it is necessary to dig into fundamental societal and ecological questions in order to shift towards different ethics and values.

A NEW GAZE: THE EPISTEMOLOGICAL BASIS OF THE TRANSITION

The direction of our gaze in the present is often oriented towards imagining the future; it integrates images, expectations, and desires. In the framework of a "territorial turn," urbanists, urban and territorial planners should discuss the epistemological nature of design in an age of radical transformation. Starting from a close territorial reading, following an approach that deconstructs and reconstructs the complexity of contemporary extended urbanization, I consider how research developed with designers' tools can generate an original and situated knowledge (Viganò, 2016). Furthermore, I argue that there is an urgent need for a new "epistemology of design"—since nothing is as before—capable of reacting to the current marginalization of the discipline's activities and operations.[1]

Collective and individual imagery flow along lines that are undoubtedly different today from those of the past. Conceptual and operational redefinition is now required to reconsider how design produces mental and concrete urban spaces. Adaptation to climate change, for example, is rapidly and drastically altering both the traditional and modern urban grammar and syntax, as well as social uses and practices. The emerging culture of the socio-ecological transition distances itself from traditional or modern *Baukultur*, which often appears inconsistent within the current conditions.

1 In *Territories of Urbanism: The Project as Knowledge Producer* (2016), I tried to understand how design describes and how, by design, we produce concepts or develop scenarios, visions, new imaginaries, and explore the future time.

When the idea of a "territorial turn" emerged in the 1990s, it referred to a process of appropriation by populations that had been deprived of their own territory. The term was much used by geographers in the Latin American context, from the perspective of giving land back to Indigenous populations. At that time, "territorial turn" mainly referred to the restitution of land, or the re-territorialization of a people. This re-appropriation of the land, however, whether occurring in spontaneous or institutional frameworks, concealed a privatization process, often establishing new enclosures, critiques of which were also developed. The notion of territory thus proved to be somewhat Janus-faced, the prospect of inclusion always accompanied by the risk of generating new exclusions.

Today, I believe, the term "territorial turn" can be reformulated, and should deal primarily with the construction of the *territorial subject*, exploring subjectification and its implicit or explicit process of definition. André Corboz wrote about the "territory as a subject," highlighting its function as a recipient of the discourses and intentions we project onto it (Corboz, 1983). But the "territory subject" I would like to discuss today is more than a recipient; rather it is an individual, with specific characteristics and rationalities.

It has a name or many names, it expresses logics, and it contains more than our imaginaries. We do not even need to enter the "deep ecology" perspective, which considers all living and non-living entities as peers. If the territory is a subject, then we can investigate its rationalities, try to understand its behaviors. And this is, in my opinion, the fundamental trait of a territorial turn where the focus is on the transformation of the territory—from object, resource, support—into a subject: on its becoming, as defined by this shift.

However, we must firstly recognize that the territory has been modified and reformed according to human needs. Today, it is mainly a territorial machine that has been subjected to multiple logics, adapted through the "rationalization" of consecutive human interventions. A map of the Boston metropolitan area demonstrates how the logistics of water and water distribution in the different communities have created different conditions of access to fresh water, with obvious consequences for environmental and spatial justice [01]. The territory has been transformed and manipulated. Again, in the Boston area, the coexistence of forests and metropolitan suburbs creates an extremely hybrid urban condition: the forest acts as a soft control system, it can easily define enclaves and isolated sites for selected coexistence alongside similar groups.

The forest, the water, the ponds .... Together, they comprise a certain type of ecology and, at the same time, a specific metropolitan space. Other maps make the effort to represent the different inhabitants of a "territory subject" through the complexity—both geological and morphological—of various species and living bodies inhabiting and sharing the same space. These attempts to represent the "territory subject" are only at their beginning, but they are of great importance in understanding how the territory is the sum (physical, natural, infrastructural, political) of different and multiple lives/subjects; all its entities and dimensions bring their respective logics and rationalities along with them.

Projects that are able to describe such complexity are acutely important today, as an expression of the ongoing adjustment of our gaze; they reflect this shift by selecting relevant paths within the heterogeneous, sometimes contradictory mix of superposed rationalities, collective expectations, and priorities.

THE ONTOLOGICAL BASIS OF THE TRANSITION

However, this epistemological shift alone is not enough. The "territory subject", for example, requires exploring value systems that do not coincide with our current ones. The ontological basis of the transition is hard to avoid. At the foundation of any paradigm shift is a need to investigate the nature of things, to subvert the idea of the territory as a resource to exploit—as a support to rely on, or an object offering services, with no individuality of its own.

The deep ontological implication of the socio-ecological transition, however, is the renewed proximity between different forms of space and organic life, and how they interact with different forms of power. The delicacy of this rapprochement reinforces the need to debate it, to envision it and, in so doing, open ourselves up to broad and deep value negotiations. Counterspaces are crucial to systematically analyze, discuss, and practice the set of paradigm shifts required by the transition: territorial design can develop meaningful and alternative visions where such a shift can be imagined and evaluated.

Our gaze needs to be re-centered to focus on the territorial constructions we call "cities", "metropolises", "villages", a "horizontal metropolis," (**Viganò, Cavalieri, and Barcelloni Corte, 2018; Cavalieri and Viganò, 2020; Barcelloni Corte and Viganò, 2022**). We have explored these constructions across several design and research-by-design projects, addressing the functional, cultural, and spatial characteristics of the contemporary urban condition, and its variety of urban and territorial figures. Comparing an 18th-century map of the Flemish territory to present day urbanization reveals the inertia of territorial structures after centuries of change—the construction of a new harbor in Ghent, for example, with the old village situated in the middle of large industrial plants and their logistical frameworks. The fragmented, heterogeneous, persistent character of diffuse urbanization still needs to be understood in its qualities and limitations, in its structures and ecological potentials.

The horizontal metropolis, however, is not only an analytical tool with which to describe the contemporary city. It proposes a vision or, perhaps better, develops a counter project that criticizes vertical (hierarchical) territorial organizations and makes use of space to strengthen horizontal relationships. It works on micro-infrastructures and on the coexistence of their different rationalities: learning from hybrid spaces and from heterogeneous ecologies and diffuse urban conditions. It is a counter project because it consciously leaves aside the mainstream conceptual frame of concentration and hierarchization. Instead, it advocates a balanced, distributed, and decentralized project designed to revive territories that have been marginalized and forgotten in the last decades. This means abandoning the mental construct that characterizes our contemporary ideas of urbanism and territorial design, wherein hierarchy is the most familiar and only principle of order. Other principles might not imply the same type of pyramid. This horizontal vision works *against* the extreme specialization of space, *against* the creation of centers and peripheries—I insist on this point, because centers and peripheries are fabricated and not natural conditions—as well as nurturing spatial hybrids, alongside developing forms of accessibility and integration. The fundamental point of this approach is to work on spatial configurations that can boost horizontal relationships: between territories and populations, between the "Other" and us. It is a project of emancipation relying on space—or counter space, in fact—that is intellectually and pragmatically necessary, particularly when mainstream research and methodologies exclude themes that are empirically recognized as being relevant, such as relationships across space and species.

The book trilogy on the *Horizontal Metropolis*, finally published in its entirety, contains the main aspects developed in the research: from the first symposium, placing the horizontal metropolis inside the debate "between urbanism and urbanization" (**Viganò, Cavalieri, and Barcelloni Corte, 2018**), to the numerous design experiences contained in the second book (**Cavalieri and Viganò, 2020**). The latter,

[01] Territorialism, metropolitan area of Boston. Map of the evolution of aqueducts.
© Phoebe White, GSD, 2012

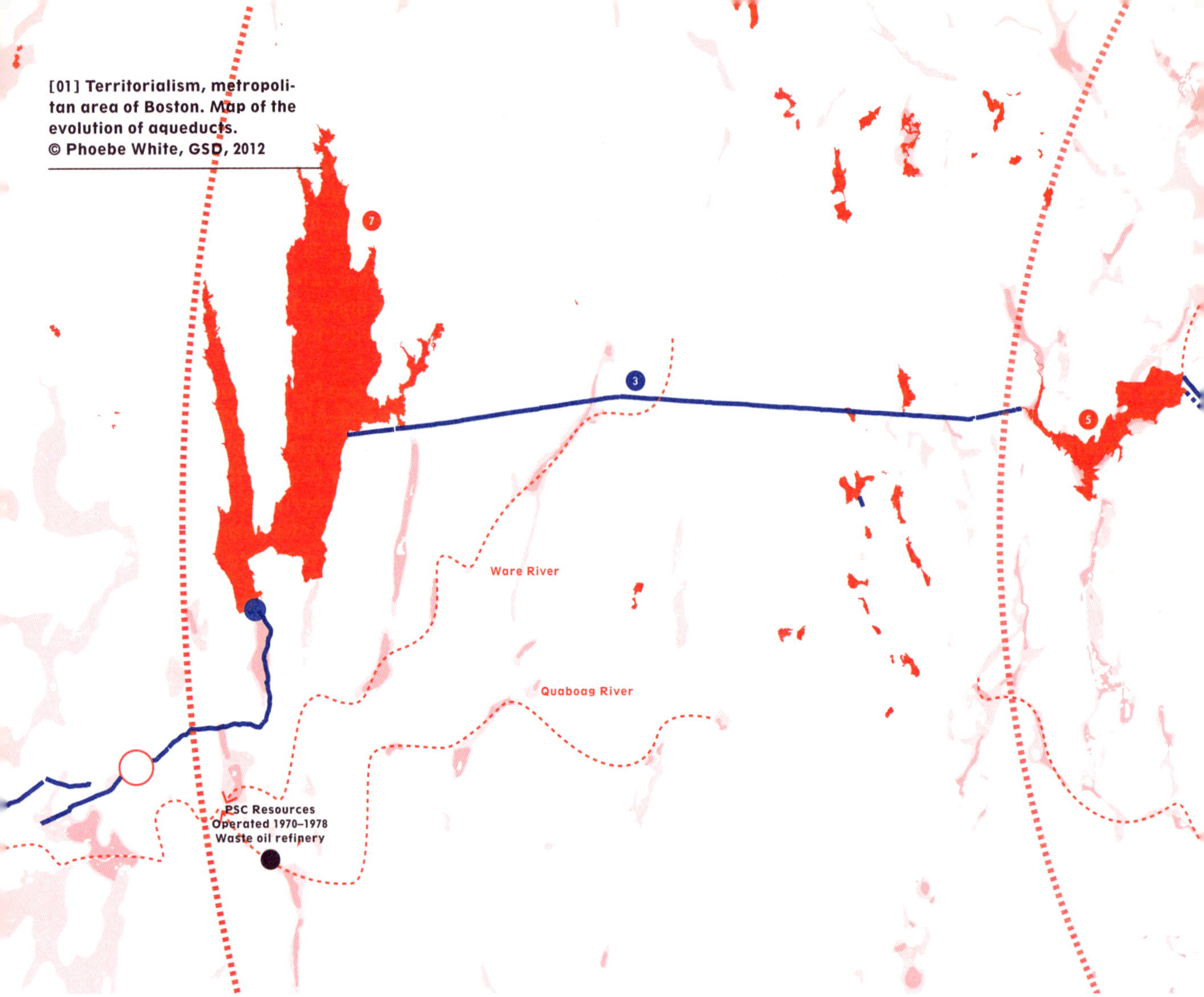

INDUSTRIES

1 **MATERIALS TECHNOLOGY LAB**
Operated 1816–1988
Ammunition production, nuclear research
PAHs and PCBs found in soils

2 **NAVAL WEAPONS INDUSTRIAL RESERVE PLANT**
Operated 1852–1984
Missile development
VOCs found in groundwater, heavy metals found in soils

3 **INDUSTRI-PLEX**
Operated 1853–1980
Glue manufacturing and paper industrial products
VOCs found in groundwater, heavy metals found in soils

4 **FORT DEVENS**
Operated 1917–1996
Military training ground
Arsenic, sadmium, lead, and mercury found in groundwater

5 **NYANZA CHEMICAL WASTE DUMP**
Operated 1917–1978
Textile dyes
Mercury and heavy metals found in groundwater, soil, sediments, surface water, chemicals discharged to Sudbury River

6 **HOCOMONCO POND**
Operated 1928–1946
Wood treating operation
Creosote found in soils, sediments, groundwater

7 **FORT DEVENS TRAINING ANNEX**
Operated 1942–present
Ammunition depot, lab disposal area VOCs, pesticides found in groundwater

RESERVOIRS

1 Cochituate Reservoir
1848

2 Framingham Reservoirs 1 & 2
1875

3 Sudbury Reservoir
1878

4 Cambridge Reservoir
1894

5 Wachusett Reservoir
1894

6 Norumbega Reservoir
1926

AQUEDUCTS

1 Sudbury Aqueduct
1875

2 Wachusett and Weston Aqueduct
1897

3 Quabbin Aqueducts Part 1 & 2
1926–1930

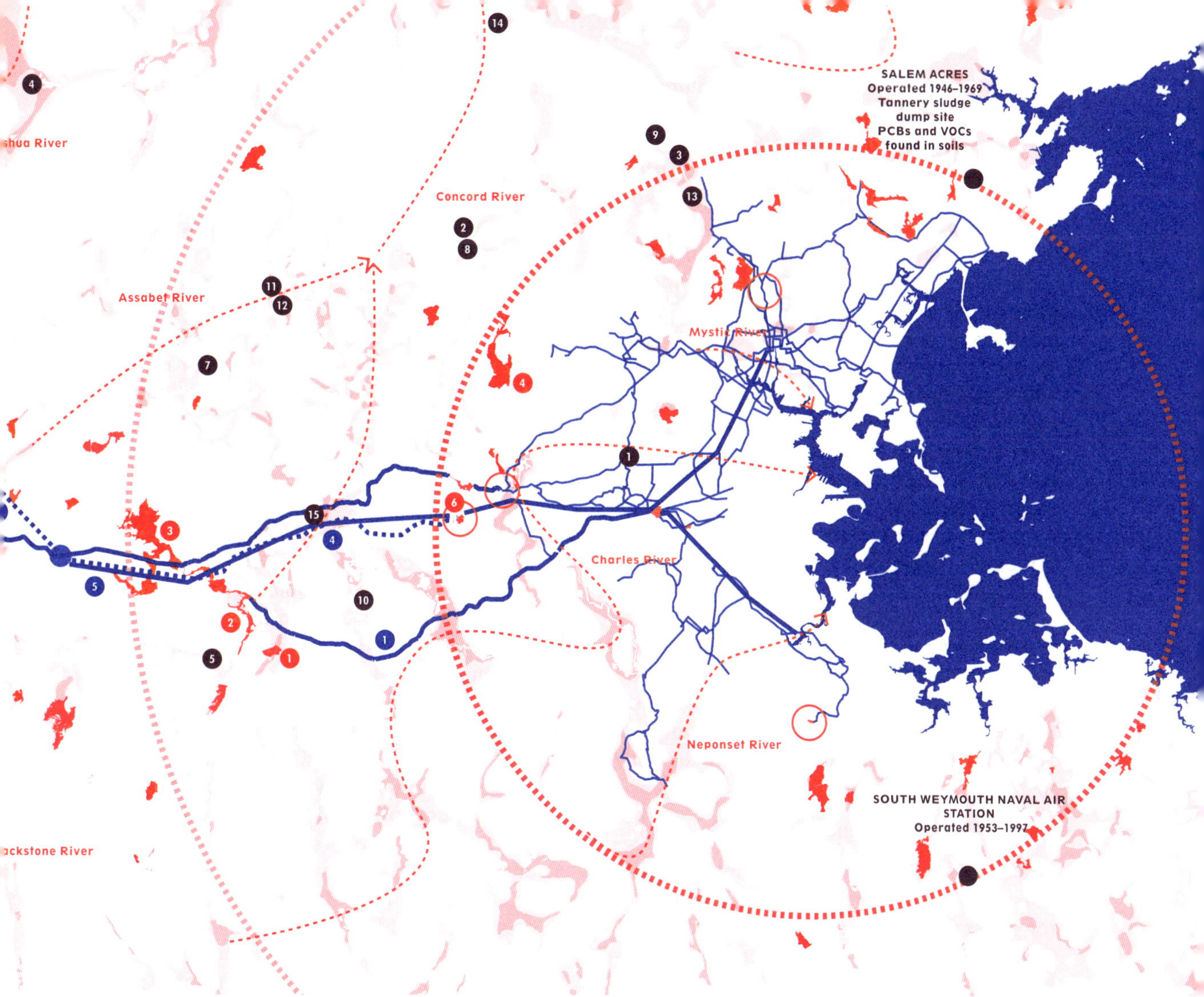

8
HANSCOM AIR FORCE BASE
Operated 1942–1973
Fire training
VOCs, chlorinated solvents, jet fuel found in groundwater and soils

9
OLIN CHEMICAL
Operated 1953–1986
Reclaimed chemical for plastics industry
Ammonia, chloride, NDMA found in groundwater, acetone found in soils

10
MATERIALS TECHNOLOGY LAB
Operated 1954–present
Textile research, aero-mechanical production
VOCs, heavy metals found in soils and groundwater

11
W.R. GRACE & CO.
Operated 1954–1980
Produced sealant products
VDCs and VOCs found in groundwater and sludge found in soils

12
NUCLEAR METALS, INC.
Operated 1958–1997
Produced depleted uranium products
VOCs and radioactive material found in groundwater and soils

13
WELLS & H
Operated 1964–1967
Public supply of water wells sited near abandoned contamination
VOCs found in groundwater, heavy metals found in soils and river

14
SILRESIM CHEMICAL CORP.
Operated 1971–1977
Reclaimed chemical wastes, solvents and sludges
Heavy metals and VOCs found in groundwater and soils

15
US AIR FORCE, FOSTER-MILLER, NORTHEAST SAND AND GRAVEL
Operated 1985–2005
Runway quick-fix
PCBs and VOCs found in soils and groundwater

7
Quabbin Reservoir
1930

4
Hultman Aqueduct
1936

5
MetroWest Tunnel
1996

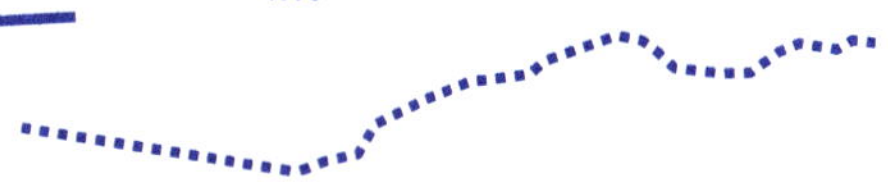

led by students in extended metropolitan conditions across different continents, tests the possibility of a just, balanced ecological and social transition. Finally, the third book, the *Anthology*, contains an amazing selection of texts; some of these anticipate a new urban condition which can be traced back as early as the 18th century, through critical responses to the assumed utopianism of the "traditional", hierarchical city or centralized territory **(Barcelloni Corte and Viganò, 2022)**. These three moments of reflection, together with the recent conclusion and publication of two doctoral dissertations **(Pietropolli, 2023; Zhang, 2023)**, are the output of a long and intense research project. These materials are now available for discussion, criticism, and enhancement. The horizontal metropolis questions how design can work effectively to reinforce nonhierarchical interactions, reconstructing a long history of thoughts and highlighting a "minor position line" that runs parallel to the main traditional urbanistic project.

To enrich and reinforce the idea of a territorial turn, the twin hypotheses of the "territory subject" and "horizontal metropolis" can embody this important shift, which has not yet entered common or shared understanding.

Greater Geneva

The territory where we initially implemented these concepts—after testing them in the vision for Brussels 2040 **(Secchi and Viganò, 2010)**—was Greater Geneva. I will only mention this briefly here, as Tommaso Pietropolli deals with this case of vision construction in his contribution to this book. The two lenses we proposed were "soil and labor"—through a series of scenarios concerning soil regeneration, work transformation, and the exploration of spatio- and socio-ecological prototypes. One of them **[02]**, the metropolitan infrastructure of socio-ecological continuity, deserves further examination—being both the first and main prototype of *weak structures* **(Vattimo, 1985)** we envisaged in Greater Geneva. The idea of the "weak structure" reveals a layer of subjugated entities within an already-existing territory: marginalized or forgotten subjects, fragile elements of the population, "weaker" territories with respect to stronger ones. By working on weak structures, social and environmental fragilities can be integrated. Weakness is a perspective and a device through which a different and more resilient design perspective can take place: regenerating the city, and reconstructing practices, tools, and positions. In the case of Greater Geneva, the weak structure of the territory is an opportunity for ecological, socio-political, and economic transformation: it is an experimental space of transition, a counter structure for the contemporary city territory. Due to its collective nature, this space represents the general interest: the common good **[02]**.

Stemming from the Greater Geneva vision, the idea of implementing a weak structure **[03]** embraces ecosystem services as well as social infrastructures. Following watercourses—including wetlands, or fragments of forest and agriculture—weak structures tend to stress ecological and functional continuity, crossing activity platforms and reactivating their relations with the rest of the territory, including villages or underused heritage and services. As such, this space can requalify and restructure the city of the 21st century **[03]**.

The weak structure is about *continuity* as a fundamental figure for the city of tomorrow **(Secchi, 2000)**: continuity of water supply, of biotic relations and climatic regulation; it is about the accessibility of places and the continuity of slow/active mobility; the assurance of wellbeing and health across different parts of the territory; the diffusion of biodiversity, together with the evolution of agriculture and its participation as a continuity factor. It is a federative project that includes social economy and the hundreds of villages that are part of Greater Geneva. It is one of the many attempts, as well, to design horizontality and represent it at the metropolitan scale **[04]**.

The weak structure responds to three fundamental ambitions: it is open to the radical alteration of the design perspective; it articulates the values of heterogeneity, coexistence, and marginality; it develops alternative eco-socio-spatial prototypes. It can help to shape a new substantial action, according to the biopolitical nature of the transition, grasping the importance of "life as a commons".

It is mainly composed of unbuilt areas: to consider the open space as a backbone of the urban system means "tak[ing] urbanism's position of weakness as its premise" **(Koolhaas, 1987)**.

Wallonia

To clarify what I mean by an ontological shift towards the "territory subject" and "horizontal metropolis", a few projects in the Walloon region (southern part of Belgium) can be useful references. Wallonia was the region where the Industrial Revolution took place in Belgium, starting from the mid-19th century through the exploitation of large coal strips. This territory is still facing a structural crisis and is currently undergoing transformation following decades of decline that have resulted in enormous social and ecological costs, including polluted areas extending for thousands of hectares and an increasingly fragile human capital. Its contemporary population—

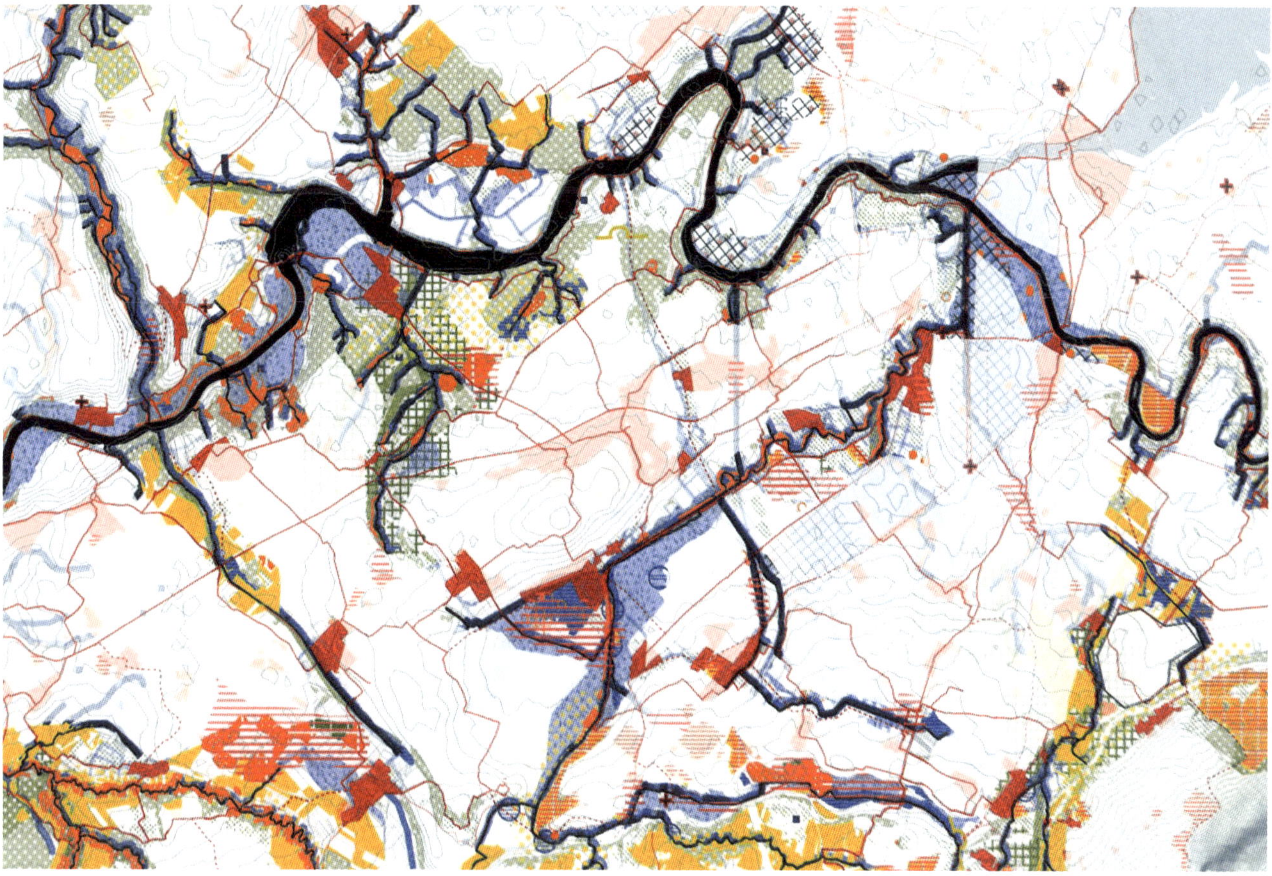

[03] Aire watershed: main territorial figures. © HRC/Lab-U: Paola Viganò, Elena Cogato Lanza, Tommaso Pietropolli

Synergic design between ecological continuity and soft mobility: spaces for wildlife and cohabitation.

- Integrating meadow fields into farming practices
- Integration of large fauna into recreational areas
- Support for the mobility of large fauna: agro-forestry areas
- Crossing of tracks by large animals
- Night-time regulation of light and vehicle speed
- Paths to raise awareness of the need to respect flora and fauna: projected
- Paths to raise awareness of the need to respect flora and fauna: existing
- Social nodes: villages and diffuse centralities
- Active mobility networks (cycling, walking): existing and planned
- Main drains
- Retention upstream of tributaries
- Re-naturation of a canalized or buried river
- River attention areas
- Flood storage areas
- Cleaning up wastewater treatment plants
- Re-injection of water into the water table using existing pipes
- Retention and filtration of polluted run-off water
- Regulation by wetlands

[02] Prospective visions for Greater Geneva, weak structures for the metropolis of the 21st century. © HRC/Lab-U: Paola Viganò, Elena Cogato Lanza, Tommaso Pietropolli

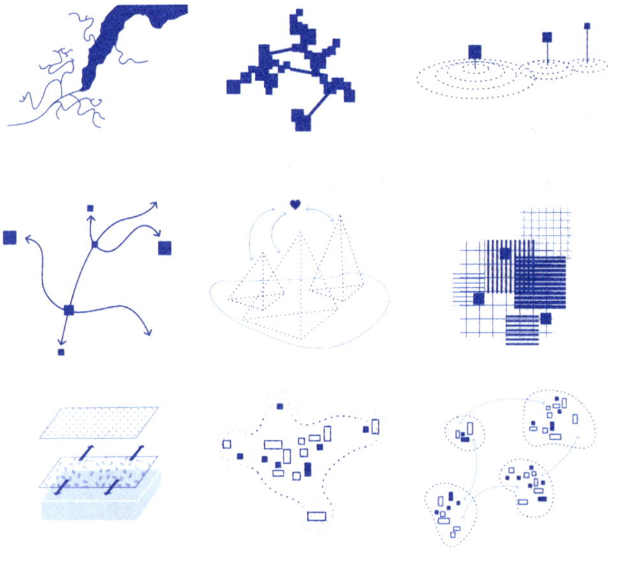

[04] Prospective visions for Greater Geneva, a metropolitan infrastructure of socio-ecological continuity. Nine declinations. © Habitat Research Center, EPFL with the students of the Design Studios BA 5-6, MA 1-2, SAR-IA

mainly descended from first-generation migrants who settled in the region at a time of industrial flourishing—are today alienated by the loss of regional manufacturing, "left over" in a post-industrial landscape shaped by exploitation. These crises remain unresolved, prompting crucial questions as to what urban and territorial design can do in a situation where deep social, ecological, and economic difficulties abound. Our projects deal with different scales, including urban regeneration projects as well as large territorial visions. In Herstal, close to Liège, an industrial site presents the opportunity to merge a program of new economies with large heritage brick buildings that have been reclaimed for reuse, also incorporating fragments of agriculture and forest [05].

In this tiny intermingling of mixed landscapes, a different image can (re)shape the presiding territorial values and innovative economies of molecules and pharmaceuticals produced out of plant cultivation in close relation with university research.

"Sambreville", meanwhile, is an in-between chain made up of small cities. An assemblage of small municipalities, collectively dubbed Sambreville in 1977, it comprises villages, large abandoned industrial areas, and workers' housing. The violet color of "industrial zone" on an outdated *plan de secteur* (zoning plan) still covers agricultural areas and a meander of the River Sambre. In regions where already urbanized and industrialized sites are available for reuse and where too many hectares of abandoned industrial space await new economies, still fertile areas cannot be lost. The inertia of rigid planning documents and ideas must be broken. The EU's ambition of "no net land take" by 2050 (namely, the attempt to reduce agricultural land consumption to zero) is a very important initiative, but it is not enough for the socio-ecological transition. Many choices and critical decisions in existing planning documents should be discarded; only then can a societal pact be reformulated.

The in-between is also urban. Sambreville is not just a patchwork of villages but, all together, forms a city of some 50,000 people. It is a scattered system connected by the river, teeming with large industrial areas awaiting the implementation of new programs. With hardly any market pressure, slow dynamics are required to transform it. This territory is not a *friche*, or fallow land, but a space of connectivity; it is not a wasteland, nor is it "available" land that can be squandered by dubious economic speculation [06]. Rather, it is a place to reuse, recondition, and recycle.

In La Louvière, one of the bigger and poorest cities in Wallonia, the vision outlined for the Val de Sambre evolves into three fundamental images for the future. First, there is an incredibly rich territory from the point of view of productivity and ecological quality. Let us call this space a "park," a term that gives an idea of its value. The "park" is defined by a chain of sequences: among them are the river and the wetlands (yet to be renaturalized) as well as the remaining industrial buildings and working-class housing, which represent a specific heritage—a testimony of how we can live collectively. In this vision, the canals (whose primary function has historically been industrial transport) emerge as works of art, while the *terrils* (slag heaps) form part of a new landscape and ecology that grew out of coal extraction. Secondly, it is a "city made of villages", not unlike the metropolis of villages recognized in Greater Geneva. The "constellations" of small settlements produce specific "civic figures" and, together, they construct different types of civic configurations. The design of everyday spaces—paths to school, the reduction of parking areas to accommodate new shops, a public transport stop designed for passengers to wait, sit, and chat—can reintroduce the civic dimension where, nowadays, there are only dormitories. The strengthening of residential economies, as well as experiential and social economies—not only the traditional industrial economy, or the more recent financial and tertiary economy—benefits from the very presence of the people inhabiting those areas. The multiplication of different types of economies unfolds in what remains of a post-

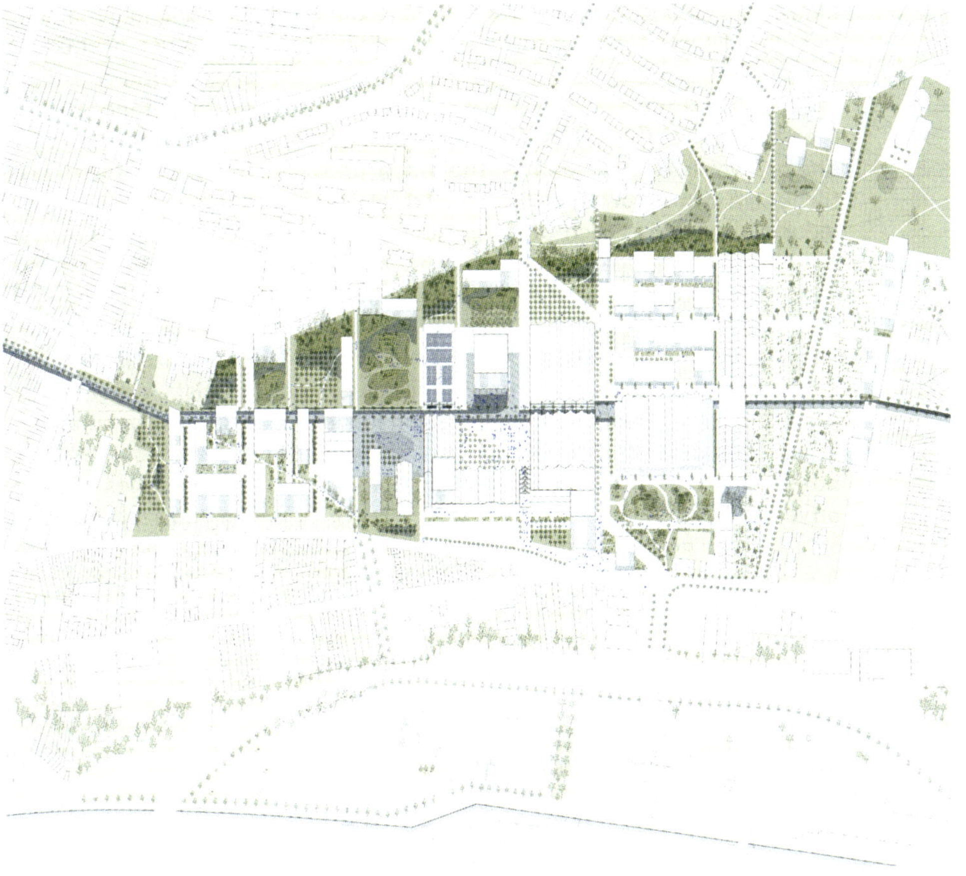

[05] Redevelopment of the ACEC site. © StudioPaolaViganò

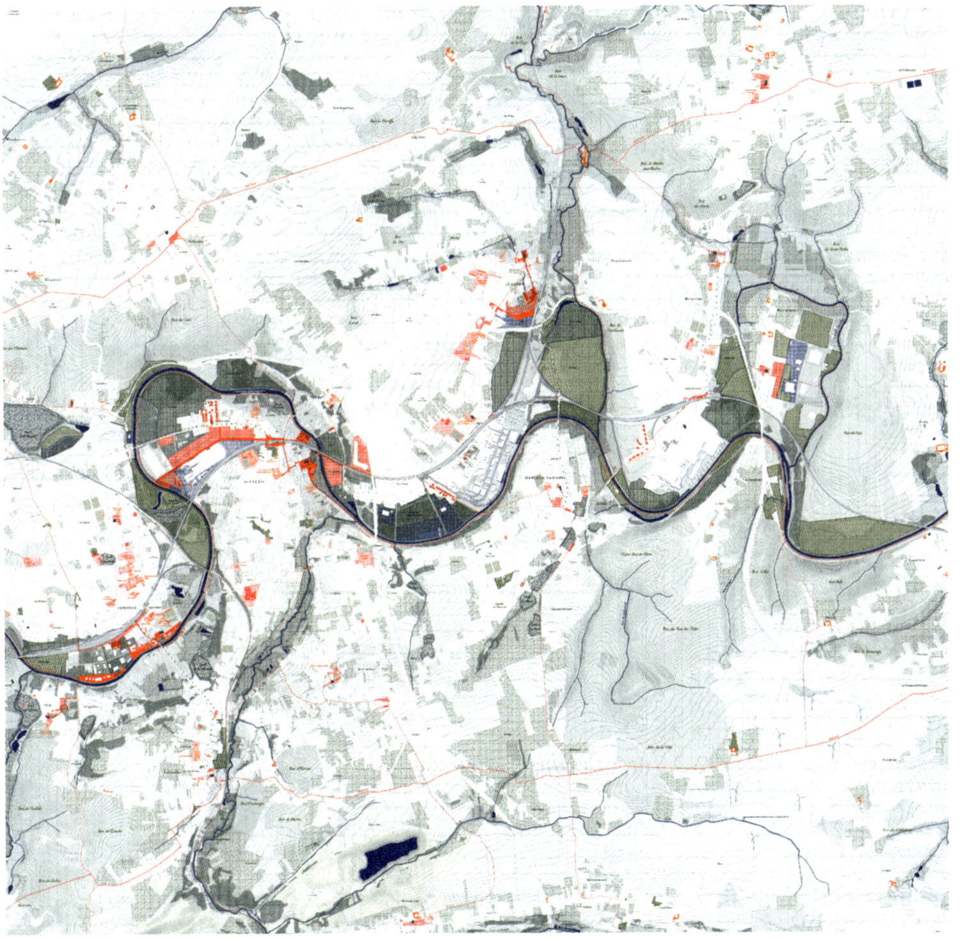

[06] Regional project for Sambreville and an integrated redeployment plan for the Val de Sambre. © StudioPaolaViganò

industrial Wallonia, overcoming the mono-functionality the territory has suffered from for decades.

Small and scattered settlements—the countryside, the *terrils*, and the canals (ground- and art-works realized against the topography through a system of water lift)—still describe the industrial machine which, although partially underused or abandoned, remains varied in terms of space and infrastructures that can be rethought and adapted. In the "central park" of La Louvière, for example, the co-existence of the highly recognizable small hills of the *terrils*, the center, the surrounding villages, and the remaining large industrial plants seem to represent a city with the potential to reimagine a space for multiple economies [07].

Large decommissioned industrial areas are now highly valuable assets for the region. This is the case with "Porte Ouest" in Charleroi: a strategic, partially abandoned industrial site where two steel industries are still operating and have become part of a new urban project that reinterprets the area, including its infrastructures and relationships with the city and the rest of the territory. There are ambitions to create new jobs and to generate a new metabolism through the re-use of the existing buildings, sharing energy and creating a metropolitan park on the existing concrete slabs. A few of the heavy infrastructural layers can be exploited to reconnect Porte Ouest to the rest of the city; some heritage buildings are capable of performing other functions beyond simplistic economic calculation [08].

From these cases, a spatial matrix for a development project emerges, which is the result of a very close and continuous exchange with citizens, politicians, urban and territorial economists, reconnecting territorial design to the economic ground and the different "capitals" (spatial, environmental, human, financial…) contained in these places. The "territory subject" and the "horizontal metropolis" concepts alter our approach and inspire concrete projects where different and renewed economies can become operational.

The final case, also in Wallonia, is still ongoing and concerns the Vesdre Valley, which

[07] Strategic masterplan for the industrial and economic development of the Porte Ouest site in Charleroi. © StudioPaolaViganò

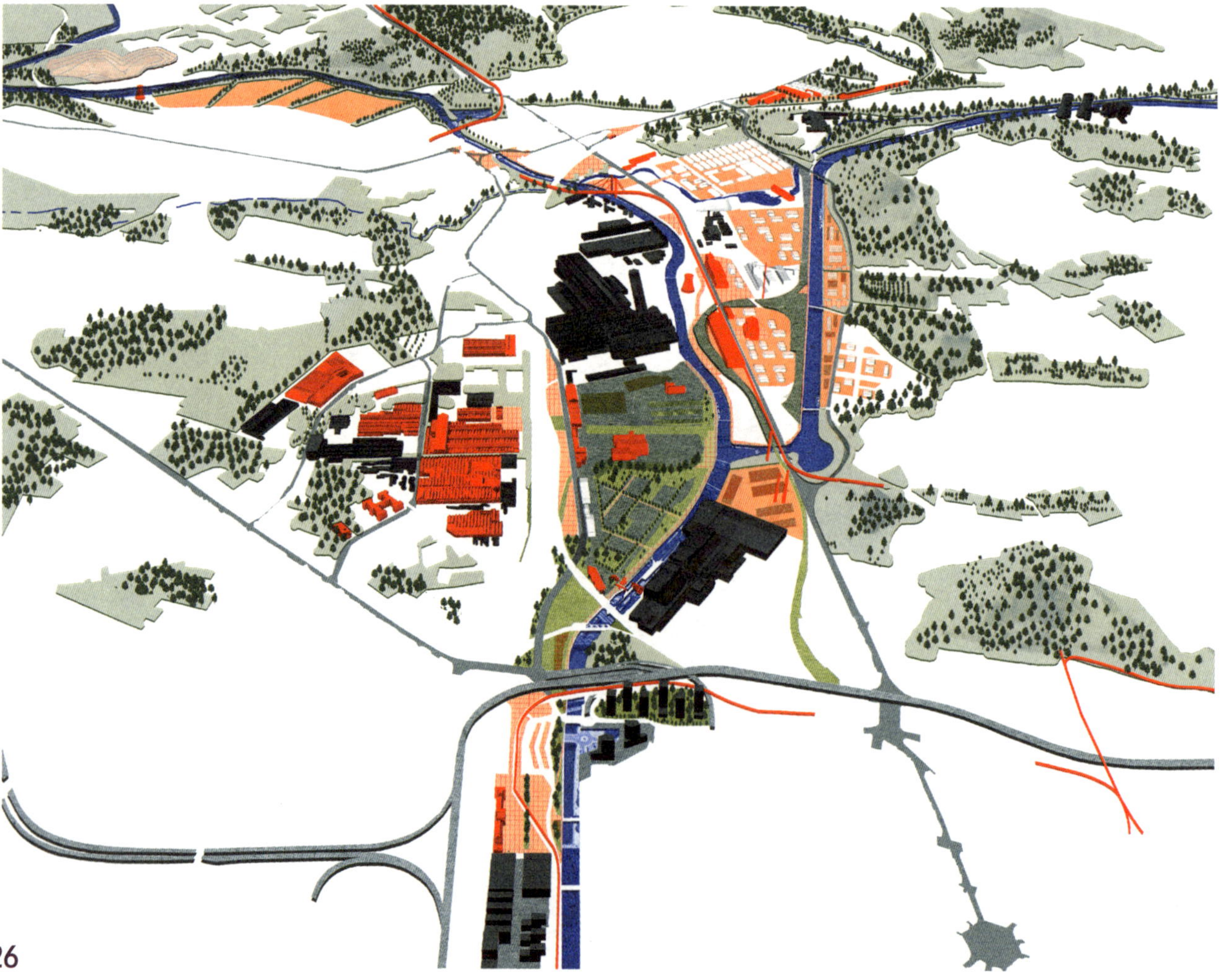

was hit by heavy floods in 2021. The "disruptive power of resilience" suitably defines what we have learnt from this case, and how revolutionary and dramatic being resilient can be.

The valley is close to the German border and in summer 2021 it flooded intensely, causing damage to people and infrastructures, pollution, and general destruction. Together with the University of Liège (a team of meteorologists, hydrologists, ecologists, sociologists, economists, planners etcetera), we are developing a strategic plan for the entire watershed. A human chain was organized a few months ago [in 2022, at the time of the keynote's delivery] and a Flemish volunteer told us: "I come from Ghent, I came the day after the floods. We had to help people, we came almost every weekend by bus. If in twenty years from now the sea covers us Flemish people, we hope that the Walloons will come to help us too." This sentence is moving: the catastrophe reintroduces the principle of solidarity in our simplified social horizon. Solidarity among populations, solidarity among territories. This is also a critical part of developing horizontal relationships—people are more and more aware that life is not only an individual concept and experience, but a collective and common one.

The subjects of the river and the valley inspired this work, reading the way the territory has been rationalized via the canalization of the river and the transformation of the heath vegetation on the plateau of Hautes Fagnes into a drained forest. The sponge effect of the previous peat areas was lost, which has implications in terms of flood resilience. Superposing the flooded area in 2021 on the principal and secondary valleys, well represented in the old 18th-century Ferraris maps, the space occupied by the rivers fills the floodplain up to its margins. The water fully occupied the available space [09].

Unfortunately, there are cities, people, activities, streets, and roads along the valleys: the risk has been produced and constructed by human intervention. Cities and industries were developed in the flood plain because of the water required by the textile industry; all hydraulic measures were planned in view of ongoing urbanization and industrial development. Reading the logic of the river, its own rationalities and the adaptation to our logics (rationalizations) is thus necessary in order to both reinterpret the complex transformation and take action. The pastoral aesthetic in the Vesdre Valley—a landscape defined by Victor Hugo as the most beautiful valley ever—was imagined working together with the dignity of industrial buildings and infrastructures. The idea of constructing a pastoral

[08] Three images: the park, city made of village-constellations, multiplication of different economies. © StudioPaolaViganò

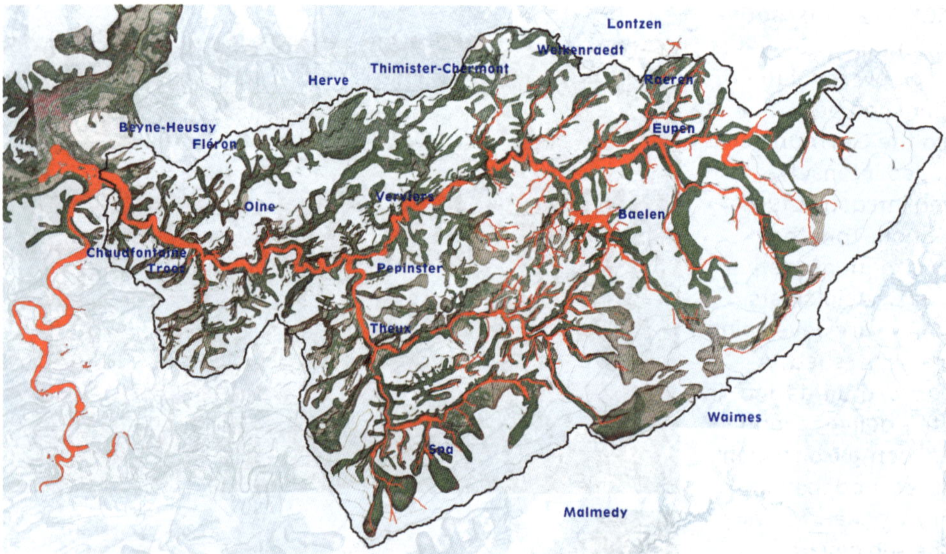

[09] The valleys of the Ferraris map (1771–1776); the hydrographic network. © StudioPaolaViganò

Industrial Revolution was extremely strong in Belgium, as well as in Great Britain: today this same idea can be reformulated as a strategy of reorganization of the flood plain and of the potential for resilience within it.

The enhancement of the ecosystemic functionalities of the territory is explained in diagrams: from the "sponge plateau" of the Hautes Fagnes (a reinterpretation of the ancient peat landscape), to the floodplain or the agricultural plateau, they form a map of the *potential resilience* to flooding and drought [10].

The scenarios we proposed work along two different axes that set the stage for a collective discussion about the future of the watershed. Along the first axis, the ontological and ethical fields are defined: on one side a "future without fracture", on the other "what the river wants", the territory subject. The second axis clarifies the possible choice between two types of urban and territorial morphologies, both present and recognizable in the valley, but part of different processes (agglutination along the north–south axes, or scattered and traditionally dispersed settlements) [11].

The scenarios have given rise to fundamental discussions with all the participating actors and citizens. Each potential element of resilience also raises other possible land-use conflicts, as well as economic or social impacts. The four scenarios transform the period following the disaster, the post-disaster moment, into a critical occasion for collectively discussing the future: in this case, for starting a socio-ecological transition instead of blindly implementing reconstruction actions.

All the experiences in Wallonia feed into a project that extends beyond the enduring mining backbone imaginary: here, the territory is the main driver for rethinking space, revising and

[10] Resilience potential. © StudioPaolaViganò

Major bed, built-up area, carbonate surface, topography, national roads, motorways.

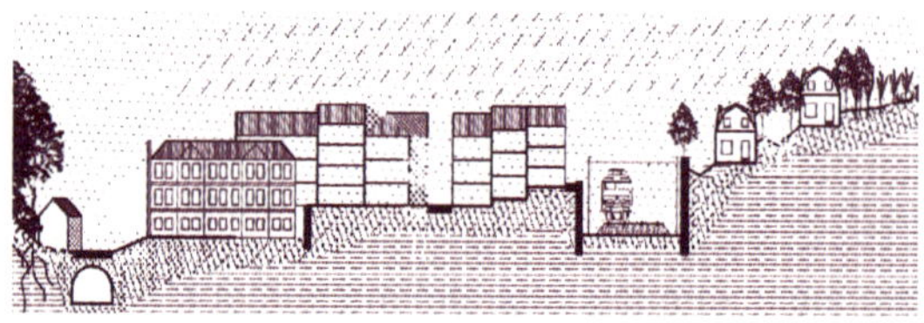

Softwood plantation on peaty and para-peaty soil, planting softwoods on hydromorphic soil, Gileppe and Eupen reservoirs, major bed, Vesdre and tributaries, run-off attenuation devices, drainage.

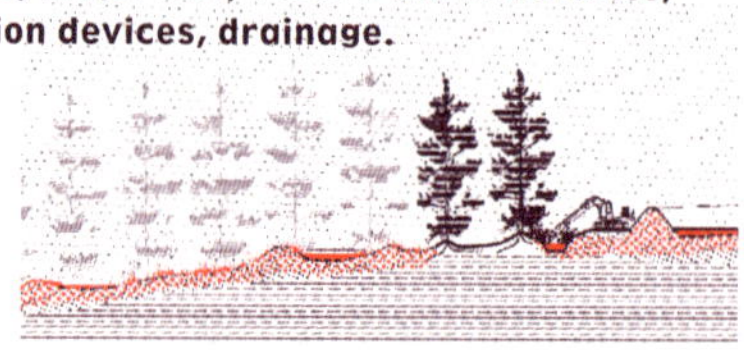

Major bed, economic zone, natural and agricultural areas, site to be redeveloped, undeveloped PdS housing zone, waterfront squares, Vesdrian Parks, railway stations, railway line.

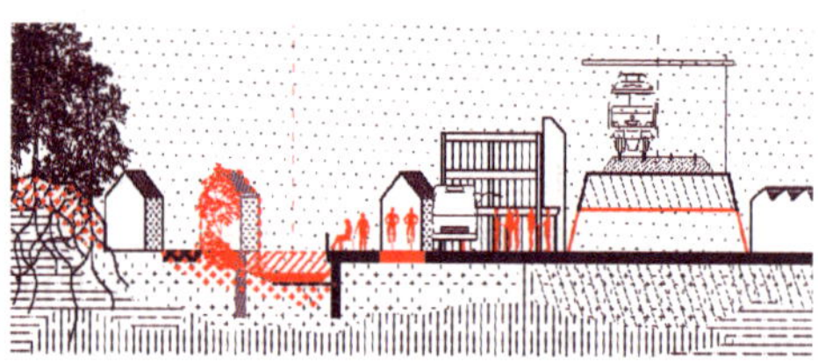

Crops and forage meadows, large agricultural plots, hedgerows and tree lines, not built ZACCs, agricultural land in residential areas, dry valleys, run-off.

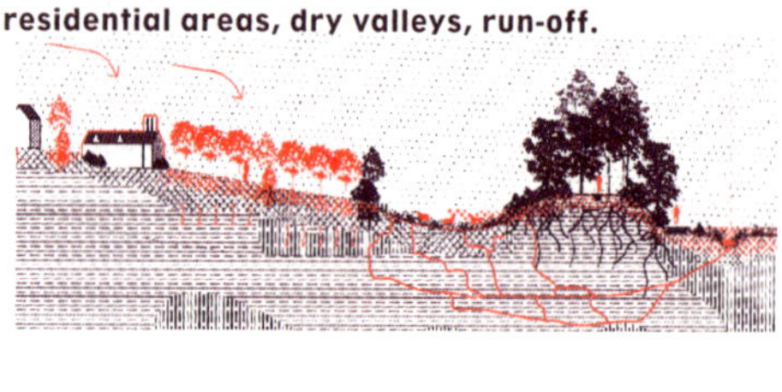

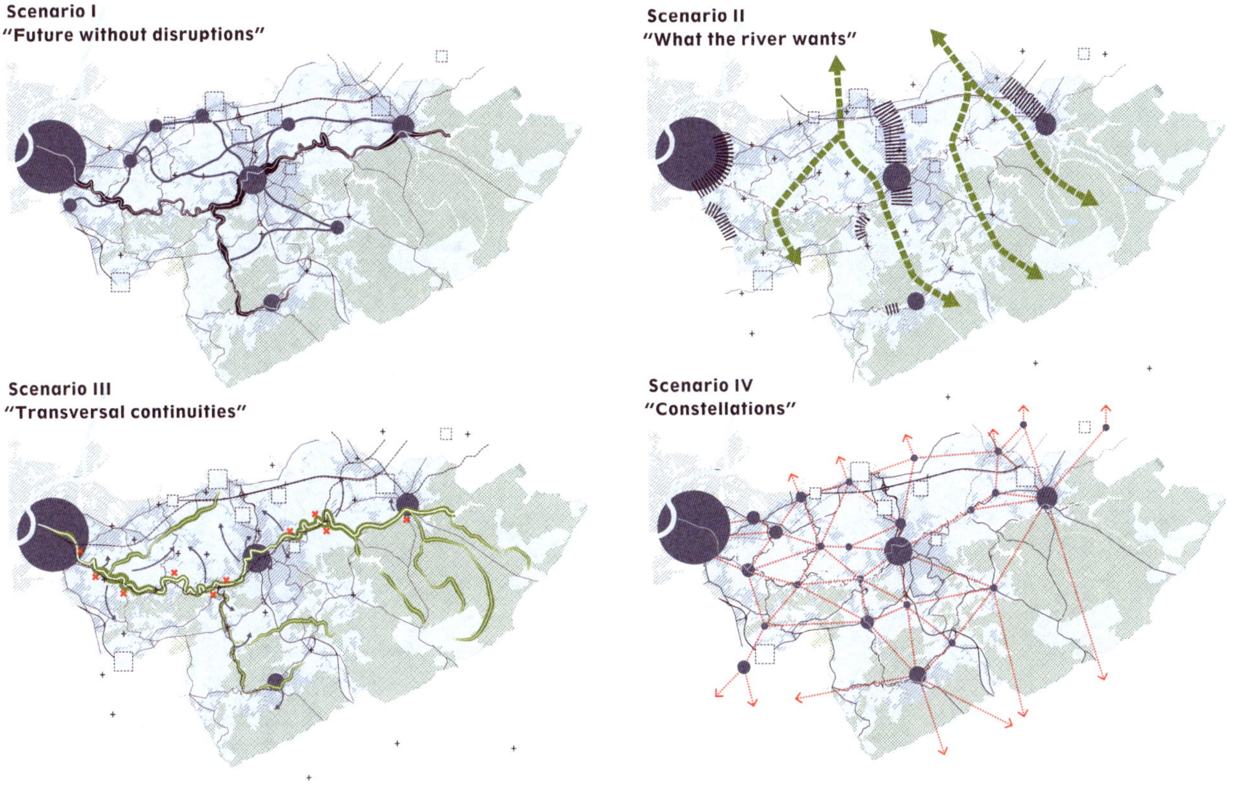

reforming it. In doing so, the backbone can be connected to other initiatives at the European scale, from Germany to France and beyond [12].

[11] The four scenarios.
© StudioPaolaViganò

- Urban hub
- Economic plate
- Forest
- to be demolished
- Village
- Free up the valley base
- Move to plateau
- Economic continuity
- Transverse continuity
- Route nationale
- Railroad
- Urbanized area and ribbon development
- valley urbanization
- Road
- Connection

Appalachia

There are other, similar territories that contain heavy marginalities, such as the Appalachian Mountain chain on the eastern coast of the United States. During its extractive and industrial development, Appalachia was still considered the "frontier": today it is situated in-between large megalopolitan areas, in the middle of very important and strong megalopolitan systems on the two sides of the chain. Extraction, however, continues and is becoming more and more aggressive in its destruction of the territory.

I had the chance to spend some time teaching at the University of Virginia, exploring one such paradox through mapping the transformations caused by extraction processes, including old underground mining and recent surface mining (the technique of mountain top removal) to extract high quality coal.

The destruction of the territory is rapid and ongoing, triggering the immediate pollution of waters and valleys. In the mining plateau, people have found a way to live alongside the minor valleys and paths leading to the entrance of the mine. The "hollows" are characteristic of how Appalachia is inhabited, forming part of its very dense and specific culture.

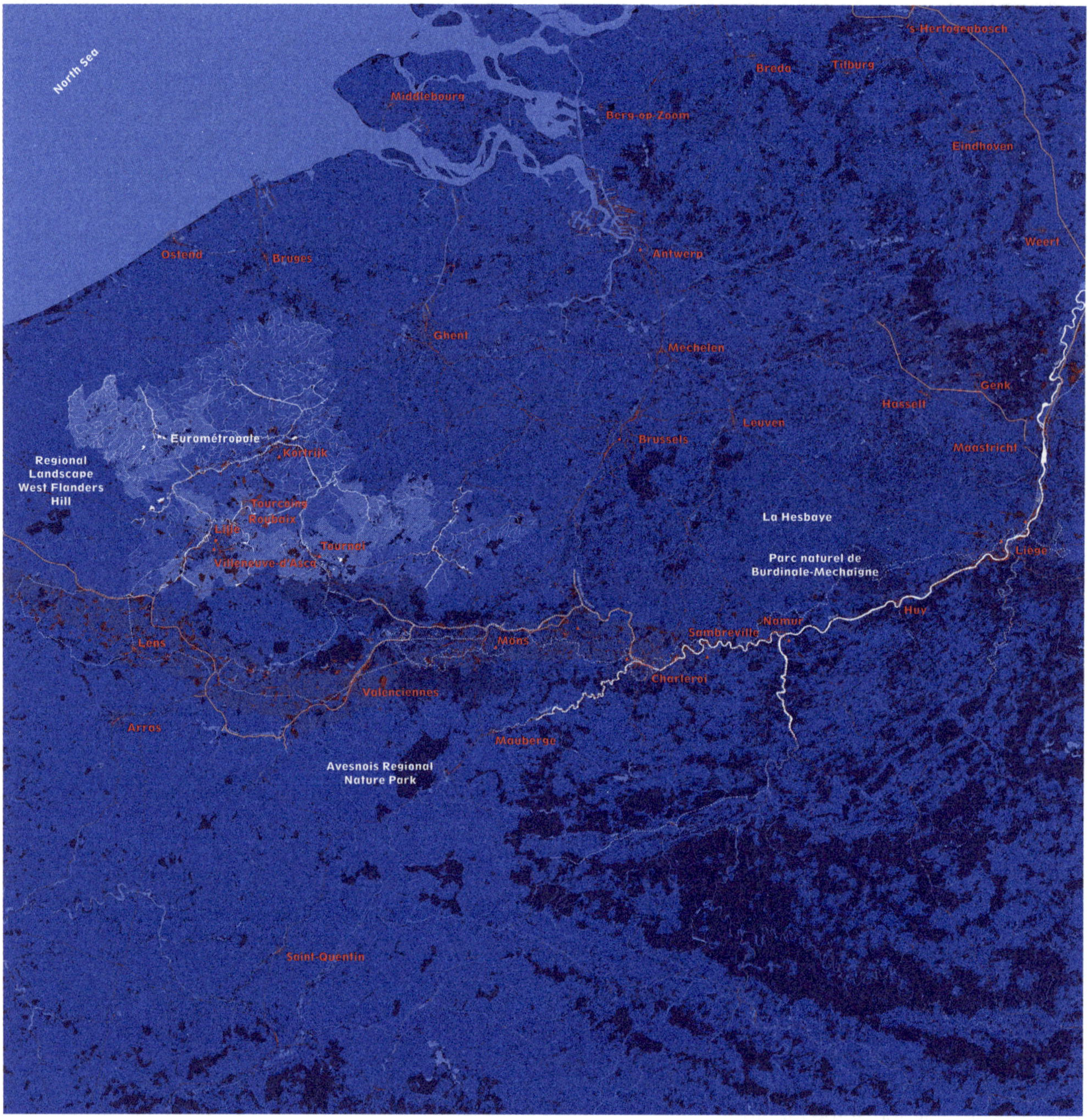

[12] Rethinking Wallonia.
© StudioPaolaViganò

On a larger scale, its marginality is more pronounced today than in past decades of decline. The correlation between politics and geology is striking and there exists a clear correspondence between the Republican vote and the mountain chain. Considered by some Americans the epitome of a "white ghetto," Appalachia has also been extremely afflicted by the opioid crisis. Walking onsite, the usual answer from residents when questioned about a "future vision" has always been a negative one.

For all these reasons, one possible starting point for researching Appalachia is to imagine and follow changing trajectories. We should consider, for example, how material extraction is still crucial to the region, a dichotomy discussed in the scenario "Extracting Appalachia, the Paradox of Plenty," which explores how the production of wealth in the territory is definitively disconnected from job creation. This scenario has a slightly cynical side, but it is just a means of bringing the real processes to the fore and defining our position in relation to them. There is a need to understand what design might be able to add and (re)solve if extraction cannot be stopped [13].

A second scenario models the idea of an autonomous, self-supporting region, an "Autarchic Appalachia" where people searching for alternative lifestyles, for instance the "preppers" (a US movement preparing for catastrophes), might find their place—along with ensuring the protection of biodiversity's richness, its ecosystem being one of the hotspots for species diversity in the country [14].

Finally, a third scenario, "One, No One, and One Hundred Thousand," develops new multiple images of Appalachia, belonging to and influenced by the megalopolitan spaces around it. This scenario conceives of Appalachia not as the margin of these agglomerations, nor as their backyard; rather it locates the region in its specific context, placing it in generative dialogue and exchange with other areas. The unicity of the Appalachian culture should not reject its progressive belonging to open and larger systems, nor refuse to participate in their dynamics [15]. Here, the idea of a horizontal metropolis could also be interestingly tested.

PROVISIONAL CONCLUSIONS

Today, it is crucial to understand the position of urban and territorial design in instigating a transformative and affirmative relationship among forms of space, life, and power. A vision cannot be constructed without considering the biopolitical dimension of the current social and ecological transition, which requires redefining the old biopolitical project and re-examining its most negative consequences. Often, this means working on difficult, ambiguous, and risky concepts. However, I share with other thinkers the conviction that not only negative forms of biopolitics exist, but other dimensions are possible, and that an "affirmative biopolitics" (**Esposito, 2008**) is possible. The question of life addressed by Foucauldian biopolitics does not end with the administration and rationalization of life and its processes; beyond this, it also concerns the (speculative) existence of a politics *of* life, a sustaining politics that operates in life's service, the importance of which cannot escape anyone.

The Biopolitical Garden, the book I have recently concluded, starts from the hypothesis that we must urgently rethink the project of the city and territory in transition as a biopolitical task. The city and the territory are concrete spaces but also mental ones, in which to reflect on contemporary biopolitical frameworks in the wider socio-ecological transition. The hypothesis of an affirmative biopolitics thinks about space—and the relationships it can establish with different forms of life and power—in a new context of radical mutation, where it can once again assume its full importance.

[13] Scenario I: "Extracting Appalachia, The Paradox of Plenty." © University of Virginia, 2017

[14] Scenario II: "Autarchic Appalachia." © University of Virginia, 2017

[15] Scenario III: "One, No One, One Hundred Thousand Appalachia." © University of Virginia, 2017

BARCELLONI CORTE, M. and VIGANÒ, P. (2022) *The Horizontal Metropolis. The Anthology*. Berlin: Springer

CAVALIERI, C. and VIGANÒ, P. (2020) *The Horizontal Metropolis. A radical project*. Zurich: Park Books.

CORBOZ, A. (1983) 'The Land as a Palimpsest', *Diogene*, 31(121), p. #.

ESPOSITO, R. (2008) *Bíos: Biopolitics and Philosophy*. Minneapolis: University of Minnesota Press. (or. (2004) *Bíos. Biopolitica e filosofia*. Turin: Einaudi.)

KOOLHAAS, R. (1987) 'Surrender, now' in R. Koolhaas and B. Mau (1995), *S,M,L,XL*. New York: The Monacelli Press.

PIETROPOLLI, T. (2023) *Another possible order. The figure of horizontality between contemporary space and disciplinary urban traditions*. PhD Thesis, EPFL, Lausanne.

SECCHI, B. (2000) *Prima lezione di urbanistica*. Bari-Milan: Laterza.

SECCHI, B.,VIGANÒ, P., HANIN, Y., DAWANCE, B., VANDENBROUCK, I., ROUSSEAU, L., DANEL, F., HAUSLADEN, G., BAUER, J., JACOBSEN, C., BONNET, C., VERHEYEN, J., FRANCK, P.-A., LELOUTRE, G. and LIONNEZ, H. (2010) *Bruxelles et ses territoires, Plan Régional de Développement Durable. Elaboration d'une vision territoriale métropolitaine à l'horizon 2040 pour Bruxelles, first report.*

VATTIMO, G. (1985) *La fine della modernità*. Milan: Garzanti.

VIGANÒ, P. (2016) *Territories of Urbanism. The Project as Knowledge Producer*. London/Lausanne: Routledge/EPFL Press (or. (2010) *I territori dell'urbanistica. Il progetto come produttore di conoscenza*. Rome: Officina).

VIGANÒ, P., CAVALIERI, C. and BARCELLONI CORTE, M. (2018) *The Horizontal Metropolis. Between Urbanism and Urbanization*. Berlin: Springer.

ZHANG, Q. (2023) *The Elemental Metropolis*. Berlin: Springer.

Paradigms Adrift: The Room for the River Program in the Netherlands

Eric Luiten

[01] The distribution of selected project areas in which river discharge capacity measures were expected to have most effect on the critical water level of the Rhine's downstream branches. © Rijkswaterstaat

A process of many centuries of organized landmaking in the Netherlands—motivated by the agricultural potential of the rich fluvial and marine soils—laid the foundations of the Dutch lowlands, which comprise roughly half of the country's surface. Through an ongoing civil-engineering strategy based on the construction of dams and dykes, together with the introduction of sophisticated water management systems, the dry surface of the country substantially grew in size. Nowadays, we tend to define this part of the Earth as a collectively organized, yet delicate equilibrium between land and water.

Increasing concern about the consequences of climate change around the turn of the millennium highlighted a new concept in flood risk control. After extremely high winter water levels were experienced on branches of the Rhine and Meuse rivers in the Netherlands in 1993 and 1995, respectively, it was decided that reinforcement of dykes would not be a sufficient remedy to safeguard private and public propertie in the river hinterland. The Ministry of Infrastructure and Water Affairs launched a program called Room for the River that was elaborated by the State Service for Traffic and Water Management (Rijkswaterstaat) between 1995 and 2000. The research was scientifically supported by the hydrologists and fluvial experts of Deltares, a publicly funded independent knowledge institute for water management challenges. By means of a computer model that simulated the seasonal dynamics of the river branches, a series of locations were analyzed to determine their hydrological position in the whole river system.

Assessments led to conclusions about the extent to which widening of the riverbed at that specific location would contribute to the double aim of the program: firstly, to lower the critical water evel by extending the discharge capacity of the river forelands—the quantitative goal; and, at the same time, to develop a renewed topography that would function more sustainably and offer improved scenery in comparison to the existing conditions—the qualitative goal. In 2006, the entire program was adopted as a National Planning Decision by the Dutch Parliament [01].

The fact that the program had to be based upon this double aim was foreseen by landscape planners and designers who participated in the program's preliminary explorations. It became obvious that the creation of more open space alongside both river branches would encroach on the continuity of privately owned farmland. Additionally, it risked compromising the qualities of established and protected natural areas in the river forelands, the conservation of historical patterns and objects, and the use of recreational and touristic infrastructure. The second aim of the program was therefore defined and summarized as the creation of landscape quality. It was this decision that led to the interpretation of the Room for the River program as a trajectory of co-creation between civil engineers eager to innovate, and representatives of the utilitarian tradition of Dutch landscape architecture. The other consequence of the double aim was the installation of a so-called "quality team" that would supervise the elaboration of designs for the thirty-four selected sites as well as the actual construction of the work *in situ*. The quality team consisted of a multidisciplinary group of experts and a secretariat, chaired by the State Advisor for Landscape and Water. They were asked to follow the progress of the design work, to deliver independent comments, and to provide their best professional judgement on each design result prior to them being accepted as a starting point for more detailed elaboration by private contractors.

The total of thirty-four measures carried out in the context of the program included widening the floodplains, moving dykes, deepening both floodplains and summer beds, lowering summer quays and groynes, digging parallel channels, depoldering, removing obstacles such as bridge pillars and buildings in the floodplains, and—in case there was no other option at hand—reinforcing and/or raising of dykes. The first works of the program started in 2006 and the last work was completed in March 2019. The total available budget was 2.4 billion euros [02].

The Room for the River program marked a break with past approaches to flood risk in general, and to river management policies and engineering repertoires in particular. Three distinct characteristics of the program can be considered paradigmatic game changers:

1 A STOCHASTIC TOPOGRAPHY

Room for the River marked a shift from flood risk management using purely technical means (as seen in Dutch water management across the 20th century) to the differentiated application of spatial measures applied in the 21st century. The central idea was to transform large parts of the existing landscape into well-prepared permanent or temporary floodplains whereas before the river would take that same land by surprise. The program relied on calculations that can be defined as stochastic, i.e., having a random probability distribution or pattern. The probability of river flooding over time

LOWERING FLOODPLAINS
Lowering/excavating part of the floodplain increases room for the river in high water situations.

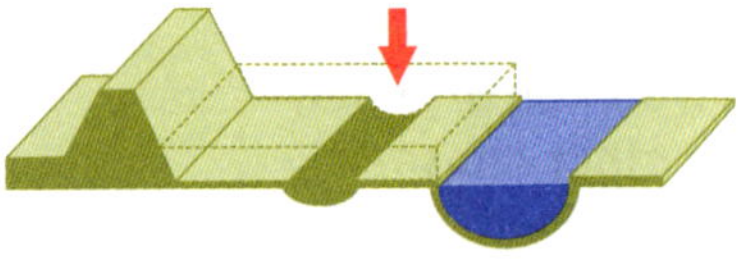

LOWERING GROYNES
Groynes stabilize the location of the river and ensure its correct depth. However, in a high water situation, groynes may obstruct the flow to the river. Lowering groynes speeds up the rate of flow.

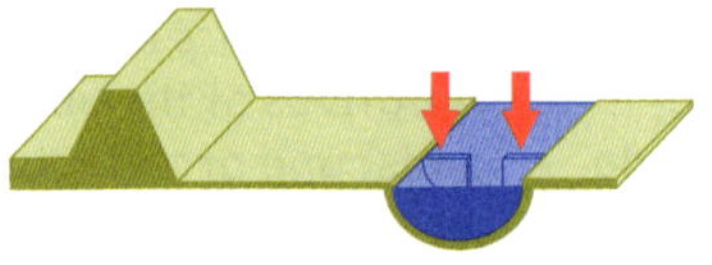

DYKE RELOCATION
Relocating a dyke inland widens the floodplain and increases room for the river.

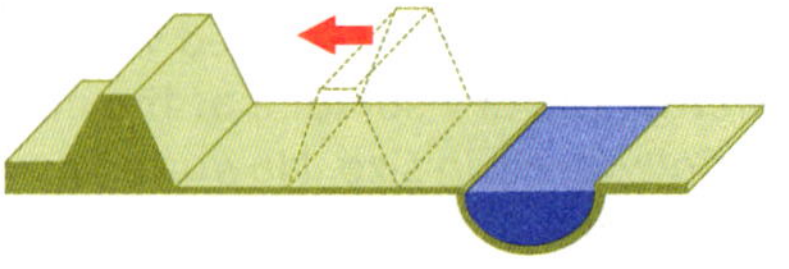

REMOVING OBSTACLES
If feasible, removing or modifying obstacles in the riverbed will increase the rate of flow.

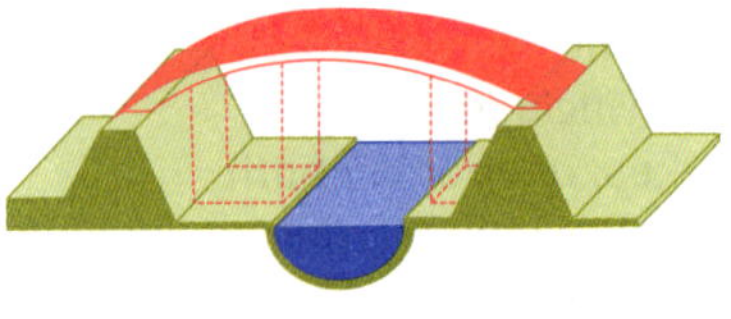

DEPOLDERING
The dyke on the riverside of a polder is lowered and relocated inland. This creates space for excess flows in extreme high water situations.

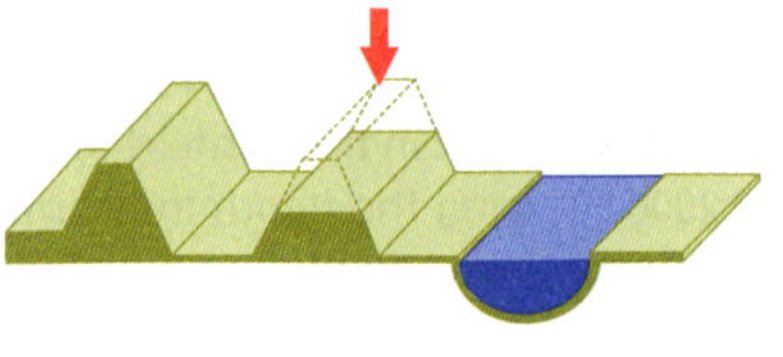

WATER STORAGE
The Volkerak-Zoommeer provides temporary water storage in extreme situations where the storm surge barrier is closed and there are high river discharges to the sea.

DEEPENING SUMMER BED
Excavating/deepening the surface of the riverbed creates more room for the river.

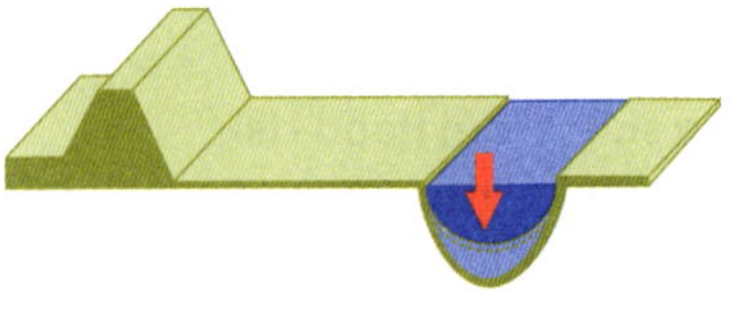

HIGH WATER CHANNEL
A high water channel is a dyke area branching off from the main river to discharge some of the water via a separate route.

DYKE REINFORCEMENT
Dykes are reinforced at given locations where river widening is not feasible.

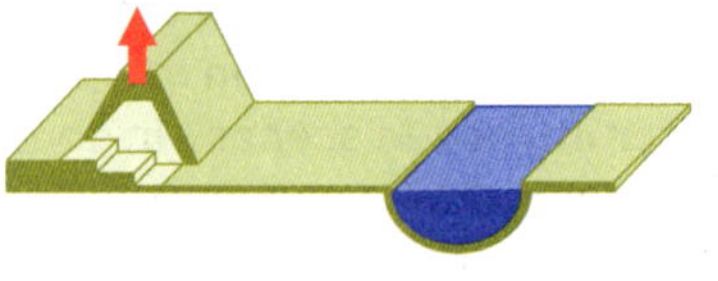

---

[02] The toolbox of measures taken to increase the discharge capacity of the river branches. It is easy to imagine the effect these modifications and interventions have on the quality of the existing landscape. © Rijkswaterstaat

steered the decision-making about which locations would most effectively contribute to the quantitative aim behind the investments. The newly created wide topographies alongside the branches of the Waal, the Lower Rhine, the Merwede, and the Ijssel now reflect the collective interpretation of water safety where previously the height of the river dykes played that role.

2 A TAILOR-MADE FUNCTIONALITY

Room for the River was conceived as a multifunctional spatial development instrument. The main purpose was to create a safer river system, but every site that was examined to assess its potential effect on riverine discharge behavior presented different land-use possibilities and restrictions. In some cases, the continuity of agricultural activity was secured whereas farmsteads had to be removed. In other cases, a substantial extension of the ecologically protected wetlands was predominant. River-related leisure amenities were created or improved over the course of the project design and in all cases new public space was provided. Proposed urban extensions were reconsidered and redirected in response to the newly defined physical demarcations between floodable and non-floodable terrains. Overall, the planning approach can be described as functionally combined and site-specific.

3 A DIFFERENTIATED PARTICIPATION

Room for the River accelerated the development of a procedure in which regional and local communities, civilians, and private entities were invited to develop a proportional level of responsibility and show engagement in the decision-making process in water management proposals. The construction of large technical water works in previous decades was merely based on a centrally organized and budgeted initiative with some political risk but almost no societal interaction. In almost all cases—after the definition of the scope of a singular Room for the River project by Rijkswaterstaat—regional water management authorities, provinces, or municipalities were asked to lead on further elaboration of the design and direct the subsequent execution. Individual citizens who would suffer substantial loss of property or interest were generously compensated. The bottom-line, though, was that the original aims of the whole program were not negotiable.

In one particular case, the involvement of a farmer's community led to a change of plans: the proposed complete buy-out of ten farms and their land was canceled in favor of continued agricultural use and the relocation of farmhouses on mounds, because this solution provided an equally effective hydrological outcome and greater societal satisfaction. Consequently, Room for the River elevated public opinion, generating a more optimistic view on landscape transformation. Many of the 20th century water management artifacts were, at the time of their construction, considered a necessary evil—especially by ecologists, environmentalists, and landscape historians. Through the experiences and results of the Room for the River program, the inevitable modification of the Dutch topography to increase climate change adaptability can be dealt with constructively.

The recently published update of the climate scenarios for 2100 describes continued global warming with more drastic impact on seasonal weather conditions, human land use, and environmental sustainability than was predicted earlier. The only way to deal with the rising sea level, and higher extremes in precipitation and river discharge, to reorganize our collective water management, especially in deltaic circumstances as the Netherlands. Room for the River has provided a combined adaptive, spatial-hydrological strategy that is based on thorough understanding of the changing behavior of water systems and on the notion that we have to live with an abundance of water instead of fighting it. Continued life in the metropolitan settlements in the deltas of the world can only be secured if we accept a reconfiguration of the urban landscape as we know it.

THE ROOM FOR THE RIVER PROGRAM in the Netherlands: https://www.rijkswaterstaat.nl/

[03] The Noordwaard looking west, alongside the Merwede River branch. This rural area turned from a monofunctional agricultural territory into a differentiated landscape. New room for controlled flooding was provided through the construction of four inlets in the river levee, visible in the middle of the aerial view. Three surface levels were introduced: permanent dry arable land, semi-floodable agricultural land, and permanently flooded wetland. The new natural beauty and scenic quality were made accessible by means of a network of bicycle roads and footpaths with bird-watch towers in well-selected locations.
© Rijkswaterstaat

[04] The city of Nijmegen is located on both sides of the most critical bottleneck of the River Waal—looking west in the picture. The river at this particular point makes a right-angled turn and was laced between the southern border of the old city and the northern dyke that protected the village of Lent. After thorough exploration and detailed modeling of the river dynamics, a decision was taken to enlarge the width of the river's foreland section. A parallel gully was created after the river levee had been moved towards the north—visible on the right side of the picture. This gully works as a differentiated support stream in times of high-water levels. Under normal conditions it functions as an attractive river branch with all sorts of recreational uses. The work resulted in the creation of a new longitudinal island that was immediately colonized by the Nijmegen inhabitants as a river park. The city is now rapidly developing a completely new spatial relationship with the Waal.
© Rijkswaterstaat

SANDRA GUINAND IN CONVERSATION WITH ALI MADANIPOUR

Ali Madanipour—professor of Urban Design, founding member and former director of the Global Urban Research Unit at the School of Architecture, Planning & Landscape, Newcastle University— brings to our attention different considerations and directions that should help initiate a Territorial Urbanism. He stresses the necessity of overcoming the dichotomy between city and countryside. He insists on the necessity of thinking and forging new spatial concepts to better grasp the realities of our surrounding environment, a task he devotes to academics and professionals. He also points towards the role (and importance) of public spaces as connecting infrastructures for our territories, which provide the potential to repair their spatial, ecological, and social fragments.

SG

The first question I would like to ask you, in the context of climate change and scarcity of resources, is how we can encourage a paradigm shift in urbanism from an urban design perspective?

AM

Well, the current organization of space is based on a careless attitude towards natural resources that treats them as if they are endless and never changing. This attitude has been developing for a long time and it requires time to change. It cannot change overnight. Much of the built environment as it is being built today—and has been built for some time—is based on this careless attitude. Thus, you could say it is the age of carelessness that characterizes this built environment. The paradigm shift that you are talking about seems to suggest the reorganization of space and a rethinking of the concepts that we currently have. In terms of spatial organization, we need to be more careful about the contextual conditions in which our cities are located, are being built, and to be more aware of our limits and the means with which we build. So, perhaps I can make two points. The first point is about the relationship between the city and the regional context.
If you think about the 19th century, many people were constantly talking about the dichotomy between the town and country, between the city and the countryside. And they thought of this as the primary tension of their time, one that needed to be resolved. If you look almost a century ago at the Charter of Athens, the manifesto of the modern movement, they talked about the necessity of integrating the city with its region. Thinking about the city not as detached from its region, but as part of it. This is a very basic insight that has unfortunately been forgotten in modern urbanism, management, and design. Today cities are basically seen as private corporations that are in competition with their neighbors, and with other cities around the world. This decoupling of the city from its surroundings, from its neighbors, and the metamorphosis of the idea of the city in this process, has been wasteful and it needs to be reversed. It is important to emphasize that cities are part of the region and for this to be acknowledged. And then you can think about the resources that this region offers and provides to the city and the capacities that are there. So, cities as part of the region can use their energies and resources more carefully.

The second point is about developing new spatial concepts. People in different walks of life may have ideas about how to deal with the issues of climate change and scarcity of resources, but they do not know how it best relates to the environment. Additionally, they may not be able to articulate their ideas in spatial terms, in design and planning terms. Thus, the role of academics and professionals is to provide the ability to articulate these ideas in spatial terms. What they need to do is to work with different groups, with different forms of knowledge and experience. This is a very rich potential source of new ideas and innovation. Then they can come up with proposals, alternative spatial concepts that can be used to organize space differently, to be more sensitive to the Earth's limitations and climactic conditions. This obviously requires a lot of collaboration and experimentation, but it can produce a series of spatial concepts which can then nurture the urban development process. Now, of course, some of these concepts have already been developed—or are being developed—through the practices of designers and developers. But many more concepts can be developed through experimental projects. At first, there will be resistance to these arguments because there are people with vested interests that these changes will compromise. There are also some people who are worried about any form of change. But ultimately, when you have a reservoir of caring and careful spatial concepts that respond to the climate crisis, that can be applied by decision makers, then those who are in charge of the urban development process will realize that the impending crisis is forcing them to change course.

SG

Speaking of innovative spatial concepts, how could public spaces improve the relationship of urbanism to the resources of the territory?

AM

If you think about public spaces as shared spaces, belonging to everyone, accessible to everyone, of course, this is a theoretical idea. Not everyone is represented here. But in practice, it means that these are spaces that are available and accessible to people who are present here, in this vicinity, in this territory, in this region. These spaces can thus act as nodes within a territory, linking and enabling people within an area to relate to each other, to mobilize their energies and to work together. It is possible in environmental terms, for example, to think of public spaces as elements of an ecological infrastructure that can link together different green and blue assets and develop a more holistic sense of territory in terms of its resources. The task of public space shifts from it being a resource to it being a facilitator of connectivity across the region. We need to think about public spaces as integrated infrastructures. In social terms, they can be a catalyst for making and connecting the social fragments that any big region will obviously have. Thus, in both ecological and environmental, as well as social terms, public spaces can contribute to the formation of a territorial context so that the repair and maintenance of that regional infrastructure can take place. Public space utilizes both ecological and social meanings as its enablers and as resources at the same time.

SG

Public spaces, as you just mentioned, are resources and facilitators of social and ecological integration. Social dimensions of cohesion and in clusion are very important elements for the dynamic of a city. What are the greatest challenges concerning social cohesion, inclusiveness, and users' involvement when it comes to developing a Territorial Urbanism?

AM

When cities grow in size and complexity, they become ever more fragmented, and this fragmentation becomes exacerbated by increasing inequality, social inequality, and diversity. So, it's about the challenge of how these different pieces can work or be linked together. And of course, challenges in terms of how those inequalities can be reduced. Basically, the big challenge is the relationship of power, the governance of the urban region. The big issue in metropolitan areas in particular, is having a tier, a regional tier of power that can coordinate issues, for example about transport, about the environment. Metropolitan areas all need that level of coordination. But what we see is that these regional authorities either do not have the necessary power or, when they do, they may not work together with local authorities—which also need to be part of the solution—because of the problem of competition. There is a the lack of coordination and institutional infrastructures that can help them to relate to one another. When social in equality and diversity grow, there is an increase of social exclusion, which has economic, political, and cultural dimensions and often finds spatial expression in particular locations, such as deprived neighborhoods, peripheral regions or inner-city areas. So, you have a large territory and a large population, which is fragmented into social enclaves—either the rich separating themselves or the poor trapped in particular locations.

Thus, the role of public space, urban design, and planning is to create the possibility of forming linkages between these fragments, thereby reducing gaps and inequalities while providing more opportunities for the disadvantaged parts of the region. Of course, planning and design are not able to do all that alone. Even the local authorities are not able to deal with those issues singlehandedly. I was recently working with some European municipalities and their complaint was that they end up dealing with problems that are created at a structural level. They are the location for the manifestation of these problems, but they don't always have the power and resources to deal with them. But if you think about public space in terms of public roads, parks, schools, education, housing and all sorts of other public facilities, you realize these are the necessary ingredients of an integrated and inclusive social life. They need to be provided through collaboration and empowerment of these local agencies, and of course in dialog with the population as well. So, again, public space has that possibility of forming linkages and connectivities across these increasingly centrifugal fragments. Essentially the big challenge of social cohesion is the growing diversity and inequality, the lack of governance arrangements—not to mention the economic challenge of reducing and coordinating these gaps and understanding systemic difficulties.

Obsolete Systems as a Resource for the Circular City

Stefan Rettich

It was only with the development of modern monument protection, and particularly as a result of the European Architectural Heritage Year (EAHY) of 1975, that the constant erosion of history was stopped. However, this preservation effort is often only applied to specific cases, namely to buildings from the period before 1914, which have been cemented as part of a supposedly "historic" cityscape. Modernism, on the other hand, continues to be up for debate, despite conservation initiatives spearheaded by ICOMOS and private entities. The fact that more and more historic architecture is now being converted—which, only a short time ago, would not have been considered worthy of preservation—means three things. Firstly, more and more professional buildings dating to the modern and postmodern eras are apparently falling into disuse—and because land, material, and energy prices are continually rising, a new market segment is now emerging. Secondly, under-appreciated, prosaic architecture is currently gaining in value over the supposedly historic. Thirdly, all this together marks a revolution in gray energy, which goes hand in hand with the theory of circular economy.

In European cities, buildings have repeatedly fallen out of use due to societal changes. However, the driving forces behind urban obsolescence have never been systematically investigated. Today, a large number of building types are under pressure to be used due to the megatrends of digitalization, the shift in transport, and changes in religiosity. While the potential of this development is already sufficiently discussed in the context of the individual architectural object, a theory of obsolescence and recycling at the level of the neighborhood or even the entire city is not yet available. In view of climate change, however, it is becoming increasingly essential to look ahead to the recycling of houses and whole areas: i.e., a strategy of the circular city.

What rules govern the phenomenon of obsolescence in architecture? Are there systemic connections? And what does this mean for the current situation?

FORTIFICATIONS: A HISTORICAL NARRATIVE OF OBSOLETE SYSTEMS

Urban societies produce different socio-technical systems of supply and disposal, transport, industry, or military defense at different times. When these conditions undergo a fundamental change, these systems become obsolete. The residual building structures themselves—which often manifest a vast amount of energy as well as political and economic willpower—then become of interest as a new system for transformation. This speci-

[01] **Anton Radl, *Ostertor-Wall with bridge at the Bischofstor and Contrescarpe*. Bremen, 1820**

[02] Spatial impact of megatrends on urban typologies.
© Rettich and Tastel, 2022

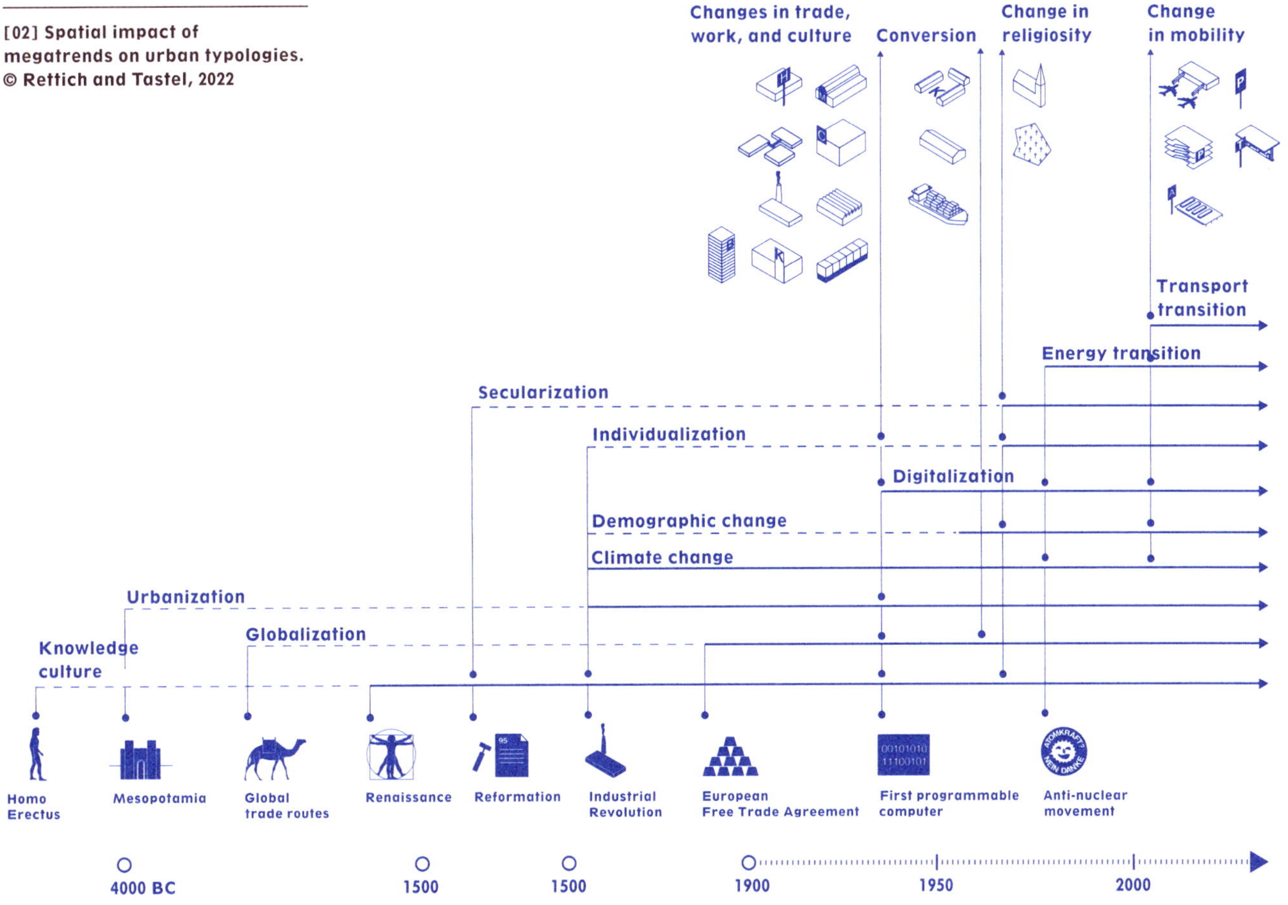

ficity cannot be repeated in any other form, at any other time—in the best case this is the starting point for social innovation.

This can be impressively described in terms of major upheavals in urban development, such as the way cities deal with their historic fortifications. Once designed as massive structures to protect the population, these could no longer serve their original purpose in the face of urbanization and the invention of new military technologies. These structures that have become obsolete released enormous potential for space. Throughout Europe, the ramparts in cities such as Frankfurt, Bremen, Hamburg, but also in Kraków or Graz, were transformed into public green spaces that still serve the urban population and thus the common good [01].

In Vienna, the opportunity was also taken to construct monumental buildings for political and cultural representation, which have shaped the city's collective image to this day. Paris missed this short window of opportunity for a green transformation, but later used the systemic space to build the Boulevard Périphérique—a transformation now set to be corrected. The plan is to convert the congested ring road into a "city-friendly" facility with lots of greenery by 2030 (see Johannes Bernsteiner's contribution to this book).

GLOBALIZATION AS A FORMATIVE DRIVER OF URBAN OBSOLESCENCE IN RECENT DECADES

In 1956, the freight forwarder and shipowner Malcolm McLean used containers to transport goods for the first time, on a specially converted tanker, known as the SS Ideal X. His invention not only revolutionized global logistics, but also had disruptive effects on port use. Many port facilities in European cities were no longer suitable for the steadily growing number of container ships and, consequently, were either abandoned altogether or relocated. Such obsolescence in the city—i.e., sites whose designated function falls out of use, but still harbor great potential—is nothing new. There are numerous other examples, such as the abandonment of barracks after the fall of the Berlin Wall, old industrial sites from the Wilhelminian period that have become defunct in the course of globalization, or centrally located freight stations that have been replaced by freight centers on the outskirts of cities. Other formerly urban functions—such as slaughterhouses, breweries, or wholesale market halls—were also relocated to so-called high accessibility points because they are integrated into international,

Stefan Rettich

[03] Level parking spaces in Hamburg.
© Rettich and Tastel, 2022
Source: Open Street Map, 2021

POTENTIAL OBSOLESCENCE
■ Parking spaces (approx. 730 ha)

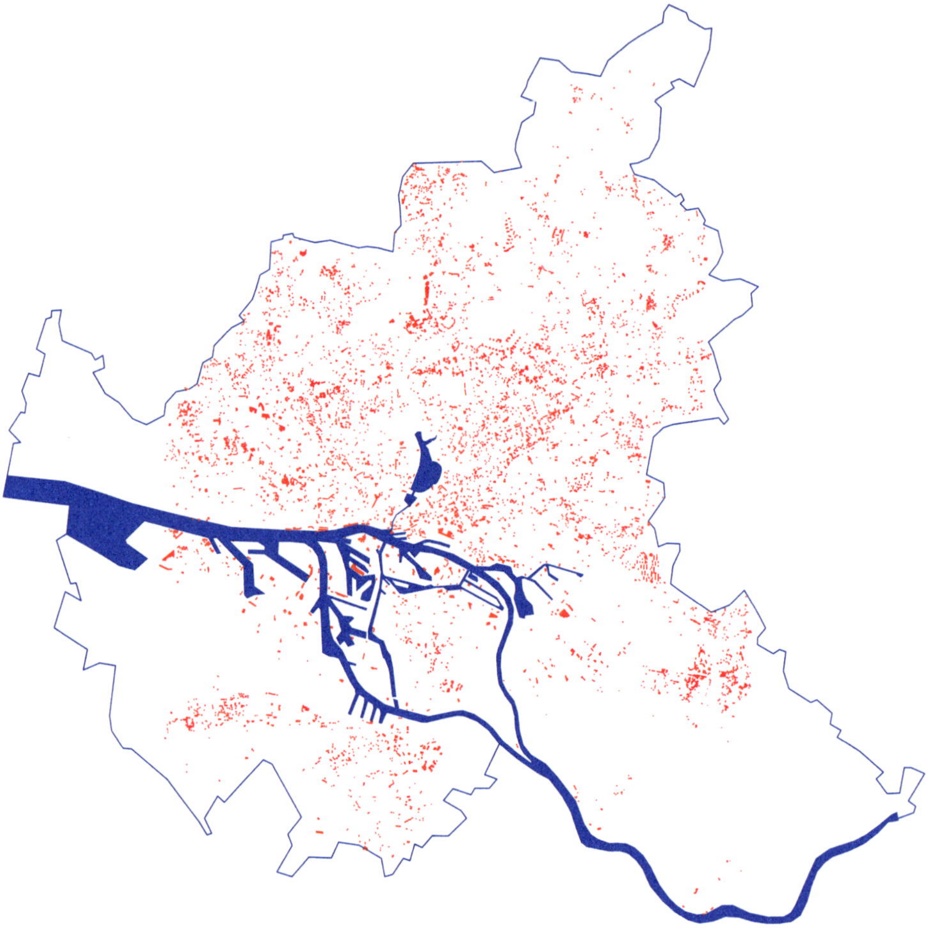

[05] Churches, parish halls, and cemeteries in Hamburg.
© Rettich and Tastel, 2022
Source: ALKIS, Geo-Online Hamburg, Freie und Hansestadt Hamburg, Landesbetrieb Geoinformation und Vermessung, 2021, Datenlizenz Deutschland Version 2.0.

POTENTIAL OBSOLESCENCE
⊟ Cemetery area (approx. 900 ha)
⬟ Churches (approx. 300 pcs.)
■ Community centers (approx. 210 pcs.)

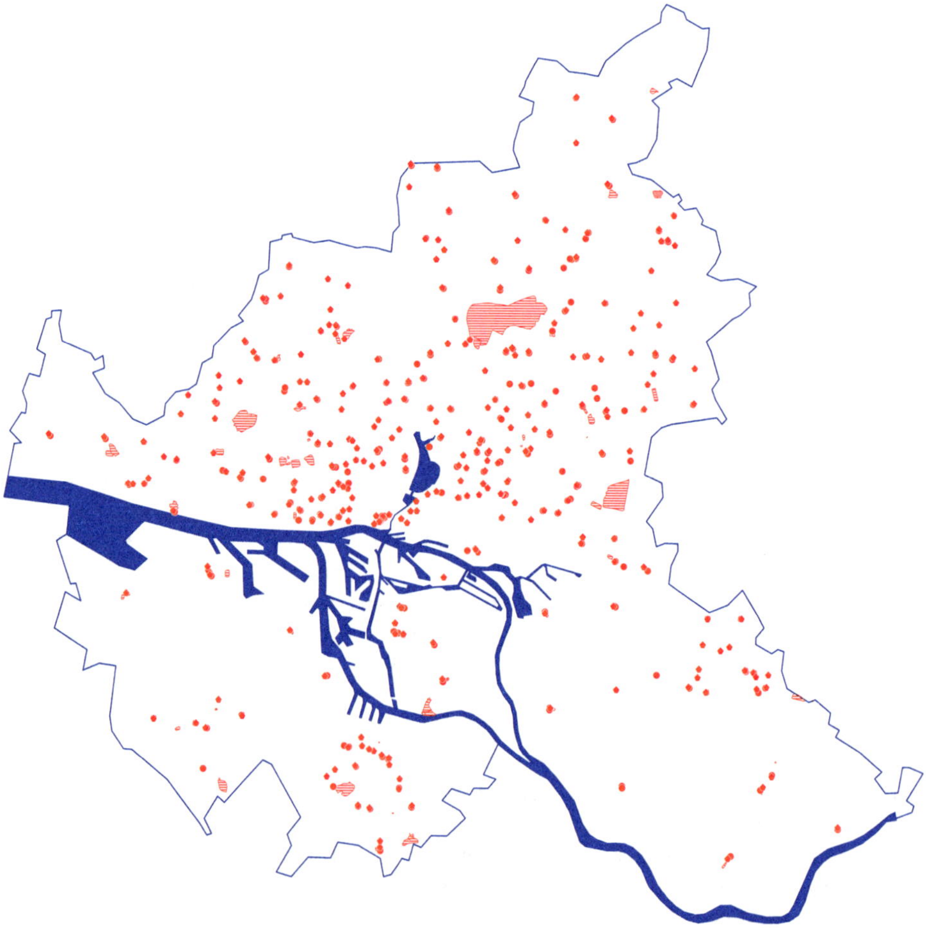

or at least supra-regional, production and supply chains.

All in all, these were large and valuable areas for the inner development of cities. They were centrally located, well developed, and relatively easy to redevelop, because the land was owned by the public sector or by the sole owners of the industry. Whole city districts, such as Hamburg's HafenCity, Bremen's Überseestadt, Munich's Ackermannbogen, or creative districts such as Leipzig's Baumwollspinnerei, were developed around these spatial resources. Such areas were also urgently needed, because since the 1990s most large cities and smaller university towns (swarm cities) have been growing rapidly, and the discussion about housing shortages and rising rents shows no signs of abating. A megatrend is at work here in the background: knowledge culture and the knowledge society are driving a structural change in the labor market. Creative industries and important centers of research and development with attractive, well-paid jobs are often concentrated in large cities and university towns.

MEGATRENDS AND THE TRANSFORMATION FIELDS OF TOMORROW

Fundamental social developments, so-called megatrends, thus have an indirect effect on the use of space, triggering space shortages, but also spatial vacancies with the potential for new uses. Is it possible to use past experience to discover which areas of the city will become obsolete in the future and which building types will be affected? To do this, current megatrends must be examined for their spatial impact [02].

During the lockdowns of the COVID-19 pandemic, for example, it became apparent—as if under a microscope—how strongly digitalization affects almost all areas of life and thus also the transformation of work and commerce. COVID-19 only acted as a catalyst here, not as a trigger. Stationary retail has long been under pressure from platform economies like Amazon. In the cultural sector, meanwhile, streaming services have been putting cinemas under pressure for quite some time; elsewhere, in the office and service sector, it is professional videocall software programs that are challenging the classic office tower.

Digitalization processes are also leading to reorganization in the productive sector. The growing use of IT and robotics is leading to a surplus of space. For the so-called Industry 4.0, fewer skilled workers will be needed, but more IT specialists required. Single-story factory halls could give way to software forges that can be organized vertically—space will then be freed up for other uses. However, the impact on the labor market and thus on the spatial requirements depends on the industry and varies considerably even across different manufacturing sectors.

THE ARSENAL OF THE CAR-DEPENDENT CITY

In addition to digitalization, it is climate change and the associated energy and transport changes that will have a megatrend effect on urban functions and thus on spatial development. Particularly in the case of stationary traffic, space could be saved, because far fewer parking spaces are needed. The only question is when and whether this will require further disruptive events, such as the Dieselgate affair, until comprehensive political action takes hold. The space gains would be immense—in a city like Hamburg, over 700 hectares of floor space are currently devoted to ground-level parking alone [03].

Calculations by the Federal Environment Agency show that, depending on local conditions, one car-sharing car replaces four to (sometimes more than) ten private vehicles (**Umweltbundesamt, 2021**). Assuming all car traffic was to be shifted to a sharing model, ideally over 90% of parking spaces could be saved. In terms of daily mobility practice, the actual value will likely settle somewhere in between this. Projects like Gröninger Hof—the conversion of a multi-story car park into a cooperative housing development in Hamburg's city center—or the deconstruction of the Büchel multi-story car park in Aachen in favor of a park are still relatively isolated cases. The fact that about 600 car dealerships go bankrupt every year throughout Germany (**Fassnacht and Vollmar, 2022**) is another indication that the whole arsenal of the car-dependent city is under scrutiny.

Applying Geels's method of the multi-level perspective (**Geels, 2002**), it is possible to graphically represent how the different levels of transformation interact and how the city would change for the better by taking advantage of the present window of opportunity [04].

CHANGE IN RELIGIOSITY

The development in church institutions is particularly dramatic. According to forecasts, membership in both major churches will decline by almost 50% by 2060 (**Evangelische Kirche in Deutschland, 2019**). All church districts and dioceses are desperately looking for strategies to convert church properties. These special places of assembly have a high social significance, and the issue is correspondingly difficult. In addition to the churches themselves, this also applies to the associated parish and community halls [05].

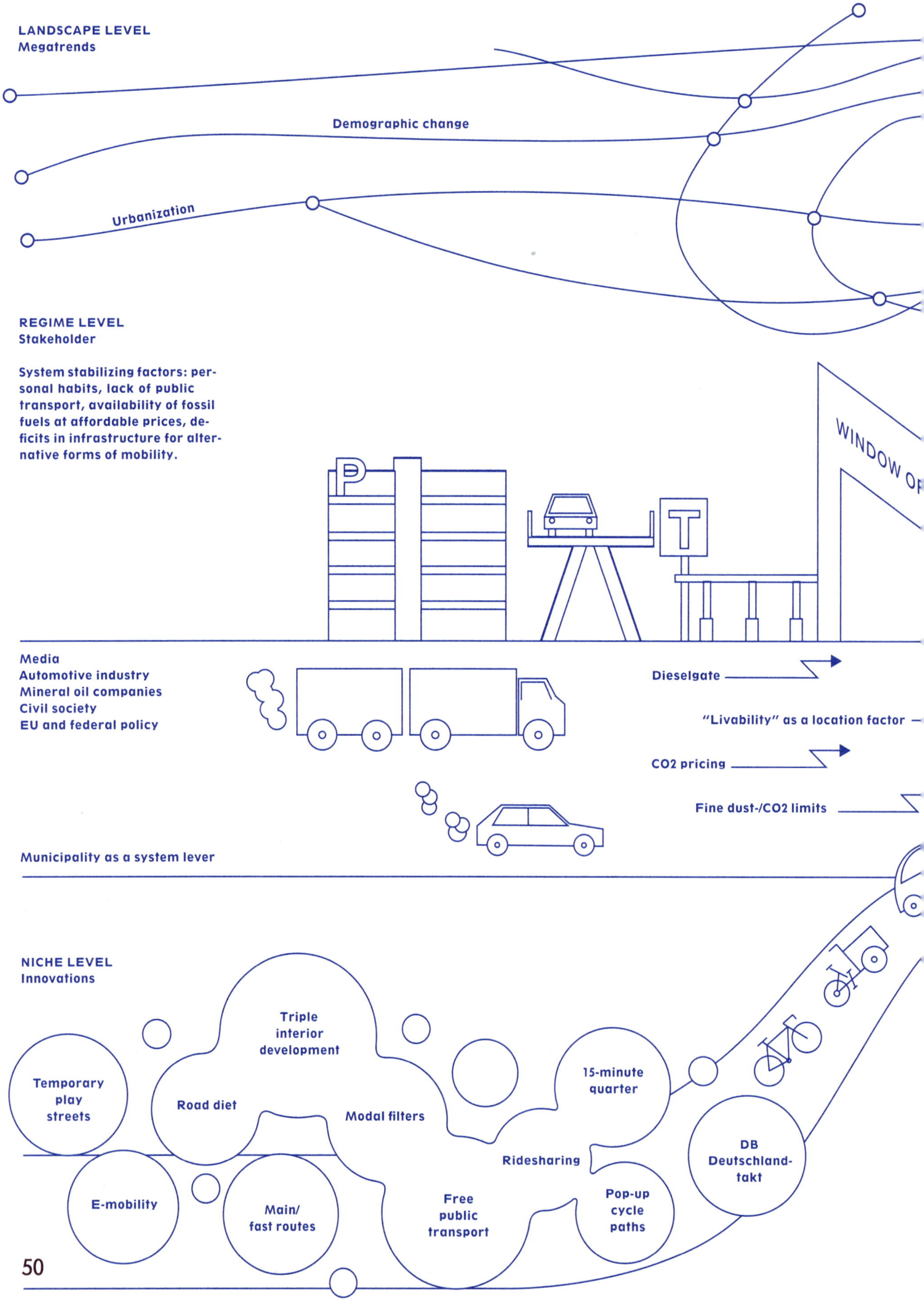
LANDSCAPE LEVEL
Megatrends
Demographic change
Urbanization
REGIME LEVEL
Stakeholder
System stabilizing factors: personal habits, lack of public transport, availability of fossil fuels at affordable prices, deficits in infrastructure for alternative forms of mobility.
WINDOW OF
Media
Automotive industry
Mineral oil companies
Civil society
EU and federal policy
Dieselgate
"Livability" as a location factor
CO2 pricing
Fine dust-/CO2 limits
Municipality as a system lever
NICHE LEVEL
Innovations
Temporary play streets
Triple interior development
Road diet
Modal filters
15-minute quarter
Ridesharing
DB Deutschland-takt
E-mobility
Main/ fast routes
Free public transport
Pop-up cycle paths

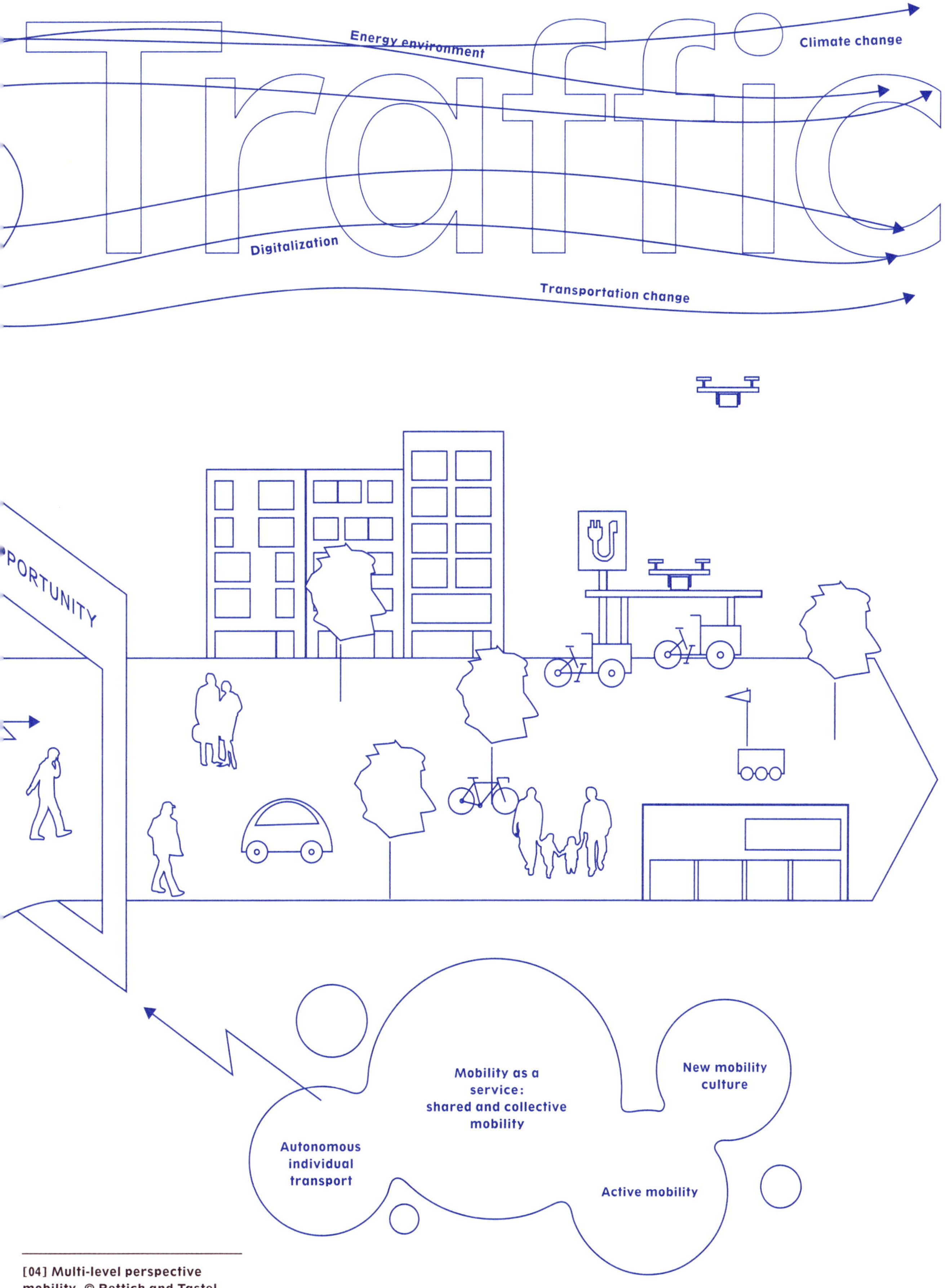

[04] Multi-level perspective mobility. © Rettich and Tastel, 2022

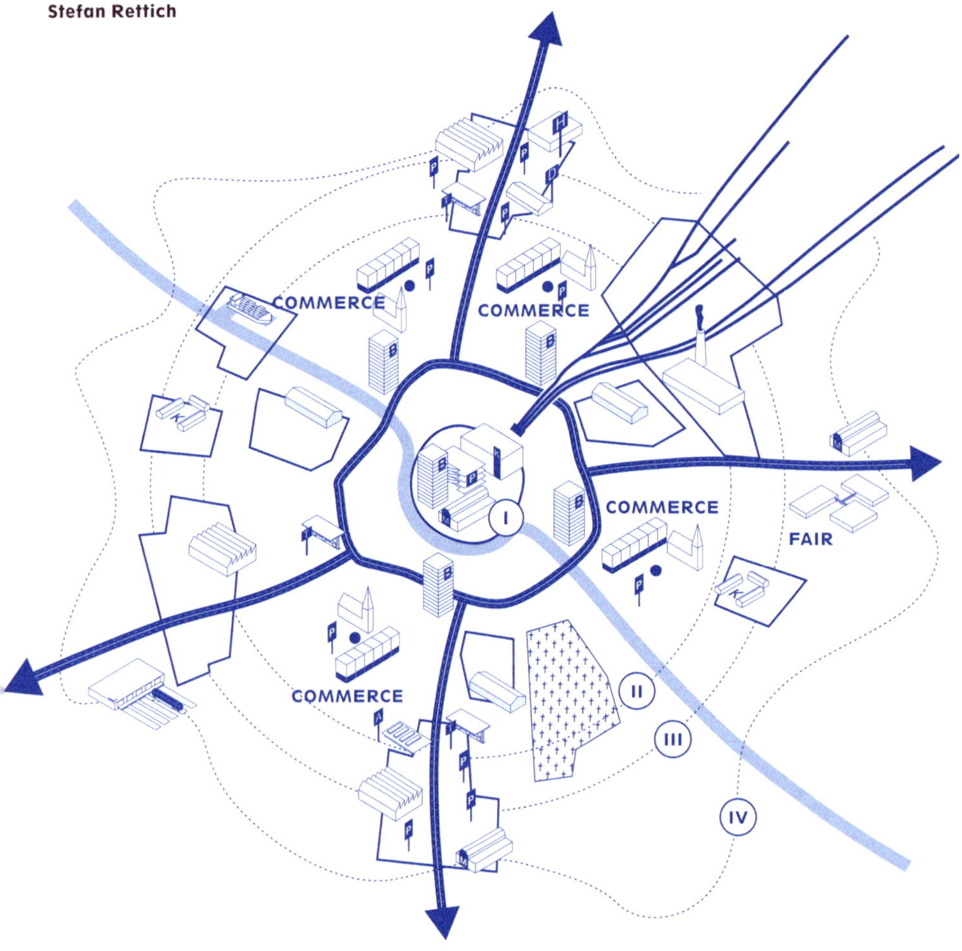

[06] Scheme of obsolete city. © Rettich, 2022

(I) Center
(II) Inner city
(III) Urbanization area
(IV) Outer city

[07] Potential spaces with accumulations of obsolete types in Hamburg. © Rettich and Tastel, 2022

ACCUMULATIONS OF POTENTIAL OBSOLESCENCE
■ Urbanization area

These sensitive properties are usually centrally located within neighborhoods and are firmly anchored in the collective consciousness of the residents. They could therefore also be used for socio-cultural purposes or for other important neighborhood functions.

In the meantime, there are several excellent examples of the transformation of churches. These range from the day-care center now hosted in the former parish church of St. Sebastian in Münster to the König Galerie in Berlin, housed in the Brutalist church of St. Agnes, or the bookshop now run out of the former Dominican church in Maastricht.

The second phenomenon in this area is a change in burial culture. More than a third of the cemeteries in Germany are now surplus areas. They are not actively used but must be maintained at great expense (**IKH, 2015**). The driving reason behind this is the change from coffin to urn burial, which requires only about a quarter of the space. Large sections of these cemeteries could therefore be converted into leisure and recreation areas after a period of reversion (**Rettich, 2017**).

In the above examples, location is crucial because the obsolescence risk of an urban function is not present (or not equal) in every location. However, identifying those resources with foresight and systematically transform them seems to become an essential task of urban development due to the acute shortage of land within cities.

CIRCULAR CITY: OPPORTUNITIES AND NECESSITIES

Digitalization, climate change, a shift in transport, and a change in religiosity are thus the drivers that are causing obsolescence in urban functions and precisely definable building types, in some cases with disruptive effects. Objects and spaces in the categories of commerce, work, mobility, culture, and religion are affected.

It is possible to draw a systemic map of an average European city and to develop an overview of urban obsolescence based on the principles of their location [06].

But where are these specifically located in the cities and to what extent will the individual building and land types be affected? This requires an approach spanning several different levels. The basis is formed by differentiated georeferenced data sets, which most cities now have access to. With them it is possible to map the objects in their location and to determine their size. For Hamburg, Hanover, and now also for Mannheim, these data have been mapped and overlaid for all potentially obsolete types, and external studies on the empirical development of individual segments have been evaluated (**Rettich and Tastel, 2022**). The areas in which they cluster can be read as the transformation areas of tomorrow. There, the public sector should proactively invest in communication, planning, and the purchase of land before prices and uses are dictated by the market. In Hamburg, twenty-four potential areas were identified using this method [07].

It is also essential to address the uses that need to be integrated into cities in the future—indeed matching these with the potential of obsolete building types is key to the circular city strategy [08].

However, in order for this to be implemented efficiently, planning law also needs to be made more flexible. Old and new functionalities must be allowed to co-exist, with new activities occupying the space even when the old ones are still (partially) operational. In the case of the much-praised Spinnereigelände in Leipzig, studios and flats were already being built when tire cord was still being produced in some of the factory halls—though this transformation was nonetheless illegal according the current planning law.

The text is based on findings from the research project *Obsolete City*, funded by the Robert Bosch Foundation (www.obsolete-stadt.net), as well as a text by Stefan Rettich published in 2021, in the book *Post-pandemic Urbanism* by Doris Kleilein and Friederike Meyer (eds.). A longer version of this source text has also been published in *archithese* 02/2022 (with Nicolas Beucker and Sabine Tastel) and a shorter version in *Bauwelt* 7/2023 (with Sabine Tastel).

UMWELTBUNDESAMT (2021) *CarSharing nutzen*. Available at: https://www.umweltbundesamt.de/umwelttipps-fuer-den-alltag/mobilitaet/carsharing-nutzen#unsere-tipps

FASSNACHT, M. and VOLLMAR, J. (2022) 'Warum unsere Autohäuser überleben müssen,' *FAZ*, 11 June.

GEELS, F.W. (2002) 'Technological transitions as evolutionary reconfiguration processes: A multi-level perspective and a case-study,' *Research Policy*, 31(8/9), pp. 1257–1274.

EVANGELISCHE KIRCHE IN DEUTSCHLAND (2019) *Langfristige Projektion der Kirchenmitglieder und des Kirchensteueraufkommens in Deutschland. Eine Studie des Forschungszentrums Generationsverträge an der Albert-Ludwig-Universität Freiburg*. Available at: https://www.ekd.de/ekd_de/ds_doc/projektion-2060-ekd-vdd-factsheet-2019.pdf, p. 8.

IKH – INSTITUT FÜR KOMMUNALE HAUSHALTSWIRTSCHAFT (2015) *Wirtschaftlichkeit im Friedhofswesen*. Helsa, p. 23 f.

RETTICH, S. (2017) 'Berlin denkt weiter,' *Garten + Landschaft*, 5/2017, p. 42.

RETTICH, S. and TASTEL, S. (2022) *Modellannahmen für Hamburg*. Available at: https://obsoletestadt.net/wp-content/uploads/2022/09/03_Hamburg_Modellannahmen_220808.pdf

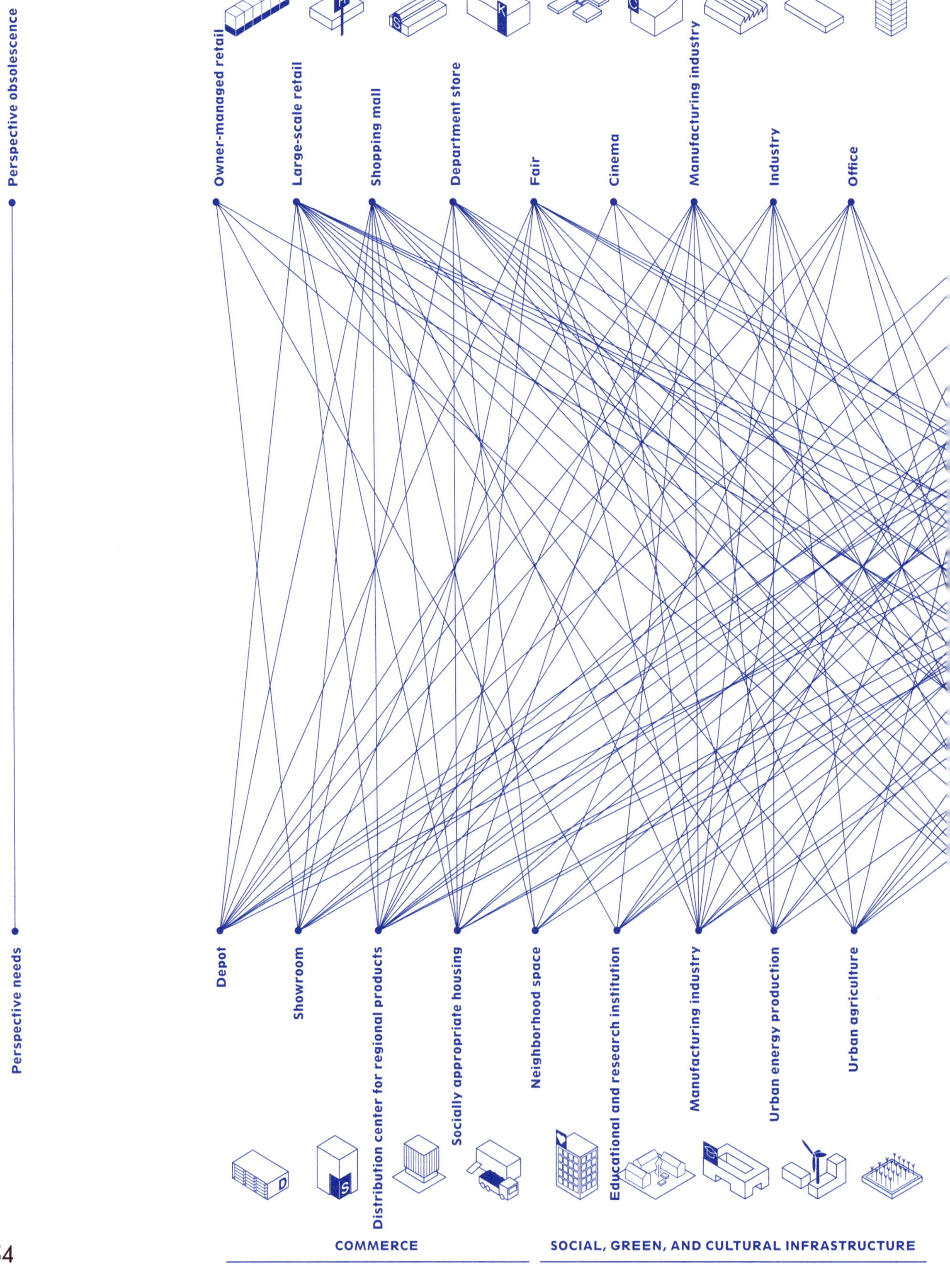

[08] Matrix of future needs: new urban functions and transformative talents of obsolete types.
© Rettich and Tastel, 2022

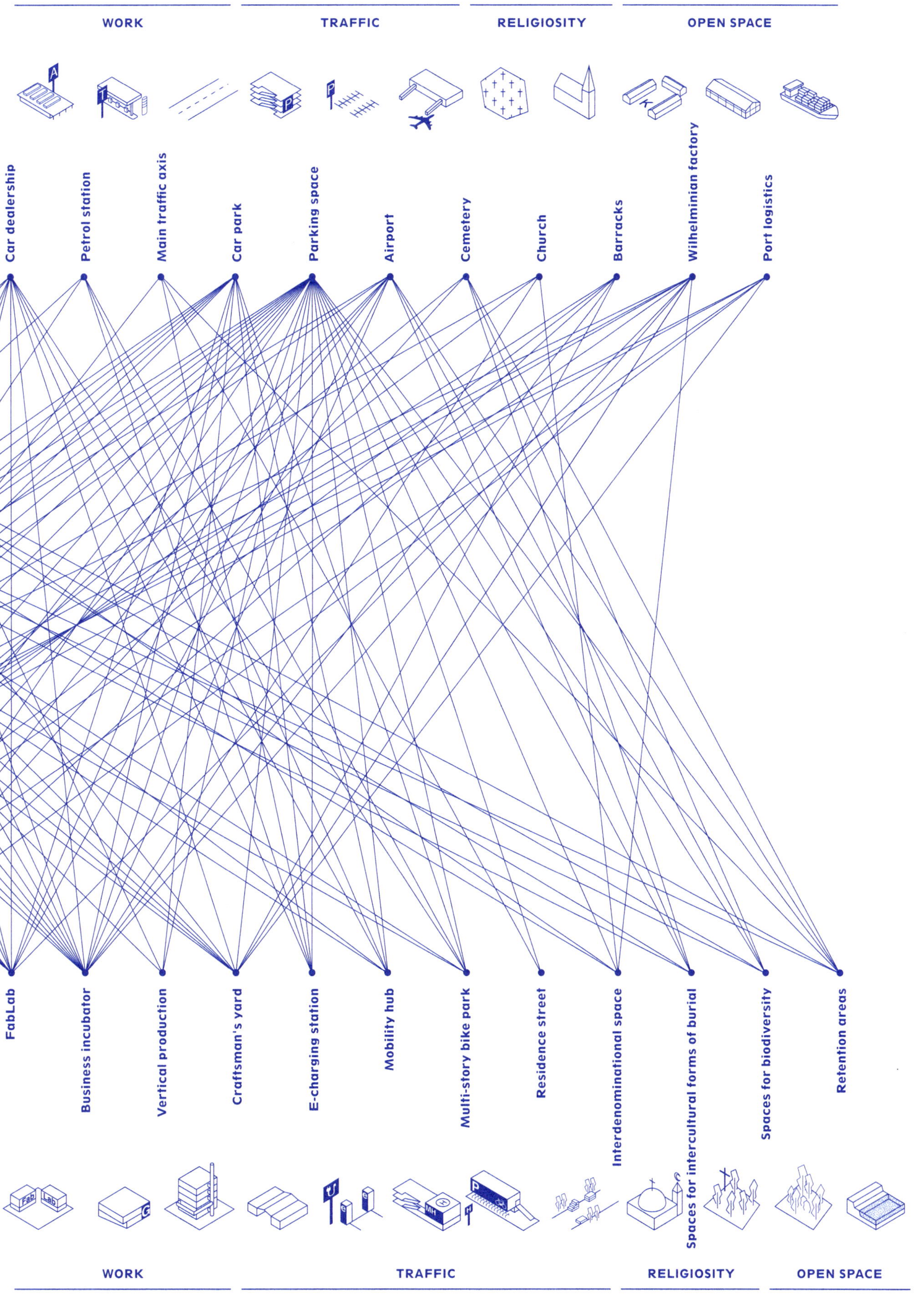
WORK
TRAFFIC
RELIGIOSITY
OPEN SPACE
Car dealership
Petrol station
Main traffic axis
Car park
Parking space
Airport
Cemetery
Church
Barracks
Wilhelminian factory
Port logistics
FabLab
Business incubator
Vertical production
Craftsman's yard
E-charging station
Mobility hub
Multi-story bike park
Residence street
Interdenominational space
Spaces for intercultural forms of burial
Spaces for biodiversity
Retention areas
WORK
TRAFFIC
RELIGIOSITY
OPEN SPACE

SANDRA GUINAND IN CONVERSATION WITH CHRIS YOUNÈS

Chris Younès—professor at the École Spéciale d'Architecture, professor emeritus at École Nationale Supérieure d'Architecture Paris-La Vilette, founder and deputy director of the Gerphau laboratory (Philosophy, Architecture, Urban Studies and Research Group) as well as chair of the international thematic network PhilAU (Philosophy, architecture, urban)—considers that we must change the way we, as a collective, represent and interact with the world. She explains the political and ethical dimensions associated with the concept of regenerative synergies and how it can be a driver to change our values and ways of cohabiting with the environment. Chris gives us insight into the notion of "inhabiting" and how it can help us (re)think the paradigm shift in urbanism.

SG

Given the context of climate change and scarcity of resources, how can we look at the current situation? How can a paradigm shift be fostered in urbanism?

CY

This is a very important question. I would say that a radical paradigm shift moves us away from the modern project to face a devastated world by humans. We have to reconsider the ways we represent and transform the world. Representation of the world is very key. It means reconsidering our conceptions of the cosmos and of society. It is a very civilizational question that we cannot avoid. The representation of this post-anthropogenic period in humanity's evolution is really a collective challenge—and it is not an easy one. It is not only a question of economic changes, of rethinking our cities, our society, and so on. But it is a question of systemic and collective thinking about interrelationships: natural and cultural versus conquest and domination of Gaia.[1] We have too long neglected this aspect of man and the collective representation of humanity at the level of species. And thus, the Cartesian vision of man as the master and owner of nature can no longer be accepted. The colonial tradition we inherited alters the way we relate to nature. We need to move beyond this attitude of domination over the living and exploitation of resources. A new attitude of caring should be our new compass. This caring orientation and attitude are built on the fundamental vision of vulnerability, fragility, and solidarity. This is not a naïve or romantic position. It is an epistemological position and, of course, an ethical and political one. Not only this, but it is also an ontological position. It renews our systems of thought and value. It is about the contemporary making of the city. It raises questions about our current positioning and about other, more relational modes of thinking about our cities, or the possibility of creating more relational cities. It is about cohabitation with all living forms, about preserving vulnerabilities and reconsidering the otherness of nature. I know a lot of researchers say there is no more duality between nature and culture. I do agree with this. But at the same time, I think we must reconsider the otherness of nature. This means that we acknowledge that something is bigger than us. As you see, it is an orientation that is about existing and coexisting.

SG

You mentioned a new ethical position. So how could ethical but also political considerations help improve our relationship with territories? Especially in light of implementing regenerative synergies, a concept that you brought up.

CY

This is a very important question too, of course, because implementing regenerative synergies in territories is at the heart of new ecologies. And since I am a researcher, I came to this idea of synergic design step by step. For me, it was obvious that we need to think about regenerative synergies in urban and architectural design because it is the art of new ecologies that goes beyond the nature–culture opposition. This orientation of regenerative synergies is not only bio inspired, but is also about ethical and political considerations. It is

1 Gaia is understood in the Latourian (2017) sense as the habitat shared by all human and non-human actors, in which humans see themselves as part of nature.

cosmopolitical in its orientation. And the challenge is to adopt an ecosystemic approach in which mental, environmental, and social dimensions are joined. This approach echoes Félix Guattari's position of *ecosophy*[2]. The question of representation, ideals, and the mental is very important. Thus, ethnology and anthropology must be at the center of the city, not only as technical or organizational questions. They need to be at the center of the city to care for it, to repair the urban fabric and to ensure its flourishing. The caring attitude rooted in feminist and eco-feminist struggles is very often, in urbanism, about several synergic levels. I will mention five of them. The first level is renewing our ways of thinking, our values, and our imaginaries. I began with this in your first question. I think that students today in our universities hold and carry this new compass about imagination and values. It is not easy because it is not a utopia. It is something emergent, still very fragile. The second level is about focusing on cohabitation between all lifeforms. It is about biodiversity but not only about knowledge concerning biodiversity. It is about the cohabitation between all forms of life. It demands a very different way of making the city because we must think about wildlife and not only domesticated life or lifeforms. The third level is about experimenting with multi-disciplinarity, collective intelligence, and the capacities of collaboration. This means that we have to stop creating separation between disciplines and expertise. We must work together. Another level has to do with articulating our thoughts and actions. We are used to separating, in a way, science from action. But we have to be able to find bridges between the two. The final point is about being able to build bridges between all these dimensions. It is a huge challenge, but it is also very exciting because it requires inventing a lot of things together.

SG

The new stance regarding our environment, living beings, and resources means reconsidering the way we inhabit the planet. What meanings can we give to the notion of "inhabiting" that could orient us towards a Territorial Urbanism?

CY

We have to consider not only what it means to inhabit but also the condition of habitability itself, because we do not know if we are going to be able to go on inhabiting the planet. So, the condition of habitability is a real question. It's a very new thing that humans are asking themselves how it's possible to live on Earth. As such, we need to consider the vulnerability of life, of human life, the vulnerability of all sorts of life in a way. We must also consider the diversity of ways of inhabiting. What is unique to humanity is that we have such diversity to inhabit: it is not the same for birds, for rabbits, for ants, etcetera. Humans also have different cultures and different ways of inhabiting. But today, with the challenges facing us in terms of the conditions of habitability, it is crucial to pay attention to the contextual situations, and to the diversity of situations. It is necessary to pay attention to existence, to what exists, and to take into account multiple scales: from the local to the planetary and from the planetary to the local. In a way, I prefer to speak of this bridge between the local and the planetary instead of the local and the global because when we speak about the global, we tend only to refer to the economic dimension. Thus, to bridge the local and the planetary is one of the challenges for Territorial Urbanism. It is also about taking into account questions of social and spatial justice. This is very important since it is about facing poverty. Thus, it is about ecosystem restoration, but it is also about the commons. This is a very important question today. Territorial Urbanism has to be very aware of shared gardens, participatory housing, third places, etcetera, because it is about building new commons, not only re-energizing the forms that existed in rural societies. We must also speak about scales of proximities. Synergic Territorial Urbanism should also speak about territorial continuities. We speak about blue and green continuities. But we should think in terms of fresh continuities. This means thinking about air but also atmosphere. Territorial continuities are very important for sustaining life. In fact, we see that we need to re-engage with sense and meaning as a part of everyday life.

2 Félix Guattari (2019) understands ecosophy as an ethical-political connection between three areas: the environment, social relations, and the human subject.

GUATTARI, F. (2019). *Die drei Ökologien.* 4th ed. Vienna: Passagen Verlag.

LATOUR, B. (2017) *Facing Gaia: Eight Lectures on the New Climatic Regime.* Cambridge: Polity.

Fringe

INTRODUCTION BY SABINE BAUER

The (urban) fringe has been long neglected in urbanistic discourse, in part because it is hard to define in absolute terms. As a spatial entity it can be characterized by social and spatial fragmentation, the prevailing presence of transport infrastructure as an organizing element, as well as its functional heterogeneity. Despite these characteristics, the fringe is above all relational—it is not a strict border but rather a transitional space linking urban and rural areas. This status determines its potential: regardless of the substantial complexity of the task, it is precisely engagement with the fringe and its comprehensive spatial challenges that is of central importance in—and holds enormous possibilities for—responsibly transforming our environment. This is due to the fact that its problems manifest at several levels simultaneously: across the ecological, the infrastructural, and the social.

A territorial approach offers a way to spatially capture the fringe using a relational definition. The scale of a project's territory depends on the context of the project and its respective focus, which has the capacity to reveal the necessary territorial connections on different levels (infrastructural, ecological, social, etcetera). The following contributions impressively demonstrate the specific manifestations of the fringe—whether it's a village in Flanders, an agricultural zone outside Skopje, the south-eastern peripheral zone of Madrid, or the French-Swiss cross-border area of Geneva.

What these scenarios all have in common is that the various challenges and opportunities they present can only be met by an urban planning approach grounded in engagement on the territorial level.

Weak Structures for the Transition: Reflections on the Habitat Research Center Greater Geneva Consultation Proposal

Tommaso Pietropolli

A VISION FOR GREATER GENEVA

Greater Geneva, a vast area stretched between the shores of Lake Geneva, the Arve Valley, and the slopes of the Jura and Salève mountains, is an original but not unique case of a cross-border institution currently rethinking its development in the face of the many challenges posed by the ecological transition. It is inscribed into a larger urban territory that crosses most of the Swiss plain, a *"ville territoire"* (Corboz, 1990) offering extended conditions of urban habitability across the whole territory; today, it is an attractive metropolitan area.

When looked at closely, this metropolitan context is characterized by a great heterogeneity of distinct urban conditions: minor centers marked by extensive abandonment; exclusive lakeside villa zones; dynamic villages that have been continuously transforming over centuries; peripheries in need of requalification; and a hyper-center subjected to extreme pressure, to name just a few. Similarly, the region's beautiful landscapes intertwine and alternate to create—in the words of the competition organized by Geneva-based Fondation Braillard Architectes to imagine its future vision[1]—a *"ville-paysage"* (Mantziaras, 2008): comprising protected forests, agricultural fields, the wide landscapes of the Rhone and the Arve, the slopes of the mountains and the Mont Blanc, the lake and its lakeshores. Landscapes characterize all urban situations, articulating their diversity, and ensuring their recognizability.

But Greater Geneva today is also an area of strong polarization; despite its impressive landscape situation and its considerable affluence, it is incapable of taking advantage of its strategic position, its geopolitical role, and its territorial scale. The spatial and economic relations between France and Switzerland are particularly problematic in this transboundary, non-compact context: the inequalities between one side and the other of the border are marked and growing. They are particularly felt in the imbalanced distribution of job opportunities (most of them concentrated in Switzerland) and in the uneven availability and affordability of housing (demand has in recent decades been largely resolved on the French side, at the cost of numerous hectares of fertile or cultivated land). Several "agglomeration plans" have been implemented since the establishment of the Grand Genève cross-border cooperation entity in 1973. To varying degrees these have all simplified the complex heterogeneity of the situation by bringing it back to a radial spatial organization with Geneva at its center, attributing to public transport infrastructure the role of regulating wider growth schemes and development strategies. These consolidated policies have somehow lost their relationship with the distributed spatial capital that has historically shaped this region, in favor of a hierarchically organized system—vertical and highly dependent—constructed around Geneva's city center.

As happens in many other metropolitan areas, particularly in the Western context, Greater Geneva in fact represents a place where collective hopes and ambitions tied to the ongoing social-ecological transition are stashed, a site from which to draw renewed growth and generalized development (Katz and Bradley, 2013; Katz and Nowak, 2018). Such a transition is charac-

1 Launched in 2018, the international competition "Visions prospectives pour le Grand Genève. Habiter la ville-paysage du 21e siècle" selected seven international teams to elaborate seven visions for the Greater Geneva area. The Habitat Research Center at EPFL elaborated a vision entitled "Du sol et du Travail. La transition, un nouveau projet biopolitique", directed and lead by Prof. P. Viganò, with Dr. R. Sega and T. Pietropolli (team co-coordinators), Dr. M. Barcelloni Corte, Dr. Q. Zhang (HRC/Lab-U); Prof. V. Kaufmann (HRC-LASUR), Prof. A. Buttler (HRC-ECOS), MER. L. Pattaroni (HRC-LASUR), Ass. Prof. C. Fivet (HRC-SXL); Prof. P. Boivin (inTNE-HEPIA, HES-SO Genève), Prof. O. Crevoisier (Université de Neuchâtel), Prof. W. R. Stahel (Product-Life Institute), J. Normand (B Lab Switzerland), I. Claus, M. Velardi.

terized by complex, sometimes paradoxical dynamics, which our spatial reflections have tried to confront and react to. Firstly, its ecological dimension (represented by the consequences of climate change, environmental risks related to agricultural exploitation and pollution, loss of biodiversity, and depletion of ecosystems); secondly, there is the social dimension (reflected in growing social imbalances and demographic trends toward population aging, but also in strong pressures created by population growth in the region, or changes in family structure); finally, the not-irrelevant economic dimension (the demand for durability of products that contrasts with the capitalist logic of consumption, a growing interest in remote working, the unsustainability of business models based on commuting between the two countries, and the fragility of an economic system largely based on the tertiary sector, to the detriment of any other form of productive economy). These three dimensions raise questions with respect to what kind of project we might imagine for the metropolitan development of the territory.

In our research, we put two questions—soil and labor—at the center of the scene. These allow us, on the one hand, to go beyond national particularisms (precisely because they transverse borders), and on the other hand to lend more complexity to the image of a Greater Geneva that is too-often reduced and flattened by the current planning tools, and the political objectives that underlie them. Looking at soil, going beyond its interpretation as a neutral surface **(Viganò and Guenat, 2022)**, allows us to extend the themes of the environmental crisis, questioning a complex subject that also concerns food sovereignty, forms of settlements, and conflicts between ecosystems and their different functions. Nonetheless, we considered any radical reflection on the transition possible only by also tackling labor, namely the economies of the future, and their social and ecological adequacy. In fact, the question of jobs in Greater Geneva is very much a spatial one: while the border is obviously national it is, above all, an economic and monetary one.

First we explored the imaginary of this region, including its literature, its artistic production, and the iconography of Greater Geneva. In parallel, we produced an atlas of the transition (a trans-scalar set of representations revealing the paradoxes and potentialities of this city-territory as it faces the transition), developing some different transition scenarios. By exposing the paradoxes that emerged through the atlas construction, we then examined and evaluated radical possible futures. In developing these moves, our hypotheses became more defined, slowly allowing us to move towards a vision and clarify the three positions/ambitions that were our founding proposal. These positions constituted the theoretical background against which each prototypical design exploration was subsequently confronted.

Pays, Paysages: Territory as a Subject

In the first instance, our vision considers the territory, in its different parts, as a subject **(Corboz, 1983)**. To be effective and to properly face the ambitions of a sustainable ecological, energetic, and socioeconomic transition (short circuits, local energy production, reduced mobility, carbon emissions reductions, etcetera) the project will have to move through a process of re-territorialization, recognizing and enriching the extreme variety of situations and landscapes characterizing the region, beyond simply offering flattened solutions. The large model we have made supports this hypothesis, according to which the different "*pays-paysages*" of Greater Geneva retain their own independence based on their geographical and physical characteristics, as well as on available resources and capitals (hence the insular representation). Simultaneously, they remain united among themselves, both ecologically (for their capacity to globally provide ecosystem services) and economically (in terms of employment possibilities and the potential to reinvest in place-generated wealth).

Emerging Urban and Territorial Figures: Economies and Capitals

This re-territorialization might also provide an opportunity for new territorial and urban figures to emerge; today only partially readable, these figures are constructed by grouping together different *pays-paysages* and can take on a structuring role at the metropolitan scale, by reinforcing their plurality. It is from these figures, in fact, that the different metropolitan economies and capitals can be rearticulated; the richness of Greater Geneva's own resources offers many precious assets for meeting the challenges of the transition towards a sustainable, inclusive, and prosperous economy for all, on the condition of accepting a less centralizing behavior in the management of resources themselves.

A Metropolis of Villages: An Image with no Project

The awareness of being faced with a "metropolis of villages"—generated by long-term territorial construction and maintenance of small villages and urban centers—clashes early on in the elaboration of our vision with the observation that current agglomeration plans interpret metropolitan development as essentially vertical/hierarchical, focusing all their investments in the main urban areas to the detriment of the rest of the territory. The planned transit-oriented development (TOD) structure reinforces the dependence of marginal territories on Geneva. However, about half of the region's population lives today on the edges of these development projects, in the network of villages characterizing the ancient structure of territorial settlement that is currently experiencing the most significant proportionate growth in the region. In our vision, we propose considering them as an active agent of metropolitan transformation, without ignoring their paradoxes and their limits, aiming instead at valorizing their spatial capital.

WEAK AND STRONG STRUCTURES, A PROTOTYPICAL SPACE

[01] To consciously go through the project of the social and ecological transition, as designers, we must question the very nature of contemporary metropolitan and urbanized territory. Additionally, we must rethink the conceptual and operational tools of its design, redefining the habitability, accessibility, and legibility conditions of Greater Geneva's cross-border space. In our proposal, this implies a radical re-discussion of paradigms of verticality and hierarchy as devices for ordering and stabilizing the city-territory, reflecting on the consequences of such a conceptual shift in a design perspective. Our vision aims in fact at altering the spatial imbalances between the different parts of Greater Geneva. Further, it hopes to prevent those inequalities arising from the essentially vertical interpretation of metropolitan organization and those recurring dichotomies—such as city–countryside or center–periphery—that shape in imagining its development. It does so while trying to avoid the rigidity of a "planning" and regulatory approach; rather it focuses on the practices and structures of the transition. Specifically, two types of structures support the prototypical actions and practices we explored: weak and strong structures. They represent possible ways in which more horizontal relations could be organized in space.

The Strong Structure

The strong structure for alternative forms of mobility reshapes transport in its various forms: reopening dismissed railway lines in the Pays des Gex region in France, extending tramway lines across the Swiss border, but also

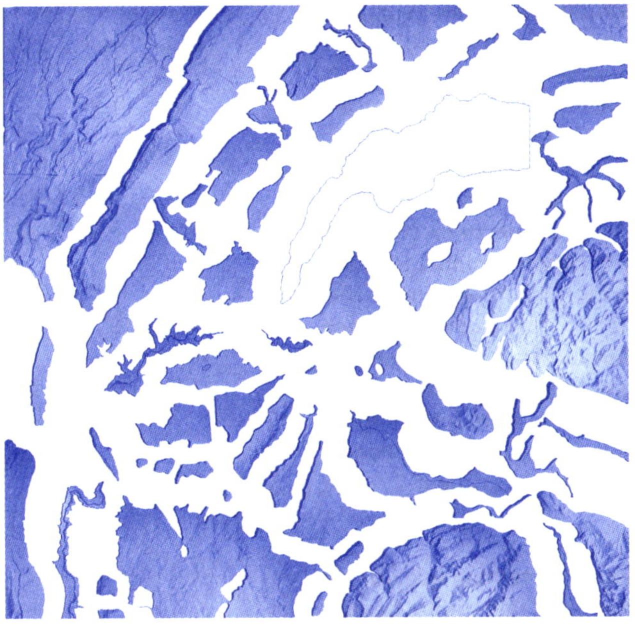

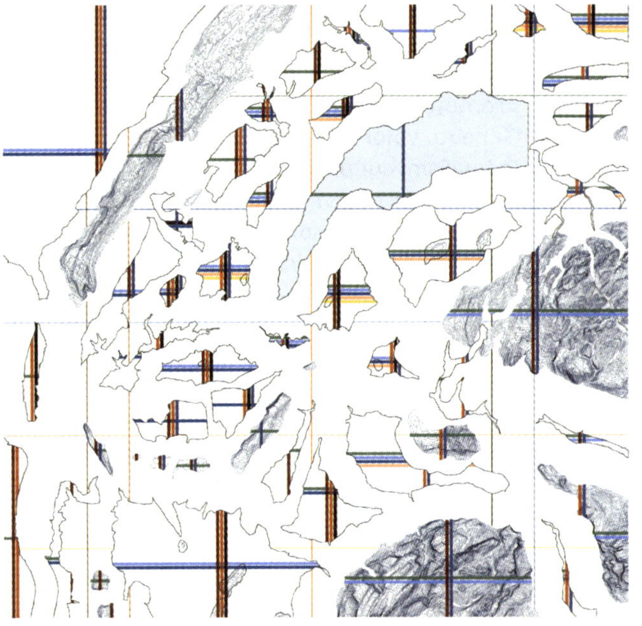

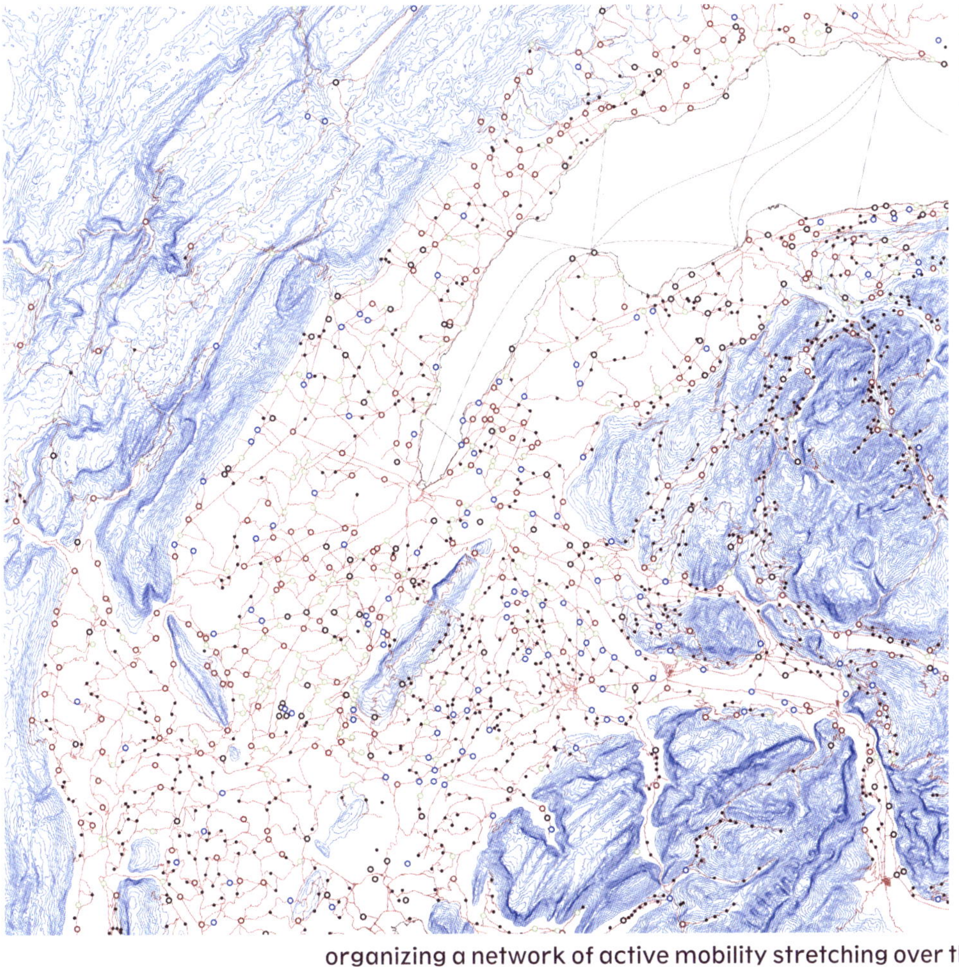

[01] *Pays-paysage*; economies and capitals; a metropolis of villages. © HRC-Lab-U, EPFL 2020

organizing a network of active mobility stretching over the entire territory, in part taking up the traditional network of minor roads connecting historical villages. Questioning the current transit-oriented planned development (concentrating investments in a few axes connecting peripheries to the center), and abandoning the centered territorial construction it generates, this structure would not only rebalance mobility conditions but also highlight the need to promote local forms of work (not just digital) in all parts of the territory. By doing so, the proposed model improves the level of habitability in the region by connecting previously abandoned places and villages. Moreover, it takes advantage of demographic growth and densification needs, rethinking the welfare conditions of a heterogeneous metropolis; it promotes, for instance, local forms of work in the French side of Greater Geneva, valorizing the different economic capitals they contain (relating to tourism, culture, agriculture, but also manufacturing and the secondary sector) and allowing for less dependent territorial development.

In doing so, a process of extensive territory regeneration can take place: by reconnecting every part of the territory to a metropolitan network of active mobility and public transport, the strong structure makes the different forms of urbanity already present in the territory part of a larger metropolitan system. It resists fixing *a priori* minimum levels of density or urbanity, instead recognizing and valorizing the qualities of habitability in the smaller centers and enhancing the variety of situations and related lifestyles that these allow; the aim here is not to reopen the conflict between compact and diffused cities, but rather an attempt to overcome it.

The Weak Structure

[02] The weak structure, however, is the real laboratory for testing ecological, social, and economic transition. The conceptualization of this spatial device in our vision has been gradual and incremental, enriched by numerous attempts and exercises. It is the transcription and reinterpretation of Maurice Braillard's vision for a public space, operating at the territorial scale and using the tools of contemporary design. It is thus proposed as an experimental action. The *Maille Braillard-Bodmer*—proposed in 1936 as a project to reform cantonal planning tools at the regional level, but never realized—is a concept with no clear representations, and yet a fascinating proposal in the Genevan urban tradition. Organized as a continuous mesh of public spaces crossing the city and the countryside, it aims at preserving the territorial heritage, organizing the cultivated and wild landscape, and equipping the growing city (**Cogato Lanza, 2007**). It was conceived as a minimum public surface to be conserved against the modern "growth" of the territory and its destructive nature, but capable at the same time of self-determination and forging its own path. Stretching across the entire cantonal area, this mesh relied on topographical and morphological rationales, incorporating historic villages and local architectural heritage, while also providing privileged viewpoints over the landscape.

Our transcription of this diagram aims to go beyond the idea of conservation and heritage, instead imagining an original device organizing the territory by proactively participating in the process of transition and putting spatial design at its center. The hypothesis is to create a space-laboratory in which to address the different facets of the transition: a "weak structure". A structure, however, that succeeds in interpreting the specificities of a city-territory, which does not possess all the traits of a traditional metropolis but requires an alternative approach geared towards rediscussing territorial hierarchies. Three dimensions characterize the weak structure, and could be helpful in unraveling its complexity:

— Firstly, its ecosystemic nature: the weak structure considers the potential of the spaces that compose it in order to strengthen ecological continuities, to increase the capacities for mitigation and adaptation in the context of climate change. It is in fact composed of forests, waterways, flood zones, vegetation, cultivated space... Spaces in which to organize and solidify different ecosystem services. The soils that participate in the construction of this new ecological and spatial continuity, both agricultural and urban ones, should all be adapted and enriched to increase their capacity to stock CO_2 (thanks to agriculture of conservation strategies), sustaining and reinforcing ecosystems. The extension of forests

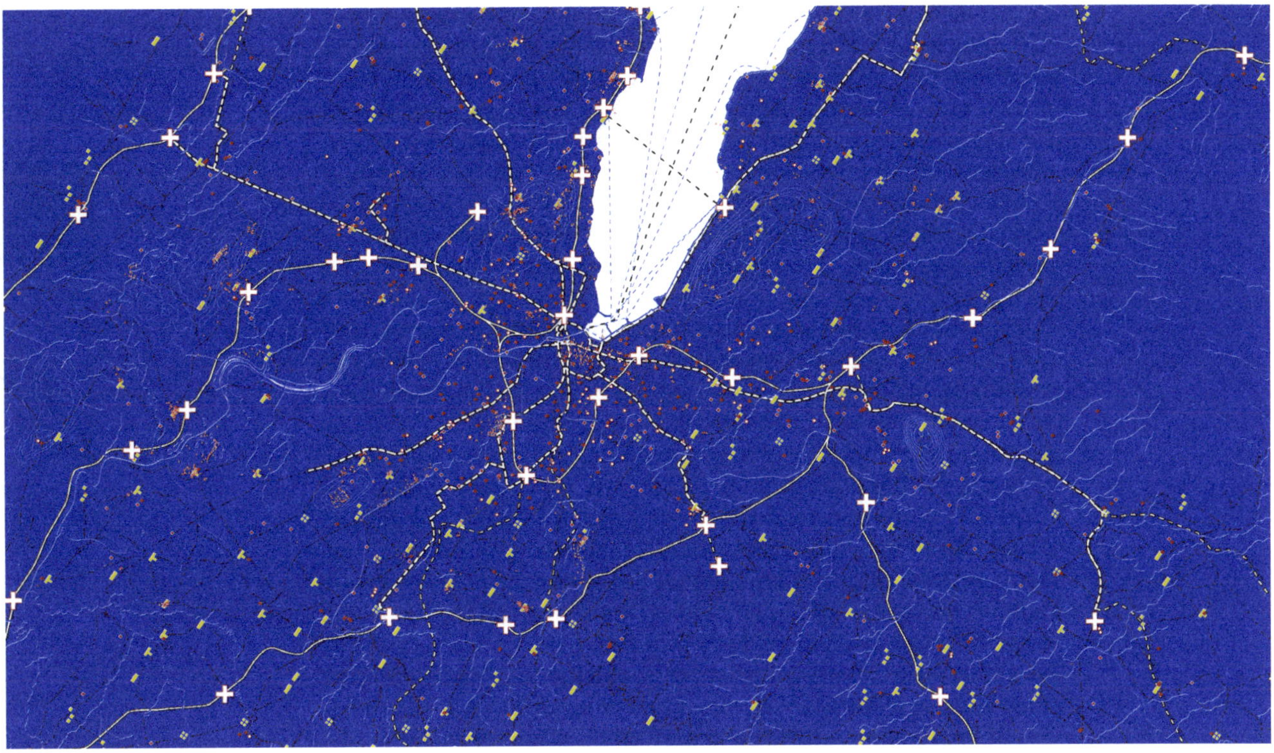

[02] Strong structure for the transition. © HRC-Lab-U, EPFL 2020

and wetlands, accompanied by a paradigm shift in agricultural practices, would therefore transform the metropolitan landscape. To these eco-systemic functions, we added a support system for soft and active mobility: through the weak structure, a metropolitan system of slow mobility extends widely over the Greater Geneva area.

By giving space back to canalized or covered waterways, by recreating wetlands to absorb CO2, by welcoming non-emitting forms of mobility, the weak structure constructs new ecological and spatial continuities, acting as a prototype for a regeneration project that should be extended across the whole territory. Public as well as private actors are called upon to take responsibility for it, enhancing the human capital of the wider territory and producing new economies related to the care and maintenance of ecosystems.

— The second dimension is that of public space, rooted in Braillard's hypothesis of a "*surface publique territorial*". Consisting of surfaces and buildings that are already public and others that are private, but in which we recognize collective interest and values, the weak structure is a space through which to explore new dimensions of a territorial governance of the commons. It integrates spaces that are today marginal or awaiting transformation, as well as the problematic and fragile ones. Such spaces are often situated in outlying territories that are far removed from the economic investment in urban "centers"; in recognizing and highlighting them, the project reinvests them with the objective of becoming prototypes of transition, proposing to finance and support their transformations while leaving space for the different actors involved to imagine their own contributions.

Indeed, experimenting with transition strategies and economies requires conditions that are unlikely to be found in the traditional market space; the weak structure is therefore conceived as a "special zone", in which a certain degree of freedom to experiment is allowed. Giving space to socio-solidarity economies, reclaiming the value of local productive and manufacture activities as well as cultural economies, it hosts and supports the practices of transition. These include collective and individual practices in which a common *savoir faire* is represented. In this sense, the weak structure associates the most evident ecological question with the social one, mobilizing actors who are currently latent, disconnected, or marginalized. It can be realized incrementally, through light and definitive interventions, and by a plurality of actions and actors for whom it operates as a relational spatial device.

— Representations and imaginary are at the center of the third dimension. The weak structure in fact accentuates and valorizes territorial and landscape heterogeneity; indeed, the expression of these differences is considered a key element in the construction of an imaginary for a metropolitan area that does not want to reinforce the opposition between city and countryside. The urgencies of the ecological and socioeconomic transition call for a radical rethink in terms of lifestyles, spaces, and society; the weak structure has the ambition of becoming an icon—however multiple and open—of this change. Actualizing the Braillard mesh, it becomes an instrument for producing original landscapes in which the accumulation of fragments, and the re-composition and interweaving of differences, substitutes the flattening that a more "traditional" interpretation of a metropolis might produce.

[03] The weak structure is thus both a conceptual device and a prototypical space; it is dedicated not only to the development of ecosystem services that will facilitate adaptation to climate change, but also to welcoming, testing, and supporting economies that are still in the process of forming and are therefore not definitive and not exact, such as social and solidarity economies. It seeks to redefine the role of the commons in the 21st century metropolis by appropriating spaces within existing fabrics that are disused or undergoing transformation. It proposes to reorganize the city-territory starting from a space of coexistence in

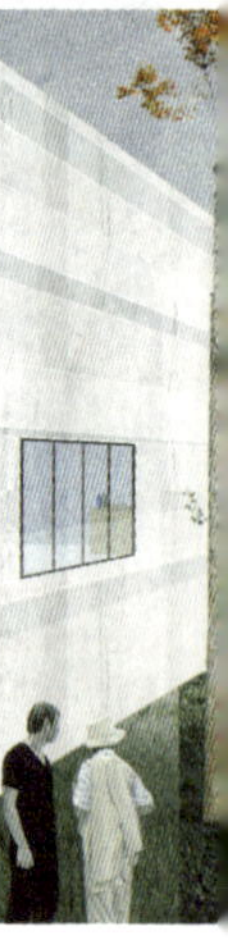

[03] Weak structure for the transition. © HRC-Lab-U, EPFL 2020

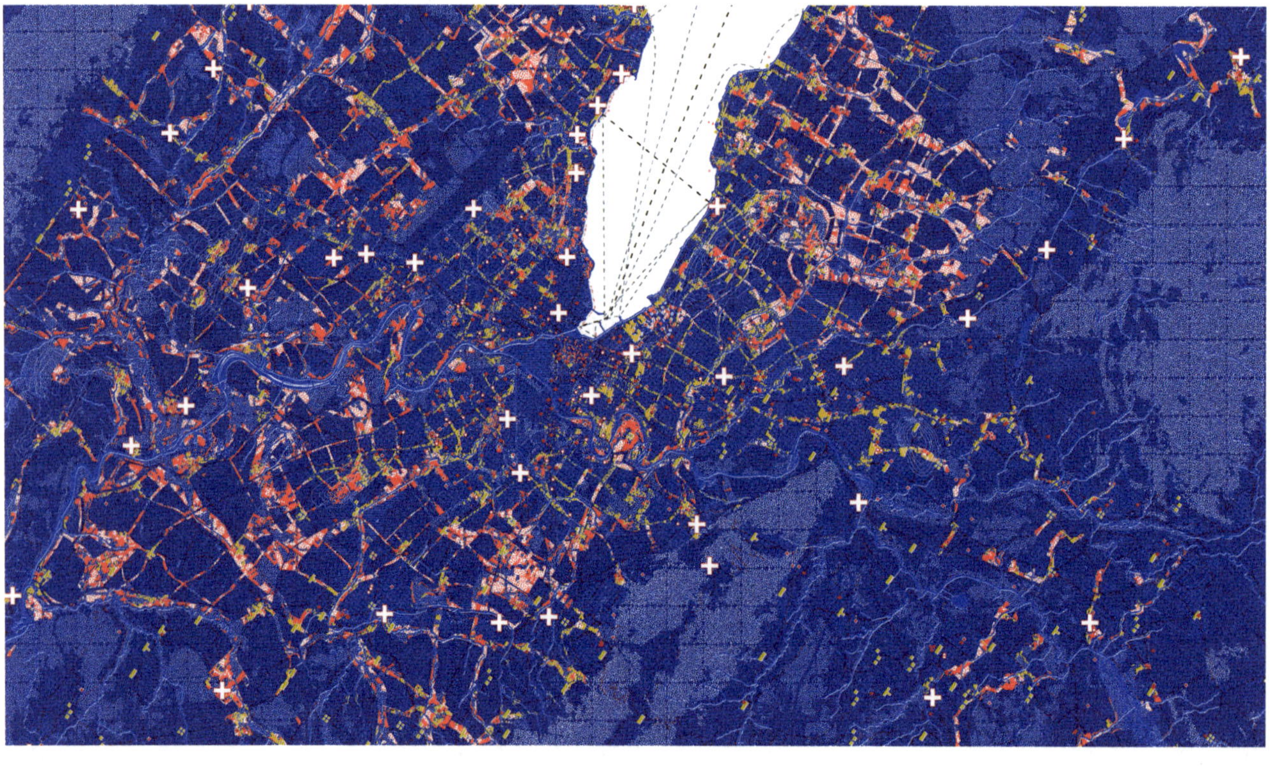

[04] An agropolitan development based on the weak structure. © HRC-Lab-U, EPFL 2020 Design studio MA1_2019, EPFL prof. P. Viganò, T. Pietropolli, Q. Zhang—students: G. Ravera, T. Nakamura

which the priorities of water, soils, and animals are intertwined with the wider ambition to bring about the radical metamorphosis of contemporary society.

WEAK AND HORIZONTAL, A PROJECT FOR THE TRANSITION

The spatial relations and the forms of spatial organization that our vision proposes for Greater Geneva are openly horizontal. [04] The reference to this figure—that is, horizontality—has to do on the one hand with the dispersed, low-density nature of the contemporary city-territory, which our proposal does not deny. On the contrary, it seeks to respond to it appropriately by enhancing its different forms of urbanity, different landscapes, and different densities. On the other hand, it also refers to the specific type of relationships that characterize horizontal systems, and to the specific forms of order they possess—not necessarily informed by strong rationalities or hierarchies. In a horizontal system, in fact, all elements are equal and do not depend on the power of some central controller/governance, with all the paradoxes that this entails **(Rosanvallon, 2011)**. As such, extending the concept and referring to its scientific interpretation, horizontality would define the behaviors of an acentered system **(Petitot, 1977)**, not governed by the center–periphery relationship but rather by the complex relations its components entertain. Such a system is based on weak hierarchical—or even a-hierarchical—relationships in which the supremacy of some elements over some others is not fundamental for the stability of the system itself **(Leonardi, 1988)**. Its elements organize themselves by finding continuous forms of provisional stability—dynamic and non-static—acting without global awareness of what the system is doing, as blind elements **(Vaccaro, 1981)** or weak forms of organization. In spatial terms, vertical systems could be conceived as spaces organized by the center–periphery relationship, and by the vertical dependency of the peripheral parts of a city on the pre-eminence of the center. In contrast, a Greater Geneva in which the dominance of the center alone is rethought, envisioning a territorial system in which every territorial part participates (and is invested) in a metropolitan project, would represent a different kind of metropolitan reality—namely, a Horizontal Metropolis **(Cavalieri and Viganò, 2020)**. This research on the Greater Geneva area and the vision it proposes are not exhaustive and do not produce certain conclusions; they do suggest, however, some paths for reflection.

Horizontality calls into question traditional forms of hierarchical order not only from a moral perspective, but from the stance of pragmatism—by observing territories with little hierarchy and their integrations, complementarity, and solidarity, it appreciates how they operate, their flexibility, and adaptability **(Viganò and Pietropolli, 2021; Cavalieri and Viganò 2020; Grojean, 2010)**. In several ways our vision for Greater Geneva explores the horizontal nature of an alternative approach to urbanism. In fact, the two structures that organize our vision act as devices of horizontality at the scale of the territory and thus allow us to propose a project that moves beyond the city–countryside dichotomy. In addition to having recognized the inadequacy of the city–country or center–periphery models in understanding contemporary metropolitan dynamics, our project is an (albeit incomplete) attempt to put forward a new proposal for structuring territorial relations that does not reproduce this same paradigm, instead hypothesizing a horizontal one.

A horizontal city–territory project can take different forms, and in the case of Greater Geneva we have explored at least two that are complementary and coordinated with each other. A voluntaryist dimension—aiming to build conditions for territorial balance through explicit development choices, with a long-time horizon and requiring intense collective support—underlies the reflection on the strong structure. A much less controlled dimension, on the other hand, characterizes the weak structure and its "special zone," in which individual action is left to participate in an overall change for which there is no clear and definitive plan, but for which there is nevertheless a minimum of agreement, a shared vision.

But the proximity of horizontal and acentered systems (blind elements, apparent chaos, uncertain action) to the general characteristics of ecosystems suggests a second consideration. In attempting to organize and manage the objectives of ecological and social transition, the weak structure is configured in fact as a space of coexistence between different species (humans, animals, plants, organisms, all of which use and take advantage of spaces differently). It interprets spatially complex logics, not simply hierarchical ones, and therefore attempts to construct original ways of living together. It is not a space that privileges the reasons of the strongest, but rather listens to and integrates the reasons of the weakest **(Pelt, 2009)**.

Hierarchical relationships within a weak structure are not those of dominance–control (typically vertical) by one element over others, but rather those of integration–emergence which characterize many living organizations, both horizontal and acentered **(Morin, 1980, cited in Morin, 2015)**. By rethinking humans' supposed "supremacy" when confronted with the risks of climate change, horizontal relations in space reframe the very notion of "spatial justice," by freeing it from the typically anthropocentric mindset through which it is normally approached. It is no longer so much a question of imagining a spatial project reducing inequalities, but of doing so by succeeding in differently integrating the other actors of change—that is, other living species. Putting the living—both human and non-human—back at the center of spatial thinking, and abandoning all forms of anthropocentrism, forces us to reveal and expose the biopolitical dimension of any project aiming at designing a sustainable future **(Secchi, 2015; Viganò, 2023)**. In our case, the assumption of moving towards forms of radical decentralization **(Dryzek, 1987)**—of space, of the actors involved in its transformation, of local politics, etcetera—is not without consequences, since it involves questioning stable positions, static designs, representations, and well-established power relationships.

Moreover, the research trajectory explored by the figure of horizontality tends to focus on the weak side of the notion of structure. A "weak" project does not reject the idea of organizational elements and order. Rather it critically rethinks the very concept of order, in particular the "inevitability" of strong modern structures that are unambiguous and rigid; it reveals coherences that are already in place and reconnects what has been separated and fragmented **(Viganò and Pietropolli, 2021)**. In its explicit reference to the multiple dimensions of weak post-modernity **(Vattimo, 1985; Branzi, 2006)**, weak structure enhances the condition of "weakness" by assigning to it a structuring role. The elements that constitute it are "weak", because they are typically ignored and marginalized by major metropolitan development projects. They are also weak, however, because they are fragile subjects facing the impacts of climate change and other social challenges, and often those who, unintentionally, will suffer its earliest consequences most acutely—marginalized and overlooked populations, non-human lifeforms, etcetera.

The design of weak structures moves with an uncertain attitude. It adjusts itself to the conditions of a specific site, in relation to which it is deformed but which it also helps to re-interpret and modify. While retaining the emancipatory will that also characterized the modern project, it instead assumes its own uncertainty and establishes forms of dynamic balance between its components. Its definition—as well as its representation—is in a constant state of flux, not stable or fixed. It assumes the conditions of a dynamic equilibrium, resisting predefined configurations.

Our vision for Greater Geneva contains a strong radicalism while also seeking to seriously investigate some of the challenges the contemporary city-territory is facing: the complex relationship with "the living" in all its forms, the role of infrastructure as an expression of power relations and imbalance, as well as the forms of governance for territories that are increasingly less homogeneous yet interdependent. In our proposal, the recycling and intensification of spaces within the contemporary city-territory represents an opportunity to rethink the wider conditions of habitability for Greater Geneva and its inhabitants. In line with its spatial and political project of decentralization, territorial balance, and horizontal relations, the/our proposal ultimately advocates for moving beyond the traditional binary of centers and peripheries altogether.

BRANZI, A. (2006) *Modernità debole e diffusa. Il mondo del progetto all'inizio del XXI secolo.* Milan: Electa.

CAVALIERI, C., VIGANÒ, P. (eds.) (2020) *The Horizontal Metropolis: a radical project.* Zurich: Park Books.

COGATO LANZA, E. (2007) *Maurice Braillard et ses Urbanistes.* Geneva: Slatkine.

CORBOZ, A. (1983) 'Le territoire comme palimpseste,' *Diogène*, 2.121, pp. 14–35.

CORBOZ, A. (1990) 'Vers la Ville-Territoire,' in M. Haller, H. Hauser and R. Zaech (eds.) *Ergänzungen, Ergebnisse der wissenschaftlichen Tagung anlässlich der Einweihung des Ergänzungsbaus der Hochschule St. Gallen.* Bern and Stuttgart: Verlag Paul Haupt, pp. 631–635.

DRYZEK, J. (1987) *Rational Ecology: Environment and Political Economy.* New York: Basil Blackwell.

FOUCAULT, M. (1997) 'Il faut défendre la société,' Cours au Collège de France 1975–1976. Paris: Gallimard/Seuil.

GROSJEAN, B. (2010) *Urbanisation sans urbanisme. Une histoire de la "ville diffuse".* Brussels: Mardaga.

KATZ, B. and BRADLEY, J. (2013) *The Metropolitan Revolution: How Cities and Metros Are Fixing Our Broken Politics and Fragile Economy.* Washington, DC: Brookings Institution Press.

KATZ, B. and NOWAK, J. (2018) *The New Localism: How Cities Can Thrive in the Age of Populism.* Washington, DC: Brookings Institution Press.

LEONARDI, C. (1988) 'Struttura Reticolare Acentrata, ovvero la frantumazione del centro,' *L'arredo della città*, 5, pp. 2–38, republished in *Domus green*, 972, 2013, pp. 14–23.

MANTZIARAS, P. (2008) *La ville-paysage. Rudolf Schwarz et la dissolution des villes.* Geneva: MetisPresses.

MORIN, E. (2015) 'Il metodo anarchico,' in L. Guzzardi (ed.) *Il pensiero acentrico.* Milan: Elèuthera (originally published in Morin, E. (1980). *La Méthode. 2. La vie de la vie.* Paris: Seuil).

PELT, J. M. (2009) *La raison du plus faible.* Paris: Fayard.

PETITOT, J. (1977) 'Centrato/Acentrato,' in *Enciclopedia*, Einaudi: Turin, ii, pp. 894–954.

RELLA, F. (2004) *Pensare per figure.* Rome: Fazi Editore.

ROSANVALLON, P. (2011) *La société des égaux.* Paris: Seuil.

SECCHI, B. (2000) *Prima lezione di urbanistica.* Bari: Laterza.

SECCHI, B. (2015) 'La tradizione Urbanistica Europea. Culture e politiche,' in G. Fini (ed.) *Il futuro si costruisce giorno per giorno. Riflessioni su spazio, società e progetto.* Rome: Donzelli Editore.

VACCARO, S. (1991) 'Il cerchio e la rete,' *Volontà*, 4-1991/1-1992.

VATTIMO, G. (1985) *La fine della modernità.* Milan: Garzanti (Engl. Transl. 1991, *The End of Modernity: Nihilism and Hermeneutics in Post-modern Culture*, translated by John R. Snyder, Polity Press).

VIGANÒ, P. and PIETROPOLLI, P. (2021) 'Designing Horizontality,' *disP – The Planning Review*, 57(225-2).

VIGANÒ, P. and GUENAT, C. (2022) 'Urbanism of the living soil,' *OASE*, 110, pp. 53–66.

Rethinking the Urban Edge of the City: Skopje's Northeast Peri-Urban Fringe

Elena Andonova

[01] The complexities of urban overflow. © Elena Andonova, 2019

In contemporary cities, relations and services are intense and interconnected. Often transcending spatial, functional, and administrative boundaries, their interaction creates liminal conditions that sometimes make it difficult to distinguish the inner city from its limits or its outskirts. This is what Edward Soja (2000) calls "a state of post-metropolis," referring to today's urbanized areas where boundaries are porous and ill-defined—hence the growing shift towards regional thinking.

[01] The changes that occur along the borders and the dynamics that play out in peri-urban zones cannot be regulated solely through traditional planning strategies that are dependent on zoning, since these zones are constantly under different forms of (mostly economic) pressure and thus in an uncertain state of transition. It is no longer a question of *if*, but a question of *how* the urban fringes can be better equipped to handle the overflow both reasonably and consciously, without transforming peri-urban zones into mere containers. Instead, there is a need to instigate authentic models of urbanity that are capable of forming socioeconomic and cultural connections within the narrative of ecological urbanism.

[02] With the city already exceeding its development capacities and expanding towards peri-urban zones, the rural landscape increasingly merges with the "inner" urban space of the city, blurring the boundaries between rural and urban areas. This phenomenon creates a unique peri-urban situation, which offers significant opportunities and challenges for the development of those zones as well as for the future transformation of natural and built environments. In such conditions, peri-urban areas serve as an interface between urban and rural areas, performing characteristics of both. When compared with urban areas, peri-urban areas are generally less planned, and their inception tends to resonate with a more informal kind of growth. As the conditions in Skopje demonstrate, the growth of peri-urban spaces is often promoted not by municipal authorities and strategic development plans, but by residents (landowners). Thus the main development of the area is brought about by less formal individual initiatives, rather than by organized community and/or institutional efforts. Therefore, in the processes of planning these peri-urban zones, a reverse planning approach is employed, wherein plans for urbanization are conducted *after* their actual emergence on site. Instead, the role of planning is more reactive towards the dynamics of the situation onsite and less oriented towards reaching certain long-term strategic goals. Under such conditions, peri-urban regions are alternative areas that fill the gap between urban areas'

[03] The peri-urban fringe as infrastructure. © Unnatural Ecologies design studio, 2018

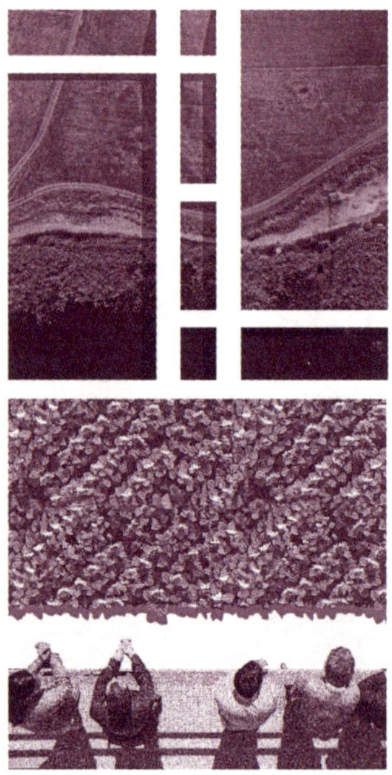

[02] Programmatic experiences at the fringe. © Elena Andonova, 2019

increased demand and supply capacity. Given that this dichotomy of urban and rural areas is now ingrained in the planning systems, institutions often fail to find adequate mechanisms for treating peri-urban zones. As Ivonne Audirac (1999) distinguishes in the notion of exurban and suburban expansion, "the concept and the territory these terms connote comprise dynamic and complex land use issues that involve more than rural to urban land conversion and conflicts between developers, environmentalists and farmland preservationists." Urban and peri-urban to rural linkages are important for both socioeconomic and cultural alleviation and for sustainable future development. In that sense, the peri-urban zone bears the capacity to become a mediator between the urban and the rural, thus eradicating the previously stated dichotomy. Whether connecting the intermediate elements or implying connections through spaces that demonstrate the cohesion of the masses, the peri-urban area can serve as a fully functional transitional interface. Such zones offer the self-sustaining growth of residential estates, simultaneously boosting their local economy and instigating sociocultural activities needed for contemporary community living.

In the case of Skopje, its peri-urban zone is characterized by resource consumption (mostly the depletion of agrarian land and land consumption through sprawl), social decay, and underused areas. Its current state is a fragmented patchwork of isolated monofunctional, predominantly household developments, or small industrial facilities, all of them built without planning guidelines. Mostly, these are inserted into existing peripheral settlements and agricultural land, instigating urban sprawl. [03]

The political and economic transition of the country from a socialist to a post-socialist system in the early 1990s rendered the urban planning field unbalanced in terms of the distribution of participatory powers, social integration, and interdisciplinary approaches. This societal shift led to the privatization of land and property which encouraged market pressure, in turn triggering the evolution of frivolous urban planning processes that could not be controlled by weak municipal administrations. This condition is especially visible at the peripheral edges of the city, which have generated a dilapidated urban tissue characterized by poor quality in the built spaces, segregation of low-income residents, and further detachment from the existing city's resources. It also contributes to an overall deterioration in both quality of life and the built environment, marked by (over-)densification of the city and the continuous sprawl of its immediate surroundings. This creates a disparity between urban and rural areas, as well as between the city's inner parts and its fringes.

[04] The urban research projects presented here are a reaction to the
[05] current state. They aim to articulate the contextual resources through strategic interpolations of autonomous yet connected fragments that conceive of a coherent urban environment within the existing peri-urban zone. They represent two concepts for newly established entities, each introducing a new structure in the actual context and providing a basic framework for investigating the collective domain within the reality of the neoliberal city. Their overall approach moves away from the common architectural fascination with big structures towards the "big picture" as a way of conceiving cohesive urban areas in the peri-urban zone. The prompt connection between the built environment and living systems is designed/intended to achieve resilient interconnected mechanisms that push beyond the goals of economic progress, modernity, or technology. The general concept for

[04] The city of Skopje with its contact zones.
© Elena Andonova, 2019

□ Testbed of 6×6 km

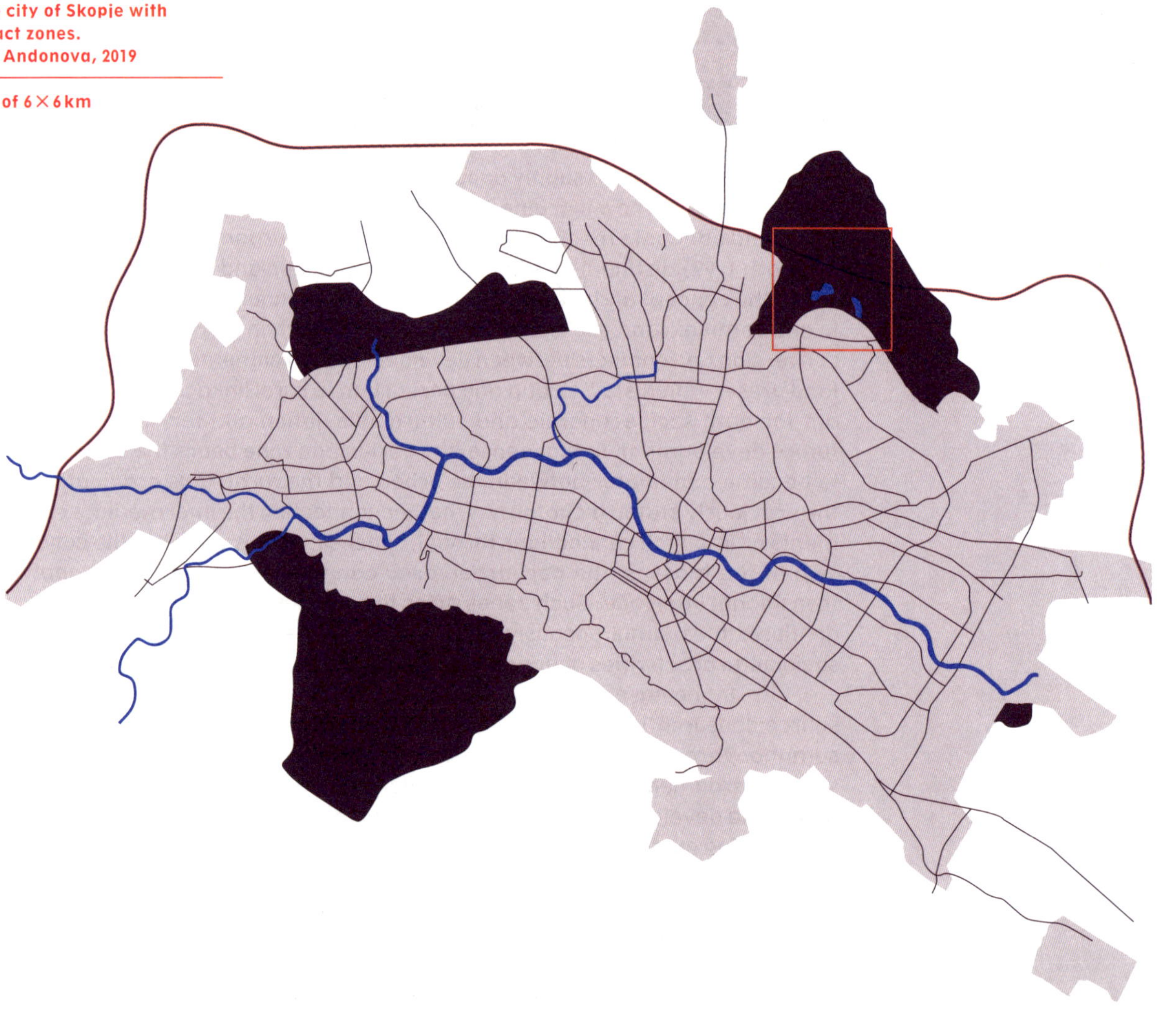

[05] Skopje's northeast peri-urban fringe. © Unnatural Ecologies design studio, 2018

the area develops possible scenarios that are enacted using speculative dynamic maps, superimposing information from natural topography onto infrastructural corridors and drafting basic spatial and programmatic structures.

The concept of a newly established, flexible, and open-ended metabolistic network is further developed and elaborated on an architectural scale. The projects stand for a holistic and cross-sectoral understanding of space that runs contrary to the conventional planning approach, which either dismisses the scale of architecture or is predominantly focused only on the buildings, (i.e., the built space), often lacking planning of the broader area. The focus shifts from the design of private spaces to designing social infrastructures and productive landscapes as the main program and development objectives. The concepts of the two projects presented here provide the conditions for achieving new local economies and improved social dimensions in quotidian life.

[06] The proposed projects for Skopje's northeast fringe derive from a design approach that defines the character of the peri-urban zone as an in-between territory and aims to attain hybrid modes of habitation through the activities of everyday life. Therefore, in architectural terms, the projects convey a specific syntax of built morphology, programmatically providing social condensers, cultural and working hubs, as well as lifestyles that encompass both urban and rural characteristics. These lifestyles anticipate densities and services that are not too distant from urban living but also include proximity to agricultural and farming land, giving the opportunity of upholding close relations to nature and food production. On a societal level, treating the fringe as a midpoint to both urban and rural life simultaneously can provide new insight into contemporary lifestyles, but also new forms of (local) economic efficiency. In that sense, urban growth scenarios give equal importance to the unbuilt as an essential space for ecological and social sustainability.

[06] A map of dynamic relations: territory of 6×6 kilometers as a testbed at Skopje's northeast peri-urban fringe. © Unnatural Ecologies design studio, 2018

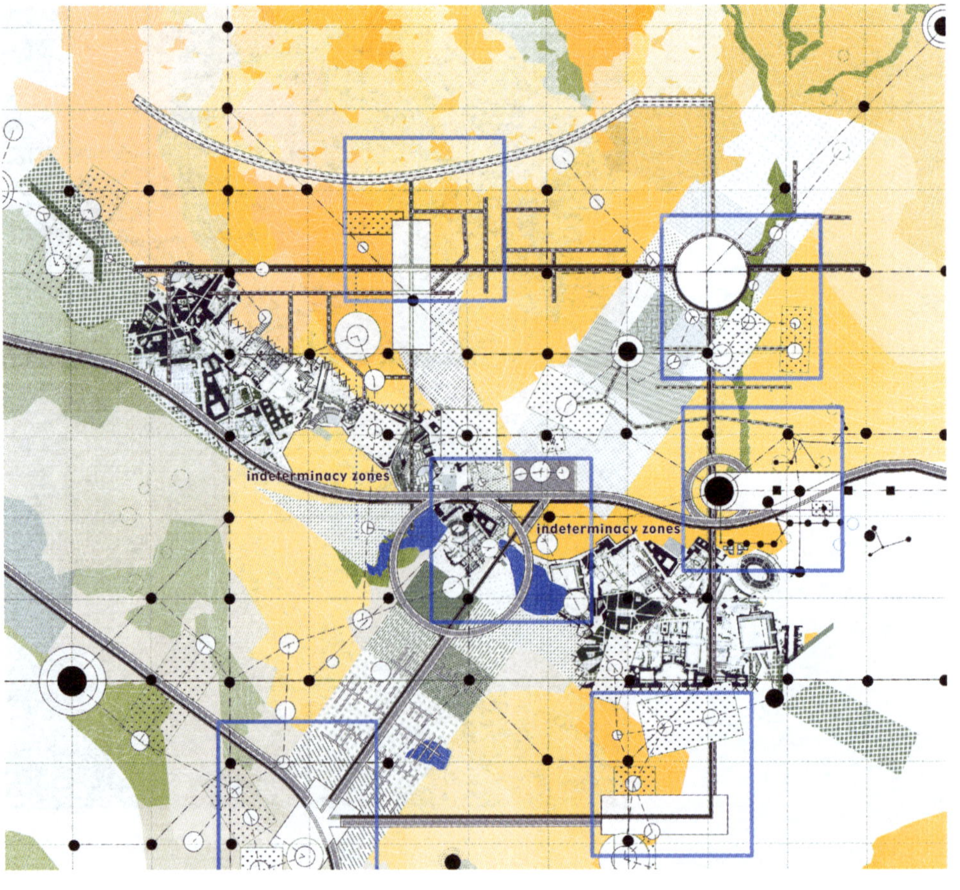

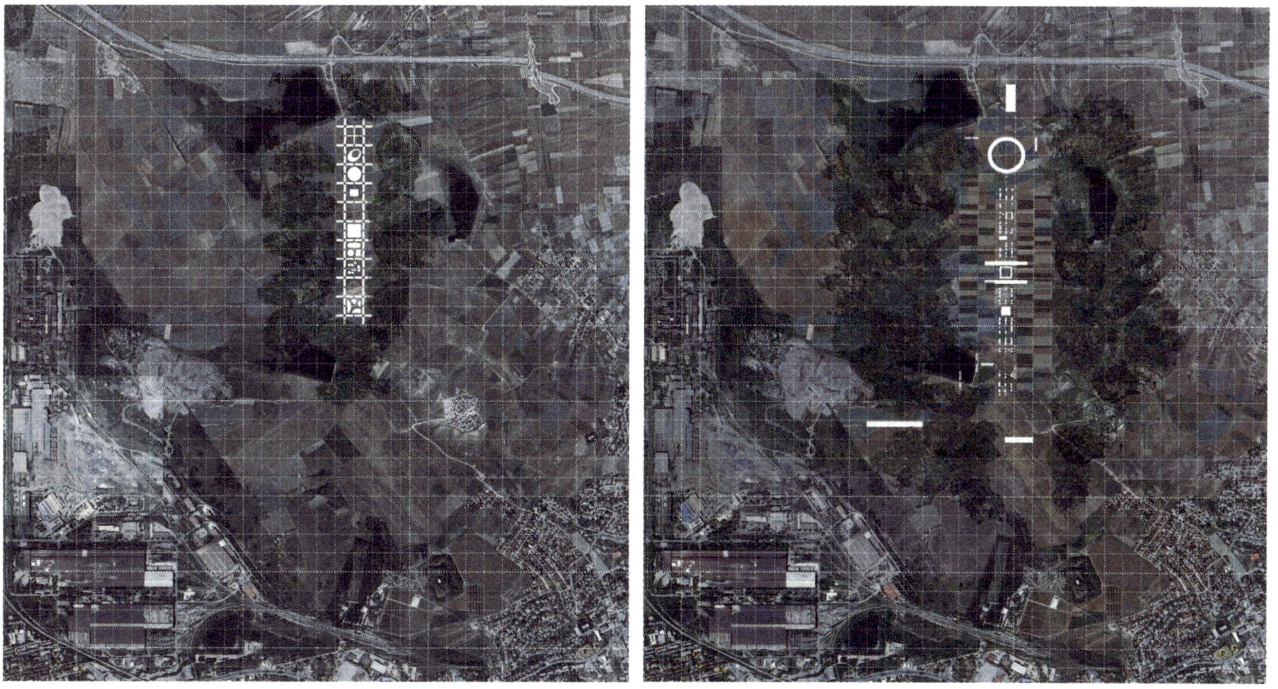

[07] Alternative models of urban living as second nature at Skopje's northeast peri-urban fringe. © Elena Andonova and Irena Milojeska, 2019

These projects represent a dialectical structure that synchronizes the essence of urbanity, its complexities, and the natural environment. Departing from the constraints of the existing landscape and its basic infrastructure, the research has the ambition to articulate the northeast edge of the city by interpolating new urban patterns. The proposals aim to confront the existing sprawl by (re)defining the production of space, following four basic conditions:

1. The contemporary urban space must be able to perform as an infrastructure.
2. The natural landscape is not just a resource but also a generative site of urbanity.
3. Architecture and landscape must create a flexible structure that has no beginning and no end (as it relates to the concept of Japanese Metabolist architecture. This is reflected in the basis of modern Skopje, which was established with the project of rebuilding Skopje's central area after the earthquake in 1963).
4. Architecture, landscape, social, and cultural production combine their strengths into a distinct performative entity.

The projects represent an approach that simultaneously operates on a larger strategic level of planning, embracing the existing infrastructure and landscape, and as a tool that inscribes new alternatives to urban living in the peri-urban zones, tested by methods provided in architectural design. These mechanisms can contribute to developing resilient systems that will extend beyond the above mentioned goals of economic progress, modernity, or technology. Instead, they bring quality of life to the urban edge, redefining the peri-urban zone not just as an in-between, ambiguous space, but as an integral part of city life. [07]

[08] Quotidian living at Skopje's northeast peri-urban fringe. © Irena Milojeska, 2019

ANDONOVA, E. (2019) *Alternative models of urban living within landscape.* Skopje: Unpublished.

AUDIRAC, I. (1999) 'Unsettled views about the fringe: Rural-urban or urban-rural frontiers', in J. F. Owen and M. B. Lapping (eds.) *Contested countryside: The rural-urban fringe in North America.* pp. 7–32. Ashgate: Brookfield.

MILOJESKA, I. (2019) *(R)urban transformations: A new landscape linkage in the northeastern edge of the city of Skopje.* Skopje: Unpublished.

SOJA, E. (2000) *Postmetropolis: Critical Studies of Cities and Regions.* Oxford: Blackwell Publishers.

VELEVSKI, S. and MANO VELEVSKA, M. (2018) *Patterns of Growth: Unnatural Ecologies.* Skopje.

FURTHER READINGS

MAKI, F. (1964) *Investigations in collective form.* St. Louis: Washington University.

MOSTAFAVI, M. and DOHERTY, G. (2016) *Ecological urbanism.* Zurich: Lars Müller.

WALDHEIM, C. (2016) *Landscape as urbanism.* Princeton: Princeton Architectural Press.

Madrid: New Proximities in the Productive Post-Industrial City

Julio de la Fuente,
Natalia Gutiérrez

[01] "La Perdiz," 1927. Escuela de Vallecas. Madrid Southeast from Cerro Almodóvar. © Benjamín Palencia/Google

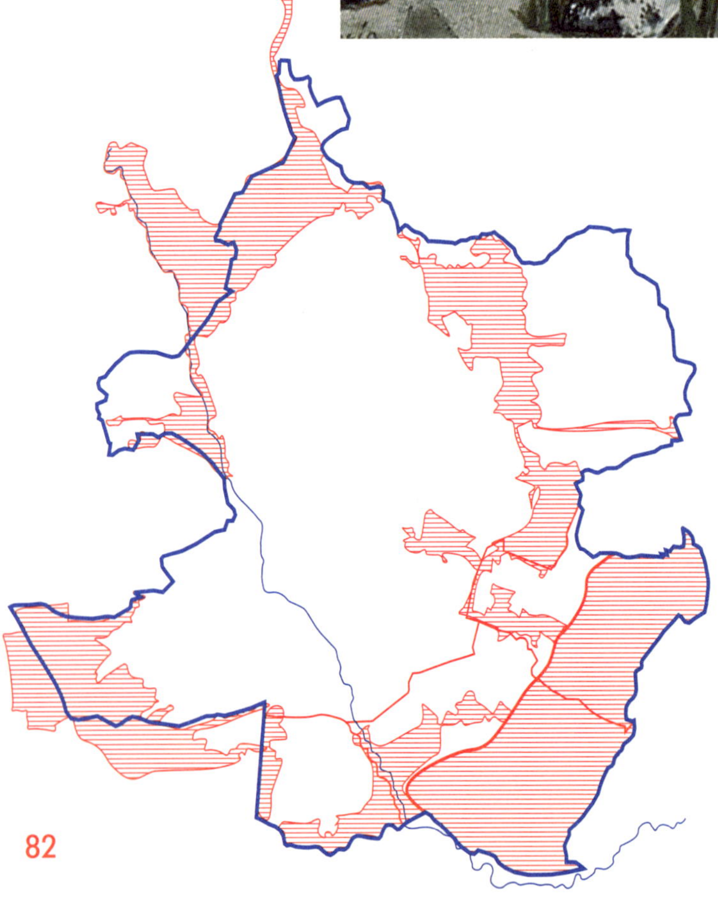

[02] Research area. Madrid Southeast area composed by the districts of Villaverde, Vallecas, and Vicálvaro, in relation to the future Madrid Bosque Metropolitano. © City of Madrid/ Gutiérrez-delaFuente

- Bosque Metropolitano
- Research area
- City border
- Villaverde, Vallecas, Vicálvaro
- Manzanares

MADRID SOUTHEAST, A SLEEPING TERRITORY

Welcome to Madrid Southeast! At the beginning of the 20th century, a group of avantgarde artists called Escuela de Vallecas used to meet at Cerro Almodóvar to paint the wild southeast landscape, sharing a very contemporary attitude towards territory originating from an ecological perspective. Almost one hundred years after, this exploration relaunches environmental thinking about Madrid Southeast territory.

This research started on the occasion of the 2019 Seoul Biennale [01]
of Architecture and Urbanism and was carried out by Gutiérrez-delaFuente Arquitectos (GdIF) with the collaboration of the photographer Davide Curatola.[1]

The southeast of Madrid serves as a unique case study, containing some of the most vulnerable areas with the greatest potential. As the only available land that will enable the future growth of Madrid, it is a territory in slow and uncertain transition. It is a degraded landscape with a history of extractive soil activities, informal settlements, and dumps, shaped by new neighborhoods in different states of development. In this blurred terrain, this research aims to recode the strategic potentials of this unknown land.

Madrid Southeast is composed of three districts (Villaverde, Vallecas, and Vicálvaro) and an ecological parcel of land included in the Bosque Metropolitano. In between these two areas, several future developments are in the process of urbanization. Although the crisis of 2008 put a stop to many of them, for some of them construction is now resuming. The City of Madrid still has time to rethink this territory from another perspective, however, cultivating a new environmental and social approach as an alternative to the traditional processes of urbanization.

The crisis arising from the success of cities produces gentrification and socioeconomic inequality. The challenge for the coming decades is to find a functional urban economy wherein employees across public services and care industries, as well as other workers, can live at reasonable distances from the city without endless commuting. Living and working must be reconsidered following the logics of circular territorial loops. But what are the scales of these new loops and what kind of collective spaces can emerge
from them? [02]

THE RESEARCH METHODOLOGY

The research is organized around a matrix of five fundamental aspects which set up new and unexpected scenarios for repairing the southeast area of Madrid: the political scale, the territorial segregation, the urban armatures, the hybrids, and the imaginary of the collective. The process included interviews with international experts such as Kristiaan Borret, Luis Fernández-Galiano, Kaye Geipel, and Bernd Vlay, among others. The exploration was supported by the City of Madrid, who exchanged data and other indicators (about social issues, incomes, education, commuting, nature, innovation...) to help build a new reality that can be implemented as a collection of plans: a new territorial cartography.

WHY NOW? THE POLITICAL SCALE

On a political level, planning strategies capable of linking knowledge, innovation, and production in a circular economy system are explored, with short chains of materials and energy flows, as well as the economic balances needed to reintroduce productive activities into the city. Why is now the

1 The work was supported by the Ministry of Development of Spain and the City of Madrid. The research was included in a pavilion in the Seoul Biennale together with Brussels Capital Region (led by Bouwmeester Kristiaan Borret) and the City of Vienna (led by StudioVlayStreeruwitz).

time to include circular models in urban agendas? What is the temporal dimension of the so-called "window of opportunity"?

According to some experts, Richard Florida among them, the economic success of a city is directly associated with the "3Ts": Technology, Talent, and Tolerance. This research addresses the question of economic success in the contemporary city and the different speeds that might be assumed according to a circular urban model. Are cities willing to grow at a lower speed? Could we consider the paradox of the artisan component (such as urban manufacturing or local food production) that shaped the pre-industrial city as one solution for improving our environments in the digital age?

[03] Industrial area of Vicálvaro, where the Tolsa company transforms local raw materials (one of the largest deposits of sepiolite in Europe). © Davide Curatola Soprana/Urban Reports

[04] Territorial exploration, Madrid Southeast DATAR. Ahijones PAU, an example of a "frozen urban development." © Davide Curatola Soprana

WHICH SYNERGIES? A SPLIT REALITY

A new urban model is currently being consolidated, where the richest areas appear scattered across the territory. The rapid growth of housing stock has produced this model. The southeast of Madrid could witness a similar transformation in the next decade, increasing the already existing gap between north and south.

The symbol of this phenomenon is the industrial area of Vicálvaro, where the Tolsa company transforms local raw materials (one of the largest deposits of sepiolite in Europe) into products for the construction sector. For years, the conversion plant was outside the city, literally hidden behind the Cerro Almodóvar. Nowadays, its new developments in the southeast exceed this urban limit, and the Tolsa industrial complex is visible as part of the new Madrid skyline. Although the original conditions may have changed, the city still needs to be "fed," also with construction materials. What territorial synergies can be triggered so that a new economy could prosper in the south of Madrid, based on a social agenda and criteria of equity and inclusion?

WHICH FRAMEWORKS? URBAN ARMATURES

[03] Infrastructures appear as agencies capable of articulating the frictions between masterplans and action plans, between production and consumption, always from a grand scale. Thinking that "the Big can also be Beautiful" is necessary to manage the metabolism of the different natural, social, and economic ecosystems, which are always embedded in bigger systems.

What spatial frameworks can be generated through infrastructures and what is their potential to negotiate the interests of different urban agents, both public and private? Very different examples, such as the Brussels Canal or the Vienna metro network, serve as spatial frameworks for the new productive city. In Madrid's case, the city is committed to studying the M-45 highway as the next model for developing infrastructure, able through a new spatial understanding to avoid a dispersed growth that generates more inequalities and greater distances.

WHICH HYBRIDS? MAKING PLACE

The circularization of urban environments is strongly anchored to the contact between urban artifacts and public space, due in large part to the new conditions of visibility of manufacturing activities and the management of resources. The visualization of "dirty" production in the city is once again accepted, opening new horizons to the often-dismissed idea of living and working in the same environment.

What new hybrid typologies can emerge between these short-distance circuits as an organic part of the public domain? What hybrid models can be negotiated between the main governance agencies: the technocratic and the emancipatory ones?

[05] Territorial exploration, Madrid Southeast DATAR. Vicálvaro Industrial Area, an example of a "hybrid land." © Davide Curatola Soprana

[06] Territorial exploration, Madrid Southeast DATAR. Villaverde, an example of an "informal production." © Davide Curatola Soprana

WHICH IMAGINARIES? THE COLLECTIVE REALM AND THE MADRID DATAR[2]

The exploration ends with a photography documentary made by Davide Curatola Soprana, spanning more than 30 kilometers of the M-45 highway. This Madrid DATAR reintroduces a series of invisible landscapes into the urban debate. This collection of realities, seen with a new sensibility about their environmental condition, are immediately transformed into the imaginary of the collective. In the words of Curatola "the M-45 hides and builds various landscapes at the same time, a new visual palimpsest. Walking through the territory with the tool of documentary photography, we have the opportunity to slow down and observe the landscape with another rhythm and, perhaps, find new ways to occupy the space and transform our environment." Territorial Urbanism is manifested here as the revalorization of pre-existing sites through a documentary campaign that aims to visibilize hidden treasures. [04]

But how can these new imaginaries be reintroduced into the city?

2 The so-called Madrid DATAR is a reference to the French DATAR created in 1963 by Georges Pompidou's government. DATAR was the délégation interministérielle à l'aménagement du territoire et à l'attractivité régionale (in English: Interministerial Delegation of Territorial Planning and Regional Attractiveness). In the 1980s, the DATAR launched a MISSION PHOTOGRAPHIQUE, whose goal was to better understand the French territory by taking thousands of photographs.

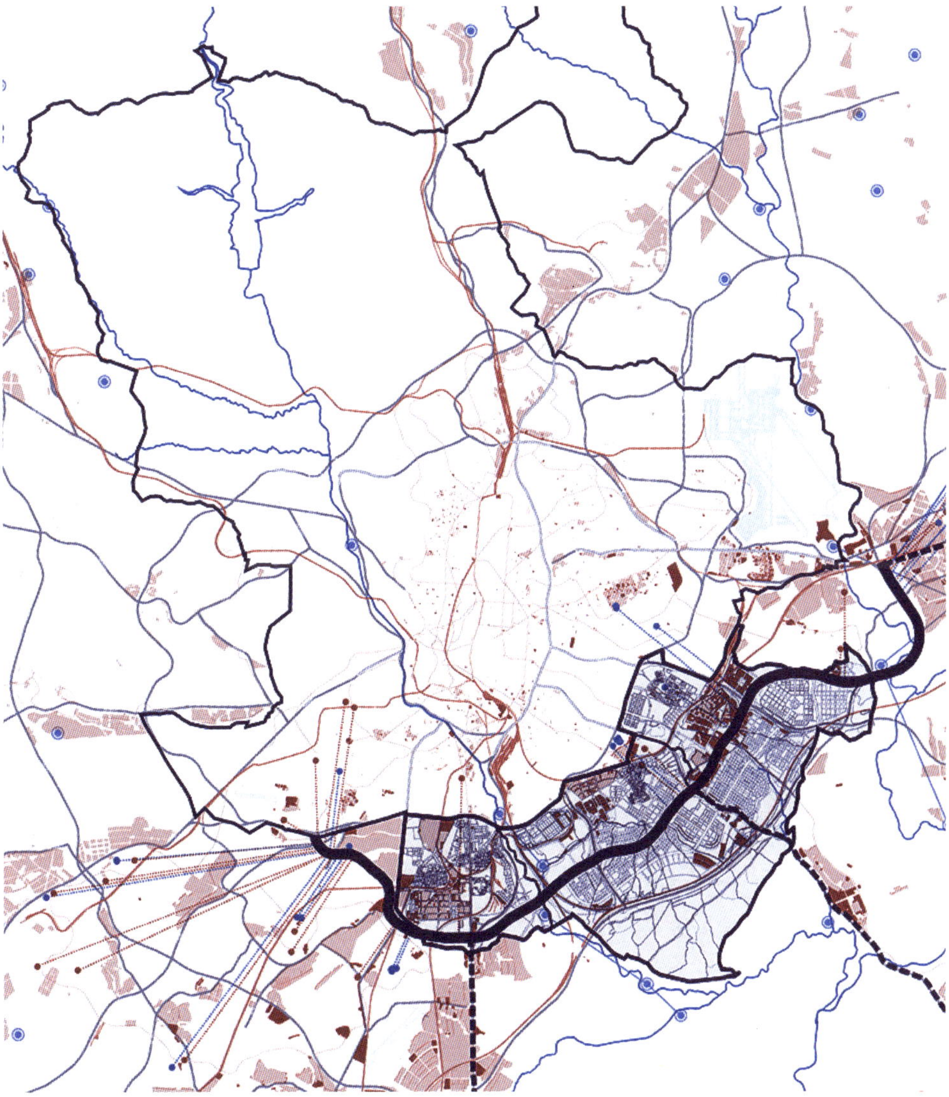

[07] A circular territory. Conclusion: "VI-VA-VI Madrid Southeast, a circular territory" is a reality. The research proposes a new model of the productive city following circular logics. As of 2022, the City of Madrid is working with this strategy as described in the research VI-VA-VI Productive City Plan (VI_Villaverde/VA_Vallecas/VI_Vicálvaro). Final research plan of Madrid Southeast and the new spatial role of M-45 highway. © Gutiérrez-dela Fuente/City of Madrid

- Vacant productive ground/opportunity
- Active productive ground
- M45: Southeast urban framework

OCEANS AND CORRIDORS

"Ideas cross corridors and streets more easily than continents and oceans" Edward Glaeser

[05] The "oceans" (following the metaphor from Glaeser) uncovered
[06] in our research attempt to reduce inequalities, distances, and segregation. But oceans are often far removed from the local, from the scale of everyday life. These oceans include findings from across the political and global scale: technocratic agencies, the 2030 Agenda, the Spanish Urban Agenda, urban development, the European context, world geopolitics, and the Urbanocene. In the scale of the oceans, we can also detect the power of infrastructures. But how to make these global issues resonate in the context of everyday life?

The other types of research findings we unearthed were the "corridors." In this category, we placed hybrid models, ambiguous morphologies, innovative typologies, emancipatory agencies, tactical urbanism, the power of self-management, communities, the blurred boundaries between forgotten territories, and the imaginary of the collective. Corridors are more closely related to the local and to the human scale. But how to make clear the impact of these "localized" issues at the territorial scale?

Only by finding the missing connections between the oceans and the corridors, between the global and the local scale, will it be possible to develop inclusive territorial models that are capable of ensuring prosperity for all.

[07] This work marks an opportunity for the City of Madrid to reorganize all agencies around a territorialization process instead of an urbanization project, presenting a chance to reduce the gap between oceans and corridors.

The Gardens of Puurs, in Search of a Village Urbanism for Flanders

Ward Verbakel

Since the beginning of the 21st century, the ratio of apartments to single-family homes in non-urban areas has been growing faster than the evolution of urban areas in Flanders. This leads to an acceleration in building activity in villages and other settlement fragments throughout the Flanders countryside. This dynamic presents us with both challenges and potential in terms of the urban context it produces, especially in light of other spatial challenges, such as mobility transition, climate change, and flood control as well as the creation of lively neighborhoods.

For one of those urbanizing villages, the municipality of Puurs-Sint-Amands, an Open Call competition in 2014 formulated the ambition to use these densification pressures to transform the village center into a qualitative and attractive place to live. The winning masterplan concept, *The Gardens of Puurs*, by PLUSOFFICE architects and DELVA landscape architects, responded with a concept that merges public space structures and gardens, presenting them as the backbone for an alternative development attitude.

The small village does not benefit from a conception of public space based on either urban renewal or classic urbanism. One cannot simply "solve" the whole village with interventions focused on singular exceptional spaces, such as the redesign of main streets, paved plazas, commercial centers, or event squares. Although projects of this nature implemented during the early 2000s have been instrumental in strengthening the core of Puurs, the recipe falls short when looking at adjacent neighborhoods and infill projects that do not present the same intensity or program mix. To preserve and accommodate the everyday, the village also needs a relaxed, possibly less infrastructural tactic which feels familiar and "village-like" to many of the residents. Urban development tailored to the needs of a small village should not avoid densification and development as such, but in our view requires another concept of public space and perhaps another form of collectivity. In the masterplans, the realm of gardens operates as the guiding image—an important tool for directing the aspirations of a community in transition processes—and offers us a collective space model that is not focused on intensity but thrives on occasional use, seasonal cycles, and informal encounters.

DE MEULDER, B., SCHREURS, J., COCK, A. and NOTTEBOOM, B. (1999) 'Sleutelen aan het Belgische stadslandschap. Patching up the Belgian Urban Landscape,' *OASE*, 52, p. 86.

[01] The patchwork of gardens and passages create an alternative structure within the existing fabric, differing in their scale, type, and level of accessibility. The gardens—in combination with a series of reinstated passages—and voids between them form a fabric of their own. The intention is not to pass through efficiently, but to invite encounters: offering a series of soft inhabitable spaces, shortcuts, and car-free connections. The village urbanism here is approached through these secondary spaces. Together, they form an organic patchwork, a soft (infra) structure or armature that operates as a rhizomatic system, growing incrementally throughout the existing fabric and adapting to future decisions and constraints. © PLUSOFFICE-DELVA

[02] In addition to the church cemetery that became a flower garden and the underused garden of the parish house with its large trees, the new *Gardens of Puurs* include the Hondsmarkt—an existing, inner-block parking lot that is reimagined as a publicly accessible green space. Anchored between two monumental red beech trees, it reminds us of the former monastery that resided here. A hidden pocket of green in the heart of an oversized building block emerges as a communal park (Dorpsharttuin). Hooiveld, a social infill project, is sited on the former hay lands and combines residents' front gardens into one linear neighborhood garden. © PLUSOFFICE-DELVA

[03] In 1999, De Meulder et al. of the KU Leuven described how "[t]he country of Belgium as a whole came to function as a phantom metropolis" (De Meulder et al., 1999), including cities, villages, and everything in between. They further suggested that it has "all the features of a metropolis, both functionally and quantitative[ly], an accumulation of innumerable differences—apart from the density and congestion that typify a real metropolis" (1999). In the villages this has produced strong juxtapositions between typologies and densities. In the village of Kessel, one finds renovated, centuries-old farmhouses next to apartment buildings, separated only by an alley leading to a landscape of back gardens and fields. © Pieter Vandenhoudt

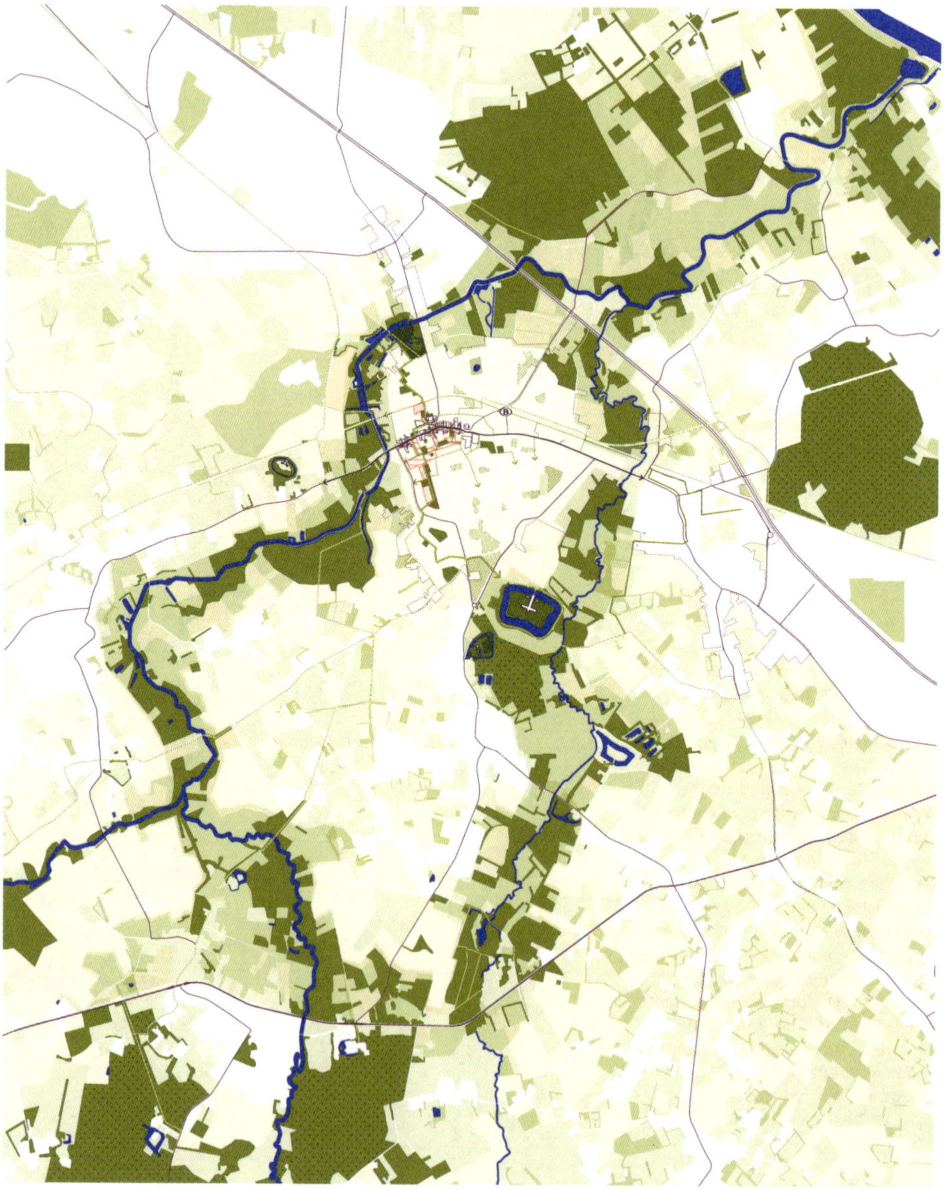

[04] The reading of the village from the gardens, the passages, voids, and landscape logics that surround them produces another guiding image for the urban layout and its open space structure. The masterplan concept *Gardens of Puurs* grafts green and intimate—sometimes even informal—spaces with a cultural and social dimension onto the existing network of alleys and paths. They serve as a space for encounter but not necessarily gathering. © PLUSOFFICE-DELVA

[05] Historical view of Puurs in the 19th century illustrates the proximity and direct relationships between the village center, the plot gardens, and the agricultural landscape surrounding them. © the Municipal Archive

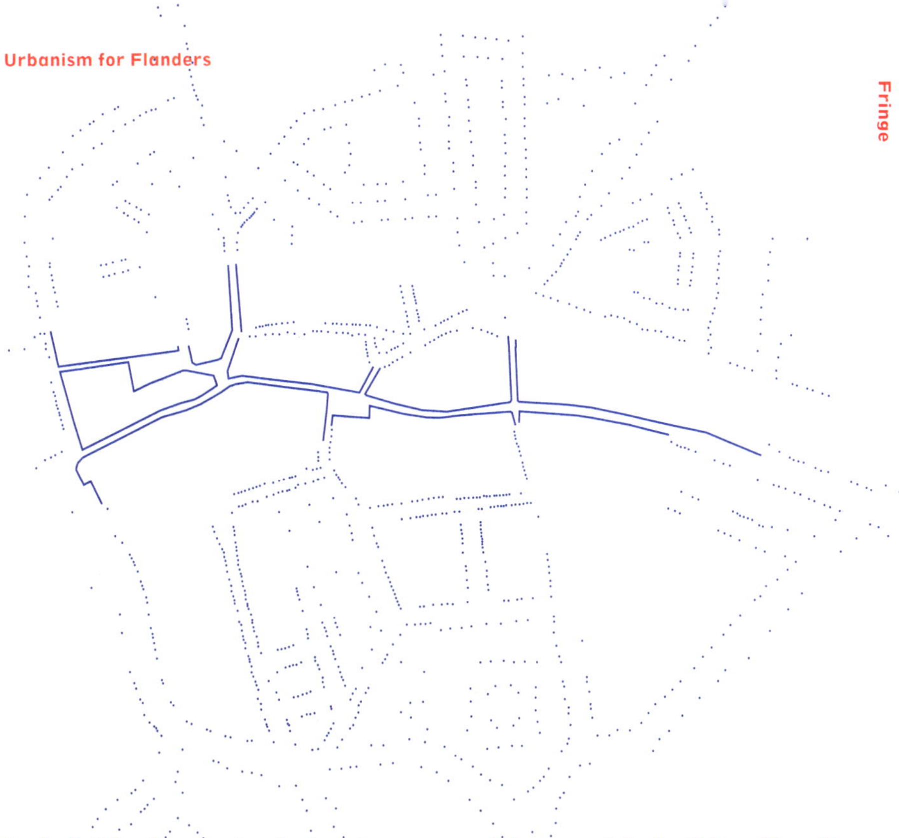

[06] Reading the building typologies of Puurs reveals the historical east–west linear street system that links the two bridges crossing the rivers. The concentric expansion of the village driven by single-family housing came later in the second half of the century. An earlier urban design project in the 2000s focused mainly on the historical armature system. It redesigned the church square and main shopping street, creating a new village plaza named "village heart" by allowing a large commercial and housing development of up to five floors. This operation alone was successful and ambitious in rethinking the public space system of the village center, its adjacent programs, and the presence of mobility in the public domain. The circulation of motorized traffic was reorganized into a one-way loop around the center, leaving space for an alternative façade-to-façade road profile that prioritizes pedestrian and bicycle users, executed using high-quality, noble materials, such as bluestone, and high-end furniture and fixtures. The church square—also treated as a continuous paved surface from façade-to-façade—was conceived as a large open event space for hosting markets and fairs. It also included a public artwork and water fountain. © PLUSOFFICE-DELVA

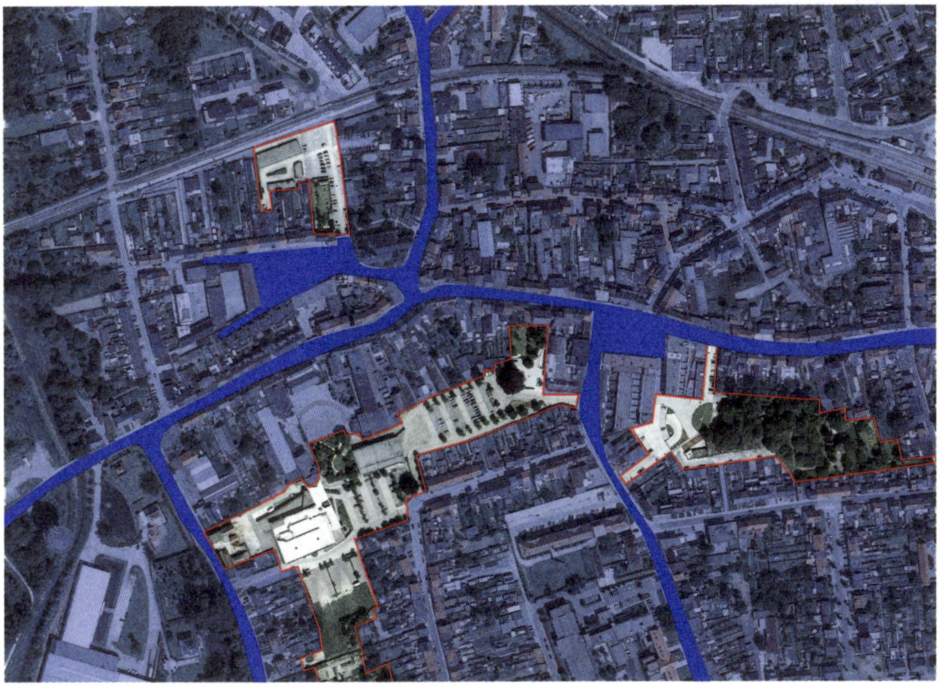

[07] While the newly built supermarket and public space investment helped revive the local economy around this plaza, the resulting space is one that relies on very urban typologies (the plaza, apartments stacked on top of commercial units with underground parking), a high-end (and high-maintenance) public space design, and the assumption of intensity (well programmed, buzzing with activity, and supported by mixed functions). The question arises whether the village's urbanization process can continue by reproducing similar interventions. How many squares can the village sustain? How many main streets, flanked by commerce and stacked apartments, can this population make use of? © PLUSOFFICE-DELVA

[08] The public services of the cultural center CC Binder and the new administrative center re-align themselves with the SJABi school (elementary and sec-ondary school) and its extension, reinstating the remaining part of the monastery garden as the public heart of the village. © Stijn Bollaert

[09] The Spoortuin is a compact housing project encompass-ing three flats and a community space organized around a col-lective garden and a small entry court, both operating as a foyer between the public domain and the individual front doors. The sequence of spaces provided is an interpretation of the alley and back door elements that often up-hold social life in villages—of-fering opportunities, but no obli-gations, to meet the neighbors, chat while parking a bike, or sim-ply nod to passersby across the garden wall. © Pieter Rabijns

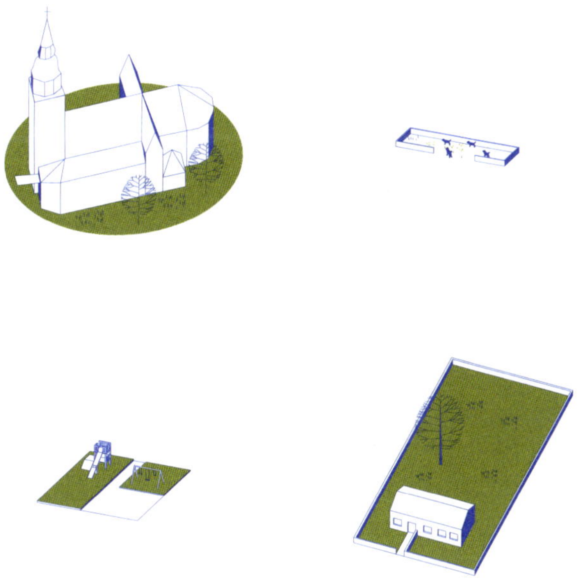

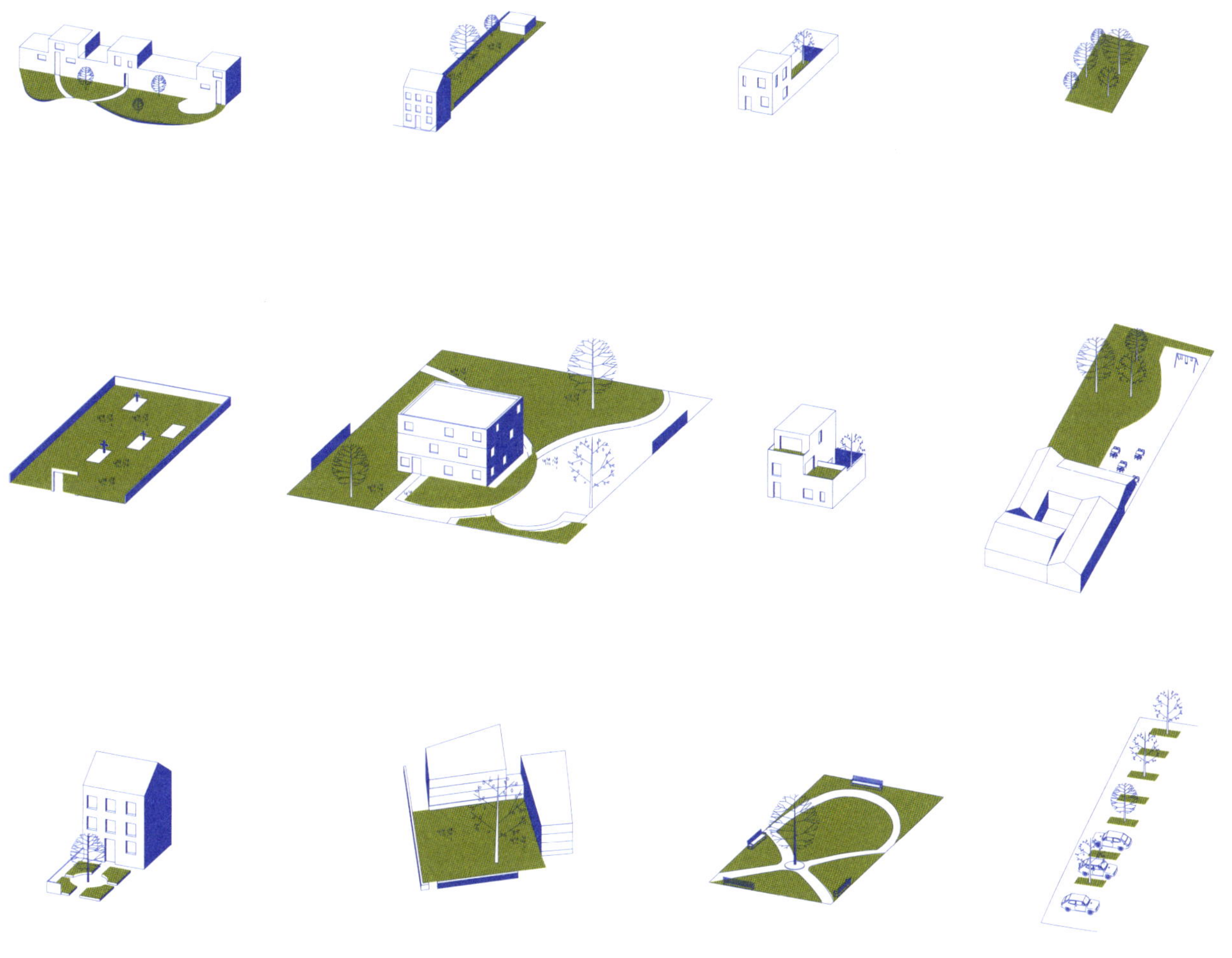

[10] The *Gardens of Puurs* masterplan approaches the urbanization process with a logic that originates from the conceptualization of the garden. It is the first step of a project: each new development should add a specific garden to the village. This builds on the strategy of an earlier project in Puurs: the landscape redesign of the church cemetery, which became a flower garden. Can the underused garden of the parish house, with its large trees, become a restaurant garden? Can the former monastery garden, part of the current secondary school campus, become a public garden? The idea is that Puurs' new gardens will expand the realm of green spaces and passages throughout the loose-knit fabric of the village. © PLUSOFFICE-DELVA

[11] The garden as a default secondary space is abundant within the Belgian provincial context, manifesting as front garden, strip gardens, fallow land, vacant lots, backyards, allotments, orchards, etcetera. This garden realm offers an array of alternative public space models which celebrate secondary nature and do not require intensity of users and activities to function. In the Hondsmarkt, the public space concept balances on the boundary between plaza and garden, dedicating at least half of the available space to vegetation and water retention.
© PLUSOFFICE-DELVA

[12] The streetscape pictured here—in a photo taken in the 1950s—shows a remarkable combination of front gardens and allotments, adjoining a street that is not much more than a passage towards the church and village center. It was retrieved from a local Facebook group discussing the transition of the village over time. When the transformation of villages is discussed, it often prompts a nostalgic reflex that focuses on ideological assumptions about the past. The *Gardens of Puurs* masterplan acknowledges this tendency but transforms it into a powerful potential for future projects, leading the discussion away from what has been lost. Instead, it offers imaginative possibilities that merge densification with quality concerns and a public space system that builds on the legacy of the village instead of erasing it.
© the Municipal Archive

SANDRA GUINAND IN CONVERSATION
WITH CHRISTIAN SCHMID

Christian Schmid—former professor of Sociology at the Faculty of Architecture ETH Zurich and researcher at the Contemporary City Institute, ETH Studio Basel—explains why the paradigm shift in urbanism is strongly related to how our living conditions, settlement settings, and building ethos are framed. He stresses how urban quality can be a means of achieving better quality of life and increasing social resources while also diminishing the anthropogenic impact on land. He calls to reduce our impact on the environment by acknowledging and working with what already exists and by making it an active component of current urban practices. Additionally, he urges us to shift our perspective on urban territories by focusing on the synergies between territories, all of them with strengths but also fragilities. These fragilities are the starting point for (re)-considering the structure and nature of our relationship with the environment.

SG
Christian, how we can encourage a paradigm shift in urbanism from a sociological perspective, particularly in the context of climate change and scarcity of resources? What's your take on that?

CS
If we talk about urbanization processes, we must first understand that they are key drivers of worldwide CO2 emissions, not just the construction process itself but also the massive increase in traffic that is generally created by urban sprawl. Attempts to address climate change in urban planning typically promote various strategies of urban densification and establish *Minergie* standards in housing construction—a building concept from Switzerland based on low energy consumption. If you look closer though, we need to admit that these might be the wrong answers. Densification may be an important means of reducing transport emissions and all sorts of inefficiencies generated by urban sprawl and extended urbanization. But the key question is how we live, and how we recenter our everyday lives towards a more collective form of living and greater sharing. We can try to increase urban qualities to reduce energy consumption for excessive urban transport and, at the same time, increase the quality of life. The use of construction materials, particularly cement, is another important issue. You may say that this is not a topic for sociologists. But it is nevertheless the key to understanding what needs to be addressed. To establish *Minergie* standards for construction as such does not solve the problem, because construction per se produces massive CO2 emissions (even if we construct with timber, for example). The main point I would like to make here is that we should first of all stop demolishing buildings. In Zurich for instance, forty to fifty year-old buildings that are often in excellent shape are being demolished to be replaced by only slightly larger buildings. This is even presented as a strategy against climate change, because the new houses are constructed according to *Minergie* standards. But the CO2 emissions of the construction process alone exceed all possible later emission savings. Thus, we need to intensify our discussions and research around how to reuse existing buildings and urban structures, and to produce buildings and urban spaces that are adaptable to changing social needs. We construct houses that have a lifespan of 100 years but, over time, the needs of people, their lifestyles and everyday lives are changing. We should think about architecture and construction in dialogue with the people who use these spaces, focusing on social needs, commonality, and sociability.

SG
You mentioned adaptability but also urban qualities. How do we apply the concept of urban quality as a means of improving the relationship between urbanism and the resources of the territory?

CS
We developed this concept in the context of a research project that was originally called "urban intensity" and was meant to propose the

densification of urban spaces. We then realized that urbanity is not just about urban intensity, but is in fact a multidimensional phenomenon. It is also a process that has very different facets and takes on very different forms. There isn't just low urbanity and high urbanity, rather there are different forms of urbanity, and each urban situation is a combination of certain aspects of urbanity. We then developed a tool that was based on a range of criteria that we linked to the question of urbanity, which could be used to guide urban analysis, urban planning, and urban design. Why are urban qualities important? It is not because urban quality is something that is a necessity for life as such. Some people may say: "We don't need that. We want to be in our nice apartment or single-family house. We don't want to have a lot of people around us and we don't need public spaces." This is their choice. But, on the other hand, we also see that more and more people are seeking accessible and attractive public spaces, wanting to have people around them, to take advantage of the possibilities to meet, to interact, to exchange. For many, being located next to public spaces becomes an important part of their quality of life. An increase of urban qualities in the neighborhood also allows us to use less private space. There are some great examples in Zurich's new cooperatives, which build additional common spaces in their settlements and reduce the size of their apartments. Because the inhabitants have access to all these great common spaces, they accept smaller private spaces. This is an effective strategy for urban densification. In mainstream discussions on densification, the everyday dimensions of lived experience and social life are often neglected or even excluded. These debates tend to look at architectural forms, but do not analyze what happens within this architecture, what activities are facilitated and enabled by a certain design or, on the other hand, what activities are impeded or even made impossible. If you look at so-called "contemporary" urban architecture, it is an architecture that is often not facilitating or enabling urbanity. We made a very detailed empirical analysis of this phenomenon in the Zurich region, which exposed that much of this new architecture isn't really urban. On the contrary, it prevents urbanity because it neglects the appropriation of public spaces, diversity, centrality, and the potential for congregation. Often, nobody feels responsible for public outdoor spaces; if someone is responsible, then they look mostly clean and tidy. But they do not invite us to gather, to meet, to play. If we analyze these spaces, we notice that they are often not made for actual use or appropriation, but instead serve to control and isolate people, to keep them in a passive role as mere spectators. These spaces do not offer use value, they offer only an illusion of urbanity—and consumption. They are made for looking at, to be shiny and have their photos published in magazines. In a similar way, indoor spaces may offer a lot of comfort—but they do not offer communal living. They are not inviting us to share and live together with others. We thus really need to change the whole approach of architecture and urban design. We must radically recenter our design efforts towards social interaction, towards everyday life, and towards use value.

SG

As you mentioned, urban quality is even more important when thinking about the extension of urbanization. How could the concept of "planetary urbanization" help Territorial Urbanism?

CS

Behind the concept of planetary urbanization is Henri Lefebvre's famous thesis of the "complete organization of society". With this thesis, formulated in 1970, he wanted to express that not only places we call "cities" but also our entire society is urbanizing on a planetary scale. This was quite a visionary hypothesis. Many decades later, Neil Brenner and I used the concept of planetary urbanization to address the key problematic of our time. It basically means that urbanization now has a planetary reach. Today, every part of the planet shows traces of urbanization in one way or another. Consequently, we need to change our perspective and decenter our position as researchers both theoretically and empirically. While we usually look from a central point and try to define the extension of an urban territory, we should now position ourselves somewhere in the periphery to understand urbanization. Brenner and I distinguish between concentrated urbanization, extended urbanization, and differential urbanization. Concentrated urbanization means the agglomeration of people, the means of production, and all sorts of facilities. But it is impossible to generate urban concentration without also producing urban extension, because everything that is needed to support the urbanization process comes from the "outside": food, water, raw materials, energy, and first and foremost the people that migrate to urban centers. In this process, the territories where raw materials are produced are also affected by urbanization processes. These are often agricultural areas, but they are not properly "rural" anymore; they have become highly industrialized and urbanized "operational landscapes". They are transformed into intensely-used production zones for food, feed, and biofuels; into energy landscapes that harvest wind and solar energy; into extraction zones for accessing raw materials; and into huge transport corridors, thus leading to landscapes of extended urbanization. How can we address these developments? We should think about these territories not as production sites, but as landscapes that need care, that need attachment—and beauty. We also have to introduce the concept of urban quality to peripheral areas. Urban design should not only be applied to urban centers, but also to extended urban landscapes. This is a real challenge. We need to look beyond the agglomerations and to understand these extended urbanized landscapes as crucial resources for us—particularly for biodiversity, but also as landscapes that people can appropriate and enjoy on their own terms.

A Plea for a Territorial Climate Imaginary

Claudia Bode,
Philipp Misselwitz

"It is clearly difficult, if not impossible, to fight for deep systemic changes if we cannot first imagine them—and the larger the systems-level change required, the more critical it is to engage society's full collective radical imagination to envision it." (Trott et al., 2022, p. 235)

The climate emergency has been described as a "crisis of imagination," mainly referring to a breakdown in our ability to grasp the scale, complexity, and true ramifications of our effects on the global climate. Yet it is also a crisis in our ability to imagine a more positive, hopeful future. To speak of an *imaginary* is to speak of shared visions that enable collective action: our dreams of a good future, but also our role in the process of attaining that future. "To imagine is to think about possibilities other than [what is] possible, times other than now, and places other than here," write Simin Davoudi and Ruth Machen (2021, p. 3).

Since the birth of the Industrial Revolution, the accelerating urbanization of the planet and the corresponding consumption of planetary resources has steadily degraded the Earth's natural systems. The building boom that will be required to house an anticipated 2.5 billion new urban inhabitants over the next thirty years promises devastating consequences. Only a comprehensive overhaul of the materials, means, and methods with which we construct the buildings and infrastructure that comprise human settlement can prevent climatic and terrestrial catastrophe. The entire life cycle of the urban realm requires drastic rethinking: the re-formation and re-materialization of the physical artifacts that comprise it, the reconfiguration of the socioeconomic structures that underpin it, and the re-engagement of the bioregions that might sustainably supply it. Can we consider the unprecedented convergence of environmental and social crises as a powerful opportunity for systemic change—to escape the defeatist and preservationist approach of "saving what we have"? What if we refuse to flatten out complexities for the sake of either administrative "legibility" (Scott, 1998) or market-based technocratic solutions?

In spring 2022, Bauhaus Earth convened an interdisciplinary and cross-cultural team of thinkers and makers from around the world—scientists, architects, spatial planners, and policy makers—to author a manifesto and serve as its initial signatories. *Towards Re-Entanglement: A Charter for the City and the Earth* is a call for radical action. It challenges all those with a role in the conception, production, operation, and governance of the built environment to address the systemic ecological, climatic, and social impacts incurred by the activities of the contemporary building sector. As discussions began—mostly virtually or via email exchanges among an interdisciplinary group that had never convened before—we began debating the purpose of the words we were using, as well as the concepts underpinning them. We acknowledged the value of a unified language, as well as quantifiable and measurable indicators in aligning global political actors, structuring multilateral processes, and pushing back against the fuzzy quality of many contemporary debates. However, we also shared a deep sense of collective frustration with the semantic uniformity and repetitiveness of technocratic language, as well as the alarmist quality of an exponentially growing number of reports, agendas, work programs, and action-oriented documents seeking to address the climate emergency. We agreed that language itself seems to lock us in—reinforcing certain ways of thinking that confine us in our disciplinary bubbles, encourage sectoral techno-fixes, and often blind us to the overwhelming urgency and complexity of the current crisis. A "good future" must be more than the mere accomplishment of sectoral aims! On reflection, we were left with the question: how can we be firm, precise, and acknowledge the need for urgent action, while also recognizing that simply aiming at the fulfillment of all sector-related targets—dressed in technocratic, actionable language—is not enough? What could be an alternative?

Research into transformation-to-sustainability processes has focused, in part, on the role of what have been called *socio-technical imaginaries*, or "collectively held, institutionally stabilized, and publicly performed visions of desirable futures, animated by shared understandings of forms of social life and social order attainable through, and supportive of, advances in science and technology" (Jasanoff and Kim, 2015, p. 4). Imaginaries are performative, and they are powerful: as they shape public opinion, they catalyze policy and inform the allocation of resources. Even those limited, sectoral approaches to transformation tend to be anchored in implicit collective understandings of the way the world functions.

This spirit became a key driver as our *Charter* and its twelve principles began to take form in the spring of 2022: to produce a motivating and guiding narrative that helps us embark upon the challenging journey that lies ahead of us. As we work on effecting deep systemic changes, we also need to develop imaginaries of a better future beyond the climate emergency, ones that inspire collective action through a clear articulation of the kind of future we might actually *want* to live in.

BUILDING BLOCKS FOR A TERRITORIAL CLIMATE IMAGINARY

Entanglement

The *Charter* deliberately begins with an acknowledgement of the disturbed relationship between humans and nature as the fundamental cause of our crisis. Its first principle is a call to "invest in nature":

"[...] Nature is the existential infrastructure of life on Earth—including human life—and the only solution to heal the planetary crisis. We must seek out, learn from, and invest in the profound intelligence and enduring lessons that a healthy biosphere can offer us. There can be no investment in cities—whether intellectual, spiritual, political, social, or economic—without a corresponding, coordinated, and continually renewed investment in the natural systems that surround and suffuse them... . Ecosystemic wellbeing, which includes humanity but is not limited to our species, must be understood as a basic right of all citizens and the organisms that contribute to the health of our terrestrial metabolism."

Crucial here is the notion of *entanglement*: of natural and anthropogenic systems, of scales, of timelines. Overlapping, contingent, and continuously evolving systems are bounded not by administrative lines on a map, but by the extents of their spheres of influence. Our own "home" region, for instance—the Berlin-Brandenburg area—is a case study in the capriciousness of administrative boundaries. Once divided by a set of hard geopolitical borders into West and East, the Berlin-Brandenburg metropolitan area is also (and always has been) much more than that. It is a set of overlapping bioregions—more or less disturbed landscapes that produce and are, in turn, produced by a specific economic and cultural context.

The notion of *entanglement* reflects, perhaps more fundamentally, Donna Haraway's call to "make kin" **(Haraway, 2016)**: to imagine ourselves as inextricably linked to the other human and non-human inhabitants of this Earth and to the Earth itself. Our kinship with the other inhabitants of this planet in fact erases the distinctions between forms of justice: climate justice is social justice, and social justice is climate justice. Just as technocratic projects that ignore social realities only exacerbate underlying issues, territorial-scale planning or design projects that fail to take into account the significance of embedded and historical power dynamics will only reinforce them **(Yarina, 2018)**.

Many signatories strongly emphasized the importance of including non-Western and/or Global South voices in these debates. Architect Ana María Durán Calisto, for instance, uses the example of the Amazon to illustrate the deep relevance of Indigenous Amazonian ontologies, in which sustainability and human welfare are fundamentally compatible, to today's world. In her work, she questions the myth of the Amazon as a primitive "pristine wilderness," separated in all ways from the urban realm and from modernity in general. Rather, she shows the extent to which the Amazon has *always* been urbanized, deeply shaped by human habitation over millennia. Understanding the Amazon in this way calls into question the assumptions many of us carry with us about the very definition of the "urban," potentially opening up space for more creative and radical thinking, in which our entanglement with nature is a basic assumption that underlies all decision-making.

Trusting traditional and Indigenous knowledge means enabling the holders of this expertise to speak, however. It is not enough to just say that someone is included: what does inclusion in a political process really look like? The call to take these embedded power dynamics seriously enables projects to move out of the realm of what Erik Swyngedouw refers to as the "post-political" **(Swyngedouw, 2011)** and into a space in which viable alternative (political and climate) imaginaries can be nurtured and developed.

Spatial Territory

The *Charter* is anchored in the concept of *spatial territory* as the appropriate arena for action. However, "territory" is often understood and used in social science as a figure for a "container" for the deployment of state power **(Agnew, 1994)**; in transformation-to-sustainability debates, it is linked to specific political jurisdictions, such as nation states or the administrative boundaries of cities. Deeply rooted in modernism, this understanding of territory has allowed our anthropocentric cities to emerge as antagonists to the surrounding landscapes, while fueling the ignorance with which our urban-centered extractive economies draw on cheap and "endlessly available" nature. A fundamental shift in our understanding towards spatial territory is therefore essential to address and repair the relationships that risk the health of our planet, and take into view the complex, systemic flows and dependencies of materials, resources, human, and non-human species that make up our habitats. Instead of seeing city and countryside as opposites, the human settlement spaces of a post-Anthropocene future must be understood as part of the

Human habitats, our buildings and cities must:

1. invest in nature
2. expand the system boundaries of design and governance and the temporal and spatial scales of our agency
3. enhance rather than deplete biodiversity
4. sink carbon by construction
5. question why we build and what we build with, prioritizing the reuse of existing buildings and materials

6 build dense and polycentric cities to restore urban community and regional wildlands

7 provide secure and dignified homes for all people to build social equity, economic livelihood, and shared respect for our common resources

8 make public space the essential infrastructure of cities and the site of socio-political discourse and innovation

9 empower rural communities and engage the traditional knowledge and practice of indigenous peoples and non-western cultures

10 welcome new urban citizens

11 redefine beauty by building with love and compassion for humans and non-humans alike

ecosystems that surround and permeate them. We are embedded in and depend on spatial systems with (limited) available material resources. Instead of continuously extracting resources from this system (extractivism) and polluting it with waste, our actions must be directed towards making a positive or "regenerative" contribution. One could therefore speak of the vision of *regenerative urban landscapes.*

When *spatial territory* is understood as a geographically anchored, dynamic network of agents and activities—rather than a "container"—it becomes a powerful and flexible framework for action. It embraces complexity, rather than flattening it out for the sake of administrative or other forms of legibility. This opens the way for a new approach towards the materials we will need to house the world's exploding urban population: thinking across urban–rural binaries opens up new possibilities to re-regionalize material flows and value chains. When we prioritize bio-based products over extractive materials, we unlock tremendous potential for decarbonization and even carbon storage. The health of the entire bioregion (not just the city), including all human and non-human species that inhabit it, should be a fundamental criterion in urban planning and development decisions. In particular, an expanded understanding of territory creates space for Indigenous and non-Western epistemologies to emerge: an expanded understanding of *spatial territory* could enable us to take into view those places which are currently disenfranchised by our city-centric political and economic systems.

Regenerativity

Out of this expanded understanding of spatial territory as the basic framework for action, the *Charter* proposes the concept of the *regenerative landscape* as the building block of a climate imaginary that is positive, action-oriented, and inclusive. Regenerative landscapes are entangled territories. They are complex, multidimensional systems of systems with shifting and amorphous edges, what Donna Haraway might refer to as "tentacular" (**Haraway, 2016**). Regenerative landscapes and territories don't flatten out complexity: in their beautiful messiness they represent a state of rich entanglement and a potential answer to the "... crisis of imagination [which] is intricately connected to a destabilization of the modernist and enlightenment tenets that have shaped our relationship with the world." (**Machen, Davoudi and Brooks, 2023, p. 1**)

The concept of *regenerativity*, moreover, enables concrete, practical action: when we acknowledge that we live in a closed system—that, as Bruno Latour so poignantly stated, "there is no outside anymore" (**Latour, 2008**), no other planet to escape to—we must think quite pragmatically about how we use the limited resources we have. More to the point, we must question the ontological underpinnings of our use of living and non-living materials and our habitual reliance on externalities to justify catastrophic decisions. It is not enough to pass laws mandating ever thicker layers of insulation or the use of certain "green" building materials, when those materials are shipped halfway around the world from places where their extraction itself causes irreparable social and environmental harm. Truly investing in regenerative landscapes means questioning our basic relationships to our environments as well as our socially and culturally conditioned norms of comfort and justice. It means moving away from a paradigm of "extraction" to one of "co-production": we get what we put in.

Our reliance on wood products for the construction industry is an arena that illustrates the potential of regenerative thinking. In Germany, as in much of the Global North, calls to switch to wood-based (instead of concrete-based) construction have been getting louder and more insistent, even as red tape and entrenched interests make this difficult to execute in practice. Indeed, there is great potential in switching to wood as *the* standard building material in large swaths of Northern Europe, since this can in theory enable cities themselves to become carbon sinks (**Churkina et al. 2020**). However, simply adjusting an existing extractivist worldview to encompass a new raw resource, albeit one which happens to be living, is not what we mean by "regenerative landscape." Trees are not merely raw resources to be mined: they are living beings entangled in ecological networks of such complexity that we have yet to begin fully understanding them. Trees are the backbone of bioregions which are inherently local and specific; as such, our territories and human settlements are entangled not only with the trees within our midst, but with the spatially-bounded ecological systems they anchor.

When we imagine Berlin-Brandenburg as a *regenerative* landscape—rather than simply a place in which policies are implemented that encourage construction using wood—we must think about what we can do to nurture the health of the bioregion that in turn nurtures us. We must, for instance, begin thinking about the complex impact of hunting laws: the careful and deliberate control of deer populations, which ensures that fragile young saplings have a chance to grow, has very little to do with the tradition of trophy hunting for sport. We must begin thinking about the regional economic factors that encourage monocultures and the international export of the plant products we do harvest. We must re-examine the regulatory mechanisms that make it difficult if not impossible to explore the use of a greater diversity of native species for construction or for other needs. We must look critically at our design and planning paradigms to ensure that they are not (willfully) blind. We must understand the need for cultures of democratic negotiation among actors clamoring for use of the same physical space and remain open to creative solutions. And, perhaps, most important of all, we must address head-on the culturally specific ways of thinking that keep us from seeing how entangled we in fact *already* are.

CONCLUSIONS

We argue that participants in the global building sector must embrace both individual and collective agency: as consumers of resources as well as producers of the most durable artifacts of human culture. The practice of regenerative design, the propagation of circular economic cycles of consumption, together with the sustainable application of renewable, carbon-storing, and bio-based building materials, can generate the necessary symbiosis between the health and wellbeing of humanity and that of our terrestrial ecosystems. We have no other option: we *must* work effectively to restore the climate while serving to rebalance the growing inequities of human society. Our imaginary favors an "and" rather than "or" relationship between the local and the global: decisive, differentiated local action grounded in a deep understanding of planetary interlinkage.

Towards Re-Entanglement: A Charter for the City and the Earth is a live, working document and will continue to evolve along two trajectories. In the first instance, several co-authors are planning to take the document to their own regional contexts and will—in new constellations of local contributors—aim to devolve more regionally appropriate versions.

Secondly, together with the *Charter*'s co-authors, we have approached cities and regional governments to engage in a dialogue about how the *Charter* could inspire concrete transformative steps. In the context of a multitude of city-centric programs and networks (NetZeroCities, C40's Clean Construction Declaration, Carbon Neutral Cities Alliance, as well as initiatives launched by United Cities and Local Governments and the International Council for Local Environmental Issues, to name just a few) which offer guidance and support towards climate change adaptation or decarbonization, it is the territorial climate vision embedded in the *Charter* that received the most traction. In October 2022, the city of Barcelona and the regional government co-signed the *Charter*-inspired "Barcelona Protocol," which focuses on bioregional cooperation to adjust material and resource flows towards a climate-positive, equitable built environment. We are currently beginning discussions with Dark Matter Labs, CNCA, and the broader NetZeroCities Initiative, led by Climate KIC, to bring territorial climate imaginaries into their transition processes. Other conversations have also begun with Bhutan, Western Cape/Cape Town, and Bali.

We at Bauhaus Earth believe firmly that the value of the initiative is its open-source character. We hope that the territorial climate imaginary of the *Charter* will thus devolve into, and merge with, a multitude of local-regional imaginaries that all point towards a better future.

Towards Re-Entanglement: A Charter for the City and the Earth; Lead authors: Alan Organschi, Philipp Misselwitz; Co-authors: Ana María Durán Calisto, Andrea Gebhard, Cade Deihm, Edgar Pieterse, Franziska Schreiber, Guiseppe Scarascia Mugnozza, Hans Joachim Schellnhuber, James Drinkwater, Marlène de Saussure, Marc Palahí, Monica Tanuhandaru, Nathalie Jean-Baptiste, Rocío Armillas Tiseyra, Tilmann Prinz, Vicente Guallart, Vyjayanthi V. Rao. Available at: https://www.bauhauserde.org/initiatives/re-entanglement

AGNEW, J. (1994) 'The territorial trap: The geographical assumptions of international relations theory'. *Review of international political economy*, 1(1), pp. 53–80.

BECK, S., JASANOFF, S., STIRLING, A. and POLZIN, C. (2021) 'The governance of sociotechnical transformations to sustainability'. *Current Opinion in Environmental Sustainability*, 49, pp. 143–152. doi: https://doi.org/10.1016/j.cosust.2021.04.010

CHURKINA, G., ORGANSCHI, A., REYER, C. P., RUFF, A., VINKE, K., LIU, Z., RECK, B. K., GRAEDEL, T. E. and SCHELLNHUBER, H. J. (2020) 'Buildings as a global carbon sink'. *Nature Sustainability*, 3(4), pp. 269–276.

DAVOUDI, S. and MACHEN, R. (2021) 'Climate imaginaries and the mattering of the medium'. *Geoforum*. doi: https://doi.org/10.1016/j.geoforum.2021.11.003

HARAWAY, D. J. (2016) *Staying with the trouble: Making kin in the Chthulucene*. Durham: Duke University Press.

JASANOFF, S. and KIM, S. H. (2015) *Dreamscapes of modernity: Sociotechnical imaginaries and the fabrication of power*. Chicago: University of Chicago Press.

LATOUR, B. (2008) 'April. A cautious Prometheus? A few steps toward a philosophy of design (with special attention to Peter Sloterdijk)', in *Proceedings of the 2008 annual international conference of the design history society*, pp. 2–10.

MACHEN, R., DAVOUDI, S. and BROOKS, E. (2023) 'Climate imaginaries and their mediums'. *Geoforum*, 138, p. 103672. doi: https://doi.org/10.1016/j.geoforum.2022.103672

SCOTT, J. C. (1998) *Seeing like a state: how certain schemes to improve the human condition have failed.* New Haven: Yale University Press.

SWYNGEDOUW, E. (2011) 'Depoliticized environments: The end of nature, climate change and the post-political condition', *Royal Institute of Philosophy Supplements*, 69, pp. 253–274.

TROTT, C. D., REIMER-WATTS, K. and RIEMER, M. (2022) 'Climate justice: In pursuit of a practical utopia: transitioning towards climate justice', in *The Routledge International Handbook of Community Psychology*. London/ New York: Routledge, pp. 229–245.

YARINA, L. (2018) 'Your Sea Wall Won't Save You: Negotiating Rhetorics and Imaginaries of Climate Resilience', *Places Journal*. doi: https://doi.org/10.22269/180327

Mar Menor

INTRODUCTION BY JENNIFER FAUSTER

Mar Menor—the largest saltwater lagoon in the Western Mediterranean—is on the brink of an ecological catastrophe. This fragile ecosystem in Spain's Murcia province has endured decades of relentless anthropocentric pressure and exploitation. Situated at the threshold of ecological wealth and economic pursuits, these pressures have unleashed a profound ecological decay, primarily fueled by eutrophication—a phenomenon driven by the excessive inflow of nitrates and other fertilizers stemming from intensive agriculture. In turn, this process has given rise to a surplus of underwater flora, voraciously depleting oxygen levels beyond the lagoon's ecological capacity—tragically, leading to significant marine life losses in 2019 and 2021.

Yet, the Mar Menor's significance transcends ecological dimensions. Its emotional resonance with the local inhabitants makes it a valuable socio-ecological space. This deep-rooted attachment has spurred the creation of various platforms and initiatives committed to safeguarding the Mar Menor and advocating for a "Territorial Shift" in planning, living, and economic practices. Out of these collective efforts emerged the "People's Legislative Initiative," leading to the enactment of a groundbreaking law that established Mar Menor as a legal entity with enforceable rights. This marked the first time within the European Union that a place received a formal legal status. The law grants the lagoon the right to exist as an ecosystem and to develop naturally.

Amid this landscape of challenges and advocacy, Davide Curatola Soprana's photographic endeavor embarks on a mission. It seeks to capture not only the contemporary landscape, but also the influential forces shaping it and the repercussions of human-centered planning. The objective of these photographs goes beyond merely documenting the physical attributes of the territory; it strives to unveil the intricate relationships interwoven within it.

By traversing various routes across this landscape, Curatola Soprana weaves a narrative that delves into the manifold histories and markings of Mar Menor. Spanning the ecologically rich coastal fringes to the vastness of the Mediterranean, slicing through the intensively cultivated northern fields via the village of San Pedro del Pinatar, and tracing the trajectories of tourist development along La Manga, these journeys offer insights into the underlying causes of the ecological decline. Simultaneously, selective explorations—such as capturing Los Alcazáres as a hub of activism or portraying Cabezo Mingote as an observation point that demonstrates the intricate interplay between water and land—depict favorable relationships between human and non-humans.

Through this immersive exploration, it becomes evident that the territory yearns for resilience, an enduring presence. The photographs reveal these imprints of the territory: the underlying systems, the dunes, the interconnected network of vegetation, the natural cycles of succession, and the memories of places that once existed and may resurface once again.

It Could Be a Paradise, Again

Davide Curatola Soprana

Mar Menor is a saltwater lagoon located in the province of Murcia in Spain. Located on an area of volcanic origin, it is divided from the Mediterranean Sea by a thin 22-kilometer-long strip of land called La Manga. Since the 1960s, the landscape has been beset by a series of pressures, leading to a general state of ecological decay within the lagoon, and causinghuge mortality events among marine fauna in 2016, 2019, and 2021. These two episodes were the result of excessive levels of nitrate in the water, which fostered uncontrolled growth of vegetation and algae, thus triggering the massive die-off of marine species through eutrophication.

These events raised significant awareness, making evident the environmental problems of Mar Menor—so much so that the citizenship, including lawyers, jurists, chemists politicians, and many local residents were involved in the formation of a platform for the defense of the lagoon. In turn, this led to the drafting and approval of the special law Act 19/2022 (passed on September 30, 2022), which gives Mar Menor the right to legal protection, conservation, and regeneration, allowing it to exist and evolve naturally. It is the first natural site to obtain a legal personality, thanks to the vision of Teresa Vicente—a jurist and professor in Philosophy of Law at the University of Murcia, who brought solidity and legal force to the feeling of citizens and activists who had already mobilized.

The following photos are selected from a wider body of work documenting the region. The photo essay comprises images of three walking routes from the coast towards the Mediterranean: one in the north, from the cultivated fields, passing through the village of San Pedro del Pinatar to arrive at La Llana; another one in the south, from the village of Mar de Cristal to Cabo de Palos; and the third following the line of the tourist urbanization of La Manga. The photographic work is completed by punctual explorations that visually connect the whole territory of the inland coast to Mar Menor: Los Alcázares, as a center of people's activism; Cabezo Mingote, a high viewpoint from where we can read the relationship between water and land; and, lastly, the Sierra Minera and the mining landscape around the village of Portmán.

The photo essay depicts the landscapes of Mar Menor, its diversity, as well as an intelligent and effective mode of activism focused on a new paradigm of legal philosophy that tends to make human and natural rights converge. Research into those places surrounding the lagoon was conducted in an attempt to show the various pressures impacting on the territory: the intensive agriculture landscape of Campo de Cartagena, the contamination of mining residues in the Sierra Minera, and the very strong anthropization of La Manga for tourism purposes. Besides the obvious pressures these sites exert, the photographic work also wants to show spaces of decompression: sites where people and activists are able to experience a feeling of connection with the sea and with nature itself, which asserts its right to exist before us and to renew itself in our absence.

before there was only
scrub and dunes

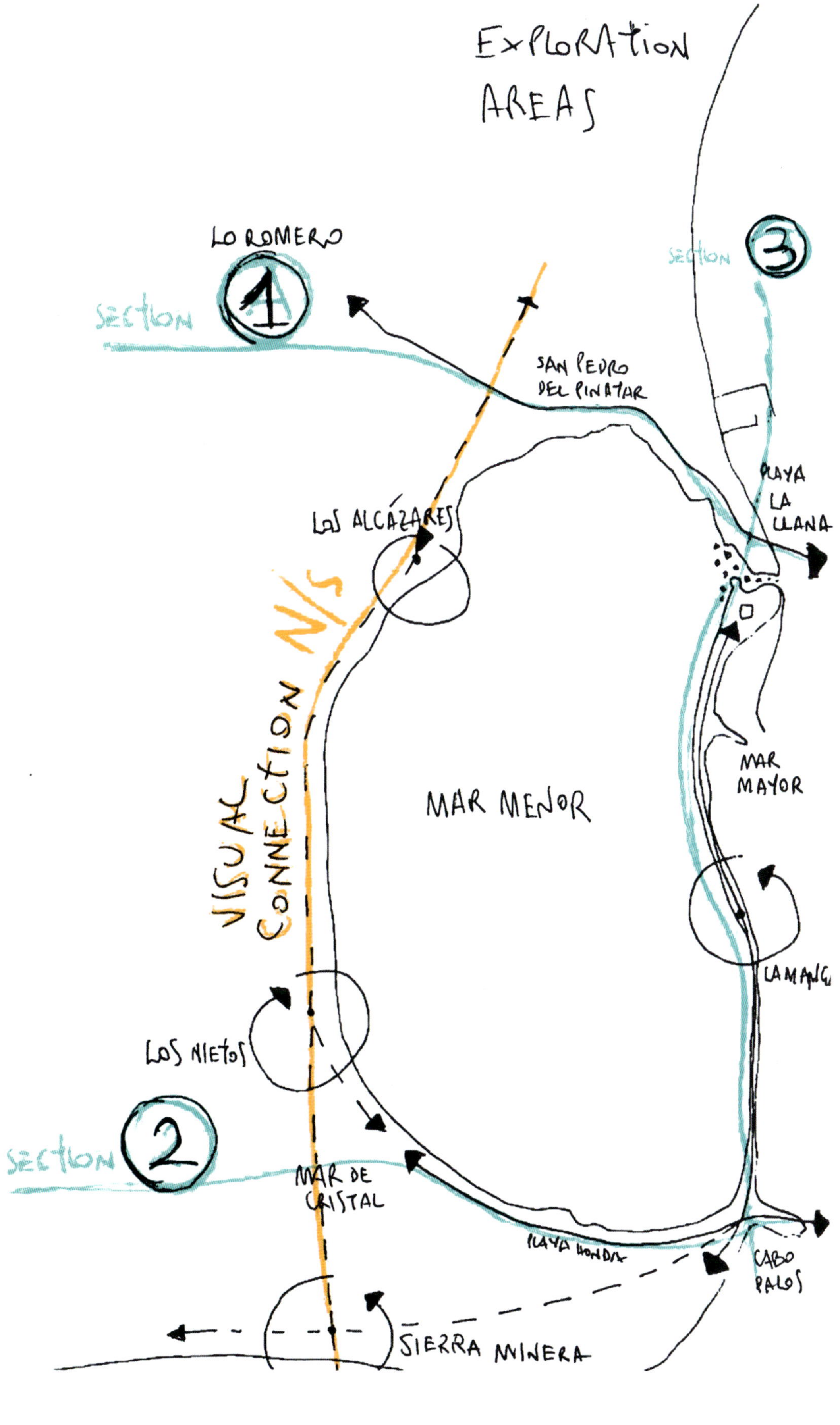

EXPLORATION
AREAS
LO ROMERO
SECTION 1
SECTION 3
SAN PEDRO
DEL PINATAR
PLAYA
LA
LLANA
LOS ALCÁZARES
N/S
VISUAL
CONNECTION
MAR MENOR
MAR
MAYOR
LA MANGA
LOS NIETOS
SECTION 2
MAR DE
CRISTAL
PLAYA HONDA
CABO
PALOS
SIERRA MINERA

[03]

[04]

ADRIÁN. Born in Valencia, Adrián's family is originally from Los Nietos, right on the waterfront of Mar Menor. Together with his partner, Neus, he has decided to return there to live in the family house. They are both involved in the lagoon's protection, participating in awareness-raising and convening information meetings on the state of the environment. He is also concerned with the urban regeneration of the village which, despite being an established historical site, belongs to the administrative district of Cartagena, thus making it an extreme periphery of the city.

[06]

JULIA. Born on the shores of the Mar Menor, Julia is the president of the association AMARME Alianza Mar Menor which—in connection and collaboration with other local and national platforms—advocates for the protection and defense of the Mar Menor ecosystem. In coordination with the promoter group that initiated the process for a Popular Legislative Initiative (ILP), she saw her dream realized with the Act 19/2022, which recognized the legal personality of the Mar Menor lagoon and its basin—turning this unique ecosystem into the first in Europe with its own rights. She feels a deep connection with the "small sea," where she learned to swim before she learned to walk, and has always considered it as part of her family. That's why she says, "How can I not stand up for my brother?"

[10]

[11]

MAYA. Born in Georgia, a few kilometers from Tbilisi. She arrived in Europe in 2018 as an "asylum seeker." After passing through Switzerland, the Netherlands, and Belgium she arrived in Cartagena, where she was accepted by the Spanish refugee system. She now lives in Playa Honda, on the southern coast of Mar Menor, where she runs a tourist guesthouse. Maya believes in simple, low-impact tourism focused on contact with the landscape. She offers her guests local, vegan cuisine served in the middle of nature.

[13]

[16]

[17]

[19]

[20]

[22]

[23]

[01] Cultivation of vegetables in greenhouses
[02] Salt production area in San Pedro del Pinatar
[03] Wetland buffer zone between the salt marshes and the beach of La Llana
[04] People in Mar Menor taking a bath in front of the Espejo Square in Los Alcázares
[06] Mar Menor wall representation in Los Nietos
[07] Abandoned glasshouses between the villages of Mar de Cristal and Los Nietos
[08] View of the lagoon from Cabezo Mingote
[10] The Portmán bay, contaminated by mining waste from the exploitation of the Sierra Minera
[11] Urbanization in Playa Honda
[13] Fishermen in Playa Honda
[14] A fishing boat amid vegetation
[15] Single-family holiday villas in La Manga
[16] Urbanization en Cabo de Palos
[17] Urbanization in La Manga, seen from Monte Blanco
[18] A hotel building, which was never finished
[19] Traces of eutrophication
[20] View of 1970s urbanization on Barón Island
[21] Dunes along the Gran Vía de La Manga
[22] Villas in Veneziola, La Manga
[23] View of the northern limit of La Manga, where the two seas meet

Mindset

INTRODUCTION BY MARIO STEFAN

Territorial Urbanism not only reconsiders the spatial reach of interventions, it also aligns with a broader shift in attitude. This new mindset emerges in ways of thinking and working within collective interdisciplinary teams, in processual considerations, as well as in questioning established functionalities and their spatial manifestations.

Rigid planning structures and thought patterns are no longer capable of generating contemporary solutions. Too often, new buildings continue to be realized in peri-urban zones with new developments geared towards car-oriented infrastructure. Project management, an operational system which has been repeated for decades, gives too little space to climate-adaptive planning. Adopting a fresh attitude will allow us to go beyond established patterns. Embracing a diversity of external influences, scales, and challenges within the project underscores the centrality of creativity and ingenuity in mobilizing solutions that meet contemporary demands.

The contributions in this section showcase how such attitudes can be applied at different stages of a project. Take, for instance, the Paris ring road which, after political decision-making, can be considered with a renewed sense of openness, the territory emerging as a potential link where it used to be a barrier. Elsewhere, in Vienna, the concept of utopia is used as a mindset for breaking out of hardened thought patterns. Such patterns are often accompanied by rigid planning processes that are typically inadequate to respond to great uncertainty or shifts in project duration brought about by global crises. As we see in Zaragoza (Spain), Apertura (Italy), and Essen (Germany), an attempt is being made to work within an approach that not only deals directly with global crises, but also draws energy from the resulting uncertainty. Meanwhile, new understandings of spatial potential, as well as the possibilities of collaboration across different roles, have animated decision-makers in Oostende (Belgium) to create new methods of planning and development in which spatial and functional co-creations can be generated, communicated, and evaluated by experts.

These innovative new mindsets are not subject to the inflexibility of long-established planning structures. Instead, they express ways of developing new ideas, of reacting more fluidly to circumstances, and of shaping a more desirable future that is worked towards collaboratively.

Territorial Design Processes and Uncertainties

Beatrice Galimberti

STAYING WITH TROUBLE AND UNCERTAINTY

Two aspects have struck me the most since I first read about Territorial Urbanism (Degros et al., 2021). The first is Territorial Urbanism's openness to incorporating ecological and social dimensions. The second concerns its attention to coexisting territorial conditions (such as the urban, peri-urban, hypo-urban, and infra-urban). I am impressed by these two commitments because they reveal an attitude of "staying with" the trouble.[1] Indeed, on the one hand, the Ecological Turn and the Social Turn share significant overlaps in their trajectories and aspirations but are also divided by conflicting interests and tensions. On the other, urban, peri-urban, hypo-urban, infra-urban, etcetera, are distinct conditions. Certainly, they are interconnected and often blur into each other. But they are different in a way that is not reducible to dichotomies such as urban–rural or periphery–center. They have different times, rhythms, densities, and needs, which may be irreconcilable and even conflict with each other. For these reasons, it seems to me that Territorial Urbanism requires a receptive eye (Akama, 2017) that is trained to notice such trouble and stay with it.

Staying with the trouble also means staying with uncertainty. Staying with uncertainties is a particularly important skill in terms of training, since design processes can face diverse kinds of uncertainty, spanning small- and large-scale situations, as this contribution tries to illustrate.

So, it seems to me that those operating within the framework of Territorial Urbanism—or working towards implementing it—may consider (also) these further challenges: recognizing the troubles and uncertainties within design processes; not trying to run away from them (in any case, escaping them is not possible); staying with them, trying to act within them, and perhaps sometimes even leveraging them.

This contribution to ongoing discussions about Territorial Urbanism seeks to reflect on how designers cope with uncertainties. The aim is not to observe territories in transformation directly. Instead, this work follows the designers involved in transforming territories, gathering some approaches from practices and research. Therefore, the following section presents some of these approaches, focusing on three design processes that resonate with the stance of Territorial Urbanism. The purpose is to try to understand their know-how in dealing with the uncertainties present in the specific and situated conditions surrounding each case. Then, the third section discusses the three design processes by embedding them in a broader framework, opening an eclectic set of concepts such as antifragility, ruse, minor urbanism, permanent temporality, and open design.[2] These concepts, though different, resonate with each other. In conclusion, this contribution suggests that the approaches and concepts gathered in these pages can be read as various aspects (complementary, overlapping, and even contradictory) of a common mindset. In turn, it explores how this mindset can support designers in staying with trouble and uncertainty, sometimes even benefitting from them.

THREE DESIGN PROCESSES

Among the three design processes described in this section, the first is *Esto no es un solar* (Zaragoza, Spain), a program formed to create ephemeral public spaces throughout the city, fostering spatial and social regeneration following the global economic crisis of 2008. The second is *Prossima Apertura* (Aprilia, Italy), the most recent of the three (2016–2021). This is the first phase of a broader transformation, encompassing not only a suburban neighbor-

1 For Haraway (2016), "staying with the trouble" means not avoiding trouble but accepting oneself as being in the middle of it, recognizing it as both specific and situated but also ambiguous and unknowable.

2 These concepts will be elaborated in more detail later in this chapter.

[01] *Esto no es un solar*: turning a crisis into an opportunity. © Grávalos Di Monte arquitectos, edited by Beatrice Galimberti

hood but also the way of doing participatory projects in Italy more widely. The third is *Zollverein Park* (Essen, Germany), a renowned and protracted reconversion of a colliery site in the Ruhr area. Developed between 2005 and 2021, the transformation is still ongoing.

Each of these cases shares some features of a territorial perspective. Indeed, they are all processes that put public space at the center: working between buildings and interweaving spatial relations at various scales. Furthermore, they are all located in territories that the binary dichotomies of urban–rural or center–periphery fail to describe effectively. These three cases each deal with uncertainty in different ways, and their approaches towards it prove meaningful.

Esto No Es un Solar: Turning a Crisis into an Opportunity

Esto no es un solar (Eng. "This is not a vacant lot") is a project by Grávalos Di Monte arquitectos in Zaragoza that has set the standard for urban and territorial regeneration through temporary, tactical, and participatory actions in public space (**Di Giovanni, 2014; Di Giovanni, 2018**). Already in the 2000s, the city of Zaragoza was experiencing economic depression and social conflict, especially in its historic center, which was inhabited by fragile and ethnically diverse populations. *Esto no es un solar* is the result of years of work between the architects and the Municipality of Zaragoza, involving many debates, meetings, and small-scale experiments. The architects had conducted an initial survey of the Old Town of Zaragoza (which includes the neighborhoods of San Pablo, Magdalena, and Arrabal) in 2004, revealing the inadequacy of the existing public spaces. In 2006, the urban art festival "En la frontera" hosted the first actions resulting from that survey: a series of artistic interventions called *Los vacíos cotidianos*, which proposed the reactivation of empty lots as public spaces. It was an initial test, a collaborative reflection with the inhabitants of the neighborhoods that sought to listen to them and encourage them to press the Municipality on this issue. At the same time, the municipal agency Zaragoza Vivienda was drafting an employment plan for about fifty unemployed people. The aim was to hire them to clean and fence undeveloped and neglected lots in the Old Town, the same ones that were the subject of "Los vacíos cotidianos".

Grávalos and Di Monte, drawing on the experience of the survey and early experiments with the inhabitants, proposed that Zaragoza Vivienda should change the type of work envisaged in the employment plan: instead of cleaning and fencing these spaces, they would transform them and temporarily open them to public use. Zaragoza Vivienda decided to support the idea.

However, a problem remained: most of the historic center's empty lots were privately owned. Convincing the owners to give over their areas, even temporarily, was not easy (not least because the Municipality had no budget to compensate them). When the global economic crisis of 2008 hit Zaragoza, however, the designers and Zaragoza Vivienda together were able to take advantage of this moment of deep uncertainty and crisis in the city's real estate market. With the arrival of the economic crisis, privately-owned vacant lots in the town lost almost all their financial profitability. At that point, many owners accepted the Municipality's proposal to hand over their lots free of charge for a limited period, allowing them to be transformed for the community's benefit, with neighborhood associations or public institutions (primarily schools) taking care of them (**Ecococos, 2012b**). Without the economic collapse of 2008 (which was felt very heavily throughout
[01] Spain), the process of *Esto no es un solar* would still be on hold.

The program itself was ambitious but relatively easy to implement. Thus, the work was comparatively rapid once the owners' approval was obtained. Between May and December 2009, fourteen spaces were reactivated in the most fragile neighborhoods of the Old Town. They became playgrounds, sports areas, orchards, gardens, meeting places for the elderly, etc. The operation was a success and was repeated the following year, extending to another fourteen locations throughout the city. In this second edition, the areas were very differentiated. Some were more urban and others more suburban, working within the materials offered by the compact city but also with nature (i.e., by the banks of the river Ebro). In 2010, the transformed areas, whether privately or publicly owned, amounted to approximately 40,000 square meters, cared for by some sixty entities, including associations and public institutions (**Ecococos, 2012b; Esto no es un solar, nd**). Interventions have always been cost-effective (around €25 per square meter) because of the limited funds available. The scarcity of resources,

[02] *Prossima Apertura*: gaining wiggle room. © Orizzontale (pictures) and Google Maps (satellite image), edited by Beatrice Galimberti

however, led to the closure of the *Esto no es un solar* office in 2011. Nevertheless, the architects and Zaragoza Vivienda continued with a more modest number of interventions between 2013 and 2014.

All the spaces part of *Esto no es un solar* shared provisional aesthetics that were open to indeterminacy **(Di Giovanni, Di Monte and Gravalos, 2020)**. But these spaces have responded differently over time: many are no longer present, while others persist in their "temporariness."

Prossima Apertura: Gaining Wiggle Room

In 2016, the Italian Ministry of Culture and the National Council of Architects announced a competition to redevelop ten suburban areas across the country. One was the Toscanini district in Aprilia, about 50 kilometers from Rome. A social housing neighborhood from the 1990s, it now accommodates about 10,000 inhabitants. However, many planned public spaces and services have never been implemented. The architecture collective Orizzontale won the competition for the Toscanini area together with a multidisciplinary team, including psychosocial researchers and urban art curators. Their proposal was called *Prossima Apertura* (Eng. "Opening Soon") and included temporary actions in the public space supported by listening to the inhabitants, running art workshops, and facilitating self-construction.

In 2019, a tender for public spaces by the Municipality of Aprilia followed the previous competition. Orizzontale won this competition as well. The project commissioned by the Municipality took the legal form of a public work, which in Italy often proves to be the most complex and slowest way to transform a space. It involved the transformation of an underused courtyard on three levels into a square of approximately 8,600 square meters. Other activities were then implemented throughout the neighborhood to activate a system of public spaces.

Historically, Toscanini is a site of social conflict due to the presence of organized and petty crime, while public services are lacking **(Orizzontale, nd)**. Therefore, Orizzontale ensured residents were listened to and involved from the very beginning of its activities.

Up to this point, it may seem a relatively conventional case. What is interesting, however, is how the project managed to instigate some crossover between the construction site's activities and the participation of Toscanini's inhabitants, which has been an unusual operation for Italian public works legislation. Indeed, in public work, one can run participatory [02]
activities in parallel with a construction site, but it is not possible to lead participation inside the construction site. Furthermore, Italian law has a regulatory vacuum around self-construction, making it complex to implement. Aware of these difficulties, Orizzontale decided to stay with the uncertainty of how to implement participation and self-construction activities in the context of this public work, defining two "families" of activities. On the one hand, there were traditional construction site activities. On the other hand, Orizzontale organized a series of actions that were complementary to the construction site. These included events nearby, visits to the construction site, and workshops led in areas of the construction site that were already completed or otherwise equipped as safe. The workshops incorporated activities such as painting, group portraits, and several self-construction activities for furniture to be used in the public space. These activities were crucial to create a sense of belonging to a public space undergoing construction. However, they are not on the list of activities envisaged by public works. The cleverness of Orizzontale lay in including these activities within the site "safety activities and charges" (*oneri di sicurezza*). Indeed, the designers identified an ambiguous point in public works legislation and were able to take advantage of it by interpreting it in an alternative yet robust way. The designers refer to this action as a way of forcing the hand of regulations to set a new precedent **(Manfra, 2020)**. In fact, including these com-

plementary works within official site activities under the umbrella of "safety" allows them to create an authorized precedent and repeat this activity in the future. Doing so thus opened a new possibility, lending the architectural collective significant wiggle room.

The construction site and its complementary activities were realized between 2019 and 2021. Orizzontale describes it as "a complete but unfinished space, which makes indeterminacy its strong point" **(Orizzontale, nd, my translation)**. Indeed, the design aesthetics embrace indeterminacy and suggest the possibility of unprecedented appropriations, which emerge daily. For the designers, being open to the unexpected means "building places that can react to the movement of those who inhabit them, experimenting with open systems as a prelude to new forms of urbanity" **(Orizzontale, nd, my translation)**.

Zollverein Park: Moving Through the Unknown

In 1986 the Zollverein coal mine and coking plant were closed and acquired by the State of North Rhine-Westphalia. The site is in Essen and forms part of the Ruhr area, the largest urban area in Germany. The Ruhr is characterized by a complex system of industrial reconversions, composed of a sequence of different spatial fragments: compact cities, industrial sites, suburbs, and forests held together by gray and blue infrastructure. The Zollverein area was fenced off and access prohibited as soon as it was closed, and nature started to (re)grow over the brownfield land. In the 1990s, there were minimal interventions in basic infrastructure and art installations, but the turning point was in 2001 when the area became a UNESCO site. In the same year, the state of North Rhine-Westphalia commissioned OMA with a masterplan defined in 2002. The following year, a complementary masterplan by Agence Ter focused on the industrial landscape. Based on these documents, a competition for Zollverein Park (i.e., the outdoor facilities of the UNESCO site) was launched in 2005 and won by a team that was led by the landscape architecture office Die Planergruppe, previously named Planergruppe Oberhausen **(Die Planergruppe, nd)**. The space for the park was approximately 80 hectares and presented an indefinite number of unknowns (for e.g., spontaneous vegetation covered all the brownfield sites, making any *a priori* assessment of their condition difficult, remediations had to be assessed on a case-by-case basis, building sites could change time and priority, etcetera).

In such a situation, one cannot know what issues will arise during the transformation, and a schedule that is too rigid in its timing and objectives would be almost impossible to fulfill. In this regard, one of the designers of Die Planergruppe writes: "In 2005 we just knew that this park cannot be built in two, three or five years. In fact, the park would rather further be developed and evolve slowly over a period of ten or even twenty years" **(Wienecke, 2018, p. 3)**. Thus, the team adopted the principle of "development by maintenance" **(p. 4)** as a compass, even before identifying spaces to transform or phases to implement. This principle involves a design process which is based first on maintenance and care, two aspects that are usually left in the background. Organizing the approach around this principle means that every design decision considers the present moment and the next step with the same value. This approach requested annual reviews of the entire process, progressively adapting to emerging challenges and changing contexts. In this way, the designers identified the essential spaces of the project (i.e., the track boulevard and the ring promenade), which emerged over time.

[03] The process has developed in four phases (2005–06, 2007–09, 2010–14, 2016–21), and the most significant elements have now been implemented. However, the area is "not finalized yet, and will probably never be finalized" **(Wienecke, 2018, p. 8)**. This openness to the state of being unfinished does not

mean giving up design or leaving choices to external agents. Instead, it means situating one's design choices in relation to perspectives of maintenance and care, while remaining open to a "pragmatic dysfunction" (Architectural Heritage Intervention, 2019). Such "dysfunction" deliberately assumes the logic (and aesthetics) of the incomplete and is also open to future interpretations and surprising directions.

Discussing the Approaches

The three design approaches presented here each deal with different uncertainties. In *Esto no es un solar*, Grávalos Di Monte arquitectos and Zaragoza Vivienda contend with the unavailability of vacant lots and the black swan event of the global economic crisis. In *Prossima Apertura*, Orizzontale undertakes the uncertain challenge of pursuing a project without any favorable regulatory framework. In Zollverein Park, Die Planergruppe works within the conversion of an industrial site where nothing is definite. These are economic, regulatory, and procedural uncertainties. Some of them are exogenous, some endogenous, and some are both. The three cases have in common that their designers are aware of these uncertainties, staying with them (although they cause problems), acting within their apparent "dysfunction," and assuming them as unavoidable conditions. Somehow, they also benefit from these uncertainties.

The design process that perhaps benefits the most from the uncertainty and trouble of its context is *Esto no es un solar*. Indeed, its capacity to turn the global economic crisis into an opportunity to reactivate some empty plots is an example of antifragility. By writing about antifragility, I refer to Nassim Nicholas Taleb's neologism, which is the subject of his book *Antifragile: Things that Gain from Disorder* (2012). Taleb, a statistician and expert on randomness, probability, and uncertainty, introduced the term antifragility to describe the "functional opposite" (2012, p. 17) of "fragility." A fragile system gets damaged by uncertainties. Its opposite, then, is a system that benefits from uncertainties. Since no word exists to describe this condition, Taleb proposes the term "antifragile."[3] Thus, antifragility is context-sensitive, adaptive, and can deal with criticalities. It leads to exploring existing fragilities. Antifragility "makes us understand fragility better. Just as we cannot improve health without reducing disease" (Taleb, 2012, p. 11). To work on existing fragility features, and thus on antifragility solutions, means having a deep acquaintance with what is present, responding to uncertainty from the resources one already owns.[4]

A deep acquaintance with the present context is also the starting condition for how the process behind *Prossima Apertura* relates to the

3 Antifragility differs from resilience in its various forms. Indeed, to simplify, it is possible to recognize three main types of resilience. The first is "engineering" resilience, where a system responds to shocks by bouncing back to its previous state of balance, restoring its initial functionality (Holling, 1996). The second is "ecosystem" or "ecological" resilience, where a system adapts to a new balance (Holling, 1996). The third is "evolutionary" or "socio-ecological" resilience, which no longer connects to any pre-existing state of balance and instead constantly adapts (Davoudi, 2012). Evolutionary resilience is the closest to antifragility because it is the only one that stays with uncertainty. As for antifragility, evolutionary resilience "considers the universe as complex and inherently unpredictable. It questions stasis and equilibrium, and defines open systems as non-linear, self-organizing, and 'permeated by uncertainty and discontinuities' (Berkes and Folke, 1998, p. 12)" (Davoudi, 2019, p. 124). However, unlike antifragility, it does not focus explicitly on the ability to benefit from uncertainty, even if evolution, adaptivity, and change are concerned.

4 In discourses related to urbanism, the relevance of antifragility is spreading. For example, Shafique (2015) proposes considering it as a possibility for re-situating contemporary urbanism. Gasparrini employs antifragility not only for theoretical reflections on the future of the city (2018) but also as the main objective for new plans he curated for Messina (2018) and the port of Ravenna (2020) in Italy. Sartorio et al. +(2021) structured a broad review of planning literature on resilience and antifragility. And Pasqui (2022) recently reflected on cities' fragilities and antifragilities during the COVID-19 pandemic.

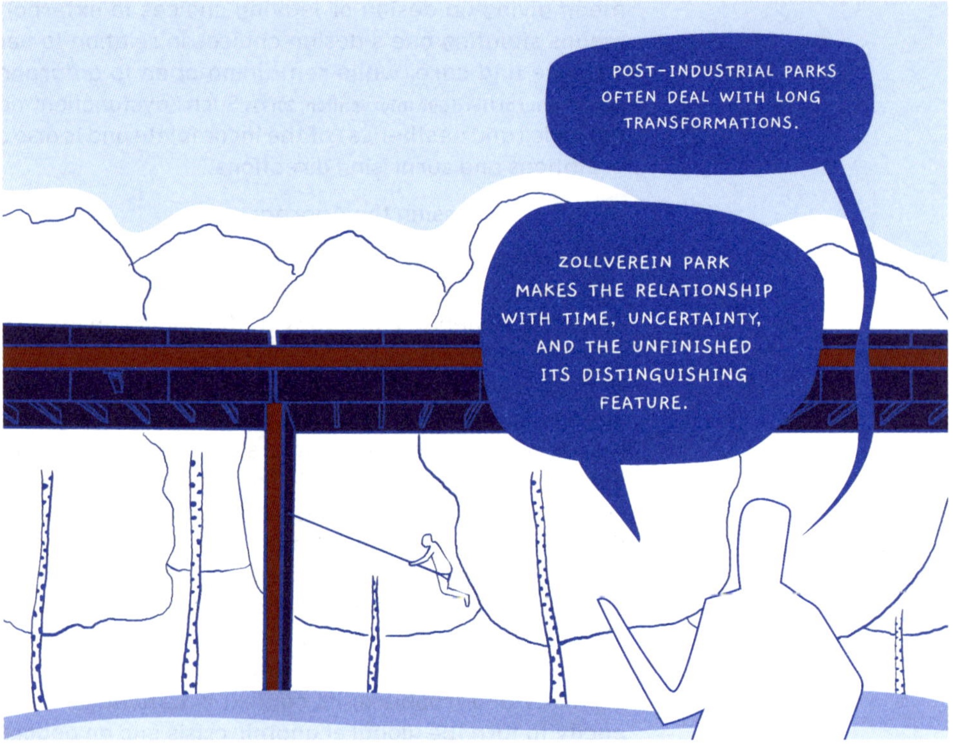

[03] Zollverein Park: moving through the unknown. © Die Planergruppe, edited by Beatrice Galimberti

uncertainty around it. In particular, the ability of Orizzontale to act subversively within institutions evokes two concepts: "ruse" and "minor." Ruse is discussed by Degros (2016) and Bendiks and Degros (2019). They refer to it as a "cunning intelligence of tricks" (p. 29). It is a type of intelligence employed by those who recognize their weak condition, understanding that they cannot face a situation head-on but need to find an alternative. For Degros (2016), in the case of urban planners, the first step is to recognize one's own weakness (that is, in the face of a rigid norm) and the second step is to have an in-depth knowledge of this norm, to find a space for unprecedented interpretation and thus innovation.

This is precisely what Orizzontale did by discovering a new interpretation of safety activities and charges. By gaining some wiggle room, Orizzontale enabled the participation of inhabitants in *Prossima Apertura* and set a precedent for future projects. Ruse has much in common with what Sandström (2019) calls "minor urbanism," which finds cracks in major urban design practices and then transforms them from within. Minor urbanism "stays particularly attentive to practices that are located outside of habitual or established modes of urbanism but inside the institutions of urban planning. This outside-inside position is the critical potential of minor urbanism: it does not act in opposition to institutional frameworks but performs a criticality from within" (Sandström, 2020, p. 109).

Prossima Apertura stays with uncertainties to discover a crack in the regulatory system and subvert it from within. Meanwhile, Zollverein Park mainly stays with uncertainties and the unknown through temporality, working incrementally and adaptively, accepting that the spatial outcome will always be unfinished. This approach seems to me to have significant affinities with the thinking of ZUS [Zones Urbaines Sensibles], which puts time at the center of design practice. Indeed, with over two decades of experience working in the Luchtsingel area in Rotterdam, they argue that "time is the new space" (ZUS, 2019, p. 170). From this stance, ZUS (2019) emphasizes the limitations of detailed masterplans which often focus on upstream processes at the expense of what may happen during a project's realization:

"Cities have a dynamic nature. Yet architecture and urban planning continue to focus on inscribing ideas into static blueprints. The desire to manage all risks beforehand is stronger than the confidence in the power of direction during the process [...]. Sustainable urban development is made possible by leaving things open instead of pinning them down—not instant urban development, but incremental and adaptive urban development. This creates a city of permanent temporality, a city that permanently develops through temporary interventions" (p. 307).

Reflections on temporary, impermanent, and unfinished interventions are increasingly widespread today. They concern both the process level ZUS mentioned and the spatial configuration of the aesthetic level. The three cases presented in this contribution show the growing trend towards transitory, simple, and light aesthetics, which are increasingly recurring in design processes and say something about the spirit of our time. Indeed, the thoughts of Sendra and Sennett (2020) resonate here. Starting from Sennett's work on the open city, they investigate alternatives to fixed spatial configurations, exploring an open design approach. Focusing more on providing support, this methodology generates conditions of possibility in which spontaneous disorder can flourish, welcoming what is unexpected or latent in a territory. Porqueddu calls this "directing rather than mastering emergent transformations" (2019).

Antifragility, ruse, minor, permanent temporality, and open design all contribute different perspectives on uncertainty, each with some elements in common. Taken together, they elicit the impression of a kaleidoscope of approaches that are in dialogue with uncertainty, engaging with it in complex and plural ways, as separate facets of one common mindset.

Juxtaposing the operations of these different approaches to uncertainty may well open new and generative spaces for research. In conclusion, I propose there are (at least) two promising directions suggested by their connections.

Firstly, they may facilitate the discovery of recurring patterns. For example, several design processes and concepts already mentioned in this contribution focus on temporary, unfinished, and indeterminate qualities. These qualities can be investigated as cues for the profound transition currently taking place across urbanism and architecture.

Secondly, they may help to identify a mindset that eclectically gathers and assembles these approaches and thus may support designers through some of Territorial Urbanism's challenges. This mindset could help hone greater awareness of uncertainty in architecture and urban planning, and train practitioners to grasp the new possibilities they offer. For wherever there is trouble and uncertainty, there is always also possibility.

AKAMA, Y. (2017) 'Surrendering to the Ocean: Practices of Mindfulness and Presence in Designing', in R. B. Egenhoefer (ed.) *Routledge Handbook for Sustainable Design*. London: Routledge, pp. 219–230.

ARCHITECTURAL HERITAGE INTERVENTION (2019) *Zollverein Park*. Available at: https://eu-architecturalheritage.org/en/archive/b/OYLjXEVPQKG5D3JLomyBMn7edW8vbr

BENDIKS, S. and DEGROS, A. (2019) *Traffic Space = Public Space. Ein Handbuch zur Transformation. A Handbook for Transformation*. Zurich: Park Books.

BERKES, F. and FOLKE, C. (1998) *Linking Social and Ecological Systems: Management Practices and Social Mechanisms for Building Resilience*. Cambridge: Cambridge University Press.

DAVOUDI, S. (2019) 'Resilience, Uncertainty, and Adaptive Planning', *Annual Review of Territorial Governance in the Western Balkans*, 1, pp. 120–128.

DAVOUDI, S. (2012) 'Resilience: A Bridging Concept or a Dead End?', *Planning Theory and Practice*, 13(2), pp. 299–307.

DEGROS, A. (2016) 'Fosbury-flop ou de la ruse dans l'espace public', *l'Observatoire*, 48, pp. 39–42.

DEGROS, A., BAGARIC, A., BAUER, S., RADULOVA-STAHMER, R., STEFAN, M. and SCHWAB, E. (eds.) (2021) *Basics of Urbanism. 12 Notions of Territorial Transformation*. Zurich: Park Books.

DI GIOVANNI, A. (2014) 'Outcropping Public Spaces', in C. Toscani and E. Dedé (eds.) *Rethinking Public Space*. Santarcangelo di Romagna: Maggioli.

DI GIOVANNI, A. (2018) 'Urban Voids as a Resource for the Design of Contemporary Public Spaces', *Planum. The Journal of Urbanism*, 2(37). Available at: http://media.planum.bedita.net/3e/56/Planum%20Magazine_Di%20Giovanni_FULL%20ENGLISH%20ARTICLE.pdf

DI GIOVANNI, A., DI MONTE, P. and GRÁVALOS, I. (2020) 'Estonoesunsolar a Saragozza. Il progetto dello spazio pubblico temporaneo come strategia di riuso e riciclo per una rigenerazione urbana sostenibile', in M. Mareggi (ed.) *Spazi aperti. Ragioni, progetti e piani urbanistici*. Rome-Milan: Planum Publisher.

ECOCOCOS (2012a) 'Esto no es un solar (I): El proyecto', *Paisaje Transversal Blog*. Available at: https://paisajetransversal.org/2012/06/esto-no-es-un-solar-i-el-proyecto/

ECOCOCOS (2012b) 'Esto no es un solar (II): La entrevista,' *Paisaje Transversal Blog*. Available at: https://paisajetransversal.org/2012/07/esto-no-es-un-solar-ii-la-entrevista/

ESTO NO ES UN SOLAR (nd) *Esto no es un solar*. Available at: https://estonoesunsolar.wordpress.com

GASPARRINI, C. (2018) 'Una buona urbanistica per convivere con i rischi', *Urbanistica*, 159, pp. 4–9.

HARAWAY, D. (2016) *Staying with the Trouble. Making Kin in the Chthulucene*. Durham: Duke University Press.

HOLLING, C. S. (1996) 'Engineering Resilience Versus Ecological Resilience', in P.C. Schulze (ed.) *Engineering within Ecological Constraints*. Washington D.C.: National Academy Press, pp. 31–43.

MANFRA, M. (2020) 'Margherita Manfra, Co-design dello spazio pubblico e attivazione di comunità', *2050 ArchiFest Colle di Val d'Elsa YouTube channel*. Available at: https://www.youtube.com/watch?v=Y9UjJnhSmEw

ORIZZONTALE (nd) 'Prossima Apertura: Un nuovo modello di rigenerazione urbana', *Orizzontale*. Available at: https://prossimaapertura.orizzontale.org

DIE PLANERGRUPPE (nd) Der Zollverein Park.Available at: https://www.die-planergruppe.de/project/der-zollverein-park/Porqueddu, E. (2019) 'Design for the Open City. Directing Rather than Mastering Emergent Transformations', *TRIALOG, 136*(1), pp. 20–23.

TALEB, N.N. (2012) *Antifragile. Things that Gain from Disorder*. New York: Random House.

SANDSTRÖM, I. (2020) 'Minor Urbanism', in K. Havik, K. Pint and S. Riesto, H. Steiner (eds.) *Vademecum. 77 Minor Terms for Writing Urban Places*. Rotterdam: nai010 publishers.

SANDSTRÖM, I. (2019) *Towards a Minor Urbanism. Thinking Community Without Unity in Recent Makings of Public Space*. PhD thesis, Lund University.

SARTORIO. F., AELBRECHT, P., KAMALIPOUR, H. and FRANK, A. (2021) 'Towards an Antifragile Urban Form: a Research Agenda for Advancing Resilience in the Built Environment', *Urban Design International*, 26, pp. 135–158.

SENDRA, P. and SENNETT, R. (2020) *Designing Disorder. Experiments and Disruptions in the City*. London and Brooklyn: Verso.

SHAFIQUE, T. (2015) 'Towards Antifragile Urbanism: Beyond the Fragility of Utopia and the Robustness of Resilience', *Studio*, 9, pp. 20–27.

WIENECKE, S. (2018) 'Zollverein Park (Essen, Germany) – A Park Evolves. Outdoor facilities of the UNESCO World Heritage Site of the Zollverein coal mine and coking plant', *Planur-e*, 11. Available at: https://www.planur-e.es/articulos/ver/el-parque-de-zollverein-essen-alemania-ZUS (2019) *City of Permanent Temporality. Incomplete & Unfinished*. Rotterdam: nai010 publishers.

Does Utopia Help? The Use of Individual Visions for a Common Goal

Lilli Lička,
Hannes Gröblacher

ACTIVIST RESEARCH

This paper reflects on the ongoing involvement of citizens in the process of implementing a park in Vienna—Westbahnpark, on the site of the former Empress Elisabeth railway in Vienna's dense 15th district, exploring the background to the initiative. The authors are initiators as well as organizers and members of the action group BLA.[1] In full awareness of the bias that this creates, they strive to critically review the project. The evaluation is intended to go beyond self-reflective analysis. Based on an action-research approach, the paper aims to develop the theoretical framework further and facilitate the improvement and evolution of the practice itself. We look at the project in the context of the current neoliberal tendencies and a wider political complacency in the planning system in Vienna, examining the self-empowering method of activism (a utopian vision as the basis for participatory and performative action). We also examine the spatial framework and potential of the site itself, viewing the city through the lens of landscape.

PLANNING OUT OF THE BOX OF THE PLANNING SYSTEM

There are several topical issues, both social and environmental, that made it into the official planning policy documents of European cities, after a longer period of constant civic and professional activism and the sustained involvement of public administrations. To date, development plans have oriented themselves towards social justice, while aspiring to greater participation, diversity, and inclusion in planning processes. Other plans focus on climate and environmental improvement, including rainwater management, the prevention of urban heat islands, and climate change mitigation.

Documents in different European cities have similar intentions centered on adapting the planning system and transforming its actual outcome in the urban fabric, i.e., the real space, for the better (**Furchtlehner and Lička, 2019**). A comprehensive global review (**Hunter et al., 2019**) gives clear evidence that many cities are striving to improve local health conditions and instigate social and environmental benefits by introducing urban green space interventions and greenways. In many of these documents of intention, citizen participation and involvement are declared as goals.

Even though the prevailing situation in Vienna regarding public participation is commensurate with pioneering countries like the Netherlands, there is some dissatisfaction with the way participation is implemented and politically instrumentalized. Following Laimer (**2020**), paternalistic traditions in Vienna see participation only in top-down organized processes, while bottom-up initiatives are generally not supported. We also observe the contradiction that the most decisive questions about the creation of public space are often taken without the involvement of the public, whereas participation processes are developed and commissioned when it comes to the design and detail of such spaces. This is in line with the shift that began in the 1970s, from planning based on a political program to more market-oriented development driven by neoliberal reasoning (**Kadi, 2018**). As a result, it has become even more difficult to argue in favor of public spaces which do not often deliver immediate revenue—despite the fact that deteriorating climate conditions have given renewed urgency to the planning of public open spaces and urban green spaces.

Apart from the question of profit maximization, the argument for housing need is also put forward. This pits two weak areas against each

1 BLA is an acronym for "Büro für lustige Angelegenheiten" (Office of Droll Concerns), which was active from 2012 to 2020 and used performative action to put societal conditions on the agenda, as manifested in public open spaces. It was founded and run by Hannes Gröblacher, Lilli Lička, and Karoline Seywald. www.bla.zone

other and negates the fact that quality housing already depends on having open space of a sufficient quality. Vienna has an excellent international reputation for social housing as well as for its quality of living.[2] The foundations for this were laid a century ago, in the interwar period—which has come to be known as "Red Vienna"—when the social democratic government realized a very ambitious construction program of city-owned social housing for 65,000 housing units. Huge numbers of apartments were realized to a high technical and social standard, while the buildings also contained social facilities such as communal spaces, kindergartens, libraries, communal laundry spaces, playgrounds, open spaces, and green courtyards. This important heritage remains the political reference point for contemporary programs which are still internationally acknowledged, despite the fact that even within the social housing sector prices for rents are rising and access is not open for everyone.[3] This period also marked the inception of a system characterized by a highly paternalistic attitude on the part of the city government, which in turn may lead to a lack of (potential) civic engagement, self-determined decision-making, and empowerment. The city government proclaims that it will implement participation but does not embrace self-organized involvement. On this tightrope walk between care and authority, the city administration tends towards the latter. It would rather "crush its citizens with love," as the editor and journalist of a local newspaper puts it (Winterer, 2019), than encourage or embrace independent bottom-up activities.

The city planning procedure in Vienna follows a similar trajectory to practices in other cities. In 2016—two city government election periods ago—participation was made one of the tasks of the vice mayor and councilor. In line with the "Master Plan for Participation," participation was defined as mandatory for decisions in urban planning on a neighborhood scale, such as the city quarter development. Looking at this document more closely, we can see that it represents a rather narrow understanding of participation in terms of where, when, and who. There are five specific criteria under which participation is mandatory: if at least 300 housing units are planned (or an equivalent of 30,000 square meters); if a high-rise construction is planned; if the site is part of a cultural heritage area; if the land use dedication changes from green areas to building areas; and if there is a legal requirement for an environmental assessment (Stadt Wien, 2022a). This, among other things, creates the impression that engagement is relatively difficult, and the extent to which participation is possible is unclear. As the authors argue, this might add to the general sense that it is difficult for citizens to influence key decisions.

In the case of Westbahnpark, presented in this paper, the authors observed, together with members of the action group, and other interested parties, exclusivity and a lack of transparency. This is shown in the creation of fixed conditions for urban development, that led to self-constraint among lay people and professionals. Both parties anticipate complying with regulations and subordinate themselves to the logic of market rules, which have a far-reaching impact on political decision-making. A plot of land within the city which is unbuilt can only be "developed" to provide buildings for the housing market. Flexibility is reduced to a narrow margin within the predefined built density, with only minor scope for decisions to be made about green or open spaces. The option of a non-built area that is

2 In its last ranking, published prior to the COVID-19 pandemic in 2019, Mercer put Vienna in first place in terms of quality of life for ten years in a row (Mercer, 2022). The city of Vienna proudly publishes a list of no less than seventeen rankings worldwide where it achieved a high position (Stadt Wien, 2022b)

3 Surveys of the private housing market, which covers 43% of accommodation, show that in the past few years rents have become unaffordable on an average salary (Kadi et al. 2021). In Vienna, social tenants pay €3.87/m2 in municipal housing and €4.84/m2 in LPHA housing compared to the citywide average of €5.27/m2 for sitting tenants (Tockner 2017, quoted in Marquardt and Glaser 2020, p. 10)

not scheduled for construction is no longer conceivable in the context of urban development. This is what this paper wants to explore: can utopian thinking trigger the imagination in a way that allows us to overcome these self-restrictions and perhaps even engender a viable new concept of urban space itself?

UTOPIA AND URBAN PRACTICE

Utopia, in this paper, is referred to as a model for imagining possible futures. When Thomas More conceived his ideal state of utopia 500 years ago (in 1516), he had social equality and justice in mind. Fernando et al. (2018) refer to the definition of utopias as "desired possible worlds—ideal worlds that may possibly exist, at least in imagination" (Fernando et al., 2018, p. 779). They also claim that utopias "can instigate individual self-regulation ... and animate collective self-regulation," making it possible for people to move their reality closer to their ideal (Fernando et al., 2018, pp. 779–80). Utopias could thus motivate people to become more engaged. As defined by Ruth Levitas, utopias serve the following functions: change, criticism, and compensation. These are the *consequence* of utopian thinking: "That is to say that imagining one's utopia may result in the motivation to engage in change, criticism, or escape behaviors" (Fernando et al., 2018, p. 780). This definition is crucial both for our actions and the process of reflecting on them. Furthermore, we would like to specify "our utopia" in terms of Sandra Meireis's theory of so-called micro-utopias (Meireis, 2021). As indicated in the subheading of her thesis, she examines the "utopian momentum in micro architectures". Small, ephemeral new sites are created using "minimal architectural techniques" as a reaction to local deficits or disparities. These newly created sites are a utopian experiment and, as such, offer a way to ponder and debate a better model for the future. The social utopia is rehabilitated in the form of the micro-utopia, Meireis suggests, arguing that: "in times of transformation, utopias traditionally have a boom. At present, they appear—realized with minimal architectural techniques—as micro-utopias against the background of urban neoliberalization processes. They can thus be understood as temporary counter-strategies in the sense of an alternative, critical architectural practice" (Meireis, 2021, pp. 220–22, translated by authors).

Such utopian experiments develop out of the lived present and can nest in it under certain circumstances. Meireis refers to sites that have been appropriated by implementing minimal built structures or making other changes to the place. In the ongoing process for Vienna's Westbahnpark, no actual changes have been made apart from presenting minimal versions of alternative uses during the walks. The theory of the power of imagination as well as the representation of the larger picture in a small intervention was the basis of the action from the beginning—as was a clear position that the green space would help to minimize existing environmental injustice. Despite the numerous utopias that would follow Thomas More's, today we are still struggling to realize a state in which disparities are diminished. One such disparity is mirrored in the urban structure and takes visible form as "green space inequality," "spatial injustice," or "environmental injustice" (Kabisch et al., 2016; Kronenberg et al., 2020; London et al., 2019). As for the equal provision of quality of life, the park project of Westbahnpark adds a crucial contribution in terms of achieving green space justice since there is enough evidence for the positive effects of urban green spaces (see Hunter et al., 2019, p. 18). Aiming at a more general Territorial Urbanism, this injustice is tackled by the authors both in theory (the reflections in this paper) and in practice (performative action, utopian visions for the specific site of Westbahnpark). Instead of the comprehensive narrative of the new society—as expressed in early utopias—we use the term "utopia" as a model of a possible socially and environmentally just urban future which is expressed through an accessible, healthy, and versatile public space that

[01] Poster for Westbahnpark. Action is taken to keep spaces OPEN for change and adjustment. Flexible development is only possible if space is provided! © Christina Kirchmair

improves living conditions for everyone and for all creatures. In the case of this ongoing experiment, the aim is to emphasize the fact that the utopian imagination is not a fixed state but an open process, or rather an "opening process": unfolding a space of thought and fantasy in order to counteract what is a current crisis of imagination, as German climate activist Luisa Neubauer puts it **(Schmidt, 2019)**.

THE CASE OF VIENNA
City Fabric

As a typical European metropolis, Vienna's density is extremely varied. It is very high in the central areas, with 27,029 people per square kilometer, and decreases towards the edges, where we find 1,429 people per square kilometer **(Dezernat Statistik Wien, 2021)**. Vienna is also still profiting from a very forward-looking decision in 1905 to conserve its forests to the west as a cool- and fresh-air corridor as well as a recreational area. Vienna's population has gone through different phases of growth and decline in the last century. Currently, it is expected to reach 2,000,000 again by 2027 and to attain a historic high by 2037, surpassing the 2,083,630 inhabitants recorded in 1910. This means that the built-up perimeter of the city is now being pushed towards the edges of the political territory and a huge effort is being made to accommodate about 20,000 more people every year **(Magistrat der Stadt Wien, 2018, n.p.)**. For the inner and outer development areas the planning processes are clearer: one-third of newly built housing is to be dedicated to social housing, with indicators and criteria set down for public spaces, mobility, and environmental standards. Even though the developments don't always live up to those high standards, it is nonetheless an achievement to establish these goals.

However, in the dense and still densifying areas, the standards don't necessarily play the same role, even though the negative effects of climate change are having a stronger impact on those areas. This has been a reason for large groups of citizens to call for action in Vienna—both on a general level and in various concrete sites (Scientists for Future Austria, Platz für Wien, Freier Naschmarkt, etc.). Demands have also been made to transform the existing street spaces into a more livable, healthier environment **(Furchtlehner and Lička, 2019; Staller et al., 2022; and others)**.

The Site

[01] The potential site of Westbahnpark is the last remaining open space in an otherwise densified inner-city fabric. In Vienna's 15th district, Rudolfsheim-Fünfhaus, we find a number of superlative aspects: it is one of the most densely populated districts, one of the poorest, one of its youngest demographically, and the most diverse in terms of housing the largest number of inhabitants from a migrant background **(Landesstatistik Wien, 2020)**. Rudolfsheim-Fünfhaus is also the least green of all the outer districts.

The district is cut in two by the railway track—the former Empress Elisabeth Railway—leading to today's Westbahnhof station. This railway line encourages the vision of a park because it overlooks an exceptional urban landscape, directly cutting across the canyons of built-up city streets towards the Vienna Woods, the protected landscape of forested hills to the west, as well as the baroque park of Schönbrunn castle. In this dense district, having a view is an exciting experience in and of itself. The narrow and straight stretch of land along the tracks is more than 1 kilometer long, which is rare for an open space in the dense city. It is accompanied by a green embankment with exceptional biodiversity, including wild bees and protected plant and animal species. In terms of urban morphology, topographical form, and existing nature, the space is exceptional and calls for a process in which the city is (re)conceived through the landscape.

In order to present convincing arguments, facts and figures were collated (www.westbahnpark.jetzt); Christina Kirchmair **(2019)** wrote a master's thesis and, in parallel to these activities, a climate analysis was commissioned and published by the City of Vienna **(Stadt Wien, 2020)**. Weatherpark—the firm authoring the analysis—located their study area in an essential corridor for the cool air that streams into the city from the west **(Weatherpark, 2020)**. All the findings gave clear evidence that the park project is an urbanistic coup with an intelligent perspective—a forward-looking measure to secure living conditions in times of densification, heat islands, and mobility transformation over the long term. Successive lockdowns in the years 2020 and 2021 made people's needs for local recreation even more evident. Public spaces in close proximity to residential housing became scarce and every square meter was used for exercise and recovery.

Utopian Action

The Westbahnpark experiment started out as an attempt to encourage people's own fantasy ideas of a possible utopia, fulfilling green space justice alongside projecting a future for this area that was intriguing, inventive, and fun. Interestingly, for the initiators, it was quite a task to break out of the box of self-restriction and it took some practice to achieve this. The landscape we chose had been on our radar for quite some time. Several studies, ideas, and projects had been developed prior to an urbanistic competition and new ones have come along since. There are countless students' design studios on the site.

This sounds like the first step in a typical landscape design, projecting a possible future onto an existing site (or rather a piece of paper) **(Kretz, 2020)**. In this case, however, the invention was not on the part of the designers, who purposefully refrained from presenting designs, realistic renderings, or other professional imagery. Instead, building on the example of Lucius Burckhardt's "strollology" **(Burckhardt et al., 2015)**, we wanted to convert the *topos* into a new utopia. Through walking and exploring the site we developed the narrative of a fictitious park project, whose implementation process and qualities we would then report on retrospectively. On several of these "journeys into the future," interested lay people and colleagues were guided through the terrain, with headphones providing explanations about how it had been changed into a park, how planning policy had devel-

[02] Activists carry air from the woods into the city: visualizing the fresh air corridor of Westbahnpark. © Harald Leitner for WESTBAHNPARK.JETZT

oped, what groundbreaking research results had been achieved onsite, and what technical innovations had been applied. The visitors' imaginations were sparked by actors in swimming costumes standing in front of the depot buildings, people reading in the steep meadow, and passers-by blowing bubbles, or carrying melons from the invented "market in the train."

Only a few posters were placed along the tour. The imagery that was shown steered clear of the ubiquitous renderings in which the space presented is deceptively real with an invariably cheerful atmosphere. The posters were intentionally misleading, both in drawing technique and in content, showing plants which would never grow there, scales which are surreal, and no equipment whatsoever. Only a 1-kilometer-long swimming pool is shown to encourage thinking outside the box.

No complete design for the area was offered, in terms of either [02]
layout plans or visualizations. This is a variation on Meireis's "micro-utopias," where the landscape itself remains untouched and the landscape-architectural changes happen only in people's minds. The aim was to be suggestive as a means of triggering people's individual imagination and encouraging them to create their own private utopias. People were passionate about the idea of creating a new park. In tours we ran for several hundred utopians, we learned that Westbahnpark had already been used as an open space for a long time by a large number of people from all walks of life. Reports about how children had learned to cycle there, what flowers blossomed in the area, and how runners used it to connect their different routes showed that this hidden site was far more than an untapped resource, or a non-site—it was a hidden gem. Since it is not easily visible from the more regular everyday paths, it is considered an insider tip and its use has been tolerated by the Austrian Federal Railways group (ÖBB), which owns the land, despite the fact that the storage halls are still rented out and used by construction companies and other firms. Biologists have even agreed with the owner that the embankment should remain unmown so as not to destroy the forage for the wild bees they are researching. This was also a welcome contribution to the green image of the railway company—or perhaps a first step towards realizing an interspecies utopia?

[03] Transparency and information are a requirement for civic engagement. Apart from tours onsite, models are a way to keep the public informed and involved.
© Johannes Hloch for WESTBAHNPARK.JETZT

FROM VISION TO IMPLEMENTATION

It is unclear how this process will end, much like it is unclear whether all the utopias will develop the strength to buck neoliberal trends and push the park through in the face of the expected development projects. However, Westbahnpark is an ongoing process. It is being lobbied for by a group of about thirty activists, all of different ages and professional backgrounds, including the founder members of the "WESTBAHNPARK.JETZT" association: namely, Hannes Gröblacher, Christina Kirchmair, and Lilli Lička. Drawing from international examples such as Park Fiction in Hamburg, Dalston Curve Garden in East London, and Park am Gleisdreieck in Berlin, we are sticking to the idea that the park has a realistic chance of being implemented.

We have contacted the landowner—Austrian Federal Railways (ÖBB)—the ministry, the city planning department, and other stakeholder groups with similar goals. Some colleagues have been critical, suggesting that the project was not feasible at a time when neoliberal planning paradigms hold sway, and that we were being naive. Media coverage and public perception, however, have been consistently positive. The district mayor[4] is very excited about the park project, and the landowner does not reject the idea entirely. In this period of indecision and transition, in which urban planning is not yet committed, the ÖBB is open and the district politicians
[03] are very much in favor of the park, suggesting that it is perfectly possible the idea will yet come to fruition.

CONCLUSIONS

Vienna's progressive planning system, dating back to the 1920s, has ensured a livable city. Such visionary thinking, however, is accompanied by a paucity of public space. Even though Vienna already has a high quality of life, as international rankings show, the city must resist "market forces" and maintain and create new green and open spaces if these standards are not to be lost. The ongoing process of the Westbahnpark has shown that micro-

4 By the time this article is published, there will be a new mayor who unfortunately is less committed to the park.

[04] Westbahnpark was essential during lockdown as a local green space and continues to underpin quality of life in the area. © Lilli Lička

utopias are a helpful tool in overcoming self-limitations and stimulating the imagination. They lead to the belief that other futures are possible, which in turn leads to active involvement within the action group. The recent announcement by the Planning Department is the beginning of a participatory development process for a larger area. The utopias are ready, but we still need to ensure that enough political pressure is built up so that when they are due, decisions are made in the citizens' best interests. Only then can the experiment be finally evaluated. [04]

BURCKHARDT, L. (2006) *Warum ist Landschaft schön? Die Spaziergangswissenschaft*. Kassel: Martin Schmitz Verlag.

CITY OF VIENNA, MUNICIPAL DEPARTMENT 18 (MA 18)—Urban Development and Planning (2014) *STEP 2025: Urban development plan Vienna*. Available at: https://www.wien.gv.at/stadtentwicklung/studien/pdf/b008379b.pdf

DEZERNAT STATISTIK WIEN (MA23) (2021) *Wien in Zahlen*. Available at: www.statistik.wien.gv.at (Accessed 16 May 2020).

FERNANDO, J.W., BURDEN, N., FERGUSON, A., O'BRIEN, L.V., JUDGE, M. and KASHIMA, Y. (2018) 'Functions of utopia: how utopian thinking motivates societal engagement,' *Personality and Social Psychology Bulletin*, 44(5), pp. 779–792. Available at: https://doi.org/10.1177/0146167217748604

FURCHTLEHNER, J. and LIČKA, L. (2019) 'Back on the street: Vienna, Copenhagen, Munich, and Rotterdam in focus,' *Journal of Landscape Architecture*, 14(1), pp. 72–83.

GRAEBER, D. (2012) *The utopia of rules: on technology, stupidity, and the secret joys of bureaucracy*. Brooklyn and London: Melville House Publishers.

HAGEN, L. and WINKLER-HERMADEN, R. (2021) 'Swimmingpool, Flowertower und entsiegelte Parkplätze,' *Der Standard*, 27 May.

HUNTER, R.F., CLELAND, C., CLEARY, A., DROOMERS, M., WHEELER, B.W., SINNETT, D., NIEUWENHUIJSEN, M.J. and BRAUBACH, M. (2019) 'Environmental, health, wellbeing, social and equity effects of urban green space interventions: a meta-narrative evidence synthesis,' *Environment International*, 130.

KABISCH, N., STROHBACH, M., HAASE, D. and KRONENBERG, J. (2016) 'Urban green space availability in European cities,' *Ecological Indicators*, 70, pp. 586–596.

KADI, J. (2018) *Die drei Phasen der sozialen Wohnungspolitik in Wien*. Published in Hungarian translation as 'A szociálislakásépítés három korszaka Bécsben,' in M. Tamáska and J.B. Kocsis (eds.) *Modell vagy külön út: bécs szociális építészete*. Budapest: Martin Opitz Kiadó, pp. 51–62.

KADI, J., GRINZINGER, E., PÜHRINGER, F. and SCHNEIDER, A. (2021) 'Das Projekt Mietmonitor Wien: Wie leistbar ist privates Mieten in Wien?', *Der öffentliche Sektor – The Public Sector*, 47(1), pp. 39–44.

KIRCHMAIR, C. (2019) *FREI:RAUM WESTBAHNAREAL: Konversionsflächen als Ausgleich urbaner Verdichtung, dargestellt am Beispiel des 15. Wiener Gemeindebezirks Rudolfsheim-Fünfhaus*. Master's thesis. Institute of Landscape Architecture BOKU Vienna. Available at: https://abstracts.boku.ac.at/download.php?property_id=107&dataset_id=19800

KRETZ, S. (2020) *Der Kosmos des Entwerfens: Untersuchungen zum entwerfenden Denken*. Berlin: Walther König.

KRONENBERG, J., HAASE, A., ŁASZKIEWICZ, E., ANTAL, A., BARAVIKOVA, A.; BIERNACKA, M., DUSHKOVA, D., FILČAK, R., HAASE, D., IGNATIEVA, M., KHMARA, Y., NIŢĂ, M.R. and ONOSE, D.A. (2020) 'Environmental justice in the context of urban green space availability, accessibility, and attractiveness in postsocialist cities,' *Cities*, 106.

LAIMER, C. (2020) 'Das Ende der Nordbahnhalle,' *dérive*, 78, Available at: https://derive.at/texte/das-ende-der-nordbahnhalle

LANDESSTATISTIK WIEN (MA 23) (2020) *Rudolfsheim-Fünfhaus in Zahlen 2020*. Available at: https://www.digital.wienbibliothek.at/wbrup/download/pdf/2999186?originalFilename=true

LIČKA, L. and FURCHTLEHNER, J. (2019) 'Changing streets: individual action, large-scale measures, and ambitious urban climate goals,' in B. Rinaldi and P.Y. Tan (eds.) *Urban landscapes in high density cities: parks, streetscapes, ecosystems*. Basel: Birkhäuser. pp. 100–116.

LIČKA, L., SEYWALD, K. and GRÖBLACHER, H. (2019) 'Für die lebenswerte Bestandsstadt,' *Architektur und Bauforum*, 25 September.

LONDON, L., JOSHI, I.K., CAIRNCROSS, E., GILMORE, J. and CLAUDIO, L. (2019) 'Environmental justice: an international perspective,' in *Encyclopedia of environmental health*. Amsterdam: Elsevier. pp. 553–560.

MAGISTRAT DER STADT WIEN, (2018) *Vienna in figures: population projection Vienna 2018; summary*. https://www.digital.wienbibliothek.at/download/pdf/2987243?name=Summary

MARQUARDT, S. and GLASER, D. (2020) 'How much state and how much market? Comparing social housing in Berlin and Vienna,' *German Politics*. Available at: https://doi.org/10.1080/09644008.2020.1771696

MEIREIS, S. (2021) *Mikro-Utopien der Architektur: Das utopische Moment architektonischer Minimaltechniken*. Bielefeld: transcript Verlag.

MERCER (2022). *Quality of living city ranking*. Available at: https://mobilityexchange.mercer.com/Insights/quality-of-living-rankings

MORE, T. (1516) *Utopia*. Released on the Gutenberg Project in 2008. Available at: https://www.gutenberg.org/files/26971/26971-h/26971-h.htm

PHILIPP, N. (2019) 'Wir schwimmen nach Westen,' *Die Presse (Schaufenster)*, 19 May.

SCHMIDT, F. and EISENHART, R. (2019) 'Luisa Neubauer über Druck und Öffentlichkeit: "Ich wusste nicht, worauf ich mich einlasse"; Die deutsche "Fridays for Future"-Vorkämpferin im Interview,' *Spiegel Panorama*. Available at: https://www.spiegel.de/panorama/luisa-neubauer-die-deutsche-fridays-for-future-vorkaempferin-ueber-druck-und-oeffentlichkeit-a-d0e1c446-5de8-4702-a341-ecba1dad5287

STADT WIEN (2020) *Stadtklimaanalyse Wien 2020: Themenkarte—Nächtliche Kaltluft*. Available at: https://www.wien.gv.at/stadtentwicklung/grundlagen/stadtforschung/pdf/stadtklimaanalyse-themenkarte-luft.pdf

STADT WIEN (2022a) *Beteiligung und Masterplan für partizipative Stadtentwicklung*. Available at: https://www.wien.gv.at/stadtentwicklung/partizipation/masterplan/

STADT WIEN (2022b) *Wien im weltweiten Vergleich*. Available at: https://www.wien.gv.at/politik/international/vergleich

STALLER, S., STUDER, H., SZEILER, M. and TERZIC, L. (2022) *Klimagerechtigkeit im öffentlichen Raum: Vision Wiener Klimastraßen*. Stadtpunkte 39. Vienna: Kammer für Arbeiter und Angestellte für Wien. Available at: https://emedien.arbeiterkammer.at/viewer/resolver?urn=urn:nbn:at:at-akw:g-5562291

TRIPP, D. (1990) 'Socially critical action research,' *Theory into Practice*, 29(3), pp. 158–166. Available at: https://doi.org/10.1080/00405849009543449

WEATHERPARK (2020) *Stadtklimaanalyse Wien: Klimaanalysekarte fertig*. Available at: https://www.weatherpark.com/stadtklimaanalyse-wien

WINTERER, M. (2019) 'Bürgerbeteiligung: Wie die Stadt Wien ihre Bürger mit Liebe erdrückt,' *Wiener Zeitung*, 6 October. Available at: https://www.wienerzeitung.at/nachrichten/politik/wien-politik/2032313-Wie-die-Stadt-Wien-ihre-Buerger-mit-Liebe-erdrueckt.html?em_cnt_page=4

Boulevard Périphérique: From City Limit to Metropolitan Center

Johannes Bernsteiner

[01] The ring road Boulevard Périphérique embodies the culmination of the historical expansion of the City of Paris. Overlapping with the administrative border, it still mirrors the image of the last city wall. With a length of 35 kilometers, it is a rare example of a ring road in the urban center of a world metropolis. Its 1,100,000 vehicles per day make it the busiest road in Europe (**Tribillon, 2015**). What is the future of this ring road, which is neither a *Boulevard* nor "peripheral" in the first place? If the city can be understood as a palimpsest onto which the structures of power are inscribed, what is the significance of this city limit and how can we make the Paris–*banlieue* antagonism disappear? What role could architecture and urban planning play in the necessary integration of the infrastructure in its urban and metropolitan context?

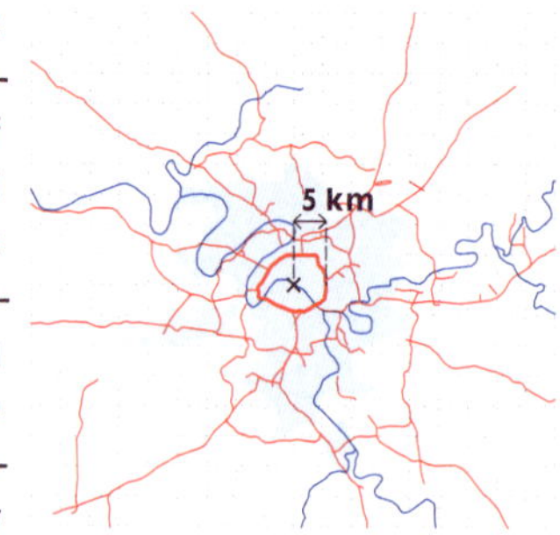

[01] Trace of the ring road as part of the metropolitan network of highways. © Johannes Bernsteiner

[02] Rather than questioning the functional and environmental issues of the infrastructure in terms of traffic and pollution, this research investigates the common idea of the ring road as a limit and a "non-place" (**Augé, 1992**), challenging its underlying paradigms. It is argued that, over the last two decades, evidence of Territorial Urbanism can be observed as the territory of the ring road has become an increasingly significant space of reinvention, strategically located in the heart of Greater Paris. This change of perspective offers a new horizon onto which the visions and expectations of the growing metropolis can be projected, thereby participating in the Territorial Urbanism of this historically neglected area. The highway thus provides, as Kevin Lynch stated in the 1960s, the "great neglected opportunity in the urban project" (**Appleyard, Lynch and Myer, 1965**).

[03] At the beginning of the 21st century, the perception of the ring road territory started to shift from marginal to central. This attitude was expressed in the political desire to re-establish links with the neighboring municipalities. The objective of the (re-)introduction of the tramway and of several "major urban renewal projects"[1] was to open up isolated neighbor-

1 **Original translation: Grand Projet de Renouvellement Urbain (GPRU)**

[02] Trace of the ring road that creates an urban threshold between the capital city and its suburbs. © Johannes Bernsteiner

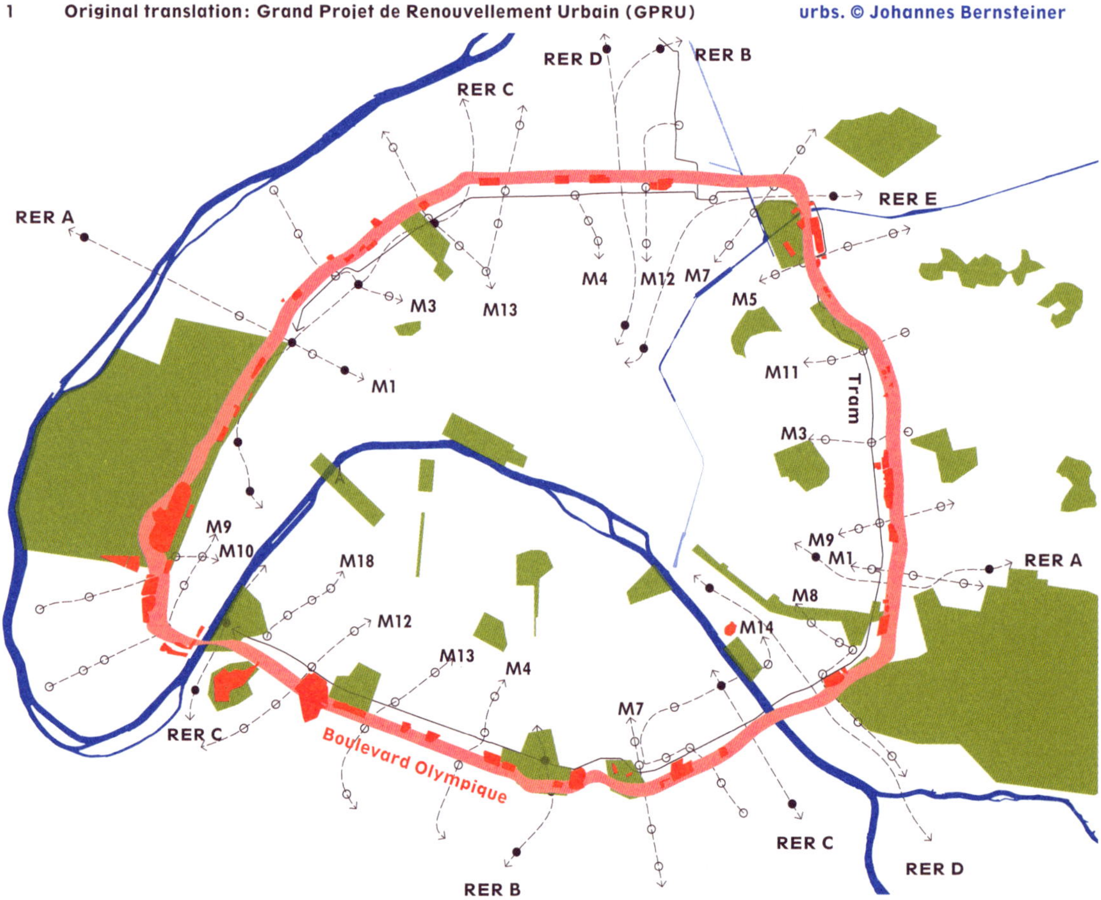

[03] View of the ring road at the Porte de Vincennes.
© Johannes Bernsteiner

hoods at the limit of Paris and to create a smoother interface with the suburbs. This territorial turn led to urban wastelands being transformed into vibrant urban spaces. Many previously neglected city gates leading into Paris have now been transformed into the public squares of Greater Paris. Between 2001 and 2020, seventy-two urban development projects near the ring road were identified identified—equating to around 10% of the Parisian territory (Hoarau-Beauval , 2021).

The idea of transversality is found in the construction of public buildings located on each side of the ring road, such as the Philharmonie de Paris by Jean Nouvel on the Parisian side, with the sports center Jules Ladoumègue by Dietmar Feichtinger on just the opposite side of the ring road. Likewise, street markets and interactive light installations by Encore Heureux and Les Arts Codés, respectively, improve the quality and animation of the pedestrian crossings underneath the viaduct. The relocation of prestigious institutions, such as the Ministry of Defense or the Paris Courthouse, to the city limits participate in changing the ring road's perception, underlining its vocation as a central space in the metropolitan area of Greater Paris. The aim of the "Linear Forest" on both sides of the ring road is to bring pedestrians closer to the territorial infrastructure, while the traffic completely disappears with the landscape cover at the Porte de Lilas, which provides a park and cultural buildings on top of the ring road. [04]

A new generation of high-rise buildings along the ring road follows decades of a *de facto* tower ban in Paris. Among the tower projects are the already mentioned Paris Courthouse by Renzo Piano, the Duo Towers by Jean Nouvel, and the heavily debated Triangle Tower by Herzog & de Meuron—currently expected in 2024. These landmarks propose vertical markers at a maximum height of 180 meters—at the risk of highlighting, once again, the demarcation of Parisian city limits and the real-estate domination of the French capital over its suburbs. On the other hand, innovation in building materials and typologies have made it possible to improve the living conditions of low-income populations suffering from external effects generated by the ring road. Some residences have undergone remarkable transformation, like the 2011 rehabilitation of the housing tower Bois-le-Prêtre by Fréderic Druot and Lacaton & Vassal. [05] [06]

While Paris's city limits have historically been devoted to monofunctional programs (the fortifications, the housing belt, the green belt, the ring road), recent developments have demonstrated that the ring road is able to generate urban intensity and complexity by introducing mixed-use buildings. Some proposals—for example *Inventing Bruneseau*, whose design makes provision for direct access to the road through its conversion into a calm, urban boulevard—prefigure the transformation of the Boulevard Périphérique and are therefore perfect examples for architectural reversibility. On the other side, so-called "bridge-buildings" (like "1000 Trees" by Sou Foujimoto & OXO) seem to counteract the idea of the ring road being transformed into an urban boulevard at some point in the future.

These projects invite us to reconsider the current purpose and configuration of the ring road itself. The City of Paris has already demonstrated a strong commitment to decreasing motorized car traffic. With the completion of the circular metro line Grand Paris Express, a significant reduction in road traffic can be expected in the wider agglomeration and especially on the ring road. A 2018 international consultation on the future of urban highways in the metropolitan region of Paris proposed a 50% reduction in car traffic on the ring road by transforming half of the lanes into a park on the Parisian side **(Mercuriali and Picon-Lefebvre, 2019)**. For the 2019 edition of the *Nuit Blanche* festival, a 1.7-kilometer section of the ring road was reserved for cyclists and pedestrians **(Razemon, 2019)**. As part of the 2024 Olympic Games, one lane of the Boulevard Périphérique will be closed to individual car traffic and is subsequently intended to be reserved for shared and clean vehicles only **(Ville de Paris, 2021)**.

The limit of the ring road—whether real or symbolic—is therefore not necessarily limiting but can trigger urban, architectural, and social innovation that will regenerate and reconnect neighborhoods. The territory of the ring road can enrich its potential (accessibility, representation, open landscape) as a central space in the agglomeration while overcoming its dysfunctions (pollution, urban discontinuities, neglect) as a monofunctional traffic space. Mixed-use urban developments create a kind of linear city that can generate urban life next to the ring road and leverage contemporary projects despite historical constraints. The transformation of the ring road itself, previously unimaginable, now also seems possible even if it is still strongly contested.

The challenge, however, lies in the articulation of relevant stakeholders, scales, and temporalities: firstly, a multi-disciplinary approach and inter-municipal partnerships are essential to reflect collectively on the future of the ring road in the context of the developing metropolis. Secondly,

[04] Boulevard Périphérique 2019, location in the trench. © Johannes Bernsteiner

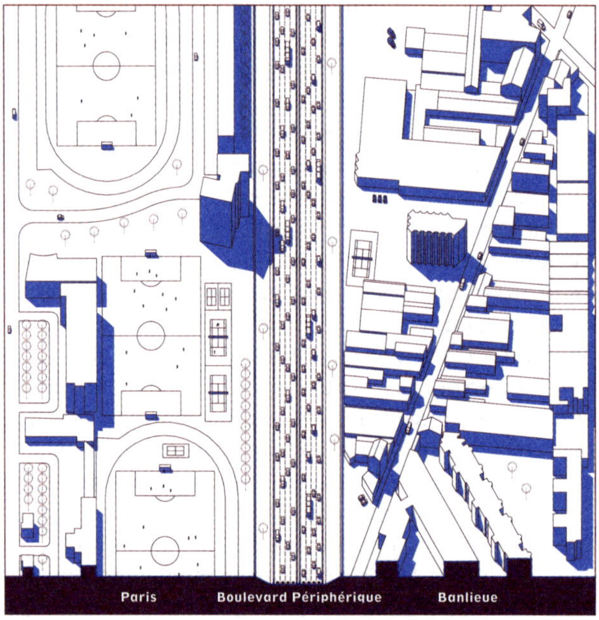

[05] The "Linear Forest" next to the ring road. (Design: Agence TER, Arpentère, Dusapin Leclercq) © Karolina Samborska

[06] Passage Miroir, Porte de Montmartre, Encore Heureux Architectes, 2017 © Cyrus Cornut

urban development that is coherent and holistic involves the scale of the neighborhood (urban regeneration, public space, accessibility, etcetera), as well as the scale of the ring (representation, ecological corridors, open landscape, etcetera), and the scale of the metropolitan region (mobility, housing, environment, etcetera). Finally, there is a risk that short term developments (buildings, landscape covers, etcetera.) may compromise or even contradict longer term visions (such as transformation into an urban boulevard, preservation of open space, creation of a circular park, etcetera).

The ongoing transformation of the historically neglected territory of the ring road into a central space for Greater Paris has, once again, shown that the discussion around the future transformation and integration of the Boulevard Périphérique comes back to the question of Paris's city limit—a political question as much as an urban one—in a highly unbalanced metropolis. Still, this example demonstrates that Territorial Urbanism in urban planning is possible—with the shift away from functional and car-centric urban planning towards the conception and transformation of transport infrastructure as an integral part of the urban and metropolitan landscape.

APPLEYARD, D., LYNCH, K. and MYER, J.R. (1965) *The View from the Road.* Cambridge, MA: The MIT Press.

AUGÉ, M. (1992) *Non-lieux: Introduction à une anthropologie de la surmodernité.* Paris: SEUIL.

BERNSTEINER, J. (2019) *Boulevard Olympique. Paris 2024.* Graz.

COHEN, J.-L. and LORTIE, A. (1991) *Des fortifs au périf: Paris, les seuils de la ville.* Paris: Editions du Pavillon de l'Arsenal.

HOARAU-BEAUVAL, C. (2021) 'Ni pour ni contre, bien au contraire.' in Collectif, G. Burgel, M. Flonneau, and F. Leclercq. *Le boulevard périphérique: quel avenir?: Seize points de vue d'architectes, écrivains, géographes, historiens, ingénieurs, paysagistes et urbanistes.* Paris: Archicity.

MERCURIALI, M. and PICON-LEFEBVRE, V. (2019) *Les Routes Du Futur Du Grand Paris.* Paris: Editions du Pavillon de l'Arsenal.

RAZEMON, O. (2019) *Nuit Blanche: On a Pédalé Sur Le Périph.* Available at: https://www.lemonde.fr/blog/transports/2019/10/06/nuit-blanche-on-a-pedale-sur-le-periph/

TRIBILLON, J. (2015) 'Dirty Boulevard: Why Paris's Ring Road Is a Major Block on the City's Grand Plans', *The Guardian*, 26 June. Available at: https://www.theguardian.com/cities/2015/jun/26/ring-road-paris-peripherique-suburbs-banlieue

VILLE DE PARIS (2021) 'Périphérique: une voie sera dédiée au covoiturage', 19 November. Available at: https://www.paris.fr/pages/peripherique-une-voie-sera-dediee-au-covoiturage-19764

Constructing a Common Vision: The Stadsatelier Oostende as a Proactive Tool for Quality in Urban Development

Stefan Devoldere

Nicknamed "the Queen of Seaside towns," in the 19th century the Belgian city of Ostend was a hotspot for a booming international tourist industry and the favorite holiday location of King Leopold II. Today, it is still the go-to place for a sunny weekend at the beach for most, and the only Belgian coastal town with a certain metropolitan allure. However, with this allure comes metropolitan benefits and challenges. Ostend is the terminus of the Belgian railway network: it has a local airport, high-quality cultural programming, and a (small) port, but it also struggles with poverty, unemployment, and unsanitary housing conditions. About 41 square kilometers in size, the city has 72,000 inhabitants, a population that triples during the peak tourist season. One of the biggest threats it faces, therefore, seems to be continuing pressure on the real estate market for second-stay apartments, and a fundamental shortage of affordable and attractive housing for young families with children.

To tackle this problem, in 2015 the city council established the "Stadsatelier Oostende" (Ostend Urban Workshop) or SAO, an expert group with a triple mission: to work on a strategic development plan for the city, to provide the framework for and help realize innovative housing projects, and to supervise various strategic development projects. The SAO operates on two complementary levels—it develops a strategic vision for the long term and, in the short term, it instigates and monitors exemplary housing projects. By working at these two different speeds, it ensures that constant feedback between the long and the short-term view is at the core of its operation. During its first years, the Stadsatelier also focused on methodical innovation, seeking a flexible set of instruments for urban development and moving from city-scaled studies to realtime building projects. I chaired it from its creation in 2015 till the end of 2020. While it continues its mission today, this paper deals with the first five working years of the Stadsatelier and with my own experiences as chairman of a city advisory body that tries to combine quality control, vision development, and negotiation planning on both large and small scales.

INTERTWINING PROCESSES AND PROJECTS

The SAO consists of both independent experts and members of the administration, resulting in a mix of practicing, academic, and administrative profiles. It was installed by the city council and falls under the responsibility of the alderman for spatial planning and urban development. As such, he and the mayor of the city are its main interlocutors. During the period of legislature in which the SAO was established, the mayor and alderman belonged to the two biggest political factions within the city council, providing a strong political mandate for the Stadsatelier. No specific quantitative criteria determine which projects need supervision by the SAO. A project can be labeled "strategic," either by the responsible alderman or by the SAO itself, if it is considered to have a crucial impact on the quality of the urban environment. The preferred method of guidance consists of workshops rather than unidirectional presentations, taking the necessary time to establish a joint working process through several sessions spent debating and judging the quality of a project. The Stadsatelier meets every two weeks for project discussions with external parties or internal workshop sessions.

The SAO was also provided with a budget for specific research, reflecting on the long-term development of the city. For these studies, which were executed by external design offices, several workshop sessions were organized with members of the city administration. In addition to these, internal workshops were set up to analyze specific districts of the city as a context for the housing projects that were supervised by the SAO. These internal workshops surpass the typical advisory function of a quality chamber. They are an efficient and effective way of harnessing the knowledge potential of the SAO members for targeted research by design, feeding reflection and counselling. Thus, the Stadsatelier functions as a workshop where the city is "made" together with a diverse selection of stakeholders; it is a place for discussions that lay the foundation for quality in urban design and a platform for synergy between city services, policymakers, and external actors. The Stadsatelier is not your classic quality chamber. Instead, it tries to weigh in on the urban development process as early as possible so as to create the conditions for a high-quality end result. As an "urban workshop" it helps policymakers and developers to think about and design the city, both in the short and the long term. It advises on current projects, but also creates a framework for future developments.

This framework can be technical, e.g., supervising procedures for innovative housing projects (see the Zilverlaan project), or it can be design research on the urban fabric of Ostend (see "Ribbons and Trajectories"). Through the supervision of several building projects, the SAO tries to set in motion a gradual transformation of that fabric, addressing local mobility issues, social isolation, and a lack of programmatic diversity, etcetera. This crucial aspect of the Stadsatelier's mission places building projects in a broader perspective, making them part of a more comprehensive reflection. The goal is to be a platform for translating urban policy into spatial frameworks and projects and vice versa, anticipating future developments and situating ad hoc actions within a long-term perspective. The vision that underpins this gradual transformation is outlined in the *Globaal Strategisch Ontwikkelingsplan* (Global Strategic Development Plan) or GSO, which is a synthesis of the first five years' work of the SAO. The GSO is a reference document that inspires policy and sets the tone for further reflection on the city. It is a perpetually unfinished document, continuously evolving and edited through the operations of the SAO. It presents a model for a future Ostend composed of three main structural elements: "Ribbons," "Trajectories," and "City Projects."

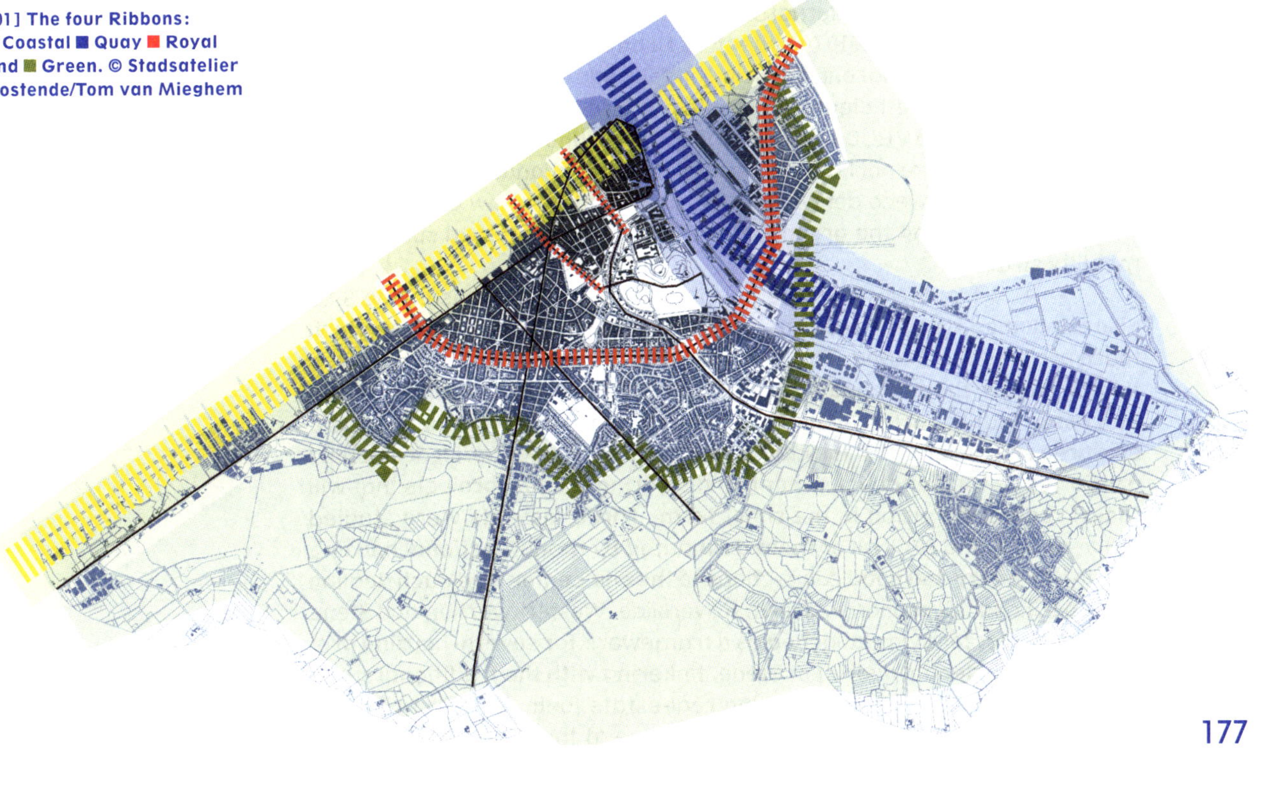

[01] The four Ribbons: ■ Coastal ■ Quay ■ Royal and ■ Green. © Stadsatelier Oostende/Tom van Mieghem

RIBBONS AND TRAJECTORIES

The Ribbons take their name from the *Groen Lint* (Green Ribbon), a recreational bicycle lane at the outskirts of the city, that was conceived as a park comprising several interlinked landscapes. It originated before the SAO was installed, when in 2010—together with the Rother District in Southern England—Ostend set out on an Interreg Europe project called "21st Century Parks." In a series of joint workshops, the issue of future-proof urban parks was linked with the emerging focus on urban agriculture, climate change, and sustainable mobility, resulting in a concept for a 37-kilometer-long ribbon that ties the various green spaces around the city together and connects the urban fringes with the surrounding open landscape. This Green Ribbon was assigned a designer via the Open Call of the Vlaams Bouwmeester (Flemish Government Architect) in 2012. Technum-Tractebel in cooperation with ADR architectes/Georges Descombes translated the concept into a collection of focused interventions in the landscape: wooden platforms, passages and plateaux, water banks and lanes, all interconnected by bicycle paths. When in 2016 the SAO started reflecting on possible forms and approaches for the Strategic Development Plan, it recognized the Green Ribbon's potential to become an important structural carrier for the development of Ostend. The SAO acknowledged its role as a structuring line, creating connections inward and outward, and fundamentally changing the organization of the city. By adding new urban programs to this Ribbon, it can define a new profile of the city in relation to the landscape that surrounds it.

[01] In addition to the Green Ribbon, the SAO identified three other Ribbons as frontlines for urban development: the *Kustlint* (Coastal Ribbon) between the beach and the city, the *Koninklijk Lint* (Royal Ribbon) between the center and the periphery, and the *Kadelint* (Quay Ribbon) between the city and port. Together, these four Ribbons form the basis of the spatial model of the GSO, reconsidering the notion of centrality in Ostend and reinforcing the coherence of the different districts—both literally and figuratively setting out the lines for the development of the city. Their potential was explored through research by design, commissioned by the SAO. Three studies were executed by external offices between 2016 and 2018. The Coastal Ribbon was explored by 1010 Architecture Urbanism as a seasonal city within the day-to-day city, not only focusing on touristic assets, but also actively searching for more efficient mobility and a circular or locally anchored economy. Posad and VELD envisioned the Quay Ribbon as a quest for space, interweaving a future port development with recreational and energy landscapes. LIST and Sweco defined the Royal Ribbon as a new central space within the city, laying the groundwork for an alternative and sustainable mobility strategy.

As a framework for the housing projects it supervises, the SAO also conducted its own research by design on the urban fabrics in which those projects are located. This combination of research and project direction resulted in the so-called Trajectories that formulate a vision for the urban tissue that lies in between the Ribbons. Each Trajectory studies a specific area or district within the city, analyzing the existing fabric, developing a vision on its further development, and steering specific projects that will (help) realize the vision in the short term. Three districts were studied between 2016 and 2019, all of them dominated by monofunctional housing, lacking diversity and good connections to the city center, and each dealing with specific social-economic issues: Raversijde, Westerkwartier, and Stene. The first Trajectory was launched as a framework for several housing projects in the residential district of Stene, tinkering with the traditional subdivision model and the accompanying real-estate logic. The first of these projects was situated in the Zilverlaan avenue at the outskirts of the city.

Its development was overseen by the SAO from start to finish. It deliberately played with the boundaries between plot and landscape, between public and private space, between individual and communal housing aspirations, between a traditional investment model and the return on collective added value. The project serves as an example of how the large-scale objectives of the SAO land on the ground and how the SAO takes the reigns on innovative housing projects in collaboration with local actors.

THE ZILVERLAAN HOUSING PROJECT

When the plot on Zilverlaan was put up for sale by the city, collectivity and affordability were key concepts. Part of the available plot was sold to Duinhelm, a non-profit organization that supports people with disabilities in the areas of living, working, and leisure. The remaining 1.5 hectares were put on the market at a fixed price, thus transferring competition from money to quality of design. The prospective buyers had to bid with a design proposal for which the SAO had prepared some ground rules through a framework. That design framework linked the plot with the neighboring parcels of Duinhelm and WoonWel, a social housing company, both of which joined the SAO in its ambition to create a common residential neighborhood. In the brief for the private developer, the overarching vision was driven by the demand for a common landscape, which included a collective lane along Zilverlaan that forms the entrance to the three housing projects, a major green area on the plot itself, and a public pathway leading to the sports park that lies to the south. In addition, the private project had to focus on the collective

[02] The "polder park" proposal by CONDOR connects the allotments of Stene with the large-scale structure of the polder landscape. © CONDOR/Bovenbouw Architectuur/CLUSTER

use of infrastructure and space: underground parking for the residents, compact and clustered housing, collective utility systems, and shared green space.

In the summer of 2016, the public presentation of this framework was attended by six private developers. Three of them responded to the invitation for an intermediate discussion with the SAO in September, and two proposals were finally submitted and presented in November. The jury, composed of the SAO with representatives of WoonWel, Duinhelm, and the city of Ostend, unanimously decided to award the land to the developer CONDOR, with a proposal by Bovenbouw Architectuur and landscape architect CLUSTER. Their alternative to the traditional subdivision arranges thirty-seven ground-level homes and thirty-two apartments around an enclosed courtyard. The front doors, the elevators of two apartment blocks, the bicycle storage areas, and a common multi-purpose room with kitchen all open onto this car-free collective outdoor space. Additionally, each row house has a small private backyard. From Zilverlaan you enter the project via a small gate building which houses mailboxes and such, passing through the collective lane where visitors' cars are parked. Next to the entrance building, a tilt gate gives access to a collective underground parking garage. Due to the compact footprint of the residential courtyard, one third of the plot remains undeveloped. If the neighbors of WoonWel are doing the same, a "polder park" measuring 60 meters in width is created in between, which guarantees the new homes a fantastic view and connects with the surrounding landscape. The plan builds up a gradation from enclosed to public green space, tailored to the needs of children: toddlers play in their own little garden, boys in the courtyard, and adolescents hang out in the polder park.

[02] Having participated in the discussions as invited jury members, both WoonWel and Duinhelm decided to join this plan and swapped their plots to adopt the landscape vision of the private developer. A shared area along Zilverlaan will be uniformly developed as a parking avenue and each partner is making 28% of its own land available to create a public park that runs across the various properties. CLUSTER was given the commission by this joint partnership to draw the plan for a common park in which each partner is developing its own residential field. The publicly accessible park is used for water management of the residential development. The soil meanwhile remains the property of the neighboring residents, while its top layer will be managed by the city as public property, thus making sure that any changes to the park in the future will have to be approved by all. The architectural office ampe.trybou architecten designed an ensemble of fifty-seven social housing units for the WoonWel plot, eleven of which will be sold via a CLT-formula (Community Land Trust). Duinhelm moved to the far corner of the site where Raamwerk architects—selected via the Open Call of the Vlaams Bouwmeester—have designed two curled residential volumes for twenty residents each. Between both volumes runs a public passage to the Steense Dijk and the Green Ribbon.

[03] For the implementation of the park, the different projects—with
[04] very different preconditions as regards assignment and financing—were coordinated in mutual consultation under the guidance of the SAO. The works and studies needed to prepare the construction projects were, if possible, linked and carried out for all three lots at the same time. The associated costs were divided according to the percentage that each plot represents of the whole. To facilitate this process, a clear calendar was drawn up with regular feedback moments. These dates were linked to Stadsatelier sessions and laid down well in advance in a cooperation agreement signed by all the partners. This agreement also stipulated the shared ambitions of the project, the practical arrangements for the masterplan, a list of studies to be paid for jointly, a provisional planning of the works, and the designation of a SPOC for each partner. After the communal phase of the master-

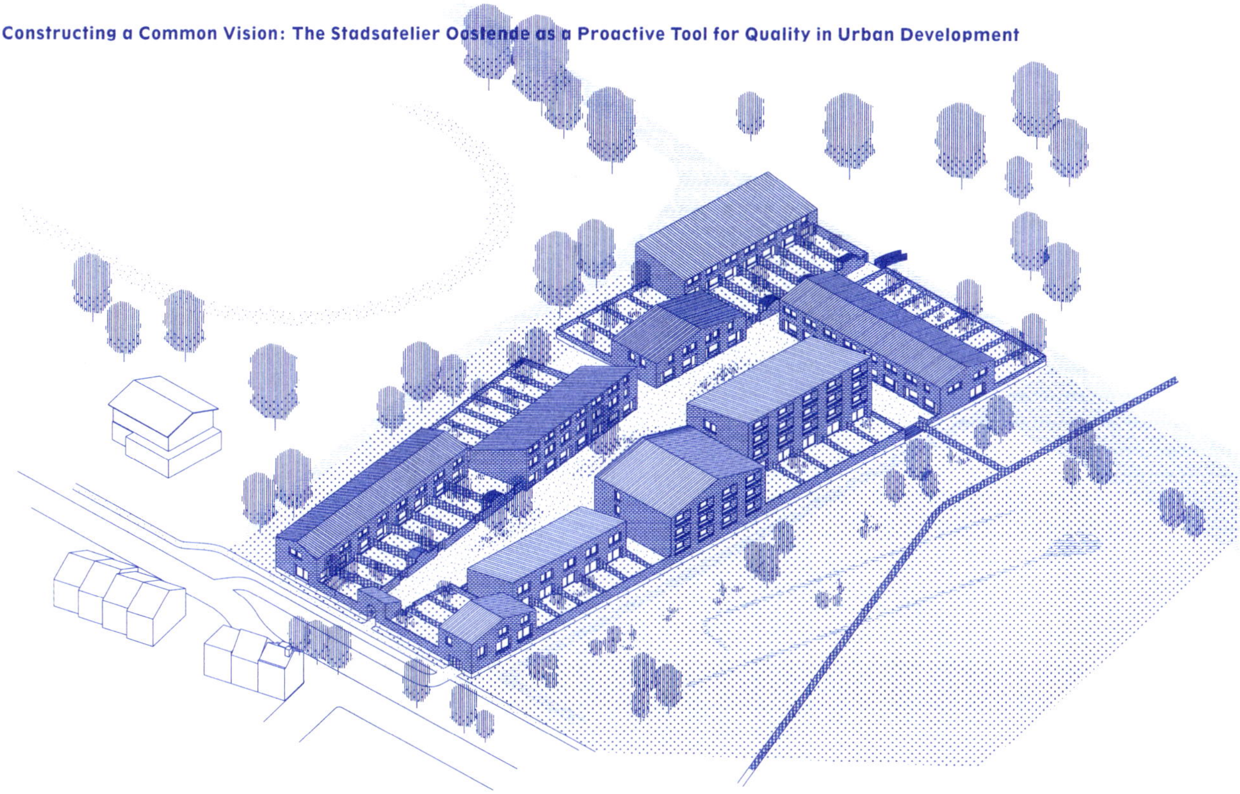

[03] The competition proposal of CONDOR: a courtyard of clustered housing and a park. © CONDOR/Bovenbouw Architectuur/CLUSTER

plan, the feedback moments served as an opportunity to keep one another informed about the progress of each of the three construction sites. What started as a shared commitment, built around an innovative housing project at the instigation of the SAO, was further monitored and followed up within the ongoing operation of the Stadsatelier, making sure that all partners met on a regular basis and that possible obstructions were dealt with together.

After a substantial delay caused by archeological findings on the site, construction of the Duinhelm project started in 2021 and the first twenty inhabitants moved into their new home during the fall of 2023. CONDOR started building a first phase with thirty-two apartments and twenty houses in the fall of 2022. WoonWel started construction one year later. The intense cooperation between the city, a social housing company, a non-profit organization from the care sector, and a private developer wasn't always easy. But the Zilverlaan project shows that a development vision which transcends both the boundaries of the plot and the traditional division into housing sectors generates benefits for the residents and the neighborhood alike. By sharing the available space, everyone will be getting more than they could have accomplished within the limitations of their own plot.

STEPPING STONES FOR STENE

In addition to the Zilverlaan project, the SAO has supervised various other housing projects on different sites in the southern periphery of Ostend. This required a proper understanding of the broader context and a coherent development framework for the area in which the various projects can play their role. The focus of the SAO supervision was expanded by drawing up a long-term perspective for the wider environment in a series of internal design sessions. This intertwined process of project development and design by research resulted in a concise vision document that was finalized in 2018, entitled *Stapstenen voor Stene* (Stepping Stones for Stene). It prompted a grant application for the Flemish Urban Renewal Fund that was honored with €2,000,000 for investments in public space and slow-traffic connections. Stene is a car-oriented residential neighborhood that is sandwiched between the Green Ribbon and the Royal Ribbon. Thanks to its central position

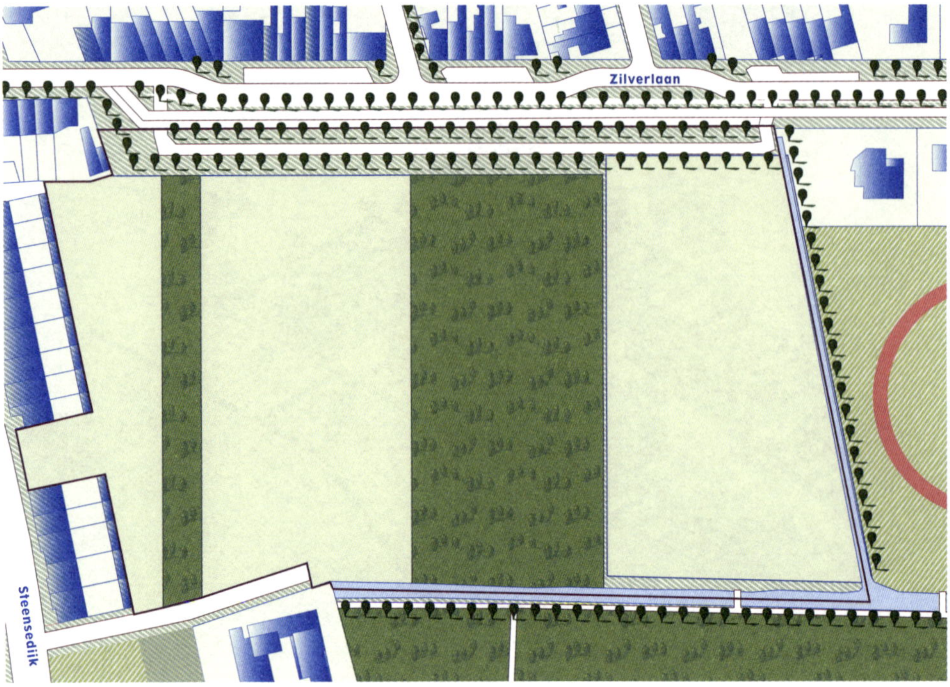

[04] A scheme was added to the cooperation agreement, stipulating built (light green) and unbuilt areas of the three properties and defining the swap between WoonWel (middle) and Duinhelm (left). © CONDOR/Bovenbouw Architectuur/CLUSTER

[05] The housing projects of Duinhelm (left), WoonWel (middle) and CONDOR (right) are creating a common public park. © Raamwerk/ampe.trybou architecten/Bovenbouw Architectuur/CLUSTER

between the old city and its 20th century expansion, the Royal Ribbon has the potential to become a new backbone of the city. The Green Ribbon, on the other hand, is the place where the interweaving of the city and the open landscape creates opportunities for a new urban make-up. What used to be the fringes of the city can become part of a new urban structure, connecting not only landscapes but also linking suburban functions within a larger, readable whole: the dunes, the Geuzen forest, the creeks, and the polders are all interlaced with a new venue location, an agricultural park, an existing sports park, a new crematorium, and a children's farm.

This new centrality on the edge of the city fundamentally changes the position of the peripheral district of Stene, instigating a gradual transformation of its urban fabric, for which three main strategies were defined. The first strategy is to create new structures throughout the neighborhood that properly connect the Green and Royal Ribbon to the local residential fabric and improve the interrelation with the city center. By establishing new connections for slow traffic, physical links are optimized and mental distance is reduced. These interconnected structures pull the district out of its isolation and form the basis for a network of sustainable mobility. The historically built-up logic of single residential areas is abandoned by identifying and reinforcing a network that integrates and connects the various districts of the city. A second strategy proposes to use these new district structures not only for bicycle and pedestrian mobility, but also as a stepping stone for urban development, adding layers of meaning and forming a basis for urban liveliness and orientation. By adding new green areas to these connections, a car-free public domain is created within the urban fabric. It introduces sustainable mobility within the urban periphery as a whole through guiding specific transformations like cutting or slowing down car flows, creating routes for public transport, or generating new meeting places for the residents of the city outskirts, where life is no longer limited to one's own plot.

The new network also enables a qualitative densification of the [05]
residential fabric. Since facilities are now close by, a greater density is justified. The new connecting structures provide excellent locations for a diverse and adapted housing supply, aiming at different target groups. The various strategies of densification, adding public space and amenities, also increase the readability of the neighborhood. From inert isotropy rises dynamic hierarchy. The uniformity of the residential districts—experienced as a maze by an outsider—is diversified and expanded in a new vision for Stene that cannot, of course, be implemented overnight. A final strategy is to set in motion a step-by-step transformation via singular public and private development projects. Some of these projects, such as Zilverlaan, are heavily steered by the Stadsatelier, while others use the strategic vision as a reference guide. Private building projects are integral to this vision and thus become a proactive tool for its implementation. The housing projects incorporate public passages, bicycle shortcuts, additional collective green space, etcetera as an imposed condition. In this way, public value is generated by private development, and the residential fabric is systematically updated through a succession of new residential projects.

THE GSO AS SYNTHESIS AND FRAMEWORK

With the morphological Ribbon studies as a backdrop, Trajectories like [06]
Stapstenen voor Stene make the link between the analysis of social and spatial challenges on the one hand, and the elaboration of building projects on the other. They explore and rewrite the fabric that interconnects the Ribbons, providing local entry points for the implementation of a sustainable development model. They are a first step towards the sustainable densification of the city, which is taking shape in the various residential projects that are supervised by the SAO. For each Trajectory, a condensed booklet

was produced, documenting the analysis, vision, and exemplary cases in about thirty pages. These *Cahiers* seek to influence policy on various levels while avoiding the weight of an official policy document. They contain maps, drawings, and diagrams that were specifically produced (by Ellen Verbiest) in a characteristic and recognizable style. They are simple to understand, thought-provoking and easily taken in hand by politician, spatial officer, and street worker alike. They complement the Ribbon studies and form the second chapter of the Global Strategic Development Plan, a light and manageable framework which presents and underpins choices, illustrating how projects and processes can be used as an instrument for preparing policy and, at the same time, testing the potential of that policy in the field.

The GSO documents the outcome of the first five years of the SAO activities, but it also aims to set the lines for spatial policy in the coming years. That delineation literally takes form in the third part of the GSO, where the urban project is put forward as a synthesis of Ribbons and Trajectories. Labeled as City Projects, twelve crucial sites were identified as important levers for the GSO's vision. They mark the spots that are pivotal to the ambitions of the Ribbons and Trajectories. They are in need of a well-thought-out design framework and clear direction to ensure quality and innovation. All future architectural and urban renewal projects located within the perimeter or in the immediate vicinity of these twelve places will be considered strategic and will, consequently, be monitored and guided by the SAO. As a final chapter of the GSO, the City Projects were presented to the city council in 2019. Six of them were selected by the council to be further studied with priority. Three of those are nodes on the Royal Ribbon, connecting it with the Coastal Ribbon, the sustainable network of Stene,

[07] Map of the Trajectory for the Stene district with housing projects in blue (project 3 is Zilverlaan) and the Green Ribbon (a) and new bicycle connections (A, B, C) in red. © Stadsatelier Oostende/ Ellen Verbiest

□ Project sites
1 Mispelplein
2 Druivenlaan
3 Lilverlaan
4 Sandershoeve
5 De Neuwe Stad
6 Mimosalaan
□ Framework and facilities
= Green Ribbon
··· New bicycle connections
A Steense dik—inner city
B Dode Kreex
C Gauweloze Kreek

0 25 50 100 150 200 m

[06] Private housing projects are creating a sustainable and car-free public domain. © Stadsatelier Oostende/ Ellen Verbiest

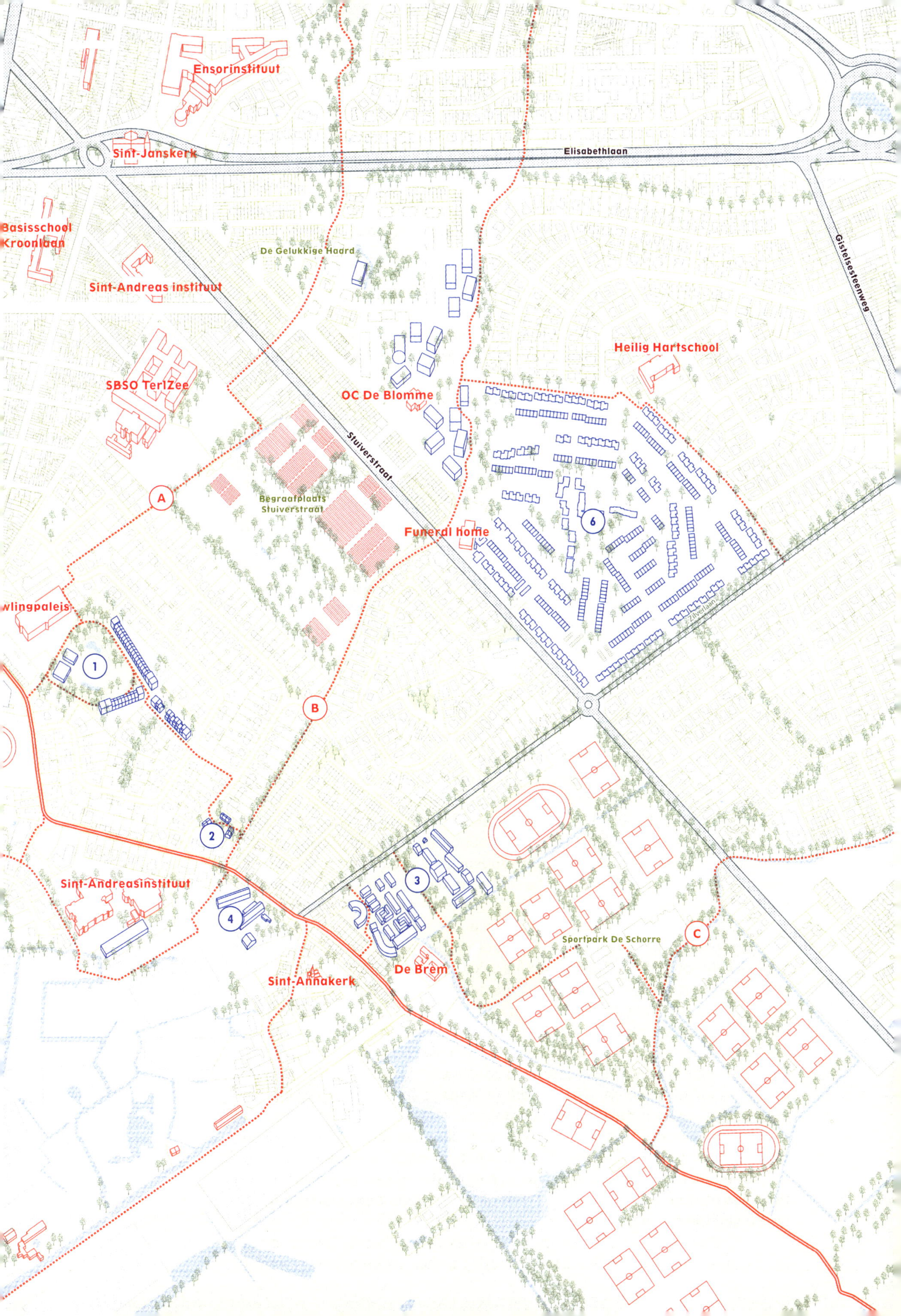
Ensorinstituut
Sint-Janskerk
Elisabethlaan
Basisschool Kroonlaan
Sint-Andreas instituut
De Gelukkige Haard
Gistelsesteenweg
Heilig Hartschool
SBSO TerIZee
OC De Blomme
Stuiverstraat
A
Begraafplaats Stuiverstraat
Funeral home
6
wlingpaleis
1
B
Zilverlaan
2
Sint-Andreasinstituut
3
4
Sportpark De Schorre
C
De Brem
Sint-Annakerk

and the motorway entering the city. The other three are historical focal points in the spatial structure of Ostend that are struggling to regain their lost centrality: these are located in the Coastal Ribbon, the Westerkwartier district, and the city center. In the spring of 2020, several City Projects were the subject for a design studio in the first master of the Faculty of Architecture and Art at Hasselt University, which added new designs and speculative images to the mix. So, the final chapter of the GSO is an open ending, as befits a vision document that seems in permanent motion, changing gears and gaining new layers as the workings of the SAO continue.

LEARNING FROM OSTEND: CONCLUSIONS

[07] The firm basis for the operation of the Stadsatelier lies in the human interaction for which it provides a stage. Its methodology revolves around setting up conversations rather than writing out and applying rules. These discussions are intended to enable the city administrators to speak with one voice when supervising an urban development project, but they also help to keep complex projects such as Zilverlaan on track by neutralizing misunderstandings between partners, keeping the level of commitment and ambition high. This way of working is intensive, but also very efficient because it eliminates parallel discussions and conflicting agendas. The focus on personal interaction is the true engine of the Stadsatelier, but also its possible weak spot. A typical problem of long-term urban development projects is the loss of the project's long-term memory due to changes in personnel. By relying on the Stadsatelier as a group, this problem is partly countered. During its first five years, the SAO successfully absorbed the departure and arrival of several members—the most challenging of these departures proved to be that of the mayor after the municipal elections of 2018. His exit ushered in a difficult period for the SAO and the GSO that was in its final stages of production. The alderman that was responsible for the SAO, however, remained in office, and after a period of speculation and uncertainty, the SAO was relaunched with the approval of the City Projects by the new coalition. The relationship with the new members of the council had to be built from scratch. The best way to do this, of course, is with exemplary projects and a powerful, well-founded story.

That narrative is well illustrated in the booklets that were produced by the SAO. The *Cahiers* circulate smoothly within the administration in Ostend, but the GSO—of which the first version was completed in 2020—was never officially ratified by a new city council that was suspicious of the political risks in some of the design proposals. As a result, the GSO is a document without strict legal value, but with the aim of stimulating reflection on the city and its design. The unofficial status of the GSO may turn out to be both a weakness and a blessing. Because it is not part of the official policy, it risks being overruled or neglected. But precisely because it has escaped the political decision-making process, the GSO can maintain its sharpness and agility, underpinning the city's official planning documents from a secondary position. Indeed, it is from this secondary position that the work of the Stadsatelier primarily takes place. It serves as a protected area where open discussions are possible, where coalitions can be formed, where agendas can be expressed and consequently (re)adjusted towards a larger shared ambition. As an addition to the regular process of the planning administration, this forum promotes confidence—or is it faith?—between stakeholders and administrators, civilians and officials, designers and users. It is not actively involved in political decision-making and public communication but nonetheless provides the necessary material for targeted participatory processes that aim to include administrations, citizens, and the general public.

Operating on a level somewhere between city architect and quality chamber, the Stadsatelier is tailor-made for the medium-sized (Flemish)

[08] The four Ribbons (left) and the twelve City Projects (right) of the GSO. © Stadsatelier Oostende/ Ellen Verbiest

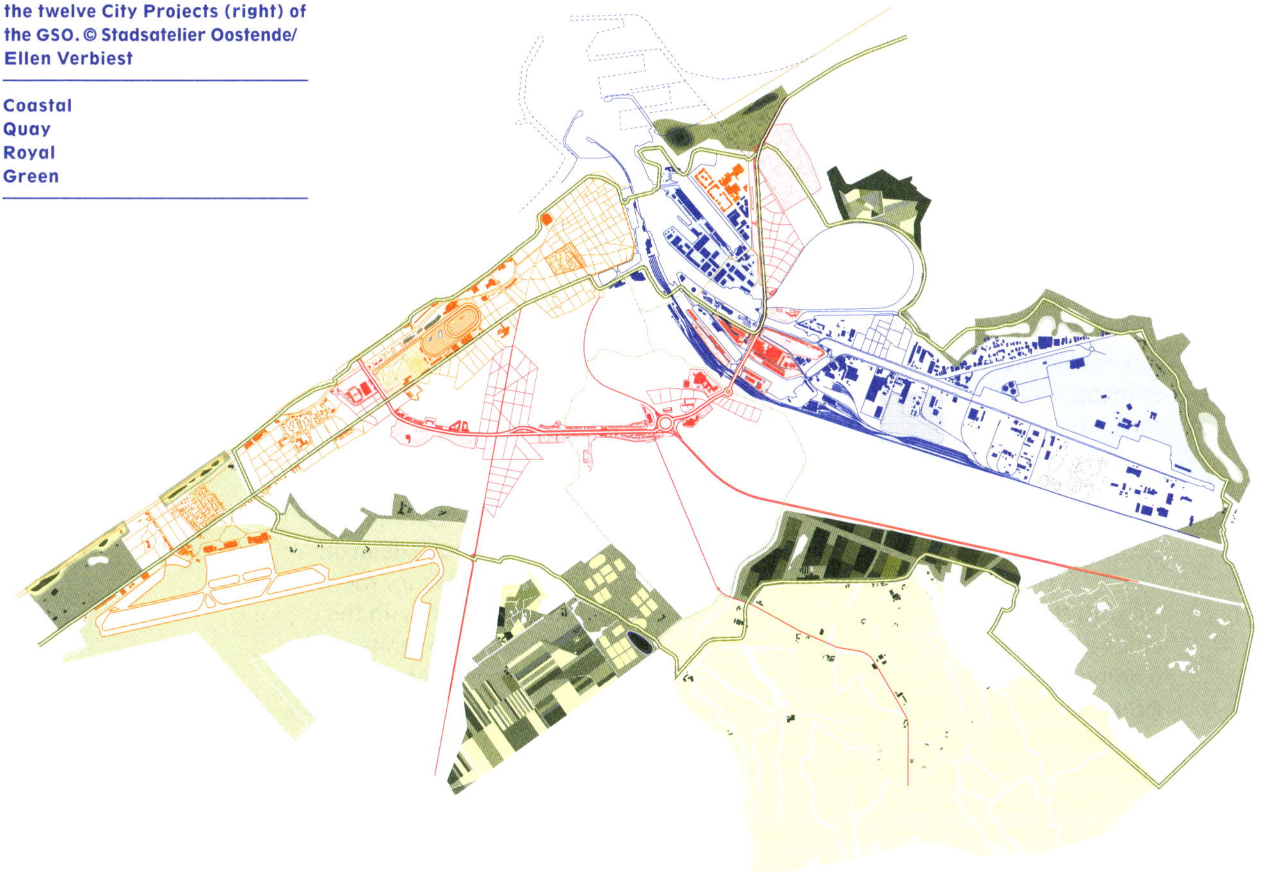

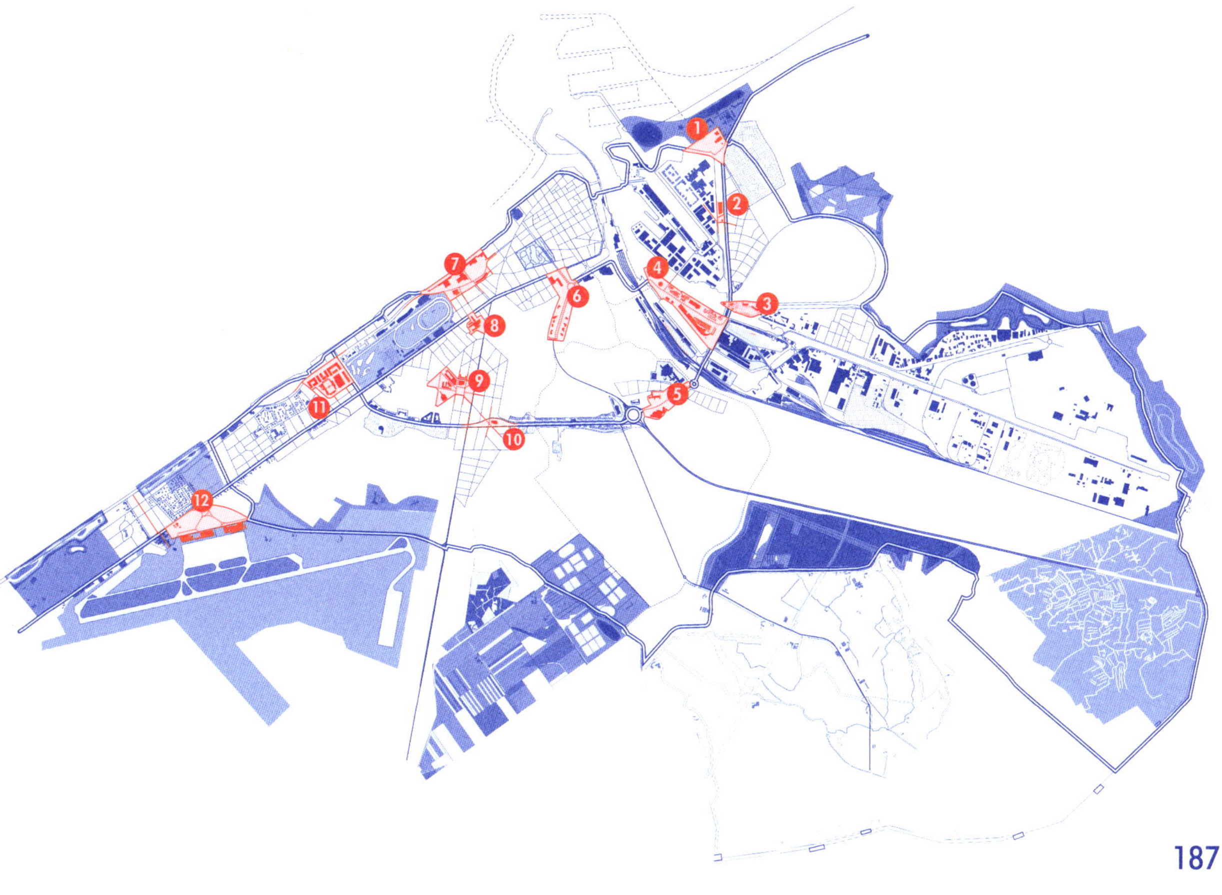

city. It uses academic and professional knowledge to strengthen a local administration that is faced with major challenges and limited capacity: too small to have a city architect of its own, but in need of a proactive urban development vision as a framework for an ambitious licensing policy. City administrations are thus given a sounding board for their operations and a platform where projects and intentions can be coordinated. An external view and expertise are combined with local know-how and understanding of the field. In addition, the Stadsatelier helps to get a grip on a development dynamic that has its own logic and speed. Such processes sometimes overwhelm the city: private developments are fast-paced and there is often no time to go through a classic planning process. By combining various processes, the Stadsatelier retains an overview and helps to respond quickly, keeping the long-term vision in mind. The particular constellation of the Stadsatelier is an excellent operating base for realizing long-term objectives through rapid and thoughtful action on the ground. It is also a model that can help local governments implement the ambitious agenda of overarching policies, such as the European Green Deal or the Flemish Bouwshift—the bold decision taken by Flanders's regional government to reduce its intake of additional open space to zero hectares by 2040, thus becoming space neutral.

The key to achieving this "Building shift"—and the necessary mental shift that comes with it—lies not only with regional policy, but with the cities and municipalities that are responsible for issuing building permits on a daily basis. Those municipalities are limited in manpower and resources. Premiums introduced by the Flemish Government for breaking up concrete and asphalt pavements and for investing in greenery certainly provide an incentive for change, but their effect in the longer term requires an active local follow-up. A Stadsatelier on the scale of a city or region could help local policymakers keep the necessary overview, weigh up where to build in order to free up space elsewhere, and thus uphold the space-neutral balancing act. Accomplishing this ambition—namely, using existing land and buildings more efficiently and sustainably—not only means weaving valuable green spaces into the urban fabric, but it also calls for new collective housing models, such as the Zilverlaan project, which aligns housing policy with overall environmental and spatial development. This is where good design can prove its value. The Stadsatelier uses design as a proactive tool for spatial policy and for realizing innovation on the field, showing which transformations are needed, and how we can make them work. It connects different agencies and perspectives at the core of its operation. It links quality control to vision development and focuses on the implementation of that vision in concrete projects. Not only by guiding them, but also by actively initiating them and bringing together the necessary actors.

SANDRA GUINAND IN CONVERSATION WITH ERIK WIEËRS

Erik Wieërs—co-founder of the Antwerp-based office Collectief Noord architecten and since August 17, 2020 Flemish Government Architect—reflects on new governance approaches in designing urban projects by focusing on the users and residents. He and his team are responsible for advancing architectural quality and innovation in public projects across the region. As such, they work with various stakeholders, including government authorities, architects, and the public, to ensure that the architectural design of public spaces meets high standards of functionality, sustainability, and aesthetics. Erik also gives tips on how this new approach could be implemented at the beginning and insists on directions rather than regulations.

SG

As an architect also involved in governance processes, how would you encourage a shift in daily practice considering the need for a paradigm shift in urbanism? And especially considering the different actors that you have to deal with, such as developers, public officials, city administration, etcetera?

EW

What is important in this shift is that it will demand the organization of actors concerned in building something or changing something within the environment. For instance, the idea that you ask a certain question and then look for designers to find a solution, this way of doing things will need to shift. You must try to start from the existing situation. You need to form a group with the people who are already concerned, local people that live in an area and their neighbors. This could represent a very big change for designing as a practice because the idea would not necessarily be to build something new or to change the environment entirely, but to start from what already exists within the environment. Thus, it will be more about "care based" rather than "project based" design. We had some experience of this with a recent pilot project. There was this group of architects and artists who wanted to transform a building. They started by looking at what this particular building could bring to the environment, by inviting all the neighbors to organize activities inside the building before they transformed it. They then looked at what it *could* be, what could be needed or demanded within the framework of this transformation. The team clearly put forward the idea that function follows form. When you look at the environment now, it's a whole different ball game. Everything that currently exists is what will still exist in the future, so you have to work with what is already existing. You should not think: I want this or that program, where will I build it? But instead, realize that you have this and that building, this and that environment. How could it be used to serve people who live around it? Who could use it? What could we do with it? I think this is a very important shift in attitudes. And I'm not sure that everybody is conscious of this change quite yet.

SG

Following the line of care urbanism and considering your experience: what is the most important process or instrument for improving the relationship between urbanism and the resources of the territory?

EW

Because this attitude hasn't reached everybody's minds yet, maybe it is interesting for us as an institution to develop some pilot projects that will get this on the public agenda. I think that's an important task. It's interesting to think about a pilot project that could be somewhere between a real project and a theoretical study. Sometimes, what we do when we develop the study is to ask commissioners and experts. Then you work on some cases together, but you also bring the people that work on those cases together. It is a learning process as well—you learn from each other. You can do this in workshops: the ideal situation is to investigate several cases at the same time. Then, by bringing together the commissioners and the difficulties encountered, you can gather a lot of information about these new processes and how they will develop. I think this kind of pilot project is something we should engage in.

SG

So which actors do we need to engage to encourage this Territorial Urbanism?

EW

I think we need everybody. Besides the usual suspects, we all also need the support of civilian movements. It is an important shift that needs to be addressed in urban planning and design, too. There should be a shift from regulations to project management. We need designers to help raise questions, not only give answers to them. When we manage Territorial Urbanism by regulation, the ball remains in the court of policy but I do not think this strategy will work anymore. Typically, the government organizes quality by regulation. You ask a designer a question, and there are some regulations to guarantee quality. In this new situation, with all those transformations ahead of us, I think we need directions instead of rules. We need a group of people that are capable of formulating the question and developing it into an answer. Take the example of the existing building I gave you. It is a whole new way of working. For me, it is very important because the Flemish government leans a lot on regulation. They believe strongly in regulation and it can be difficult to make clear to them that each process is different—that everything is contextual and that it is better to have a good team that works out the project, than having rules that apply to all projects. We need to really make this change in how we are connected to the environment.

Learning from Pompeii: Reclaiming Urban Life

Anselm Wagner

[01] Robert Otter: Café Wha? on MacDougal Street, New York City, 1966 © Ned Otter 2005

HOUSING IS THE CITY'S DEATH

In May 2023, at the invitation of the Styrian Chamber of Commerce, a panel discussion took place in Graz on the topic of "Urban development Graz—future instead of standstill" (**Kabelis-Lechner, 2023**). Apart from the head of the city planning office and a professor of construction economics, the podium was almost exclusively populated by (male) representatives of the real estate industry and various housing cooperatives. Due to its composition alone, this event was symptomatic of the wider discourse on urban development that we have been conducting for decades. Let me be clear from the outset: this discourse is not a part of the solution, but rather part of the problem. Talking to housing and construction industry representatives about urban planning is about as promising as discussing vegan food with a pride of lions. Housing is and always has been the death of the city. Whether one favors social housing from a left-wing perspective or privately financed housing from a neoliberal perspective makes no fundamental difference in terms of its ramifications on the urban fabric: both approaches have ended fatally for the city. Far too many of the guild of architectural producers are still fueling this lethal discourse when they focus one-sidedly on the housing issue instead of expanding it into an urban development issue.

Of course, there is nothing wrong with housing in principle. Logically, it is both important and necessary. But the unquestioned assumption that housing estates create cities, or that they contribute positively to the growth of cities, is somewhat surprising. No one can seriously think that cities could be created just by building roads, offices, factories, or amusement parks. Everyone would immediately see that something crucial was missing. When it comes to housing, however, this prejudice persists. People still seem to believe that once citizens have a roof over their heads in sufficient numbers and there is enough population density, everything else will more or less take care of itself and something like a city will automatically emerge—even though we have known for half a century (and as proved by countless satellite towns *à la* Athens Charter) that it simply doesn't work that way. In functional terms, only highly mixed cities are real cities, while largely monofunctional housing developments just produce housing estates that can only feign their urban character through parasitic behavior towards (mostly) historic inner cities in their vicinity. This statement is less trivial than it seems, because unfortunately we can observe that new urban districts—which nowadays are often called "quarters" and advertised as urban, dense, and mixed—are only marginally different from the housing estates of the 1960s, and in fact often fall behind them in terms of quality. Mixing can only succeed if the city is pedestrian-friendly, i.e., if it greatly reduces motorized private transport and—what is usually forgotten—if it structures this pedestrian-friendly public space on a small scale. Furthermore, it must define this public space as an open-air indoor space and, finally, clearly demarcate it from the equally-indispensable private open space. These three principles have been found in all Eurasian cities for millennia, and they are modeled in the urban structure of Pompeii [02] [03], which was well preserved by the volcanic eruption of AD 79: a dense network of narrow streets accompanied by adjoining houses with ground-floor shutters enclosing private courtyards, and public squares enclosed by public buildings—much like courtyards are enclosed by private houses (**Visconti, 2017**). For the sake of simplicity, I would like to call this urban structure the "Pompeii model."

BIG CITIES AND THE MYTH OF ANONYMITY

But first: what is the purpose of settlements and ultimately of cities in the first place? Humans, as pack animals, need social relationships beyond the immediate family circle—for psychosocial reasons, but also for very tangible material reasons. Most of us prefer to live in clusters of houses than in lonely log cabins in the wilderness, because this allows us a variety of social contacts—professional, business, recreational, and private—and has been proven to raise our standard of living. Mutual support, division of labor, and the prosperity that comes from it are only possible in large associations. That is why cities were and continue to be the engines of economic, technological, and cultural development, while purely agrarian, village-structured, or nomadic societies specializing in hunting and gathering have largely stagnated in this respect. Since the end of the 19th century, however, the conviction has been spreading in social criticism—especially in the German-speaking world—that big cities are distinguished from village life primarily by their anonymity, i.e., that they are somehow deficient in social terms. While in the countryside everyone knows everyone else, people know everything about each other and greet each other as a matter of course when they meet on the street or in the fields, in the city people often don't even know their immediate neighbors. They are completely anonymous in the largest crowds on the streets and sit next to each other on public transport without passing a word or greeting. This anonymity, initially experienced as freedom (from the patriarchal paternalism that is often even more widespread in the countryside), leads to loneliness in old age (at the latest). Regular reports that people living alone die in their flats and are only discovered weeks or months later because no one misses them, only the spreading smell of decay alerting the neighbors, seem to confirm the basic assumption of the socially dysfunctional big city.

But is this finding really true? Is loneliness the inevitable price one must pay for urban life? It seems that the anonymity and "blasé" attitude (**Simmel, 2010/1903**) of the city dweller is more the product of a self-fulfilling prophecy than the inevitable result of urban society. For the urban planning of the 20th century (which is also continuing briskly in the 21st century) did everything to excessively promote this supposedly typical urban anonymity: by building residential towers in which one climbs from the underground car park directly into the lift to one's own flat without having to meet a neighbor, and from which one can reach the workplace, the shopping center, or the leisure park via wide urban motorways. Or by constructing single-family housing estates in the suburbs, which protect themselves from neighborly glances with high hedges or noise barriers from through roads which are often only viable with the help of cars. This is aggravated by the systematic destruction of public space, which has been replaced on the one hand by sprawling, spatially undefined parks without social control, which have neither public nor private character, or by monofunctional traffic spaces that serve either only cars, only public transport, only cyclists (keyword "bicycle motorway"), or only pedestrians (pedestrian zones in old towns overused for tourism). In short, everything possible has been done to prevent neighborly contact, chance encounters in public spaces, and making acquaintances through the use of services.

THE CITY AS A STAGE

As much as anonymity is a product of modern urban planning, it is not a characteristic of cities per se. In fact, cities are "resonant spaces" (**Rosa, 2021**): they are highly capable of facilitating and fostering diverse social contacts, and they have fulfilled this task to the best of their ability throughout their many thousands of years of history until, from the mid-20th century onwards,

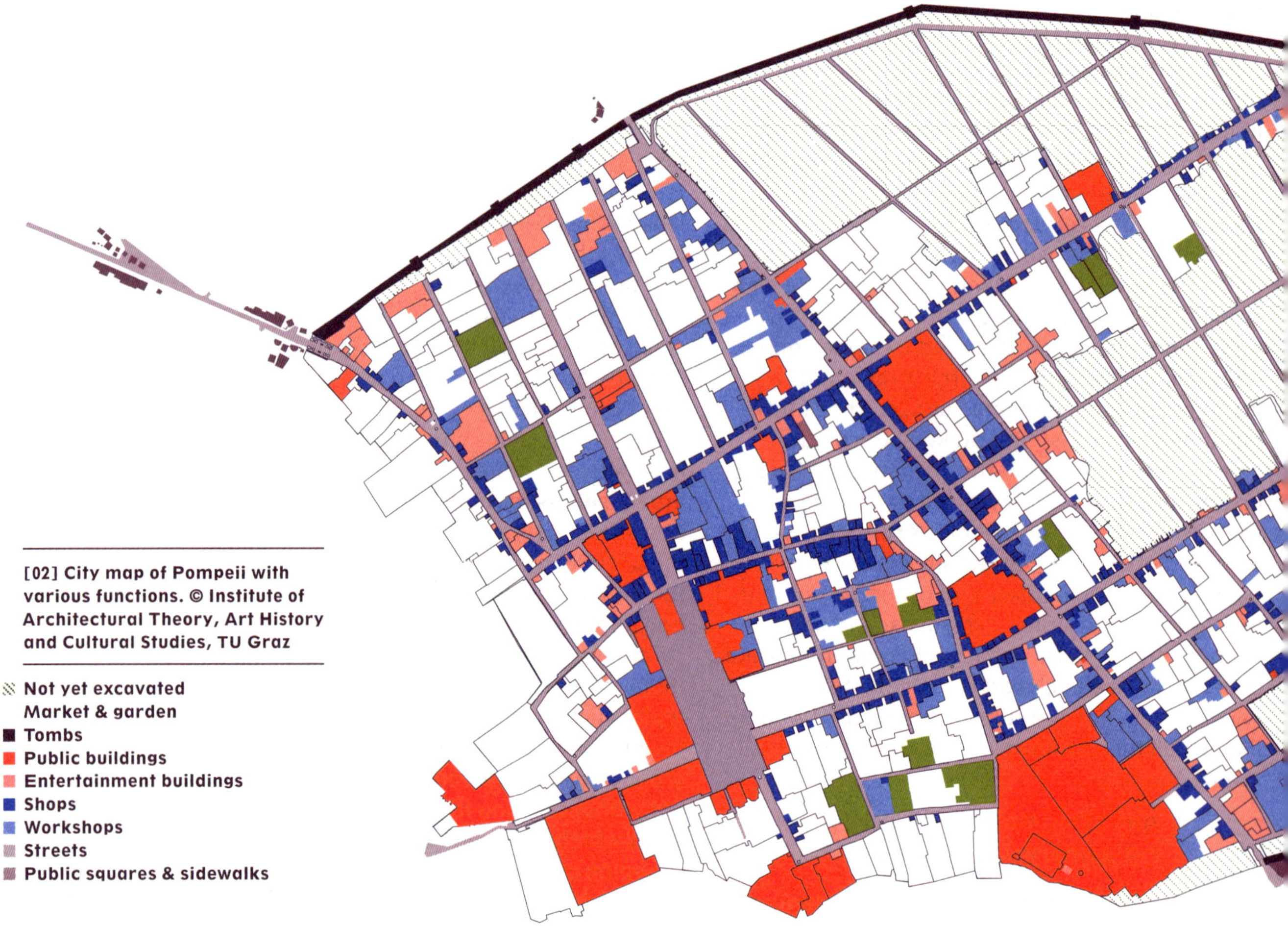

[02] City map of Pompeii with various functions. © Institute of Architectural Theory, Art History and Cultural Studies, TU Graz

they were transformed into car-friendly anonymity machines to realize their supposed purpose. Reading Jane Jacobs's *The Death and Life of Great American Cities*, which is based largely on the author's observations of 1950s New York, Philadelphia, and Boston, one is surprised by the close-knit and diverse character of street life, defined by both attentive residents and numerous strangers (Jacobs, 2020/1961). For Jacobs, street life on Hudson Street in Greenwich Village resembles a stage on which a "pavement ballet" with countless interactions is performed every day [01]: it begins when she takes out the bin in the morning and observes the schoolchildren walking by and the merchants opening their shops, the barber putting his folding chair in front of the door and then the dockworkers getting a beer in the pub next door. At lunchtime, employees and students populate the surrounding restaurants and cafés, in the afternoon the shopping strollers and, later, the teenagers stroll down the street, to be replaced later by partygoers and night workers. The residents and pub owners maintain loose but good neighborly relations, keep their eyes on the street and, without consciously setting out to do so, ensure its safety. For example, the neighbor in the pub next door leaves the flat key out for her lodger, a stranger who has obviously lost his way is given directions, or a resident who injures himself falling through a window at night is assisted by a passing stranger and rescue is called. A prerequisite for this rich urban life is a ground floor zone with a diverse, attractive offer (retail and other services) which appeals to different audiences from early in the morning until after midnight; a small-scale, varied structure with a wide pavement that is attractive to pedestrians of all ages; and street-side perimeter development so that shopkeepers and residents can interact with the street life and the public space is given a clearly defined framing. Only then can the stage be created on which such urban life can be "performed." For this does not consist in intimacy, but, as Richard Sennett has shown, in the interplay of social roles (Sennett, 2017/1977).

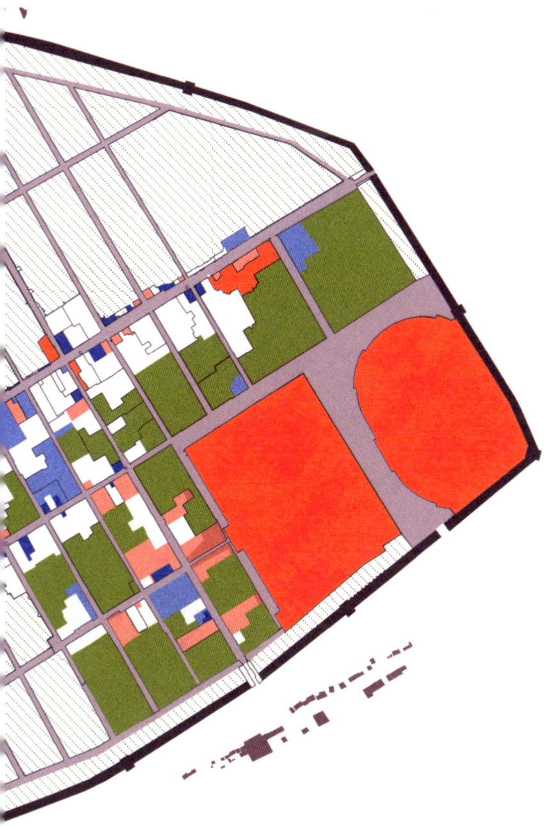

WHY ARE TODAY'S CITIES SO BORING?

All the manifestations of social life in a big city described by Jane Jacobs are still appreciated today in historic inner cities, whether in Rome, Istanbul, or Chicago. But to this day we do everything we can to successfully stifle it in newly built districts: firstly, through road cross-sections that are far too wide, allocating four lanes to individual traffic, two lanes to public traffic, two lanes to "stationary traffic," two lanes to cyclists, two lanes to avenue trees, and two lanes to pedestrians, so that crossing these monster roads becomes an expedition for children and the elderly. Secondly, through the ideologically obsessive abandonment of the perimeter block, which is replaced by isolated buildings that can no longer grasp the street space. Such buildings tend to make the interaction of house and street more difficult, and fail to create a clear separation of private and public space and their corresponding responsibilities through the omnipresent implementation of "passageways" and "greening through." Thirdly, by favoring large plots, often called "quarters," which are usually developed by a single-housing developer and designed by a single architectural firm, and whose too-large ground floor shops (if they exist at all) are rented at best by supermarkets, at worst by open-plan offices. These occupants then glue up shop windows (if they do not remain empty) and offer the pedestrian no security, only dull boredom. Certainly, such developments hardly constitute the "stage" on which Jacobs's social ballet played out.

The reasons for the frequent failure of contemporary urban planning are manifold and it is impossible to list them all here. Besides the ideology of functional separation, which has still yet to be overcome, and the fear of confinement and density, it is above all the housing business model that has a negative impact on urban development. Created by the housing shortage after the two world wars and accordingly promoted politically, both non-profit housing associations and commercial housing developers have become the gravediggers of urban life. Like the mythological King Midas, whose touch turned everything into gold, housing estates freeze urban life wherever they are built, making it very difficult or nearly impossible to get it going again. Now, one can hardly blame the housing developers for this—after all, building housing is their profession. But one can blame the city leaders for having obviously forgotten that a functioning, lively public space is not just a picturesque ingredient of urban life, rather it is vital for a city's survival. Likewise, they may have forgotten that urban streets are not primarily monofunctional "roads" for motorized individual traffic, but multifunctional "streets," i.e., the central living spaces of a city, as Johannes Fiedler points out **(Fiedler, 2014)**. But a street cannot be a living space if it has two lanes of cars travelling at 50 kilometers per hour in every direction. It is only logical that in the course of the 20th century architecture turned away from the street as a source of noise, dirt, and danger. Instead of appealing façades, houses now only jut out into the street through the intrusion of unsightly "private" spaces: rubbish facilities, underground car park exits, and arcade access for passers-by. Only when it is possible to reclaim the street as a public living space can housing be persuaded to turn and face it, to develop a public front and a private back, creating qualitative public (or qualitative private) space again.

That the street should serve pedestrians firstly, cyclists secondarily, and motorists lastly is now a widely recognized fact, although there is still a long way to go before there is agreement on how to get there. But here the question arises: is the redistribution of public space and the re-

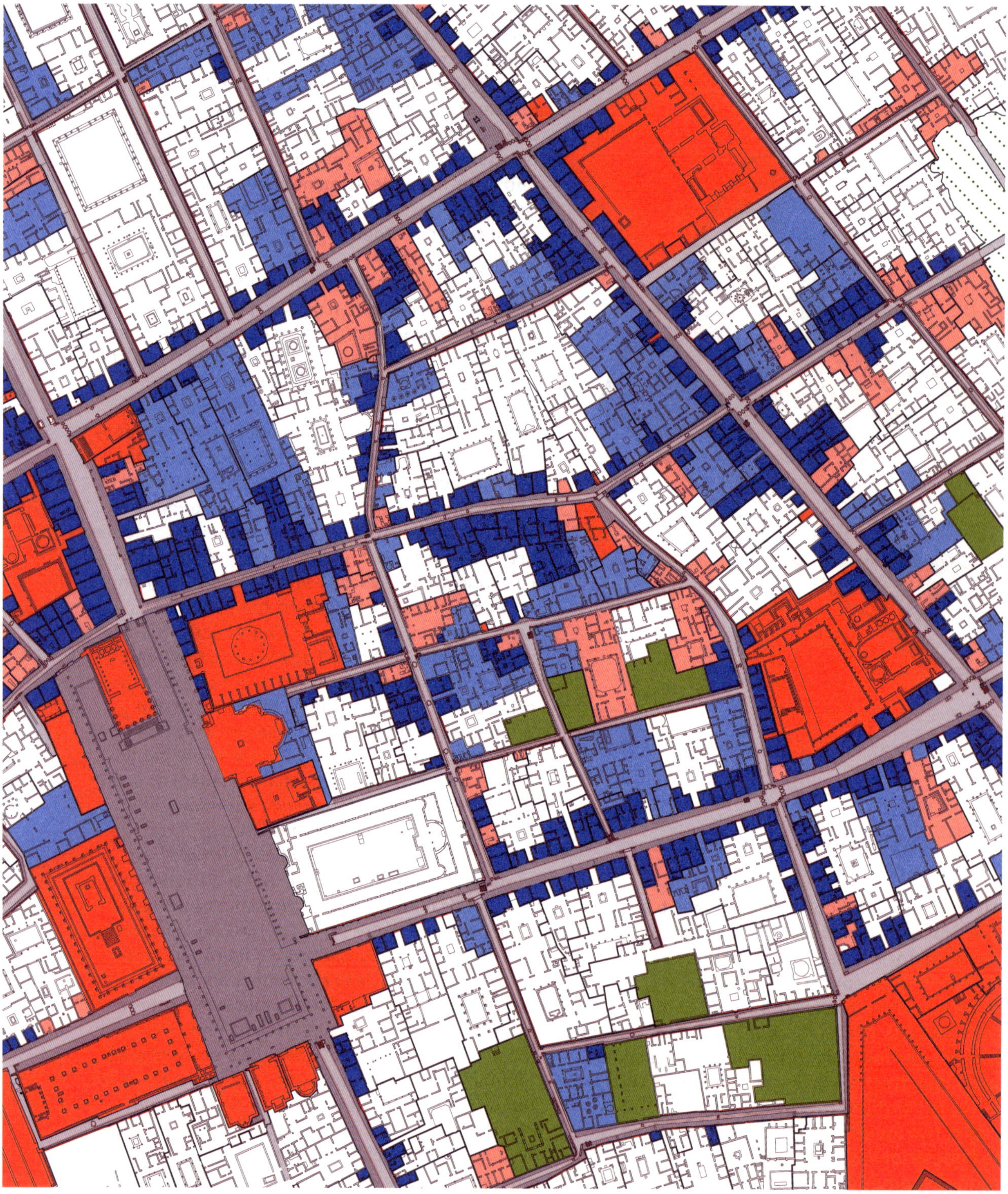

[03] Detailed view of the city map of Pompeii with various functions. © Institute of Architectural Theory, Art History and Cultural Studies, TU Graz

pression of motorized individual transport in favor of soft mobility sufficient to regain the social viability of the city? Houses and public space are communicating vessels and must not be considered in isolation. Territorial Urbanism must not mean forgetting about architecture entirely in favor of public space.

THE ENTREPRENEURIAL CITY

To understand why old cities seem so lively and modern cities seem so dull, one must first briefly consider their historical development. In the Eurasian region, cities did not generally develop because a ruler decided to settle their subjects behind walls and gates, nor because factory owners had built housing for their workers near factories—and certainly not because housing associations were building housing estates. At the origin of almost every European city is a marketplace where traders and local craftsmen offered their goods. Marketplaces are not private, intimate places per se. Trade does not presuppose a relationship of kinship, nor even one of friendship or acquaintance. It does, however, require clear rules that are accepted by all participants, and mutual trust between people who do not know each other, or know each other only in passing. The marketplace is an archetype of public space that is not simply open space or communally owned space, but rather space for social exchange taking place between strangers (in the sense of people who are not related or friends). A vibrant city is always an entrepreneurial city in the sense of small and medium-sized businesses that rely on public space as a marketplace. A settlement inhabited only by civil servants, workers, and farmers, for example, could never become a city. For a city to emerge, it is essential to have as many businesses as possible that need access to the public space as a marketplace. Pure housing not only contributes nothing to the city, it is even detrimental because it produces no public space, only private space. If, as is the case today, a large part of the retail trade shifts to online retailing, the concept of the city then comes under pressure, since analogue service providers (such as restaurants, hairdressers, fitness studios, etcetera) must occupy the marketplace alone. Though the frequently voiced criticism of the increasing commercialization of public space may well be justified, it should not overlook the fact that without a commercial purpose, not only does public space die off, but the concept of the city is also called into question.

In September 2023, a group of senior-citizens from an assisted living facility in the Burgenland district capital Oberwart demonstrated against the planned closure of a supermarket because it was the only grocery shop that they could easily reach on foot (red, 2023). They publicly lined up with their walkers in front of the supermarket, even making it into the Austrian news. This example shows how thinned out the retail sector has become in many cities whose administrations have relied on motorized mobility for decades (including shopping centers on the outskirts), making these cities uninhabitable for people who cannot or do not want to practice this form of mobility.

"A CITY IS BORN WHEN TWO HOUSES SHARE A WALL": NO CITY WITHOUT PERIMETER BLOCK

A marketplace needs a high visitor frequency, which can be increased by spatial confinement and density, among other things, which in turn increases the possibilities for social exchange. People are less likely to enter an empty pub than a well-filled one, although they would find a seat more quickly in the former and would likely be served more quickly. Finally, a marketplace as a place of rule-based exchange also needs appropriate protection, a framework in terms of space and time. In the European Middle Ages, this was initially only temporary market rights along with the municipal privilege of protecting the marketplace and the houses of the traders and craftsmen behind an enclosing wall. The clearest distinction between town and village soon consisted in the fact that only the former had a town wall. Thus the German word *Zaun* goes back to the Old Norse *tun* meaning "enclosed land," from which the English *town*, among others, developed. The clear demarcation of the urban public space not only referred to the city walls, but also to the construction of the houses themselves, which were built side by side so that their façades formed continuous walls for the streets and squares in between and thus gave the public space a clear, uncluttered form. "A city is born when two houses share a wall," Alison Brooks Architects wrote in a wall text as part of their exhibition in the Arsenale at the Venice Biennale 2021. This seemingly trivial principle can be found 2,000 years earlier in the Roman writer Tacitus, who reports in his *Germania*, written around AD 98, that the Germanic tribes did not know of cities with buildings leaning against each other, only villages with detached houses (Tacitus, 1868). The perimeter block development, which is often wrongly dismissed as a mere episode of the 19th century, is not without reason the urban typology *par excellence* and has existed since cities existed at all. The best-preserved ancient cities on the foothills of Mount Vesuvius, such as Pompeii and Herculaneum, are a good example of how Roman perimeter block development created the public space of the city as a narrowly defined interior space in the open air. The advantages of the perimeter block have been extensively presented by Wolfgang Sonne, Christoph Mäckler, and Karsten Pålsson (Mäckler/Sonne, 2012, 2018; Pålsson, 2023). Instead, I must limit myself here to the most important aspects: only perimeter block development can create a fully functional public space that has interior qualities as a dense and compact meeting space and differs from most other interior spaces only in that it is freely accessible to all, belonging to the city's inhabitants in common. The "ballet" of dense social interactions described by Jane Jacobs can only take place in a comparatively narrow, uncluttered space and would be unthinkable in the expansive exteriors of Le Corbusier's *Ville radieuse*, for instance. But the block perimeter also creates a necessary counterpart to public space, namely the private open space of inner and back courtyards, which cannot be replaced by public parks and is used either individually or communally as a protected zone—the lack of which is one of the main factors driving the environmentally-damaging desire for the detached house in the suburbs or the countryside. For one thing must not be forgotten: public space also generates stress. No one can always be on stage. Just as public space is essential for the city, so too is the private—*hortus conclusus*, as it was called by the Romans—where one can put aside one's social role.

However, perimeter block development must not mean that a large investor builds an entire block. Only in the case of small-scale parceling, with many residential townhouses built side by side, is there also a chance that the ground floor zone will be correspondingly diverse and attractive for pedestrians. Given the dominance of commercial housing, this demand seems utopian at present, but without it Territorial Urbanism would remain an unfinished project.

The "Pompeii model" outlined above does not call for a naïve return to the city of antiquity or the Middle Ages but demands a wider reflection on the fundamental principles of urban planning, which have been valid for millennia and which we must adapt above all to the challenges of climate change. For example, the cities of the future will have to contain much more greenery than the ancient city. As such, we must develop new considerations for which there are hardly any models so far. We must not make the mistake of dusting off the garden city of the 20th century as an easy historical solution (as is sometimes done today). This only initiated the separation of city functions and the destruction of public space in modernist urban planning. Only when the city is compact, dense, socially mixed, entrepreneurial, and lively with plentiful public space—doubling as a "stage" for the complex interplay of residents and strangers—and a private (or collective) open space—as a place of retreat—can it then be properly ecological.

DEGROS, A., BAGARIC, A., BAUER, S., RADULOVA-STAHMER, R., STEFAN, M. and SCHWAB, E. (eds.) (2021) *Basics of Urbanism: 12 Notions of Territorial Transformation*. Zurich: Park Books.

FIEDLER, J. (2014) 'House and Street', in: Wüstenrot Stiftung (ed.) *Ground Floor Interface*. Berlin: jovis, pp. 251–257.

JACOBS, J. (2020) *The Death and Life of Great American Cities*. [1st ed. 1961] London: The Bodley Head.

KABELIS-LECHNER, E. (2023) *Stadtentwicklung Graz: Zukunft statt Stillstand. Eine Podiumsdiskussion mit 100% männlicher Besetzung*. Available at: https://gat.news/nachrichten/stadtentwicklung-graz-zukunft-statt-stillstand

MÄCKLER, C. and SONNE, W. (eds.) (2018) *Vorne – hinten: Wie wird aus Wohnhäusern Stadt?* (8. Konferenz zur Schönheit und Lebensfähigkeit der Stadt) Berlin: DOM publishers.

MÄCKLER, C. and SONNE, W. (2012) 'Vorne und Hinten im Städtebau', *archimaera*, 9, pp. 121–138. Available at: https://www.archimaera.de/2021/rueckseiten/5216/archimaera9_maeckler_sonne.pdf

PÅLSSON, K. (2023) *Urban Block Cities: 10 Design Principles for Contemporary Planning*. Berlin: DOM publishers.

RED, BURGENLAND.ORF.AT (2023) *Rollator-Demo gegen Supermarkt-Aus*. Available at: https://burgenland.orf.at/stories/3222860/

ROSA, H. (2021) *Resonance: A Sociology of Our Relationship to the World*. Cambridge, UK: Polity.

SENNETT, R. (2017) *The Fall of Public Man*. [1rst ed. 1977] New York/London: W. W. Norton & Company.

SIMMEL, G. (2010) 'The Metropolis and Mental Life' [1903], in: Bridge, G. and Watson, S. (eds.) *The Blackwell City Reader*. Chichester/Oxford: Wiley-Blackwell, pp. 103–110.

TACITUS (1868) 'Germany and Its Tribes', in: *The Agricola and Germany of Tacitus*. Translated by Alfred John Church and William Jackson Brodribb. London: MacMillan & Co., pp. 1–33.

VISCONTI, F. (2017) *Pompeii: Città Moderna*. Tübingen/Berlin: Ernst Wasmuth.

SANDRA GUINAND IN CONVERSATION WITH MAARTEN VAN ACKER

Maarten Van Acker—professor of Urban Design at the Faculty of Design Sciences at the University of Antwerp and spokesperson for the Research Group for Urban Development—presents tools and practical insights on how to act in order to pursue a shift in urbanism. For instance, urban designers and planners should be proactive rather than reactive to urban conditions. As far as concerns pursuing specific paradigms in urbanism, like that of the "healthy" city, Maarten shows how it can anticipate better life quality but also reduce our impact on the resources of the territory. His main urban design and planning approach is to work together "with" the environment and fully consider it as a living entity.

SG

Maarten, as director of the Research Group for Urban Development, the first question we have is: in the context of climate change and scarcity of resources, how can we manage a paradigm shift in urbanism from an urban development perspective? How can we reconcile the two movements?

MA

Within our research group, we are looking at urban development and the means of implementing this shift from five different perspectives: the government perspective, meaning the policy instruments we need; infrastructure linked to mobility; healthy urban design; the legal aspect; and, last but not least, the climate and resilience perspective. I am looking at it primarily from the perspective of mobility and the healthy city. The shift required is a move away from urban design and planning which, at the moment, is most of the time focused on how we can reduce the negative impact of our surroundings on our health. Most of the spatial plans try to reduce the air pollution, reduce traffic, reduce noise, pollution, etcetera. But the question is, shouldn't we be more ambitious in our aims as urban designers and urban planners? Not striving to merely reduce negative impacts, but instead, to create a city which also makes and keeps us healthy? We are in a very good moment in history to do so. Post-COVID-19, we have never been so concerned with our health nor so aware of our environment and what is missing from it. Through combining these two forms of awareness, the recipe for a new and healthier city can be rewritten quickly.

SG

You mentioned the healthy dimensions within our cities can a healthy urban design help improve the relationship between urbanism and the resources of the territory?

MA

I am convinced that working with the paradigm of healthy urbanism can help deal with the scarcity of resources in big cities, but also in smaller cities and even villages. We were looking at what kinds of tools are at our disposal, as urban planners, to stimulate health in smaller cities and smaller communities. It starts, for example, with making a serving environment, meaning an environment that can provide healthy food. This means an environment which provides enough space for food production. It is just one aspect of a healthy village or healthy city. A biodiverse environment is another example that can answer several issues linked with scarcity of materials. This means working with "nature-based solutions." For example, working with natural pest control, recycling wood used on the sites of agricultural plots, which can be then re-used as bioenergy. It is also about having a safe environment, which protects against stress from the urban heat island effect, by greening up the concrete surfaces. In one instance, we worked with local stakeholders to build a new residential place for elderly people. We proposed not just to build apartments, but also to integrate a school and agricultural fields so that, even in old age, residents can work with their hands.The greenery, meanwhile, can educate the students on agricultural techniques. At a larger scale, we designed a couple of paths where younger and middle-aged people can take their daily walk around the neighborhoods and discover where you can buy sustainably produced food. I truly believe the paradigm of healthy urban design can help us solve the challenge of scarcity of resources.

SG

To achieve these types of projects, which new methods or tools does Territorial Urbanism need?

MA

Firstly, we need to work with the notion of metabolism. This means looking at the different flows of this city and designing it not just as the juxtaposition of functions, programs, and buildings. But, rather, looking at the flows of energy, heat, air, building materials, and drinking water. Secondly, we need to design *with* air. One of our PhD students is investigating how we can redesign our streets—in particular street canyons—so that it improves air ventilation and circulation, therefore improving the air quality on street level by weakening the roughness of the buildings, opening the ground floors and planting trees in that particular setting. The third strategy involves working with movement maps, a tool that we developed. We were assigned by the city of Antwerp to redesign a street and see how, by redesigning our streets and squares, we can invite people to exercise more, to become more fit. We came up with a typology of different layouts, different designs of street sections and squares. It is a tool which the city of Antwerp now uses each time they redesign a street or square. A fourth tool is underground urbanism. There are only a few cities in the world which have a vision and proper maps of their subterranean level. It is important to know what you can use the underground for and how it affects what is above ground. The fifth tool is place-node development. Another of my PhD students is investigating train stops, these kinds of transitional places, where there is not even a building that can be formally called a station. In our opinion we can do much more with these places. We investigate how accessible they are by bicycle, by foot, by train, by car, thinking about the development costs but also the development potential of those sites and how we can improve it. The final tool I would like to mention is the adaptive re-use of car landscapes. We have been investigating the re-use of underground parking garages. One fifth of all newly built underground car parks in Flanders are empty. So, what are we going to do with those places? What if in the future we start to drive less, ride our bicycles more? How will we then use these underground car parks? How are we going to reinvent those big motorways, which are currently cutting though all our cities? These are six tools I have been thinking about.

Living Together in the Garden Metropolis

Susanne Eliasson

Since the beginning of urbanization, cities have always been the place where people live together: for the opportunities and safety they provide, for economic reasons, to fulfill a need for social bonds, and for all the other reasons that make us come together as people. Living together in a particular environment requires a kind of collective organization that always manifests itself physically and our urban structures reflect the values and challenges faced by our society.

This text focuses on a certain urban structure, the Garden Metropolis—a concept introduced by our studio GRAU. Neither the center nor the periphery, the term refers to residential urban growth that has mainly occurred in the last 150 years as a direct extension of major urban centers. Because it arises from a liberal world order and market economy, we struggle to make sense of this growth, often considering it an uncontrollable chaos that is the "price to pay" for people to satisfy their individual desires: an environment shaped by boundaries and distance rather than the desire to live together. It's a kind of urbanization that exists all over the world around every major city center. We have produced it, in dizzying quantities, and now we have to deal with it, transforming and adapting it continuously. To achieve this, and to give it collective meaning, we have to look at it in detail and understand the specific processes that lie behind it.

Our work on the Garden Metropolis was exhibited from April to October 2022 at arc en rêve centre d'architecture in Bordeaux where we explored this urban condition from the point of view of four cities: Bordeaux, Brussels, Chicago, and Phoenix. The aim of the exhibition is to show that the Garden Metropolis is a global condition we can find everywhere but also to shed light on the vast amount we have already produced, highlighting the urgency of focusing on it and its potential for evolution. We have assembled the urban fabrics of the four cities into one single surface and room, producing a physical space for the Garden Metropolis [01].

The metropolitan region of Bordeaux provides a more concrete example of the potential of the Garden Metropolis as an urban structure. As advising architects of the city since 2021, we accompany and oversee all projects within

[01] Four urban fabrics: Bordeaux, Phoenix, Brussels, Chicago. © GRAU

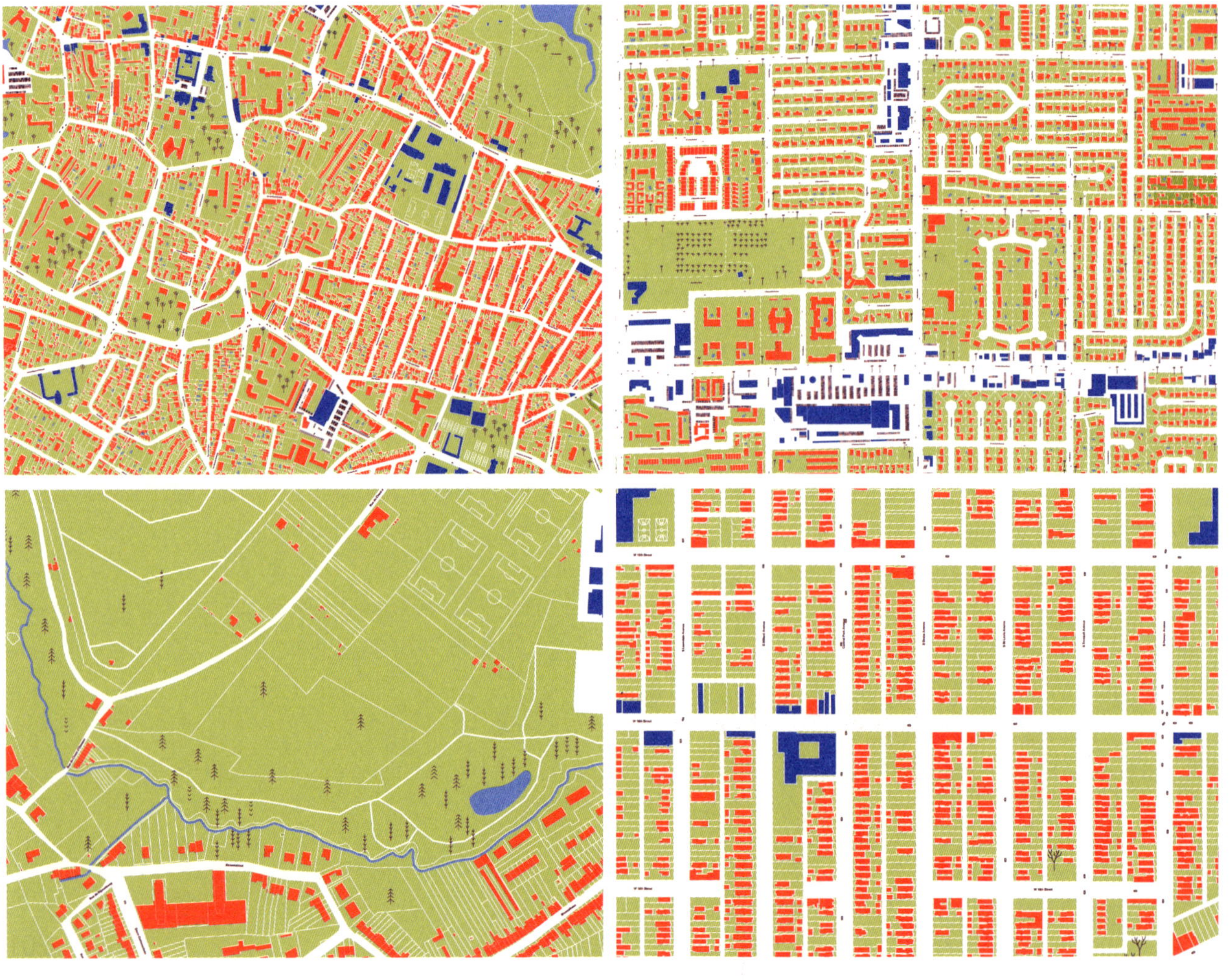

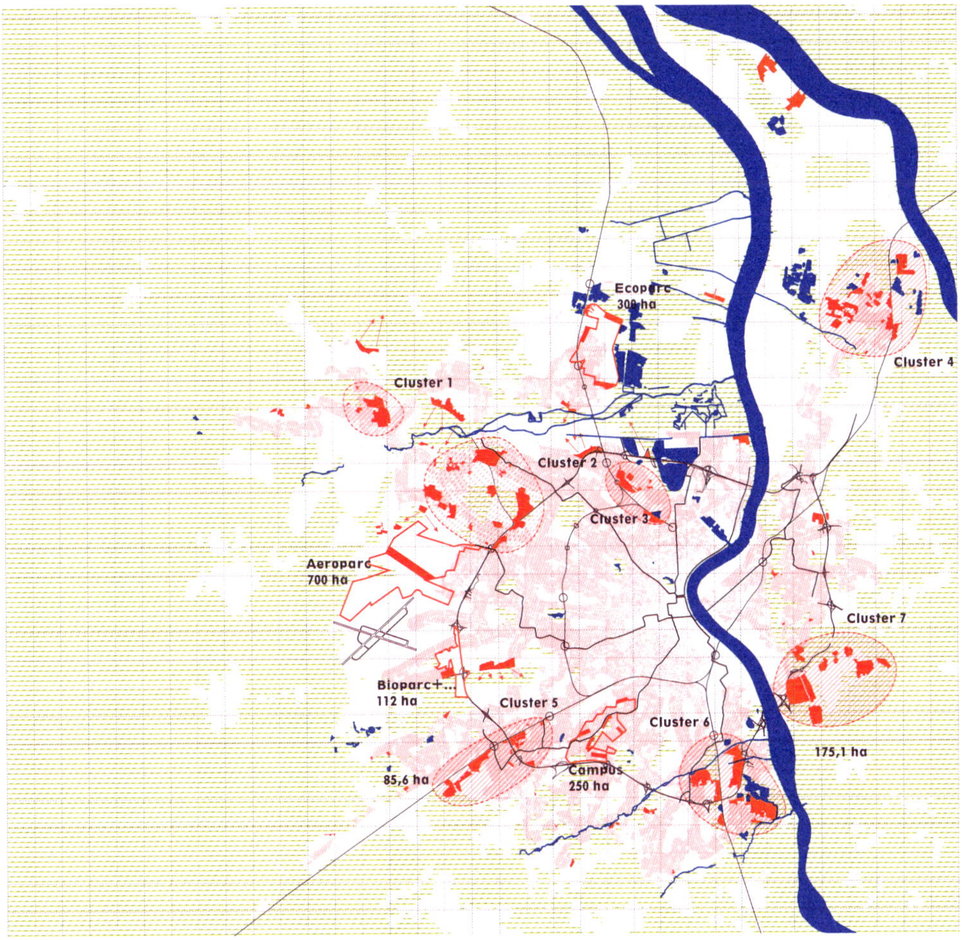

[02] A strategy for the construction of 50,000 new dwellings in the metropolitan region of Bordeaux. © GRAU/51N4E

the municipality. Our history with Bordeaux goes back to 2010 when we participated in a study with 51N4E on how to produce 50,000 new dwellings close to public transport. Bordeaux as a region has grown considerably and so has the need for housing. The city, known for its climate and lifestyle, attracts tourists and new residents every day, leading to a growing shortage of affordable housing and prices that have doubled in just a couple of years. With the "50,000" study, the metropolitan region aimed to develop solutions for building better, cheaper, and faster dwellings. Focusing simultaneously on the qualitative and quantitative aspects of housing was an opportunity to examine the relationship between housing typology and urban form in the region [02] [03].

In 2013 we were commissioned by the city of Bordeaux to design a development strategy for the district of Caudéran, together with landscape architects Michel and Claire Corajoud. Caudéran, a residential district located west of the city center (750 hectares, 45,000 inhabitants), has grown over time from a rural landscape of vineyards and small villages to a major residential area: an urbanization without urbanism but with multiple residential qualities. In Caudéran, the landscape and the built forms maintain a close relationship, working in a complementary way. In addition, the qualities of the public space are mainly produced by the private domain, through the green fences, front gardens, and trees that overflow onto the street [04].

Based on observing the existing conditions of Caudéran we identified four different types of residential fabrics, each with their own specific qualities: the individual fabric with houses and small gardens, the collective fabric with large collective buildings and parkscapes, the hybrid fabric along the main transport axis, and the *échoppe*[1] fabric with a patchwork-like "quilted" appearance.

We then asked the following question: in the context of metropolitan growth, how can each fabric evolve in time while keeping its existing qualities and DNA [05]?

This is a matter of housing typologies and the way they actively participate in the residential fabric. The main fabric of Caudéran is the individual fabric which needs to accommodate more density but also provide new potential for collectivity. Lifestyles are changing as much in the outskirts of cities as in the center; there

1 The *échoppe* is a one-story, narrow row house that first appeared in the 15th century as a space occupied by merchants and craftsmen.

[03] Four hypotheses for the construction of 50,000 new dwellings in the metropolitan region of Bordeaux. ©GRAU/51N4E

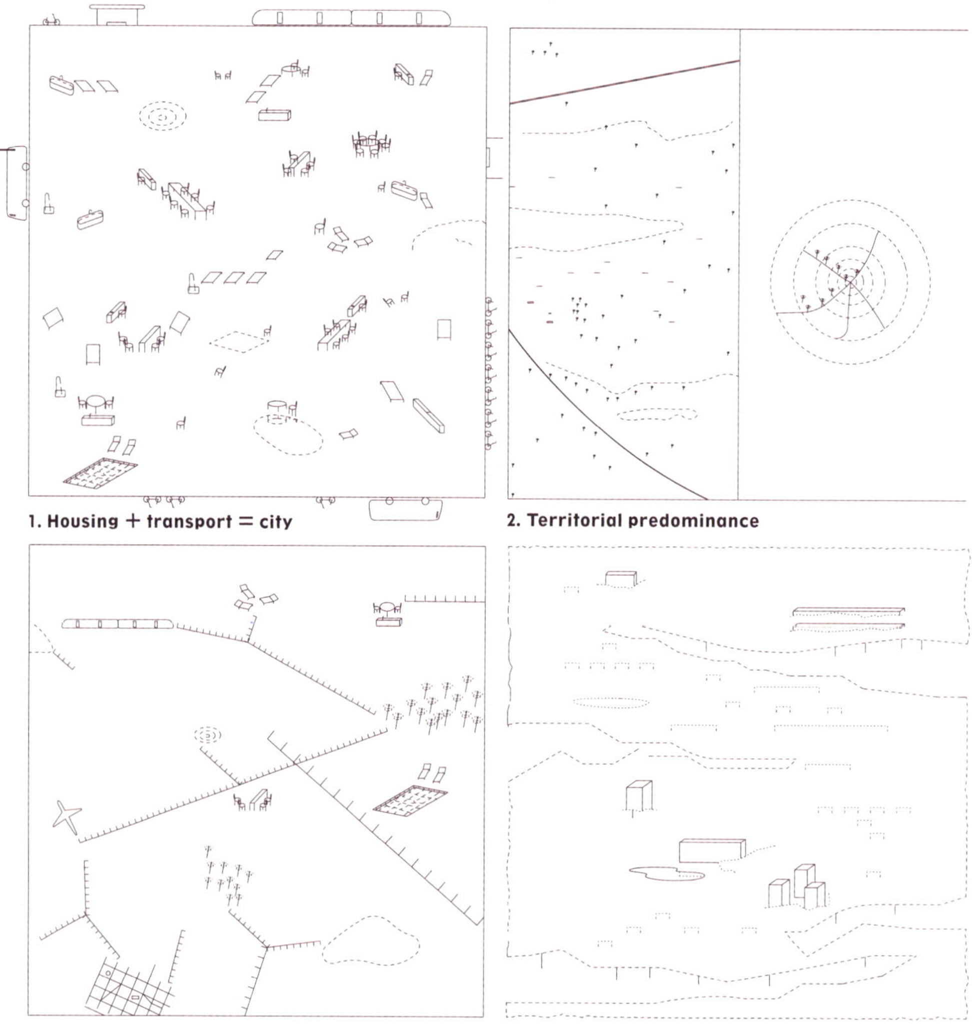

1. Housing + transport = city

2. Territorial predominance

3. Scales of mixed use

4. Horizontal and emerging densities

[04] Caudéran: relationship between built form and landscape. © Antoine Espinasseau

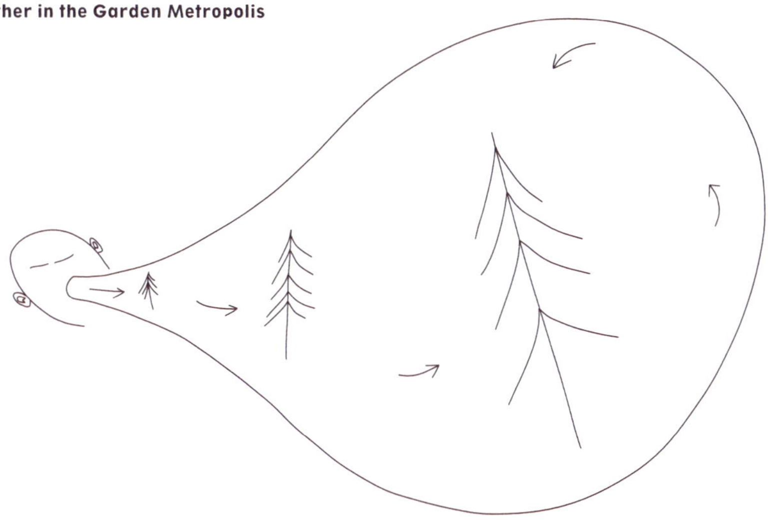

[05] Radicalizing the existing qualities of the residential fabrics of Caudéran. © GRAU

[06] The Triad Apartments, Alfred Beadle, Phoenix, AZ. © GRAU

[07] Boardwalk Apartments, Alfred Beadle, Phoenix, AZ. © GRAU

[08] The Three Fountains Condominiums. © GRAU

is, for example, a rising elderly population in need of support systems as well as single parent households looking for less (but more flexible) space. To provide the potential for collective living we need to understand and measure how close we can get to each other while maintaining individual qualities and, additionally, what role the garden can play in creating thresholds between private and public.

While researching housing typologies with a specific connection to gardens we discovered the work of American architect Alfred Newman Beadle who was active in Phoenix, Arizona from the 1950s. He built several dense, horizontal, low-cost housing projects there, including Three Fountains Condominiums, the Boardwalk Apartments, and—one of the only two multi-unit developments within the Case Study Houses program—the Triad Apartments.

Triad Apartments is a one-story complex comprised of three apartment units grouped together around a common space, a garage, and a laundry room. Each unit is organized so that the living room and kitchen look out through alarge glass wall onto a shared green space, while the back rooms open onto a small private courtyard. The Boardwalk and Three Fountains Condominiums were built on the same principles but at a larger scale and in a denser setting [06] [07].

These three projects offer qualities that allow people to get closer to each other and to benefit from it: architecture and garden form a whole that provides proximity without promiscuity and the grid is used here not solely for structural purposes, but to organize an urban model of living. Rather than an accumulation of architectural typologies, together the units form a collective fabric in which the car is no longer at the center. These physical strategies all make sense in an individual context: we call it proximate living [08] [09].

We are now developing such living structures in Bordeaux, focusing on producing a collective environment within an individual project. In Caudéran, we have designed fifteen individual dwellings for a private developer, organized around a common collective garden, a clear reference to Beadle's principles. In addition to the collective garden there is also a front garden that remains open to the street [10].

Another ongoing project, exploring the same questions, is located north of Bordeaux. It consists of twenty-two social housing units, both

[09] The Triad Apartments, the Boardwalk Apartments, and Three Fountains Condominiums: proximate living. © GRAU

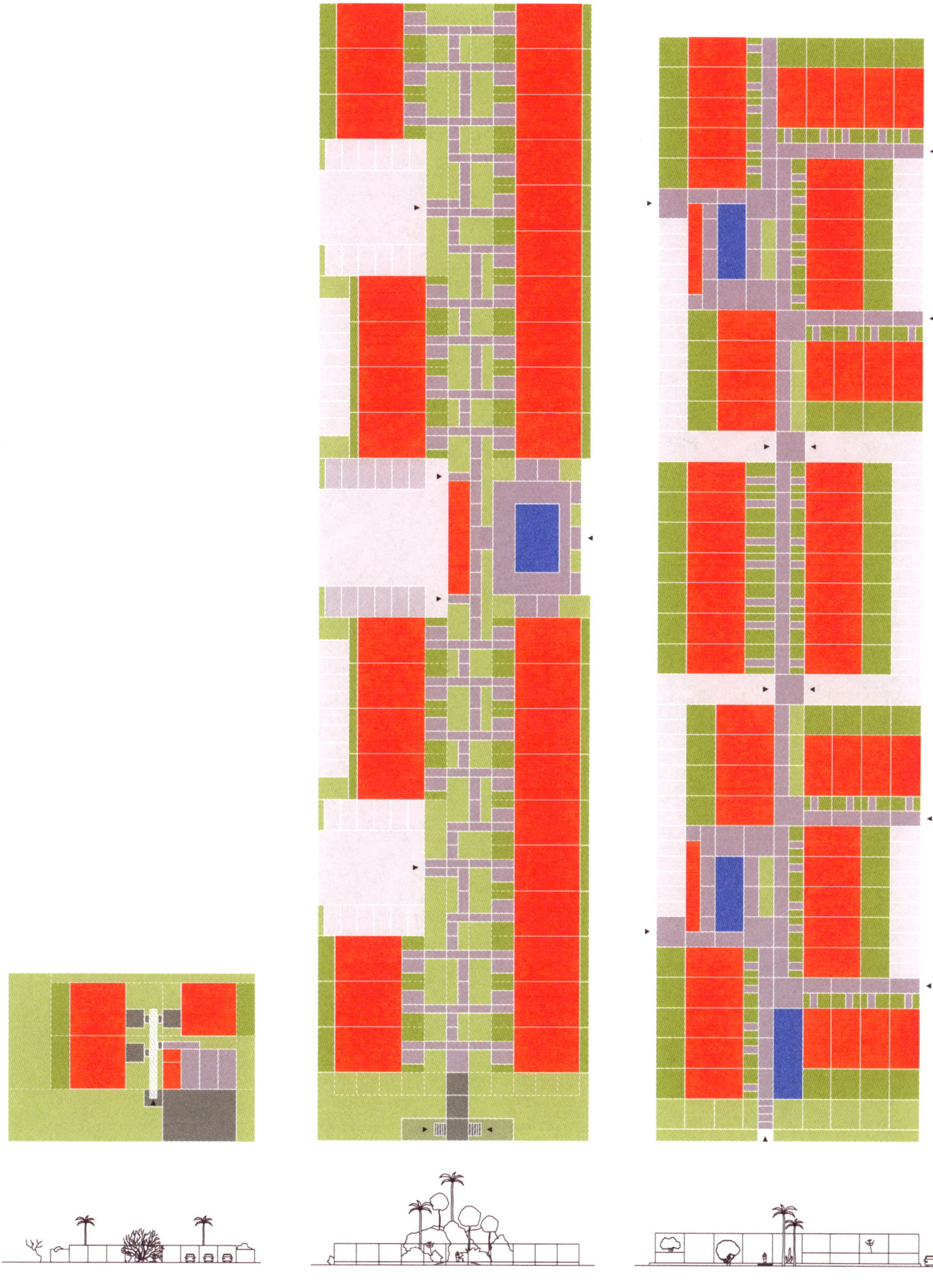

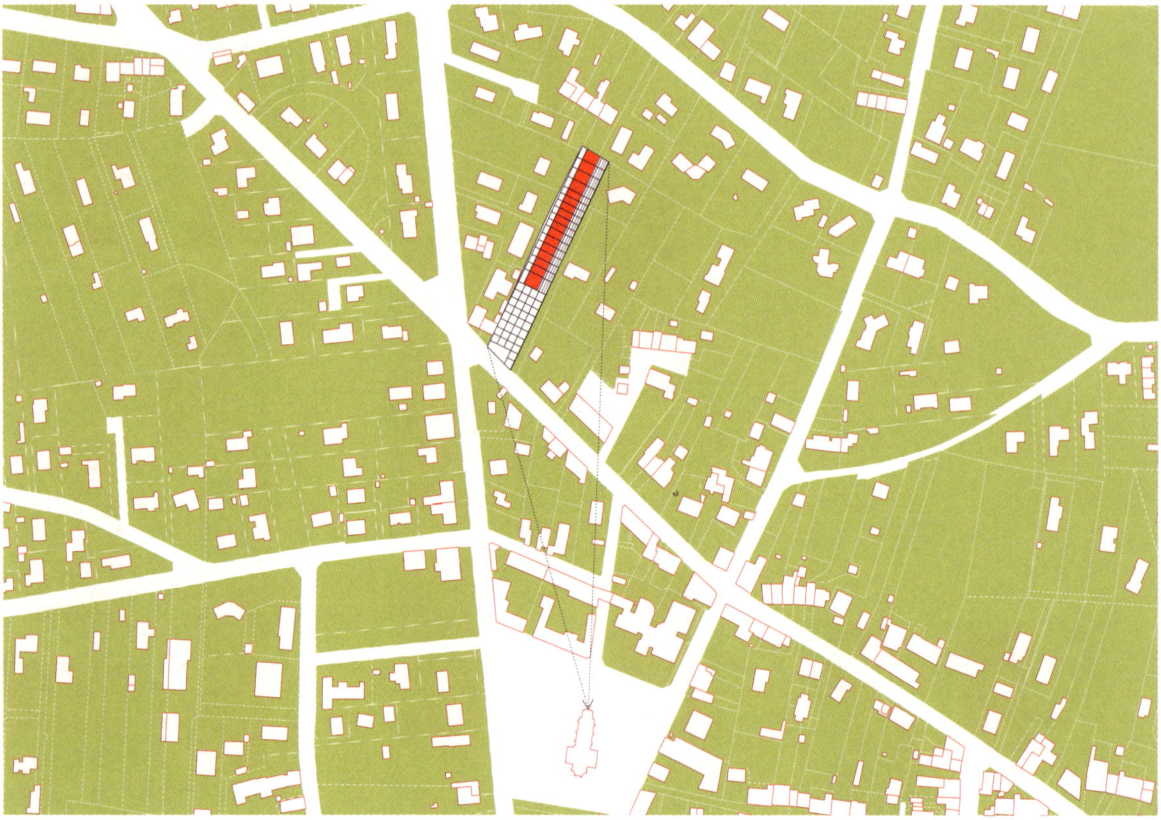

[10] Fifteen individual dwellings in Caudéran. © GRAU

[11] Twenty-two individual and collective dwellings in Parempuyre. © GRAU

[12] The private garden in the back, an exterior living room. © GRAU

[13] The garden threshold, both a filter to preserve intimacy and a place of socialization. © GRAU

collective and individual. On a very narrow and deep plot we create a single horizontal building with different housing units that open up onto a collective promenade [11] [12].

The main challenge of the project lies in the dimension and design of the garden threshold, which serves as both a filter that preserves intimacy and a potential place of socialization between neighbors, part of a larger collective environment [13].

The current discourse about the collective (what we speak of in France as the *vivre ensemble*) does not hide the fact that we live in a very individualistic world: development and transformation on the larger territorial scale is framed by planning documents but in practice we see the construction of fragmented islands next to one another, a direct result of the private sector producing more and more of the urban environment. We consider these two projects as a hypothesis for living well together in the Garden Metropolis: it is about finding the inherent structure, even when it might seem absent, and building on its specificity to produce greater wellbeing. This structure is, after all, what holds us together [14].

[14] Bordeaux: the horizontal city. © GRAU

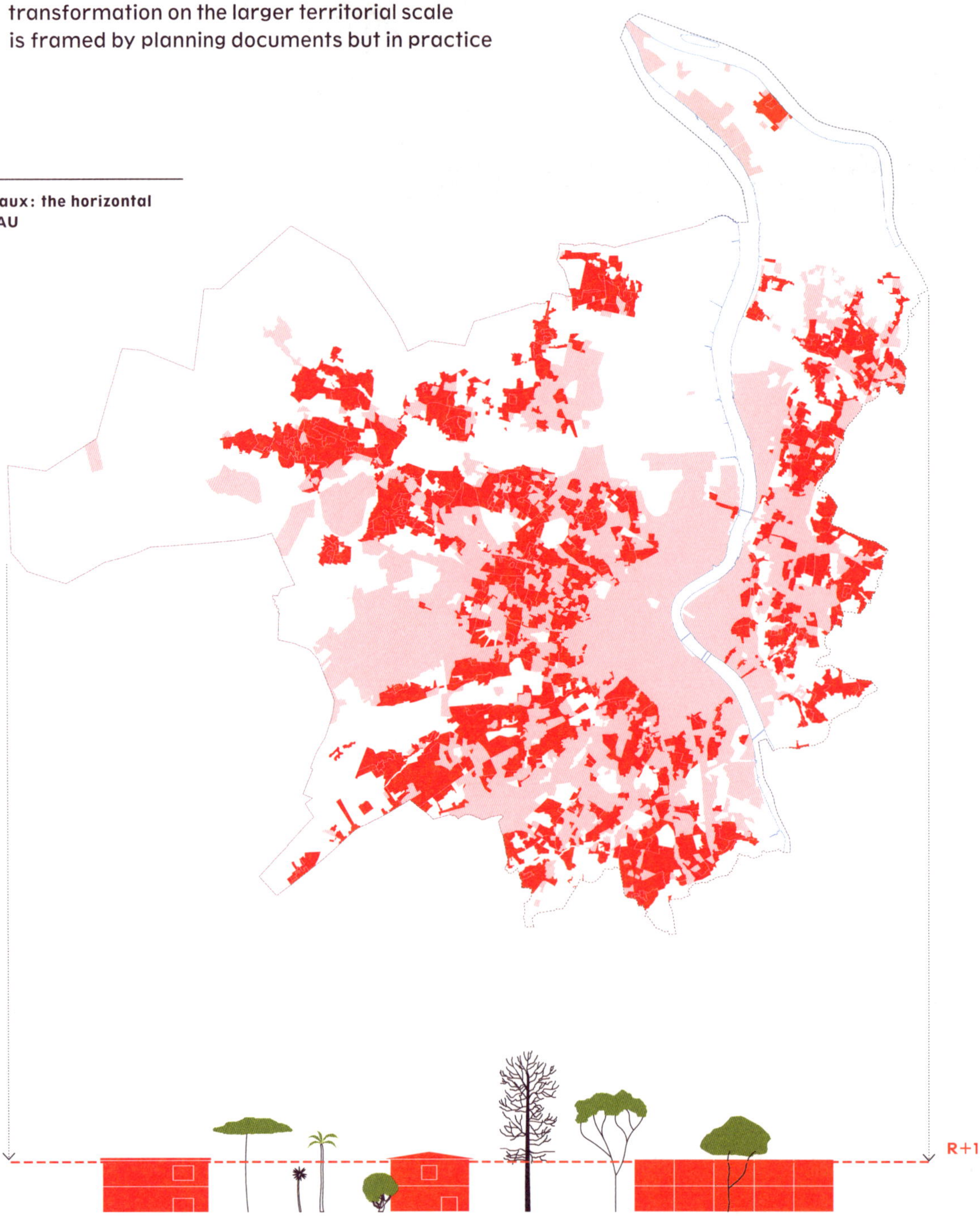

Studio Decarb Lux

Stefan Bendiks, Aglaée Degros

During the Winter semester 2022, studio "Decarb Lux" at the Harvard Graduate School of Design brought together students with diverse disciplinary backgrounds to research and design transition on a territorial scale. This studio was built around the material of the publication *Towards Territorial Transition*, published in 2023, and dealt with the territorial transition of the country of Luxembourg in the face of the various ecological, economic, social, and spatial challenges involved in navigating the shift towards carbon neutrality. It focused more on the process of achieving the goal than on the goal as such. The students were invited to think about the transition as a project in itself, existing on a scale beyond the more common ones of the building or the city. In the past, crises have always influenced spatial disciplines, just as crises have always influenced the development of various societal movements, which in turn transform the disciplines. Currently, the challenges of climate change, e.g., through increasing severe weather events, have once again confronted us with the fragility of the (built) environment—and thus raised the call for a rethinking of the goals and means of the spatial disciplines. The studio started with the idea that, in the face of immense environmental and social challenges, a paradigm shift in planning and design approaches is needed. In this respect two notions were particularly essential for the structure and content of the studio:

TERRITORY

"A territory is not a random piece of land, but it is always deeply related to a specific place with its soil, resources, ecosystems, climate, and other agents. These aspects define the size, the potential, as well as the structuring elements of a territory. Any form of economic and ecologic activity (such as hunting, consuming, polluting, etcetera), as well as social interaction and generally all life on Earth (both human and non-human), is related to a specific geography, with specific systemic and often elastic boundaries. The complex systemic relations of any activity to the ground describe a territory." **(Towards Territorial Transition, 2023)**

TRANSITION

"A transition is a temporal process of gradual change from one situation, state, subject, place, to another. The term 'ecological transition' has already been in use since the 1970s **(Bennett, 1976)**, and became more specific and operational in terms of the 'energy transition' **(Hopkins, 2008)**, highlighting that the Anthropocene and the fossil economy are strongly related, as the fossil economy ignites the Anthropocene situation. In that context, transition is largely understood as the gradual shift from a fossil-fuel dependent to a post-carbon society, a process that needs to be organized continuously, step by step, in order to avoid hard social, economic, or ecological shocks. Yet this transition is not infinite, rather it is specific in time, as it has a beginning and an end (when carbon neutrality is achieved)." **(Towards Territorial Transition, 2023)**

In the studio context, "territorial transition" stood for a holistic, cross-sectoral, and networked understanding of space in time. It implied a close connection between the built environment and living systems—an approach that replaces the predominantly building-oriented attitude in planning in favor of an increased appreciation of the landscape and its systems. It was the space between buildings, rather than the buildings themselves, that were understood as essential for ecological and social change, both at the level of the entire territory and in the immediate, environing habitat.

Although the studio specifically tackled the territorial transition of the Grand Duchy of Luxembourg as a case, the fields of study and experimentation were not defined by the boundaries of geopolitical space. Rather the investigations and ideas were positioned in the larger context of the different, existing, and future socio-ecological systems and cycles of Luxembourg.

This led to the investigation of larger, interconnected territorial systems that gain greater resilience through networked structures. The territorial transitions envisioned in the studio went beyond the usual development goals of economic and technological progress. They followed the overarching idea of working towards a more just and ecological region, with a high quality of life for all agencies involved in the transition process.

In small groups, the students started to research and map relevant, self-chosen topics in relation to the goals of decarbonization, such as: land use, transport of people and goods, the production and distribution of food and energy, building construction and demolition, waste, brownfield sites, and forestry. In this phase, the students began to get to know the territory they were unfamiliar with and discovered the particularities of Luxembourg. In a collective effort, themes that had formerly been worked on independently and specific findings were superimposed and combined. This led to the formulation of unexpected strategies for the territorial transition of Luxembourg. These were taken up by individual students and translated into tangible design tasks. Although the individual transition projects were very different in terms of the chosen territory, scales, agents, and processes, some of them also shared great similarities. Some of these similarities were more or less to be expected, as they were conditioned by the given methodology of the studio, for instance focusing on uncertainty, working between different scales, and the formation of unexpected alliances between the different actors involved.

An apparent commonality between the projects was the focus on optimizing existing systems. The spectrum of systems to be optimized covered the entire range of the analyzed topics. A common approach of the projects was to optimize and combine the different systems to gain space. Space, which was then used for processes of CO2 absorption, but also simply to improve people's wellbeing and health. This suggests that "space" is one of the most valuable but generally underestimated resources in territorial transformation. The projects all led to spatial design proposals of different kinds. More interesting than describing the students' designs in detail or their individual qualities was working out overarching findings. They can be formulated as five paradigm shifts (or transitions) that are valuable for the work on territorial transformation:

From a narrative to an epic
From actors to agents
From scale to scales
From re-use to re-fuse
From planning to uncertainty

FROM A NARRATIVE TO AN EPIC

Far-reaching transitions operating on a territorial scale, with a tangible impact on people's comfort and habits, require not only convincing facts and figures, but also compelling storytelling to bring people along on the journey. A transition to a more frugal urbanism and economy, with less consumption of resources and space, is not just about independent agencies transforming isolated components, it's about transforming networked systems. This dual transformation is complex to understand and to communicate. "Instead of promoting an instant solution which leads to us formulating answers that are often quick, simple and already proven, shouldn't we explore slow and complex paths" **(Towards Territorial Transition, 2023)**. Those complex paths often cannot be explored in a simple, compact narrative. They require a more extensive and detailed but compelling epic.

In her project, Jialei Tang is developing an epic of global decarbonization via the Luxembourg financial center. According to Jialei Tang the impact of a "local" spatial intervention to decarbonize Luxembourg's territory (regardless of how the scale of this territory is defined) is small compared to the impact that Luxembourg can exert through its global interconnections with the financial world. She proposes using an ultra-fast "edge" server system to advantage and hence encourage green stock exchange transactions that either pass through Luxembourg or are initiated there. This means that those who are faster to take action in decarbonizing will have priority over others. The new servers supporting these transactions are positioned closer to the financial institutions in order to save a few fractions of seconds, compared to a similar transaction conducted, for example, in New York.

For the exact localization and contextualization of the edge server facilities, Jialei Tang explored the city's underground system of so far unrecognized cavities, such as caves and galleries, as well as existing underground car parks that could be converted in the course of the envisaged changes in mobility. The connected underground structures are activated for recreational purposes, as well as for the collection of rainwater and the use of waste heat. The storytelling of this project goes further than a simple narrative.
It makes the otherwise abstract connections of the global financial world and its wider impact on the (de)carbonization of our globally networked world comprehensible and locates the relative interventions in a specific, recognizable urban context of the city of Luxembourg. It is an epic that literally anchors the transition of global (financial) flows on the grounds of Luxembourg's city center.

FROM ACTORS TO AGENTS

Impending far-reaching transition processes understandably unsettle the various stakeholders involved. One of the main tasks of a good transition "epic" is to overcome this unsettledness and to provide a common pathway to the future.
It is about bringing together the often-conflicting individual needs and interests of those affected, connecting them and also forging seemingly unlikely coalitions. To do this, the people concerned must move from a passive to an active role. They must become the drivers of the transition themselves, rather than just letting it happen to them. In this case, we are no longer talking about actors but about agents.

This shift from actors to agents of transformation asks for a hybridization of the making of territory. Unlike typical "visions of the future," a transformation seeks to reconcile co-creation and stakeholder involvement with the method and process of changing a territory. In this context, Anita Berrizbeitia, Professor of Landscape at Harvard GSD, questions how we can achieve far-reaching transitions and refers to Edward O. Wilson's Half Earth initiative: "a proposal to protect half of the Earth's land and oceans in order to preserve biodiversity globally. With this initiative, it will be interesting to track how they are implemented, by whom and who has the capacity to fund it." **(Towards Territorial Transition, 2023)**

Pavin Banternghansa's project investigates the carbon emissions of the agricultural and the energy sector—namely, their production and the import/export of different product groups. In the project, he combines Community Supported Agriculture with diversified renewable energy production. The concepts of silvopasture and permaculture are coupled with concepts of agrivoltaics. Based on the meteorological and agricultural characteristics of the territory, he implements a new decentralized energy and food production grid. This leads to a hybridization of the agricultural and forest landscapes. The formerly sectorally-organized actors are thus also hybridized. They are both producers of energy and agricultural products. The range of considered agents with their specific needs and demands is thereby radically extended into the non-human realm. Not only farmers, but also their livestock, their trees, and their crops, as well as wind turbines and solar cells, are seen as agents of change. Together they form a coalition that is radically changing not only the systems of production and distribution of energy and food, but also the pastoral and cultural landscape.

FROM SCALE TO SCALES

Territorial projects, as the name suggests, are defined by engaging with the challenges of transition on the largest relevant scale, generally beyond the scale of the building or the plot. Yet after zooming out, territorial transformation also requires zooming in gradually and iteratively on these scales.

Territorial projects hence evolve in a multi-scale dynamic, constantly moving between analyses of the entire territory, the definition of strategic objectives, quantitative climate mitigation measures, and smaller spatial interventions that translate the strategic objectives into the specific local context. Scale can be understood as a tool to decide, design, measure, evaluate, and relate systems to each other. The territorial scale of reflecting and designing ecology-related spatial systems is a key element for transition. Scale is not an abstract, general concept here, but is closely linked to ecosystemic resource networks such as water, energy, food, biodiversity, etcetera. Exploring the spatial implications of the chosen territorial transition strategy requires not only working and designing at several scales from the whole territory to the immediate habitat of the direct surroundings—but also making use of different forms of representation: from mappings and plans, to diagrams, sections, and perspective representations.

In his project Abhishek Desai zoomed out far beyond the geographical borders of Luxembourg to investigate the logic of freight logistics. This led to the discovery that a favorable value added tax system encourages the creation of warehouses for the temporary storage of imported goods. Owing to this, European truck traffic into and through the country increased, resulting in higher carbon emissions from the logistics sector as well as a regional concentration of warehouses in the vicinity of Luxembourg's external borders. Rather than reducing this tax advantage, in the project it is transferred to sustainable mobility: the warehouses that were previously served exclusively by fossil-fuel mobility are replaced by production and logistics hubs on the conversion sites of the former mining industry. As those are well connected to (inter)national rail networks and located close to both old and new urban developments, they can become nodes between the global rail delivery system and local networks for last-mile delivery, also including modes of active mobility. The project alternates in its scales and representational techniques from the mapping of global logistics to the urban planning of the former mining site, the landscape profile section, and the perspective visualization of a refurbished warehouse.

FROM RE-USE TO RE-FUSE

Territorial transition towards decarbonization also questions the core function of architecture and urban planning: the construction of buildings and the associated consumption of resources. Since sustainability has gained importance in the construction sector, terms with the prefix "re" are currently booming: re-cycle, re-use, re-furbish, etcetera. A term less popular among architects and planners so far is "re-fuse," which means not necessarily building anything and, avoiding excessive growth in order to save resources, land, and biodiversity. The approach of "re-fusing" implies that architecture and urban planning are primarily aimed at improving the quality of existing space rather than the production of new space. This is, however, at odds with the economic principle of constant growth and also calls for an entirely different attitude towards the real estate sector. New business relations must be explored and activated through an alternative economic and societal vision for the construction sector. In turn, this leads to the already mentioned need to develop a holistic epic about the built environment and to form coalitions of new agents.

Magic Sun's project takes as its starting point the fact that 9% of Luxembourg's carbon emissions are related to manufacturing and construction. Within this field, she identifies three main problems: the supply of building materials depends largely on imports. Compared to other European countries Luxembourg has very high construction and demolition waste volumes and the capacity of Luxembourg's landfills is reaching its limits. This leads to high carbon emissions, not only directly through construction, but also indirectly through the associated transport. Hence, Magic Sun proposes an alternative take on the redevelopment of former steelworks sites in Luxembourg. She "re-fuses" new residential areas there. Instead, she proposes transforming the brownfield sites into manufacturing facilities for products made from recycled materials. These products are then primarily used for the necessary (energetic) renovation and redesign of the existing building stock in the immediate vicinity of the site and not for the construction of new buildings. A logic of circular construction replaces the former logic of "construct and dispose." This approach also means that refurbishing and repurposing is done in close cooperation with the surrounding residential areas. Spatially, the former brownfield site becomes an integral part of the surrounding landscape. The production facilities merge with environmental and recreational systems. The refusal to build new housing also leaves space for natural agents to take possession of the space.

FROM PLANNING TO UNCERTAINTY

The current increase in extreme weather events is forcing us to look at our environment and the way we interact with it with different eyes: planning according to the predictable becomes a privilege from times past. If we stick to old routines, planning will increasingly move towards disaster management. Or we can explore new ways to plan for the uncertain. History teaches us that when a system breaks down or changes rapidly, the obsolete system creates opportunities for new uses. For example, when coal replaced wood as the primary energy source in the US, production forests became ecological forests that sequester CO2 for longer periods of time and were later used primarily for recreation. This transition shows how much long-term planning depends on the predictability of demands. What if we were to question the demand for more buildings for the real estate market and hence the current growth of the built environment? What could be done with any surplus supply of houses? When we plan and design can we already take into account obsolescence and uncertainty?

In his project "Luxembourg forest urbanism," Rongqing Liu questions the growth forecasts for the need for new buildings. Rather than accepting them and responding with new construction, the projected growth—which increasingly builds up and seals the soil—is seen as uncertain. Instead, a production forest interwoven with the urban fabric is planted as a material resource in order to insulate and transform existing buildings. The underutilization of, for example, existing villa-type residences is seen as a possible response to the future housing demand. The existing building stock can be divided up and thermally insulated with the newly planted wood. The demand for growth is replaced by an improvement of the environment through the creation of productive forests and thus the creation of a material reserve that can support slow growth. As production forests grow, so do the potential material resources for the building stock conversion. Yet in the event of reduced or no growth, the production forests situated in close proximity to residential areas can remain active as carbon sinks and fresh air generators. The forests can be preserved as valuable landscapes for recreation and other improvements to the quality of urban life. Existing neighborhoods are upgraded and given a unique look and feel that makes the urban transformation towards CO2 neutrality visible and tangible.

ARMENGAUD, M., DEGROS, A. and RADULOVA-STAHMER, R. (2023) *Towards Territorial Transition.* Zurich: Park Books.

BENNETT, J.W. (1976) *The Ecological Transition: Cultural Anthropology and Human Adaptation.* New York, NY: Pergamon Press.

HOPKINS, R. (2008) *The Transition Handbook: From Oil Dependency to Local Resilience.* White River Junction, VT: Chelsea Green Publishing.

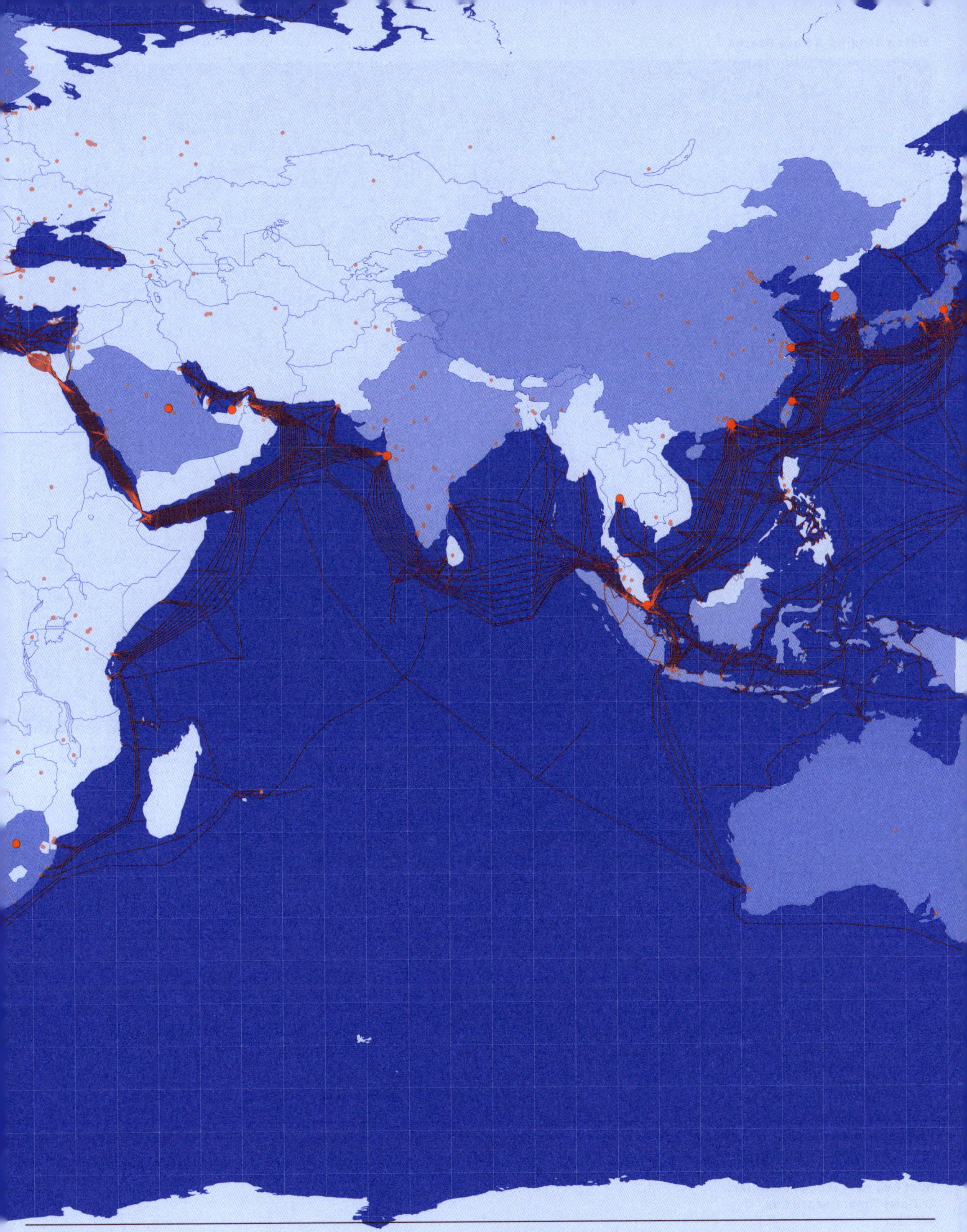

PROJECT "ON EDGE"
BY JIALEI TANG

[01] The territory of the global financial market with its physical (data) infrastructures. © Jialei Tang, Decarb Lux, WS 2022

FOREIGN DIRECT INVESTMENT (IN MILLION USD) BY COUNTRY
- 4–10 million
- 10–31 million
- 31–110 million
- 110–399 million
- 399–1,500 million

- Stock exchange
- Data center
- Submarine internet cable

Sources: Esri, Garmin, FAO, NOAA, USGS

0 375 750 1500 2250 3000 km

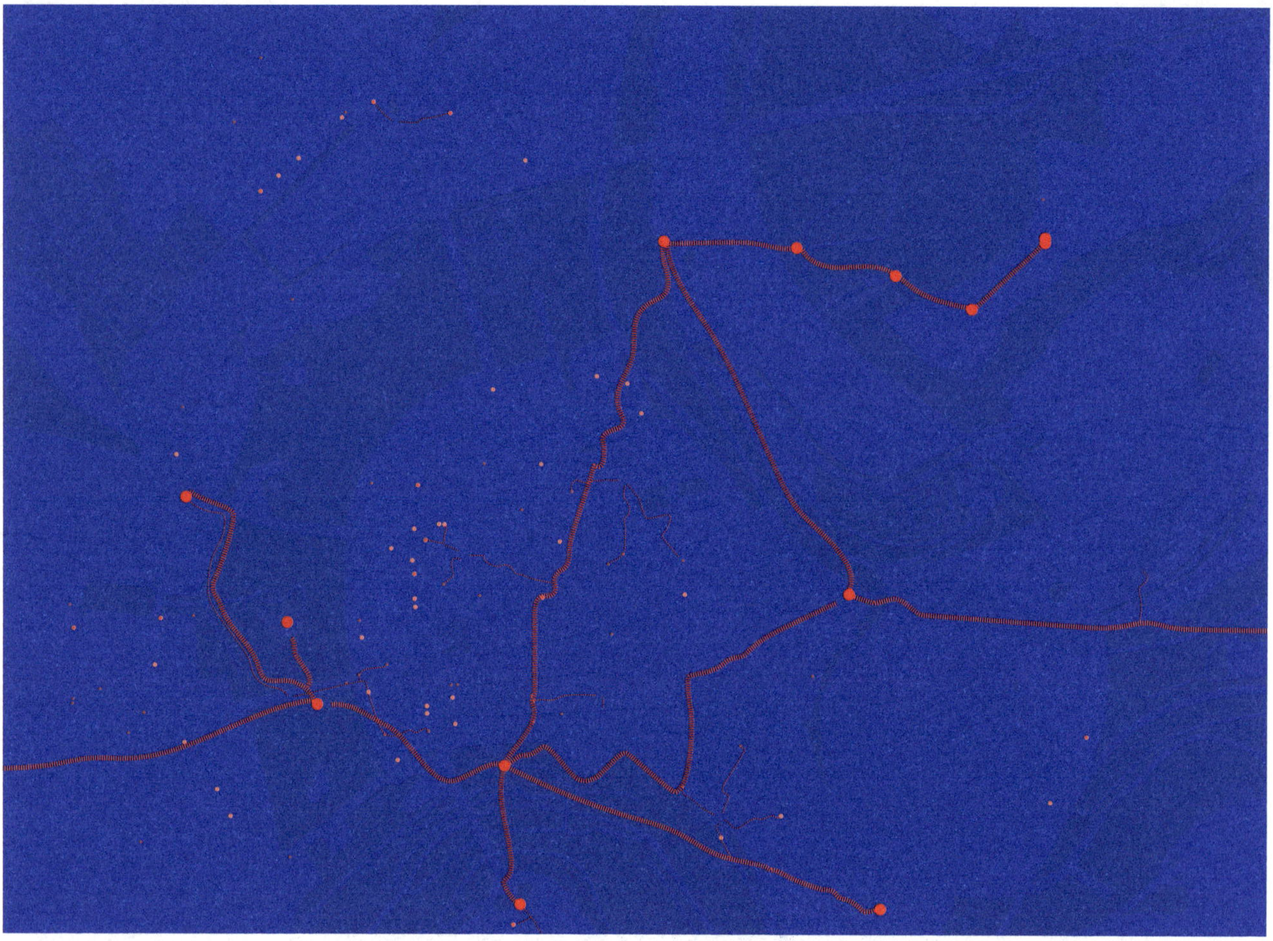

PROJECT "ON EDGE"
BY JIALEI TANG

[02] Localization of the new edge center in proximity to the financial institutions, making use of the city's existing underutilized underground structures.

Buildings
- Historical fortifications
- Stock exchange
- Banks
- Finance

Sources: Esri Community Maps Contributors, LVermGeo RP, Esri, HERE, Garmin, Foursquare, GeoTechnologies, Inc, METI/NASA, USGS

0 0.13 0.25 0.5 0.75 1 km

PROJECT "ON EDGE"
BY JIALEI TANG

[03] Contextualization of the data centers in underground car parks and their integration into a network for harnessing waste heat and harvesting rainwater.

PROJECT "ON EDGE"
BY JIALEI TANG

[04] Comparison of the carbon footprint of Luxembourg and its 100 largest funds. © Jialei Tang, Decarb Lux, WS 2022

■ Carbon footprint of Luxembourg: 9,750,000 tons CO_2 emissions (2019)

■ Carbon footprint of 100 largest Luxembourg funds: more than 39,000,000 tons CO_2 emissions (2019)

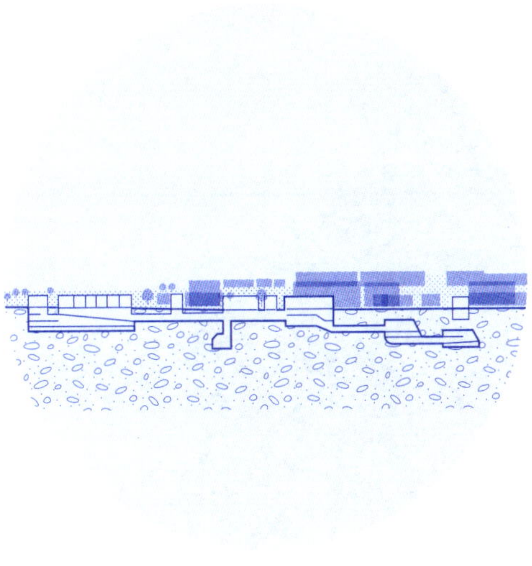

1

2

4

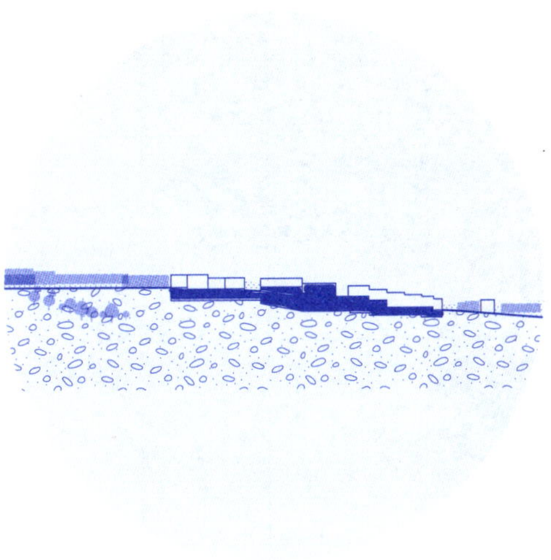

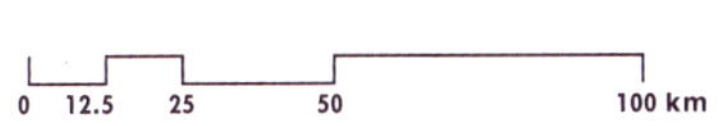

3

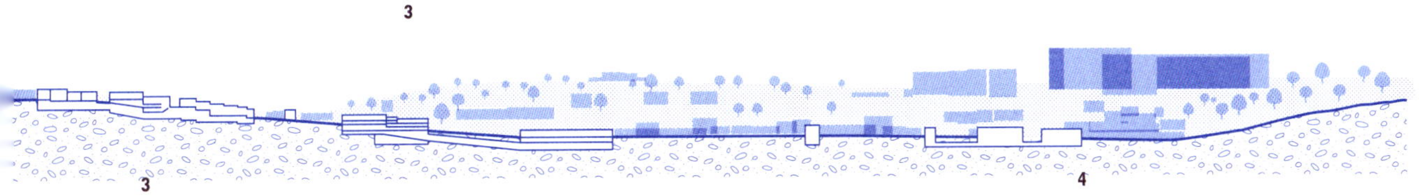

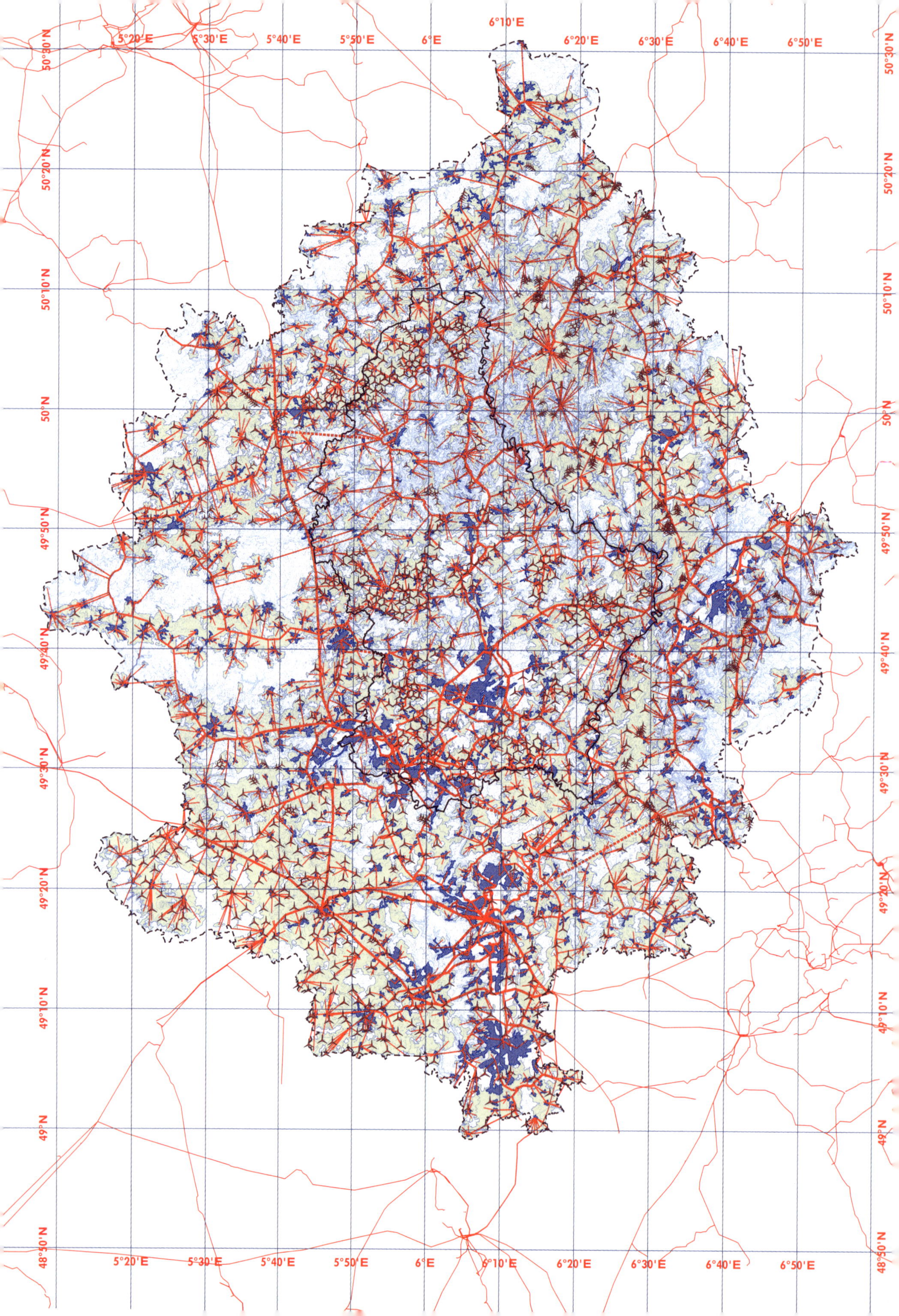
5°20'E
5°30'E
5°40'E
5°50'E
6°E
6°10'E
6°20'E
6°30'E
6°40'E
6°50'E
50°30'N
50°20'N
50°10'N
50°N
49°50'N
49°40'N
49°30'N
49°20'N
49°10'N
49°N
48°50'N

Studio Decarb Lux

PROJECT: "FOOD × POWER" BY PAVIN BANTERNGHANSA

[05] The area defined by coupling the production and distribution of energy with that of food. © Pavin Banternghansa, Decarb Lux, WS 2022

FOOD × POWER—TOWARDS A HEALTHY TERRITORY
Milieu territory
Lux boundary
Proposed wind turbine
Existing wind turbine
Transimission line
Sub-transimission line
Proposed transmission line
Urban area
Town to trans
Farm to town
Agricultural land

PROJECT: "FOOD × POWER" BY PAVIN BANTERNGHANSA

[06] Development of Luxembourg's carbon emissions under the hypothesis of a strong coalition of food and energy agents. © Pavin Banternghansa, Decarb Lux, WS 2022

Sources: Food and Agriculture Organization of the United Nations (UN FAO), IEA Net Zero Emission and LUX energy and climate plan

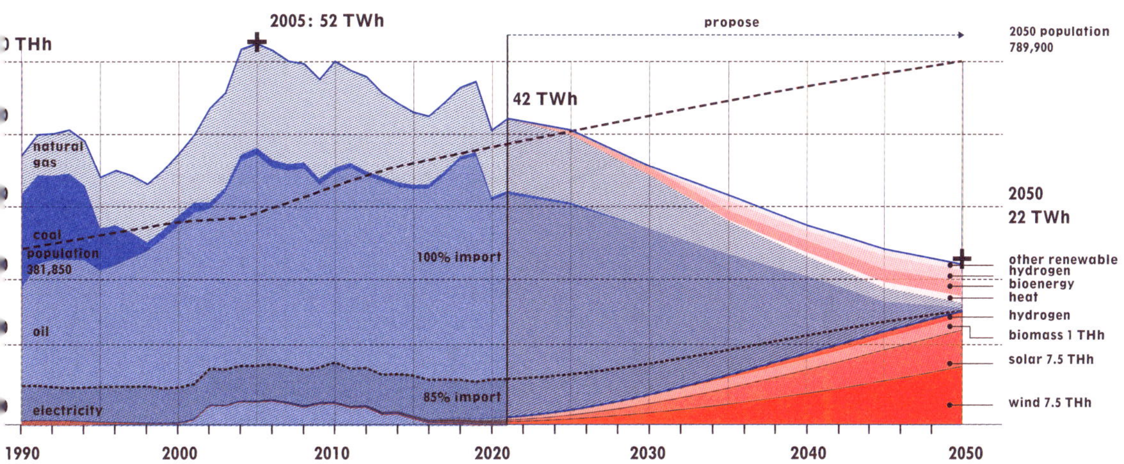

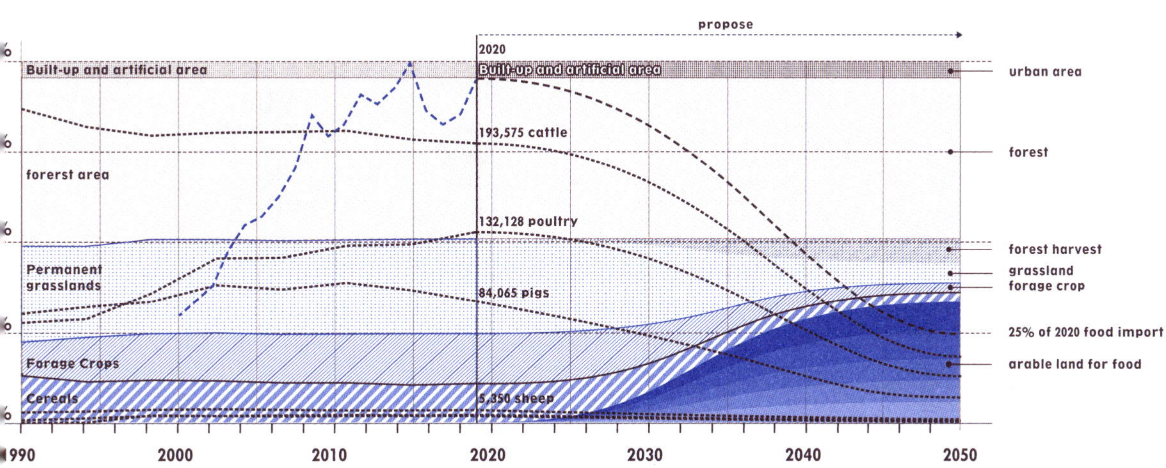

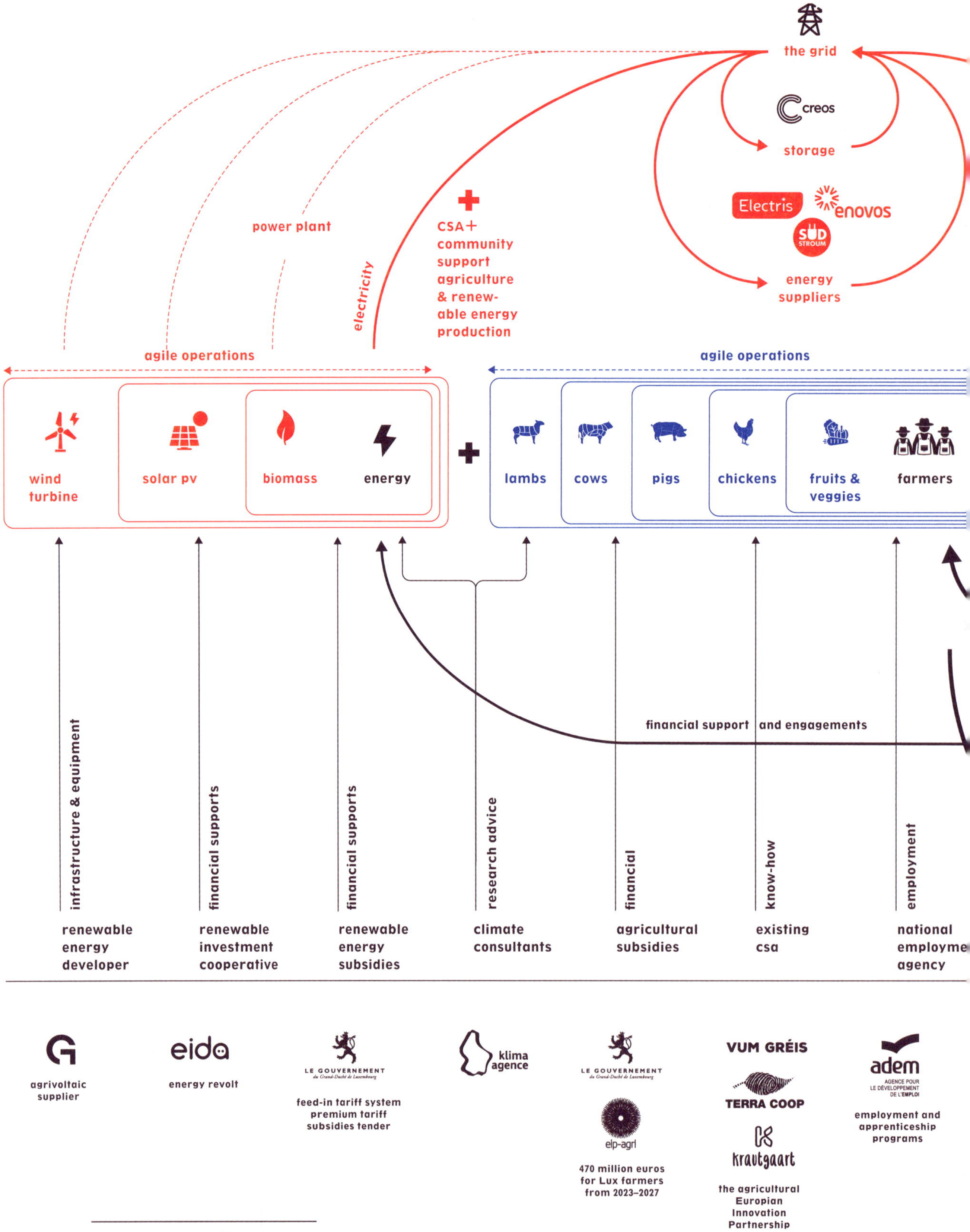

PROJECT: "FOOD × POWER" BY PAVIN BANTERNGHANSA

[07] Considered human and non-human actors and their inter-actions. © Pavin Banternghansa, Decarb Lux, WS 2022

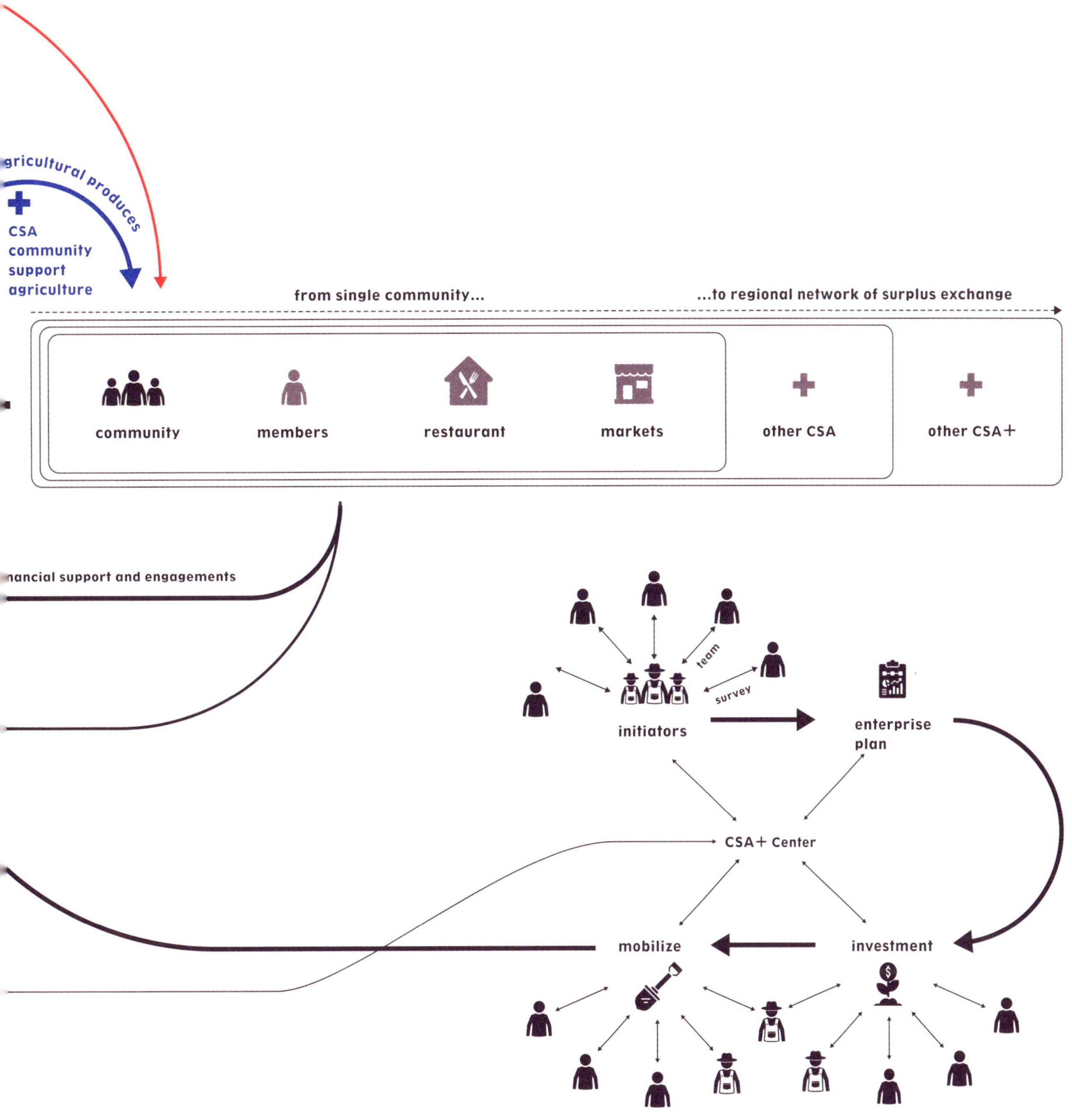

gricultural produces
CSA
community
support
agriculture
from single community...
...to regional network of surplus exchange
community
members
restaurant
markets
other CSA
other CSA+
nancial support and engagements
team
survey
initiators
enterprise
plan
CSA+ Center
mobilize
investment

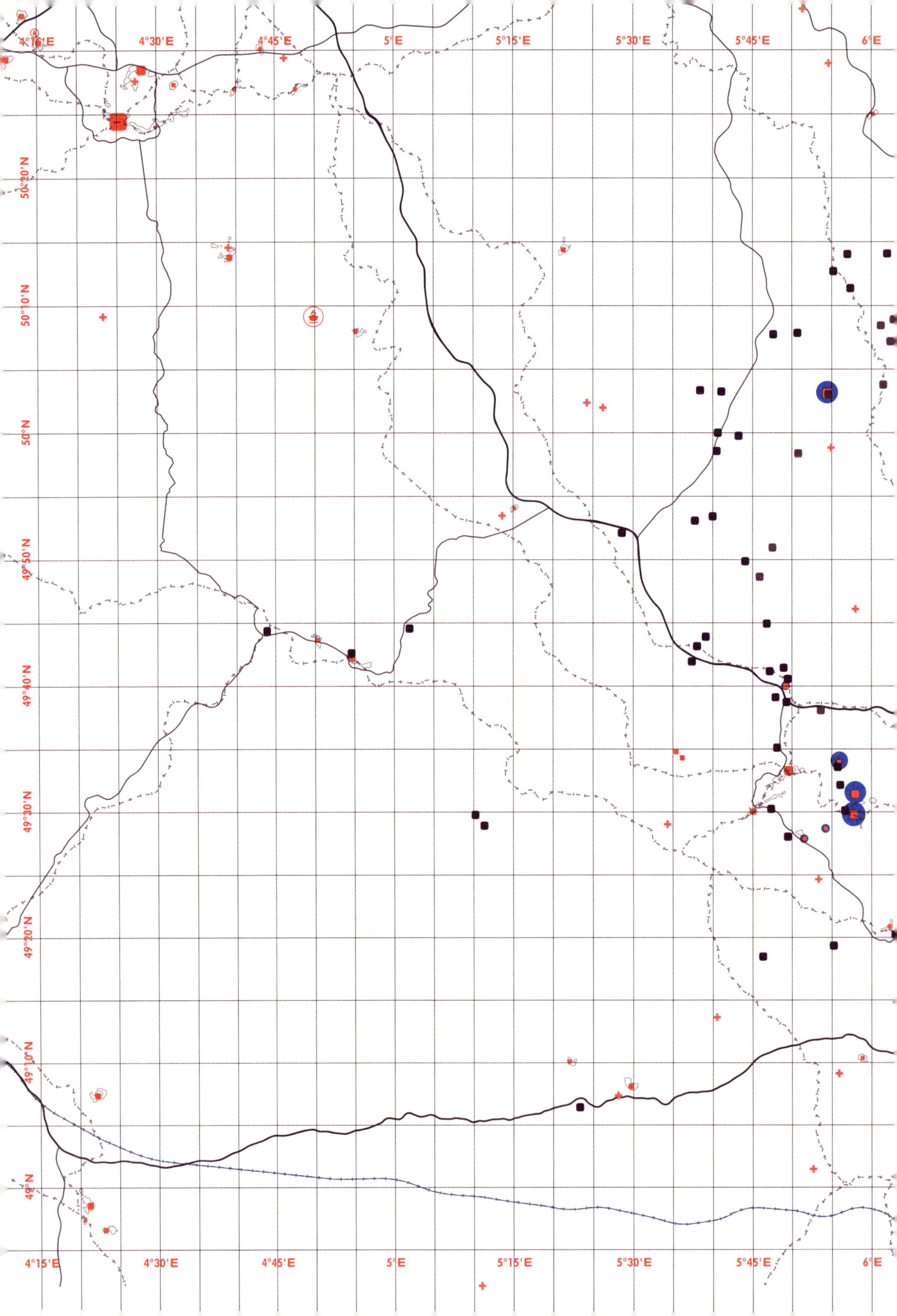
4°30'E
4°45'E
5°E
5°15'E
5°30'E
5°45'E
6°E
50°20'N
50°10'N
50°N
49°50'N
49°40'N
49°30'N
49°20'N
49°10'N
49°N
4°15'E
4°30'E
4°45'E
5°E
5°15'E
5°30'E
5°45'E
6°E

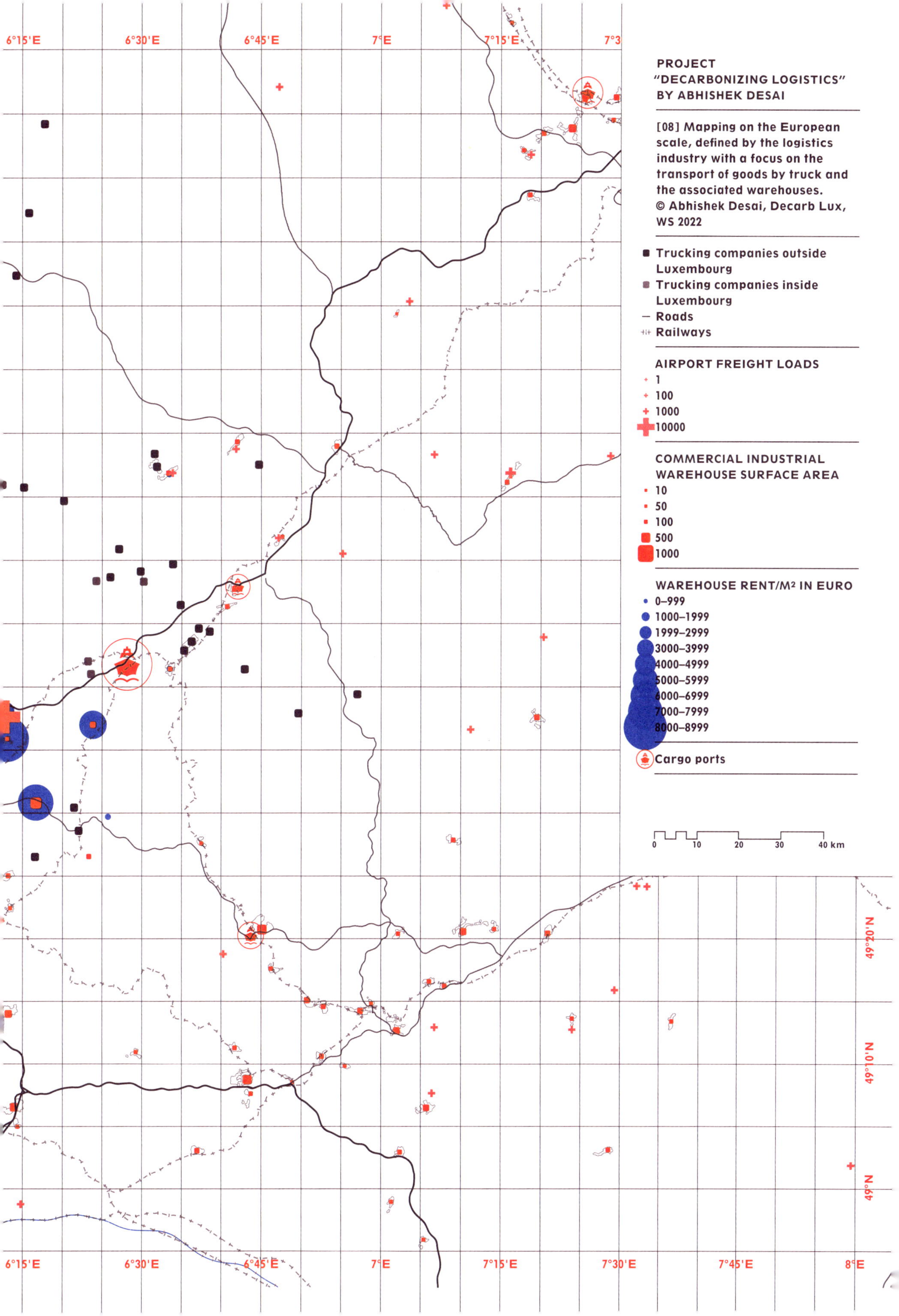

PROJECT "DECARBONIZING LOGISTICS" BY ABHISHEK DESAI

[08] Mapping on the European scale, defined by the logistics industry with a focus on the transport of goods by truck and the associated warehouses. © Abhishek Desai, Decarb Lux, WS 2022

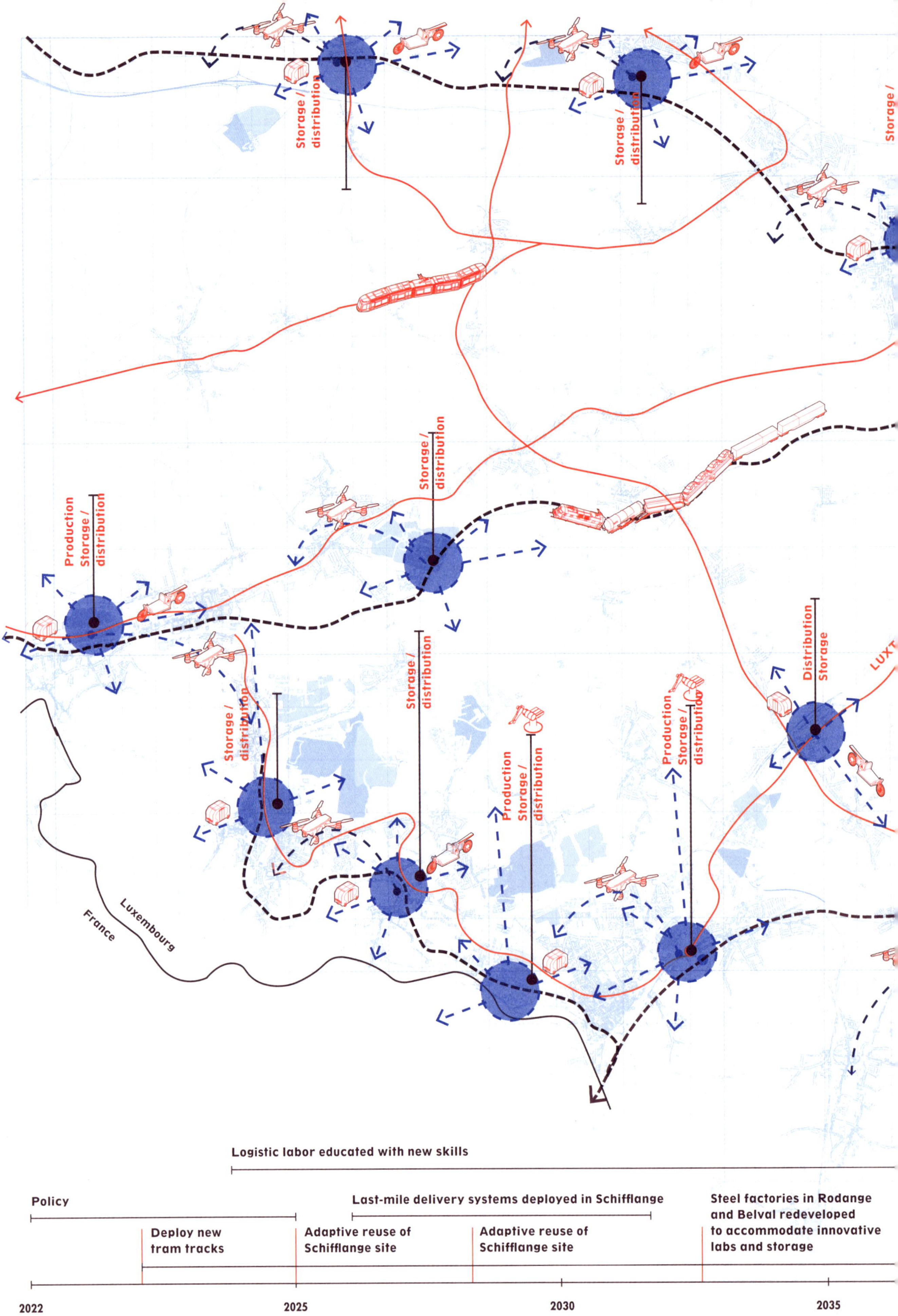
Storage / distribution
Storage / distribution
Storage / distribution
Production
Storage / distribution
Storage / distribution
Storage / distribution
Distribution
Storage
Production
Storage / distribution
Production
Storage / distribution
Luxembourg
France
Logistic labor educated with new skills
Policy
Last-mile delivery systems deployed in Schifflange
Steel factories in Rodange and Belval redeveloped to accommodate innovative labs and storage
Deploy new tram tracks
Adaptive reuse of Schifflange site
Adaptive reuse of Schifflange site
2022
2025
2030
2035

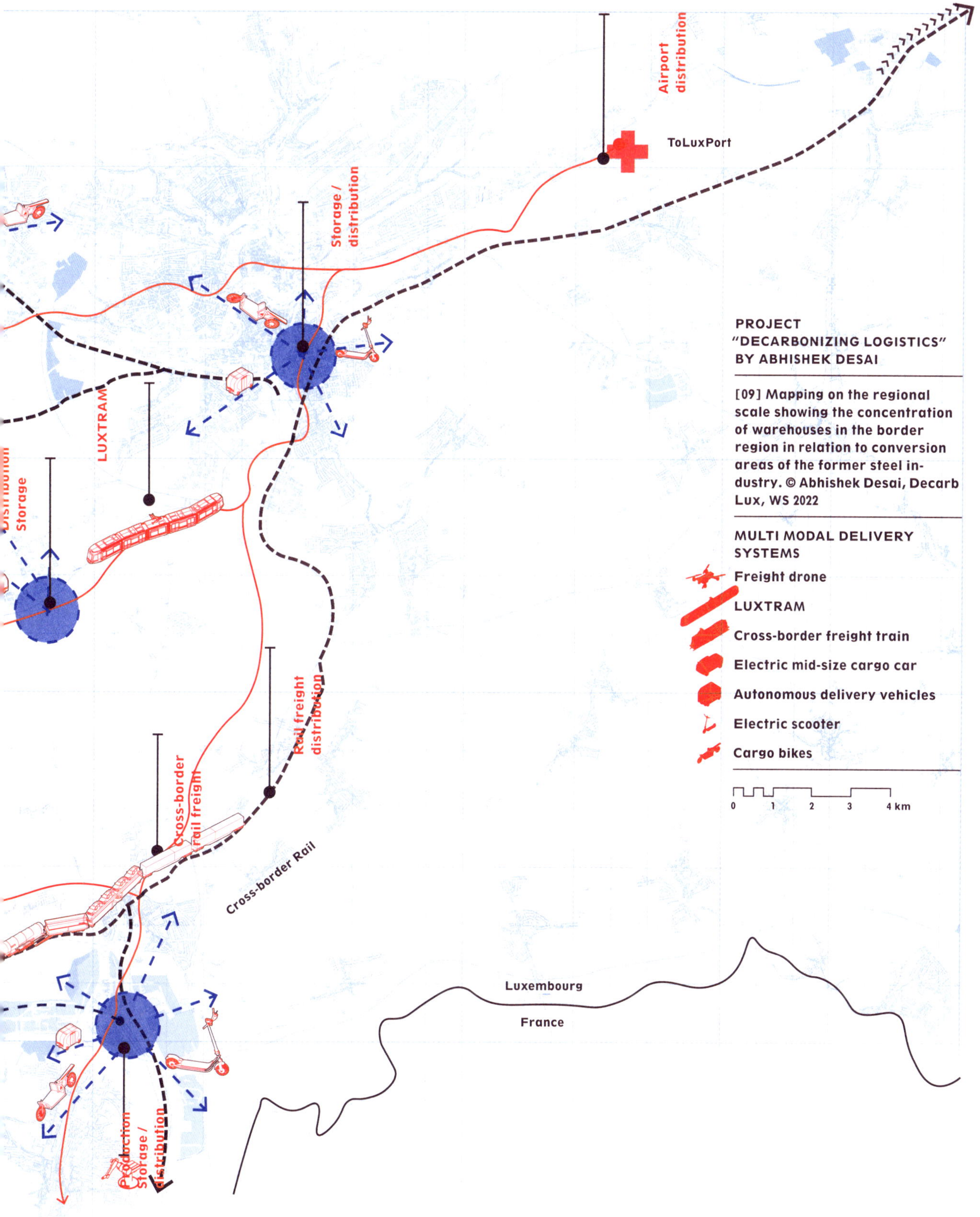

PROJECT "DECARBONIZING LOGISTICS" BY ABHISHEK DESAI

[09] Mapping on the regional scale showing the concentration of warehouses in the border region in relation to conversion areas of the former steel industry. © Abhishek Desai, Decarb Lux, WS 2022

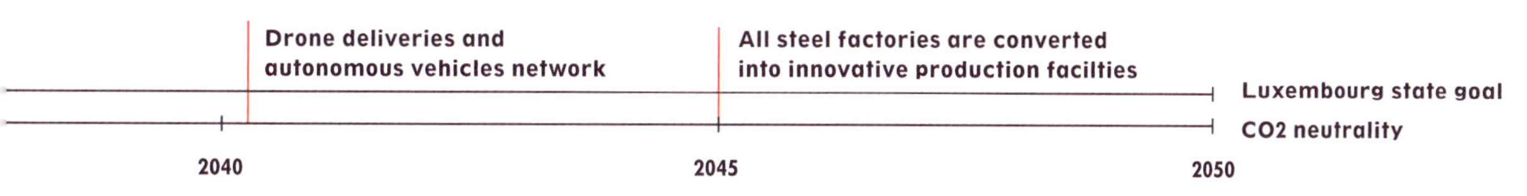

PROJECT
"DECARBONIZING LOGISTICS"
BY ABHISHEK DESAI

[11] Perspective visualization on the scale of the building, showing the conversion of a former steel plant into a hub for last-mile freight transport by tramway. © Abhishek Desai, Decarb Lux, WS 2022

PROJECT
"DECARBONIZING LOGISTICS"
BY ABHISHEK DESAI

[10] Section on the scale of the site showing the refurbishment of the former steel production site into a mobility and production hub. © Abhishek Desai, Decarb Lux, WS 2022

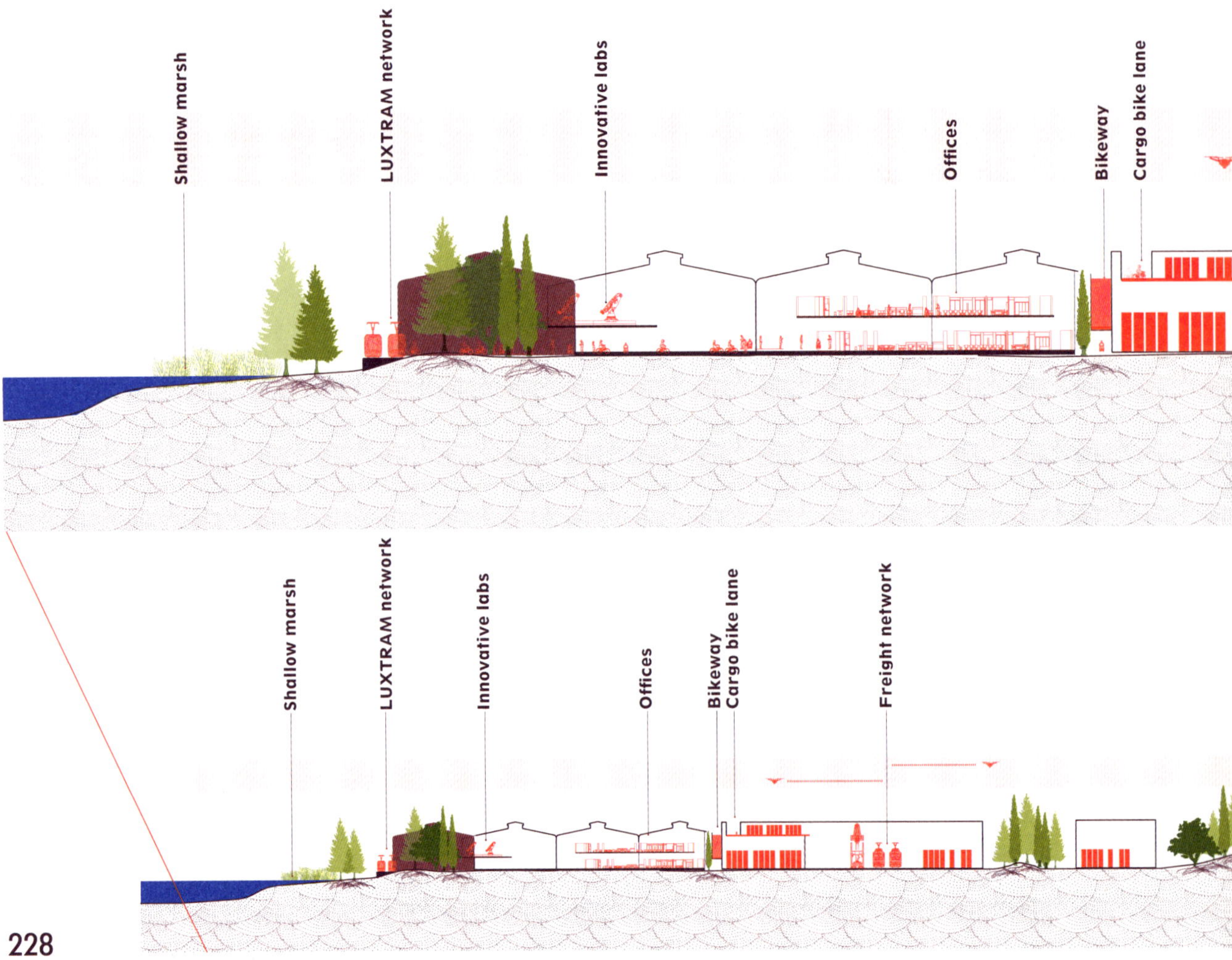

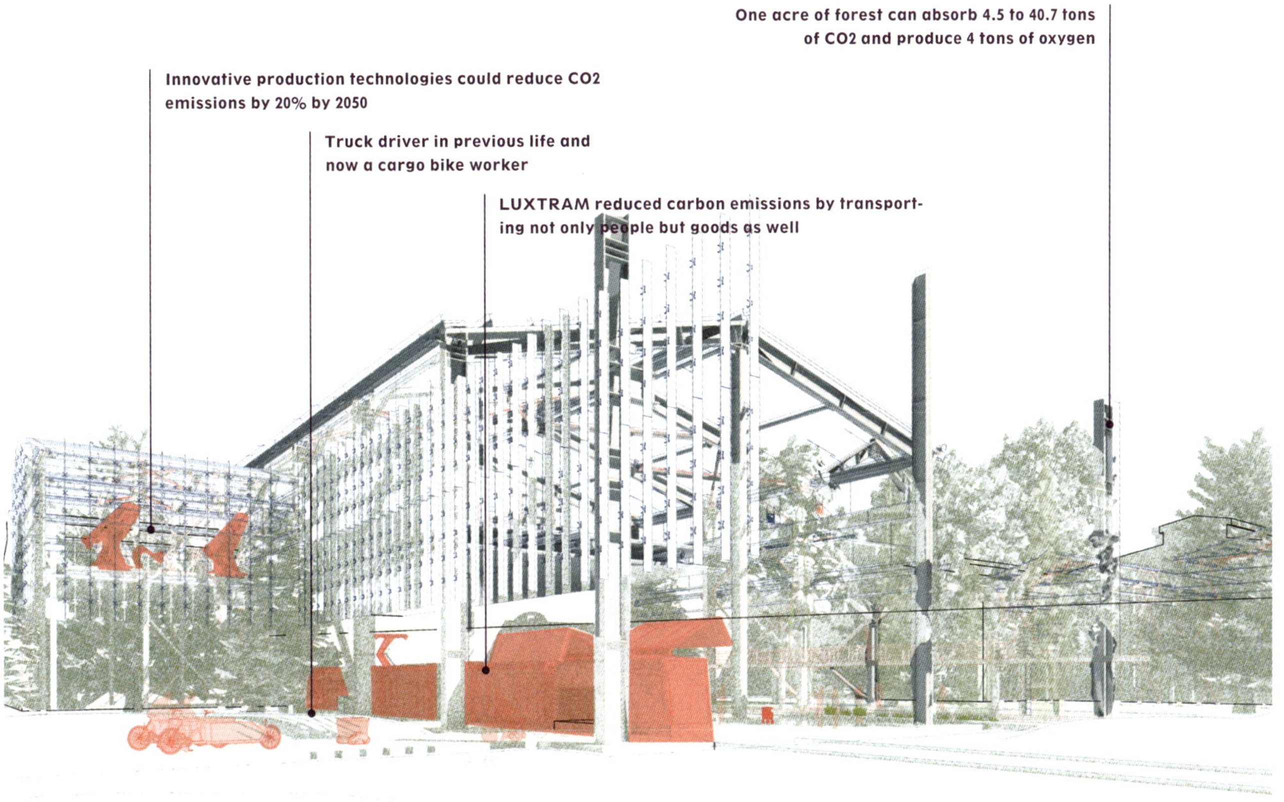
One acre of forest can absorb 4.5 to 40.7 tons of CO2 and produce 4 tons of oxygen
Innovative production technologies could reduce CO2 emissions by 20% by 2050
Truck driver in previous life and now a cargo bike worker
LUXTRAM reduced carbon emissions by transporting not only people but goods as well

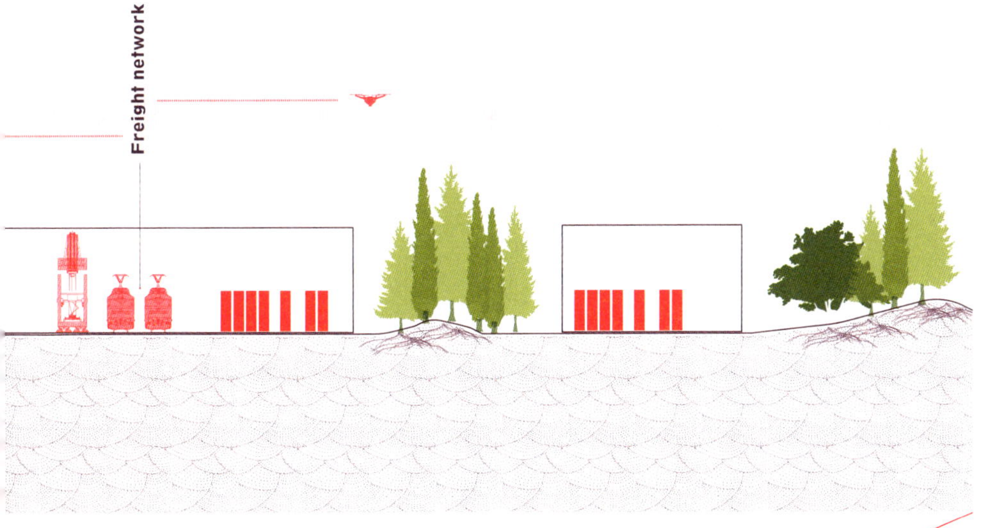
Freight network

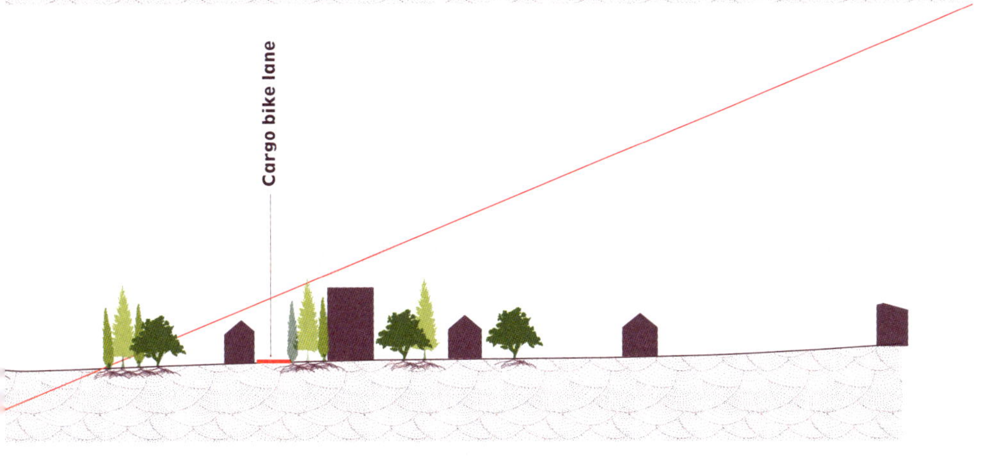
Cargo bike lane

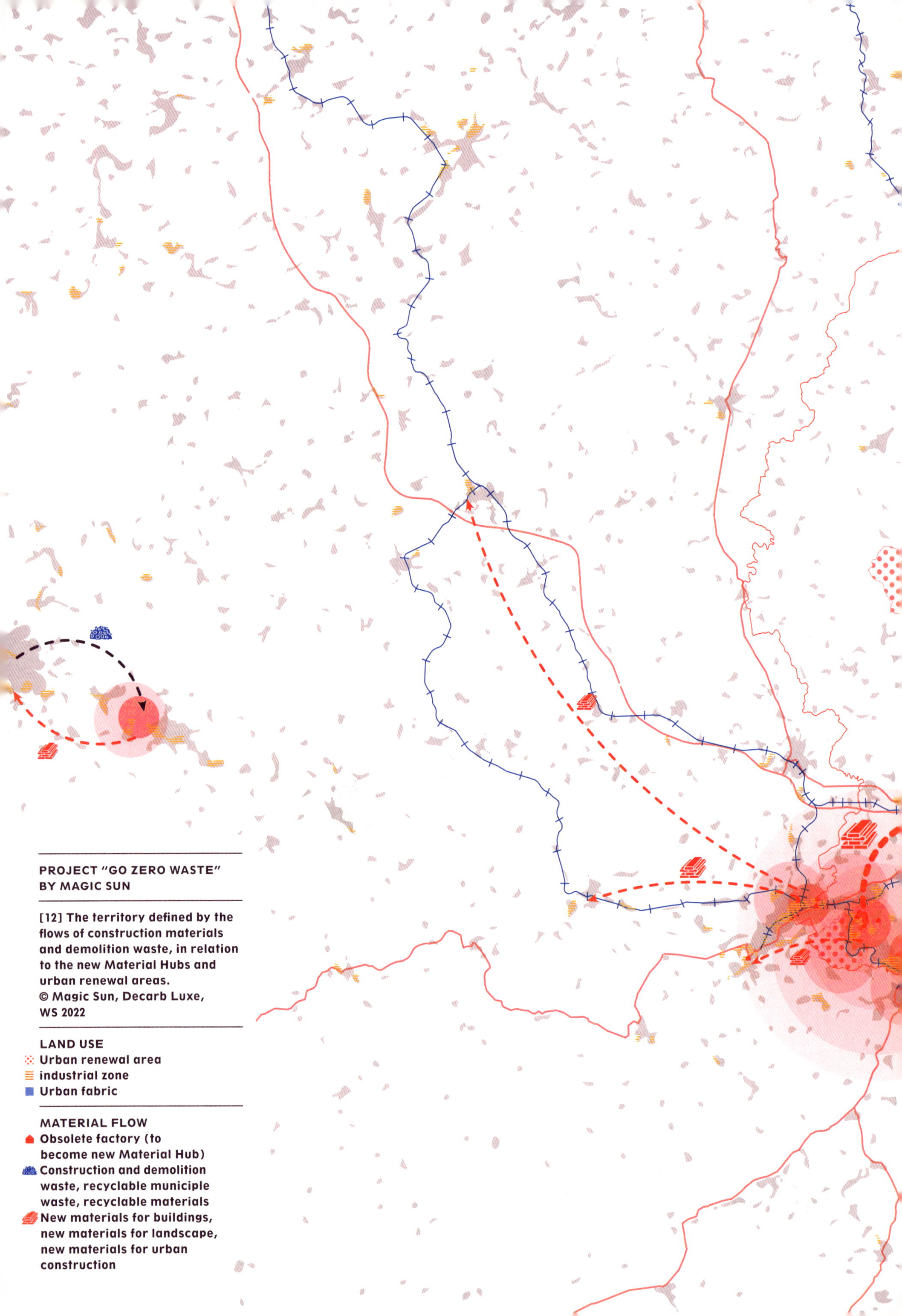

PROJECT "GO ZERO WASTE" BY MAGIC SUN

[12] The territory defined by the flows of construction materials and demolition waste, in relation to the new Material Hubs and urban renewal areas.
© Magic Sun, Decarb Luxe, WS 2022

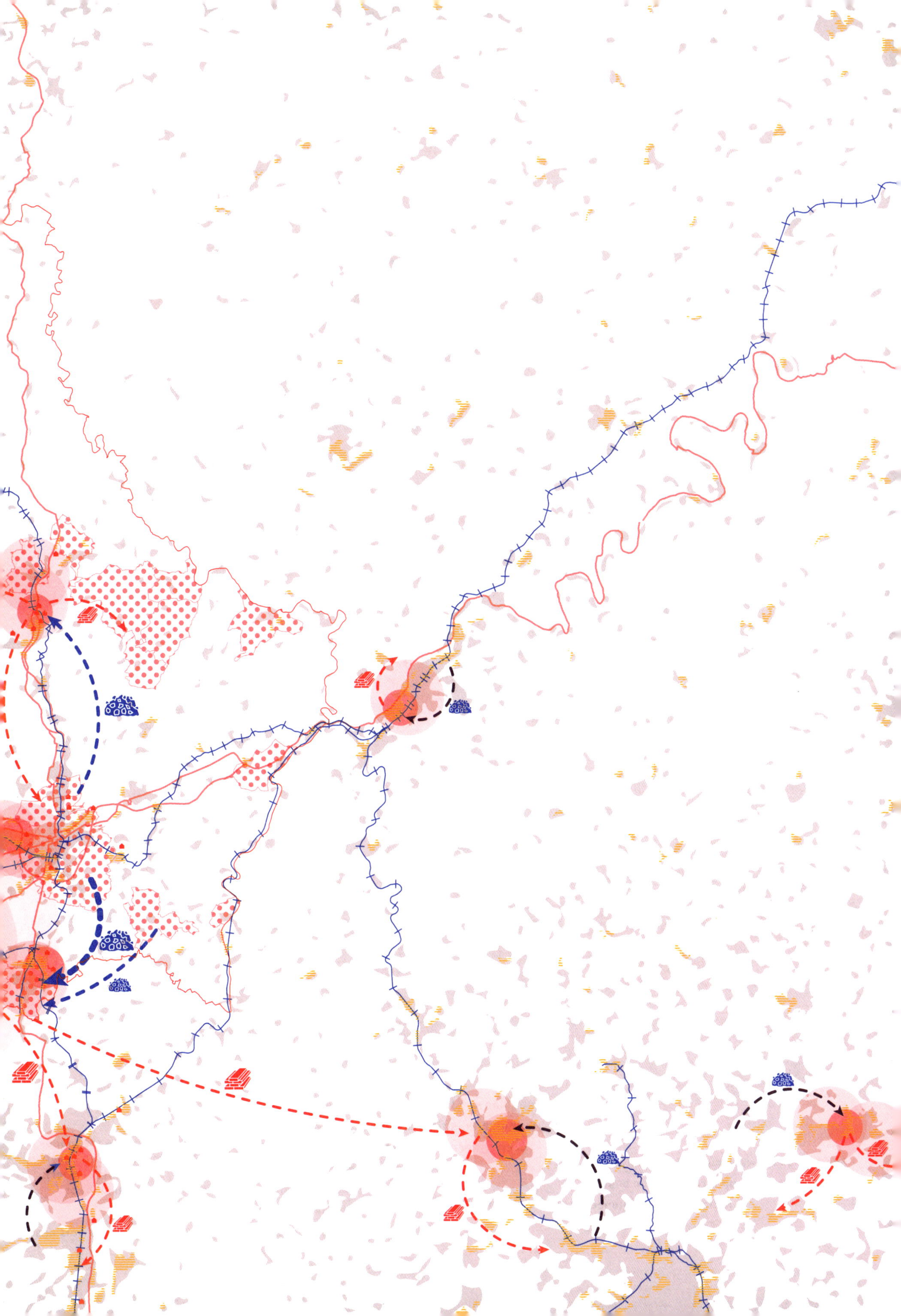

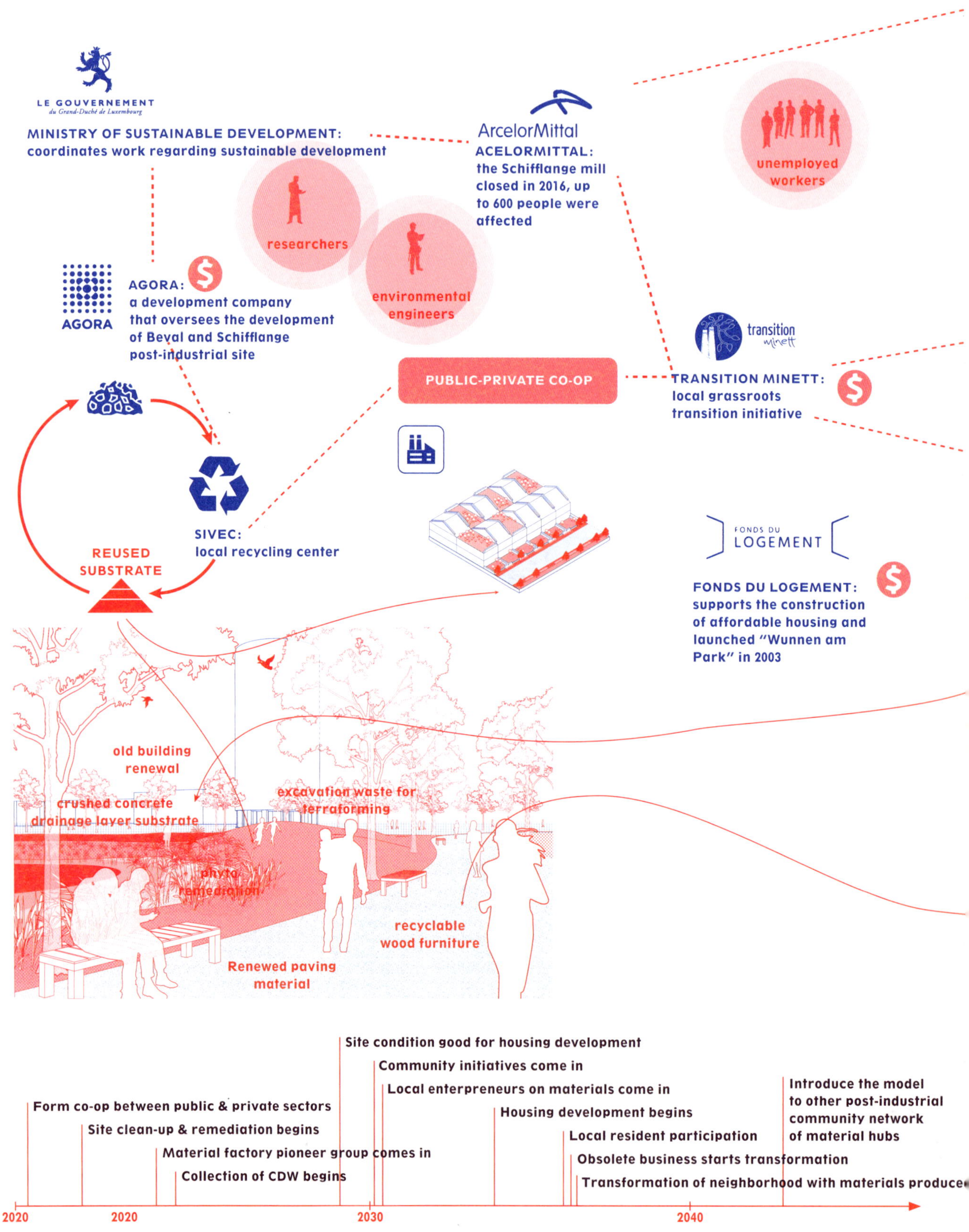
LE GOUVERNEMENT du Grand-Duché de Luxembourg
MINISTRY OF SUSTAINABLE DEVELOPMENT: coordinates work regarding sustainable development
ArcelorMittal
ACELORMITTAL: the Schifflange mill closed in 2016, up to 600 people were affected
unemployed workers
researchers
environmental engineers
AGORA
AGORA: a development company that oversees the development of Beval and Schifflange post-industrial site
transition minett
PUBLIC-PRIVATE CO-OP
TRANSITION MINETT: local grassroots transition initiative
SIVEC: local recycling center
REUSED SUBSTRATE
FONDS DU LOGEMENT
FONDS DU LOGEMENT: supports the construction of affordable housing and launched "Wunnen am Park" in 2003
old building renewal
crushed concrete drainage layer substrate
excavation waste for terraforming
phyto remediation
recyclable wood furniture
Renewed paving material
Site condition good for housing development
Community initiatives come in
Local enterpreneurs on materials come in
Form co-op between public & private sectors
Housing development begins
Introduce the model to other post-industrial community network of material hubs
Site clean-up & remediation begins
Local resident participation
Material factory pioneer group comes in
Obsolete business starts transformation
Collection of CDW begins
Transformation of neighborhood with materials produce
2020
2020
2030
2040

PROJECT "GO ZERO WASTE" BY MAGIC SUN

[13] Mapping the envisioned coalitions of the different agents involved in the renewal of the construction and demolition cycle in Luxembourg. © Magic Sun, Decarb Lux, WS 2022

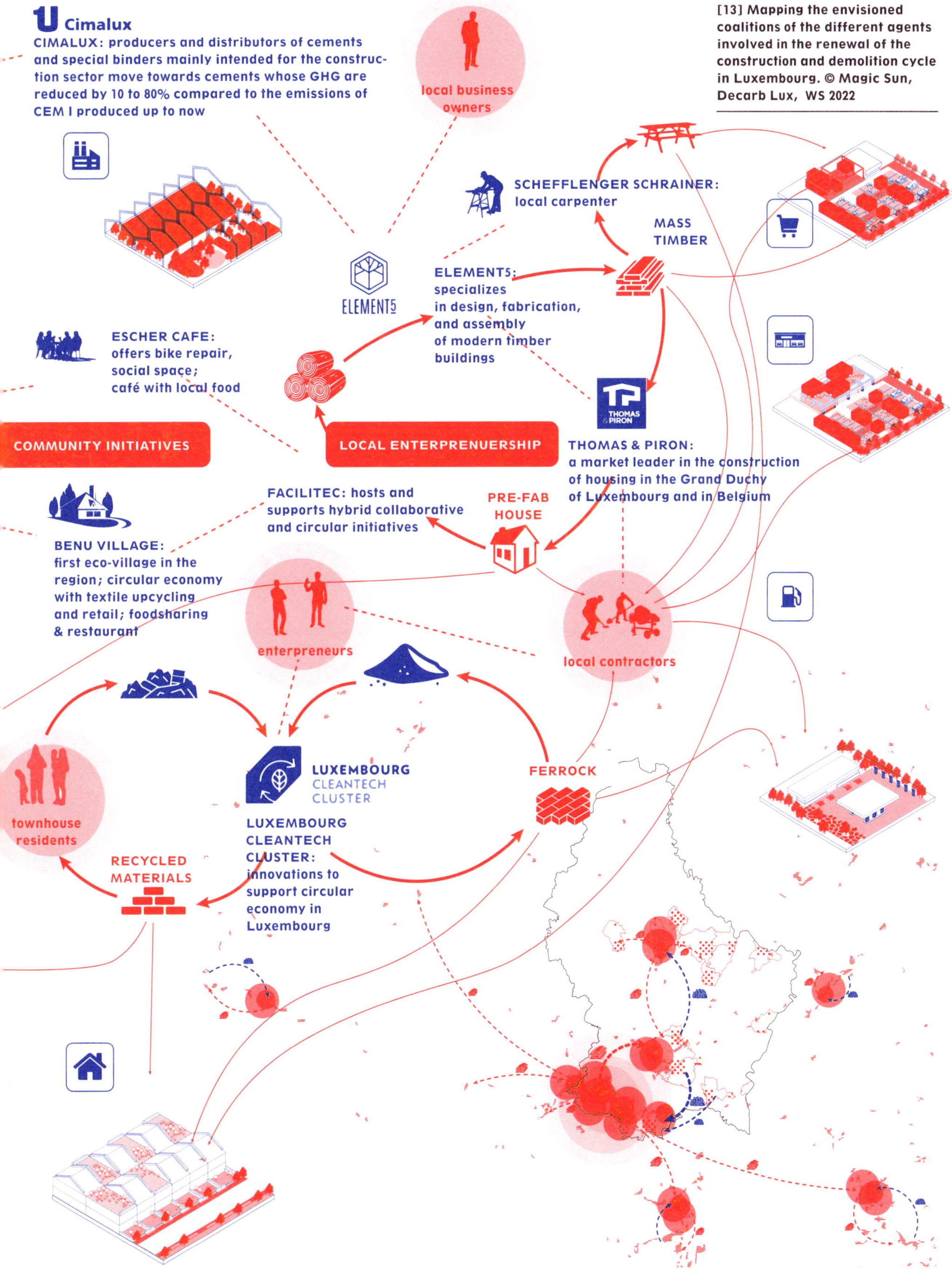

PROJECT "GO ZERO WASTE" BY MAGIC SUN

[14] Former industrial area transformed into a material hub where building materials are produced and recycled for use in nearby urban renewal areas. © Magic Sun, Decarb Lux, WS 2022

SCHOOL
LOCAL CARPENTER
Mass timber
FURNITURE FACTORY
TY HALL

Stefan Bendiks, Aglaée Degros

PROJECT "GO ZERO WASTE" BY MAGIC SUN

---

[15] Redevelopment of the waste treatment site of the steel plant into a near-natural site with new mixed office and residential use. © Magic Sun, Decarb Lux, WS 2022

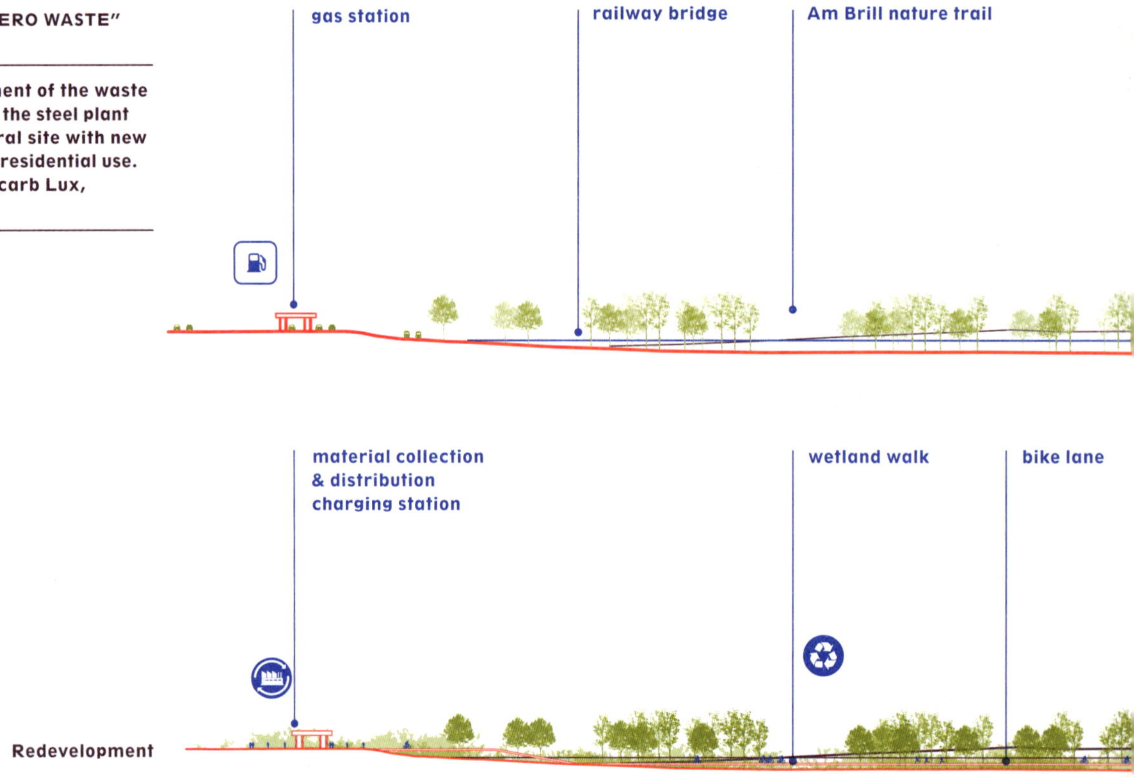

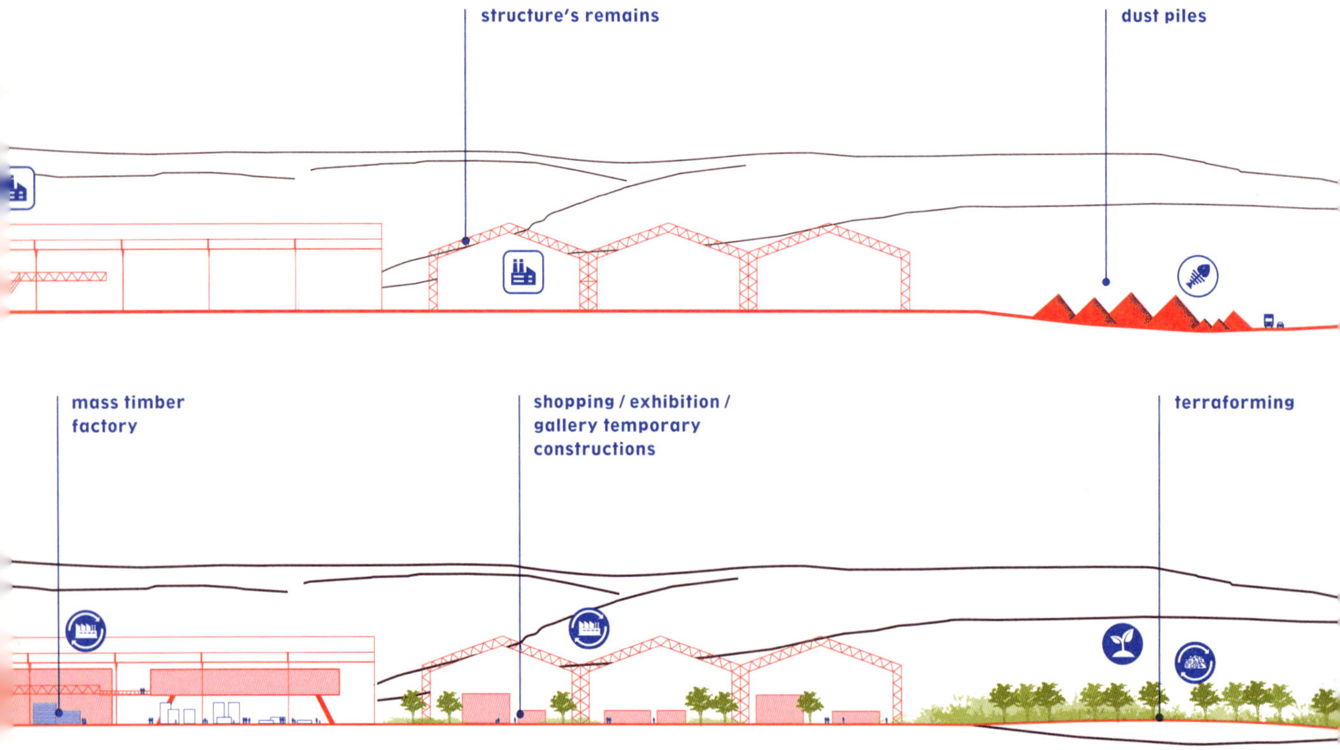

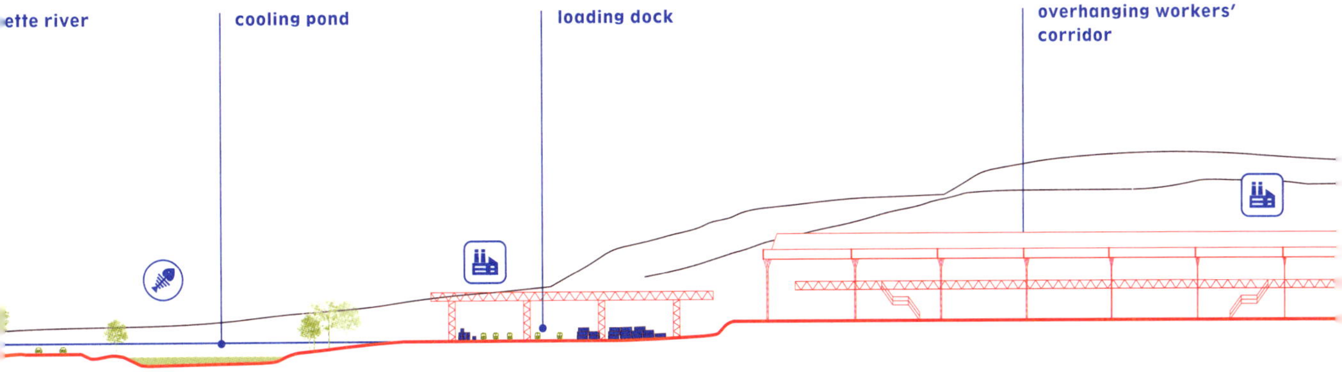
ette river
cooling pond
loading dock
overhanging workers' corridor

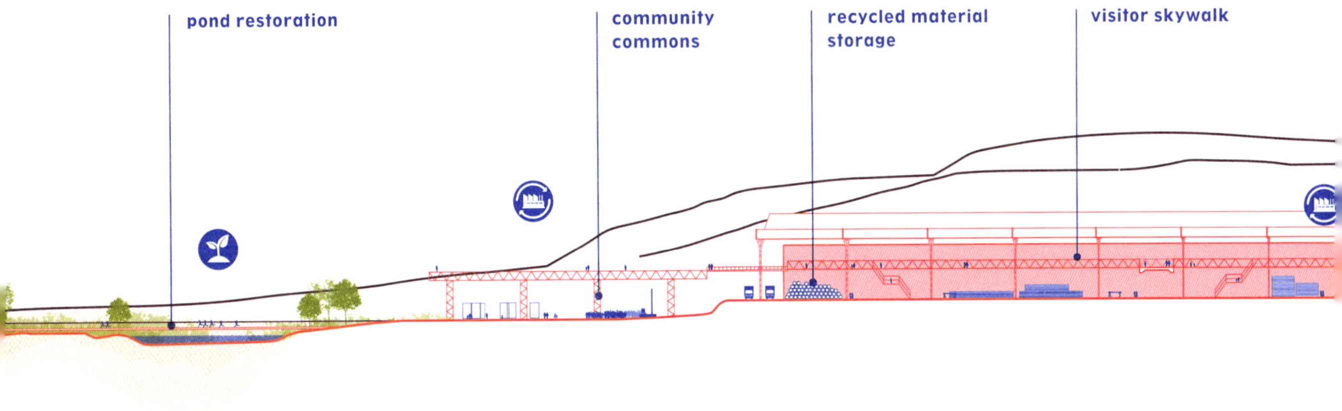
pond restoration
community commons
recycled material storage
visitor skywalk

discharge pond
Alzette river

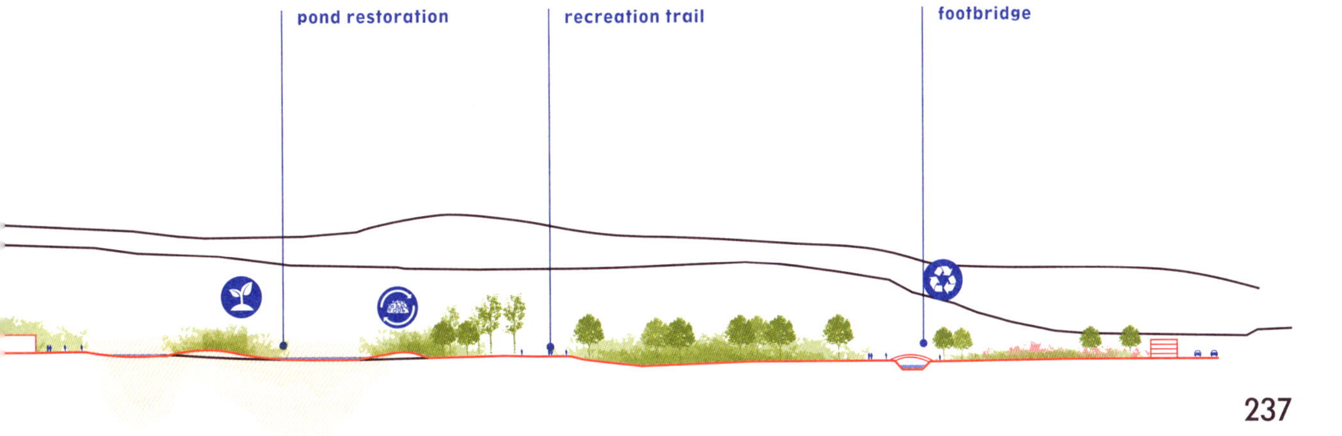
pond restoration
recreation trail
footbridge

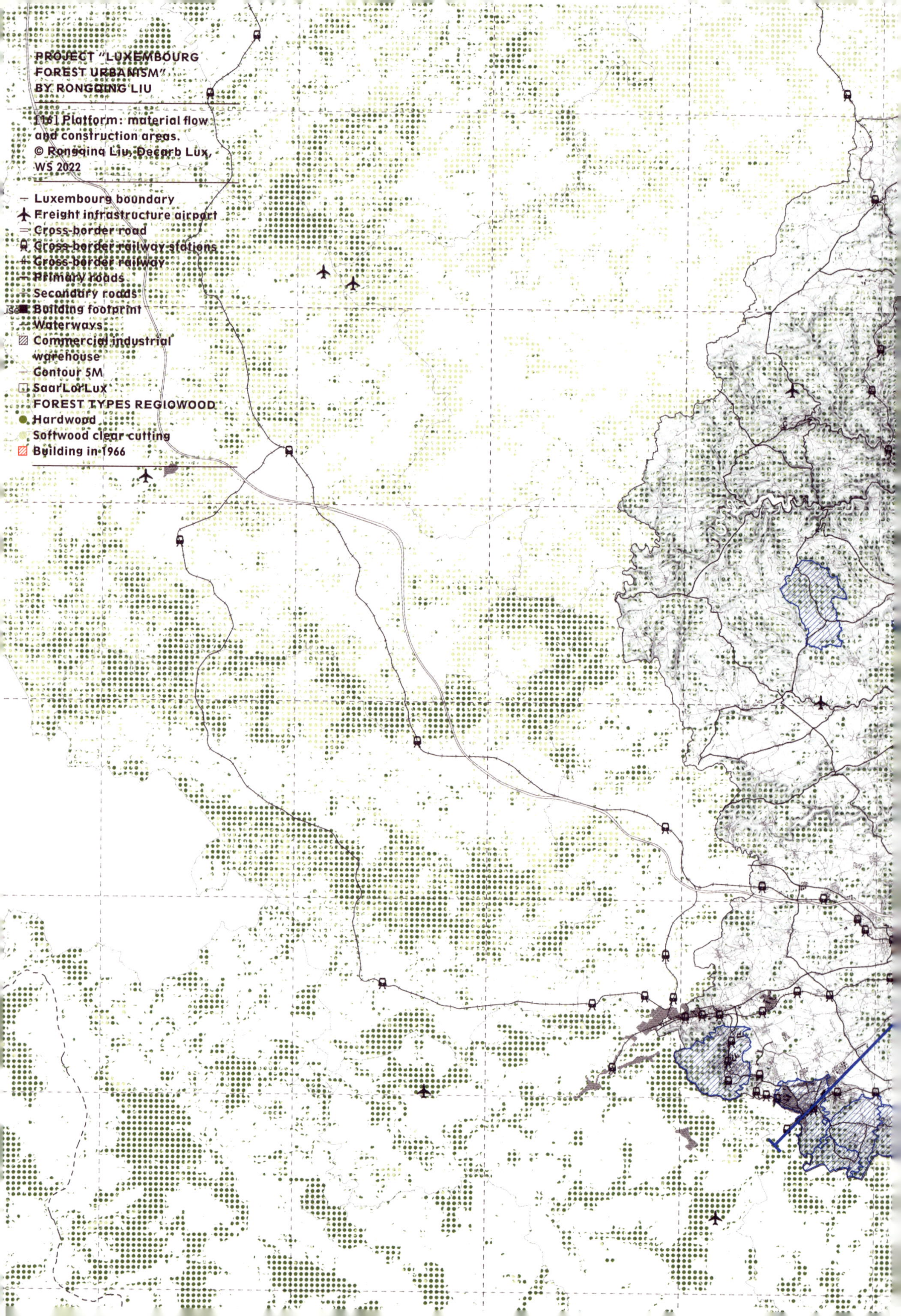

PROJECT "LUXEMBOURG FOREST URBANISM" BY RONGQING LIU

[16] Platform: material flow and construction areas. © Rongqing Liu, Decarb Lux, WS 2022

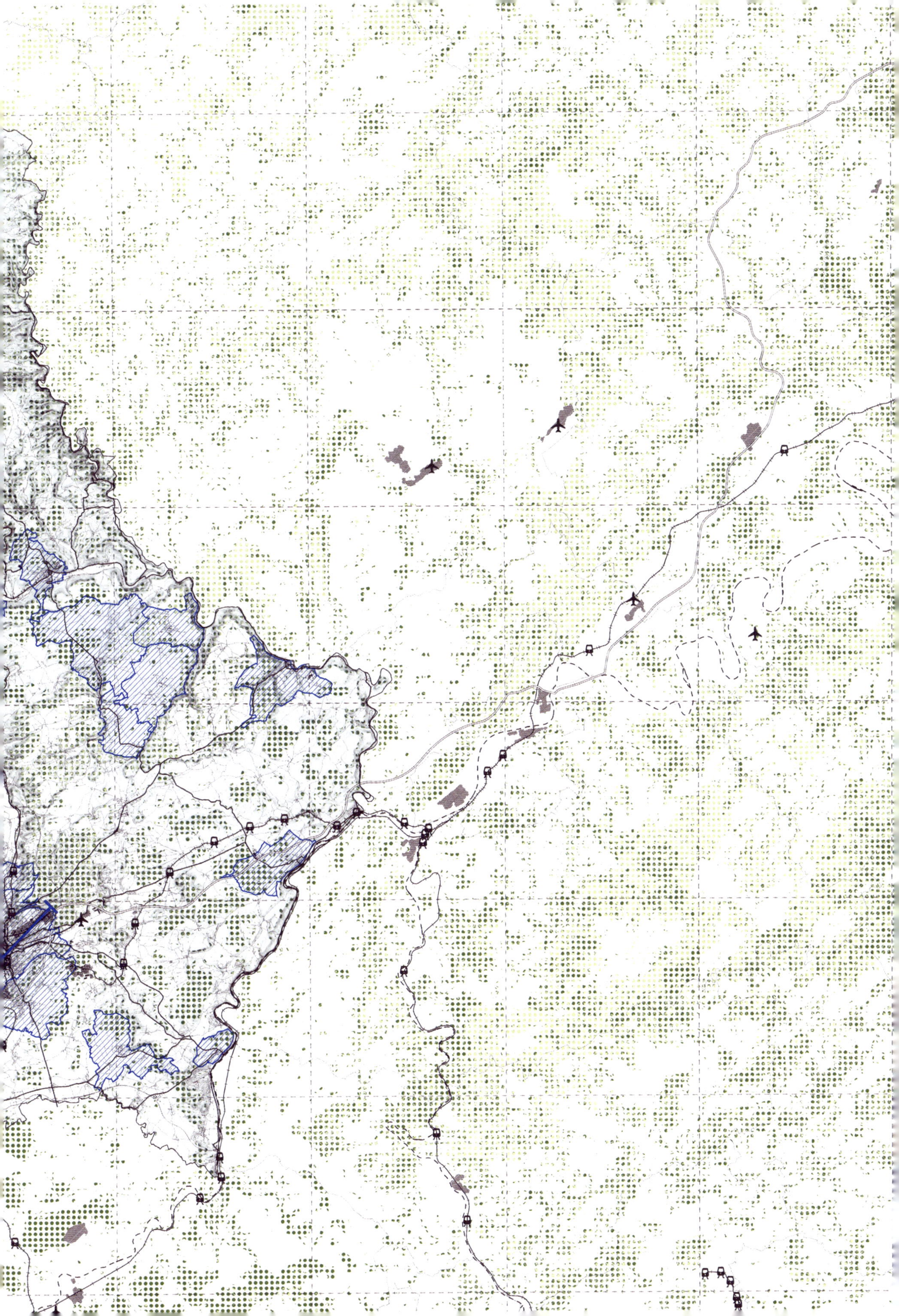

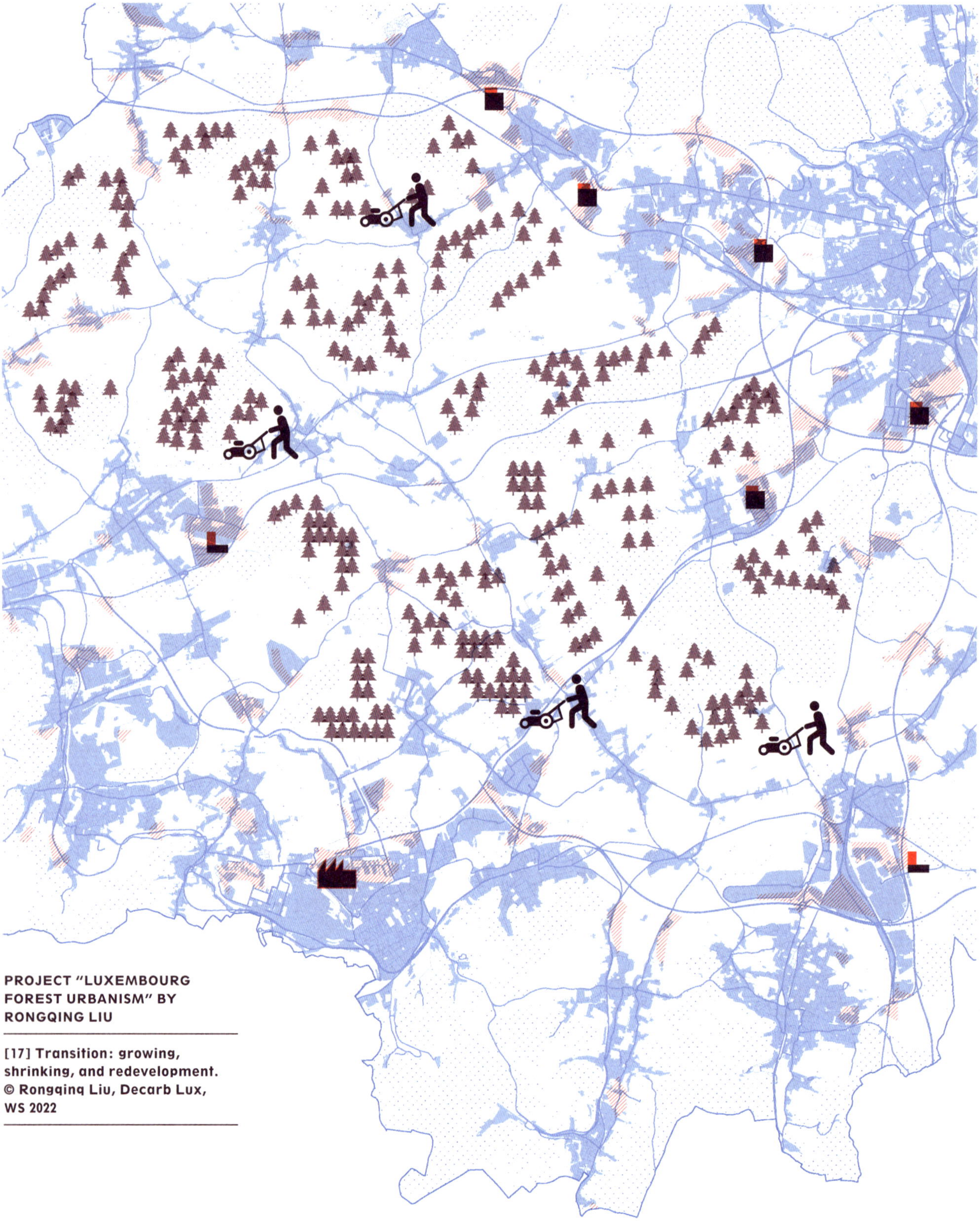

PROJECT "LUXEMBOURG FOREST URBANISM" BY RONGQING LIU

[17] Transition: growing, shrinking, and redevelopment. © Rongqing Liu, Decarb Lux, WS 2022

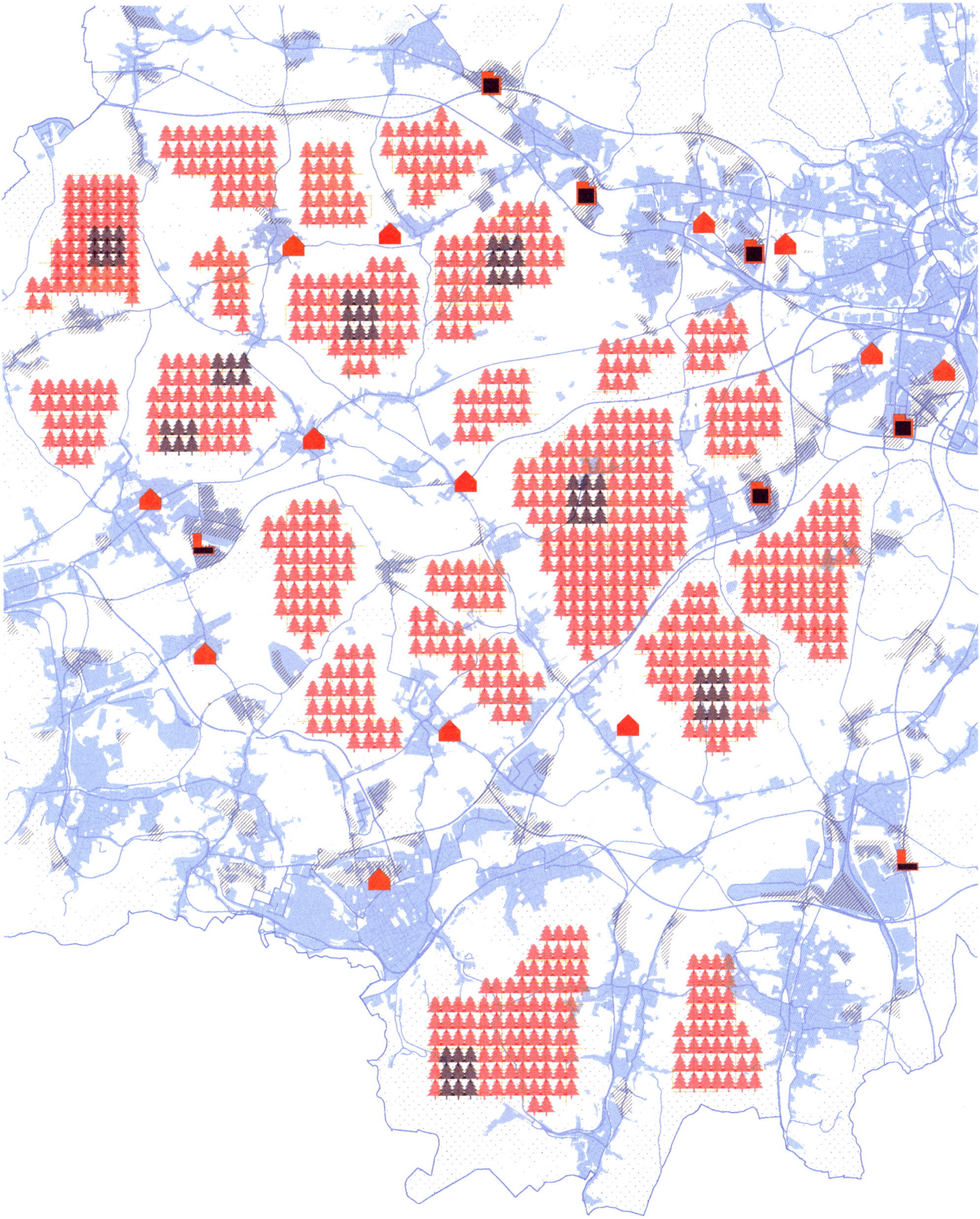

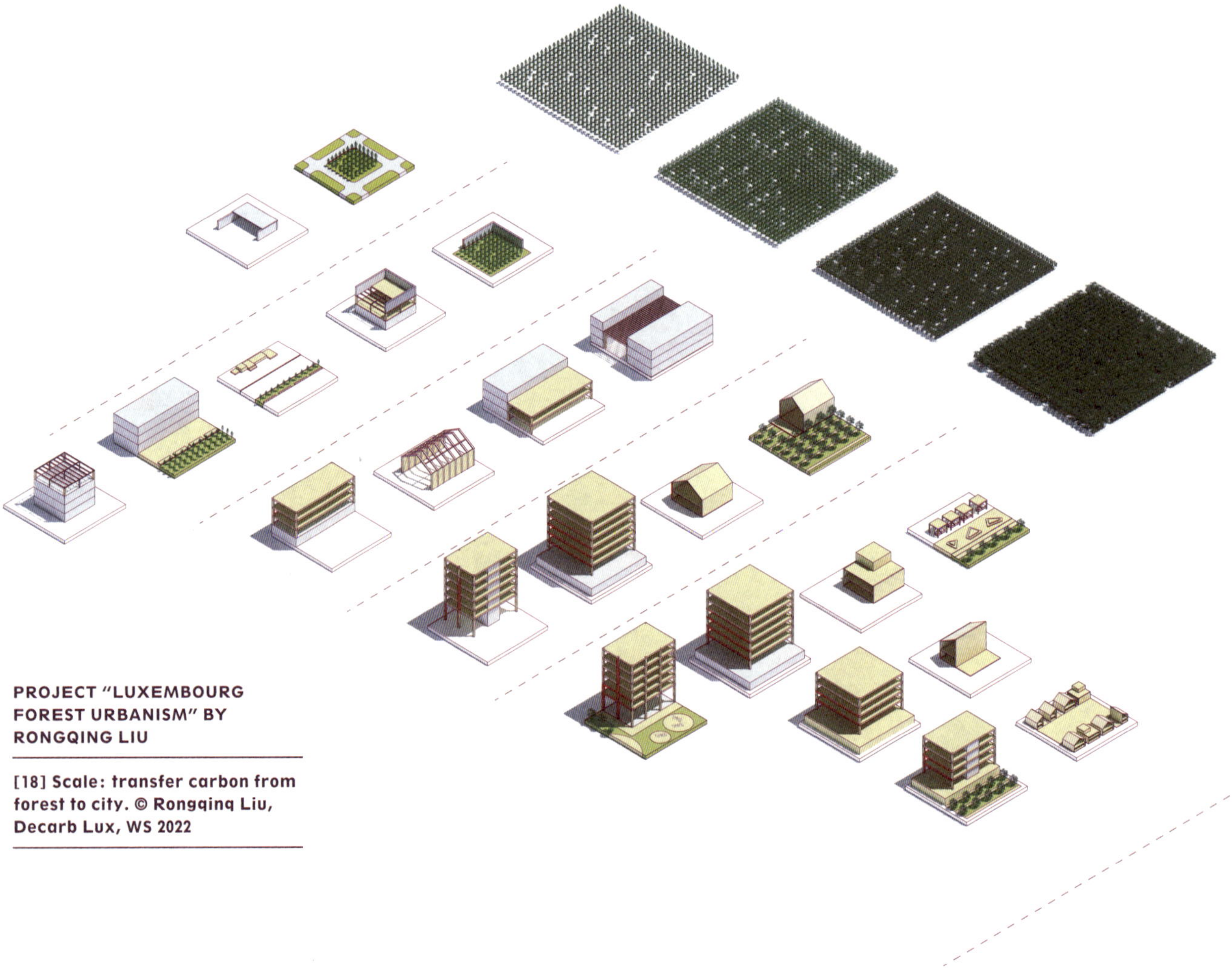

PROJECT "LUXEMBOURG FOREST URBANISM" BY RONGQING LIU

[18] Scale: transfer carbon from forest to city. © Rongqing Liu, Decarb Lux, WS 2022

The Nature of the City of Nature

Eva Pfannes, Jesse Honsa

After a long era of unprecedented economic growth generating an over-expansion of built space, now is the time to protect and reconstruct nature. In other words, to dedicate oneself fully and as a matter of urgency to the reproduction of nature as a long-term objective.

Mainstream economics relies on a "circular flow model," identifying how money, goods, and services move through the market. What is remarkably absent from this model however is nature—the seemingly irrelevant backdrop to human activity. This economic system, demanding constant growth, fails to recognize that its operations are playing out on a planet with finite resources. The conflict presents itself through the challenge of surmounting natural disasters but, even then, there is an assumption that the innovative power of humans and the regulating power of the market will fix everything. To challenge this paradigm, Kate Raworth (2017) proposes a new model for understanding economic activity that embeds the question of nature, recognizing that human welfare ultimately depends on energy provided by the sun, matter extracted from the earth, and waste produced.

But this raises another question: what is nature? Our understanding of nature has been partially crafted by Descartes's mind–body dualism. The world was composed of "thinking things" (mostly white men) and "extended things" (women, children, Indigenous communities, and nature). As Patel and Moore (2017, pp. 51–58) argue, "society" was invented in opposition to nature during the emergence of capitalism, as a handy organizing principle. Nature was pushed to the margins, taken for granted as a free resource. As they point out, Descartes (1985, pp. 142–143) himself claimed that "we must become the master and possessor of nature".

This definition of nature is only one of many. In a recent article, Ducarme and Couvet (2020) illustrate how different philosophical traditions have treated nature as a material reality independent of human activity, the whole universe, the inner character of something, or the specific force at the core of life and change. Elsewhere, in the works of Heraclitus, Hegel, Nietzsche, and Darwin, nature is concerned with the process of evolution. In our own work, we rely on this latter definition to understand nature as something dynamic, deploying natural processes to heal and repair the territory. Rather than "conserving" nature by isolating it from the city, we strive to incorporate nature symbiotically and (re)solve problems locally.

[01] *Source de Friche*: Drinking water fountain filtered by plants. OOZE (Eva Pfannes & Sylvain Hartenberg) and Marjetica Potrč © OOZE, 2013

[02] *Of Soil and Water*: King's Cross Pond Club, a natural swimming pool in a pioneer garden. OOZE (Eva Pfannes & Sylvain Hartenberg) and Marjetica Potrč © John Sturrock, 2016

[03] *Água Carioca*: inclusive public space vision in Morro da Formiga. © OOZE, 2017

We have developed several "urban prototypes" that demonstrate how natural processes can be integrated within urban processes. On an industrial wasteland in Brussels, we used helophyte plants and carbon filters which naturally treat polluted water. In the middle of this feral landscape stands a single hand pump, inviting visitors to taste the work of nature. Elsewhere, on a construction site in King's Cross, London, a swimming pond is cyclically cleaned without the need for chemicals. The joy of swimming is enriched with an awareness of how the body is connected to water, soil, plants, and the evolving city. Through such prototypes we challenge the notion of a manmade city at odds with its productive hinterlands. Rather, we seek to construct a new image of an "isotropic" city, composed of repeating patterns that allow processes to occur locally [01] [02].

ÁGUA CARIOCA

This idea of the isotropic city was also explored in Rio de Janeiro. Rio relies on an antiquated sewage system which pumps primary waste directly into the ocean just 2 kilometers from the coast, as well as treatment stations located far from the city. Within this large-scale and complex system, a great amount of waste is never dealt with, nor can

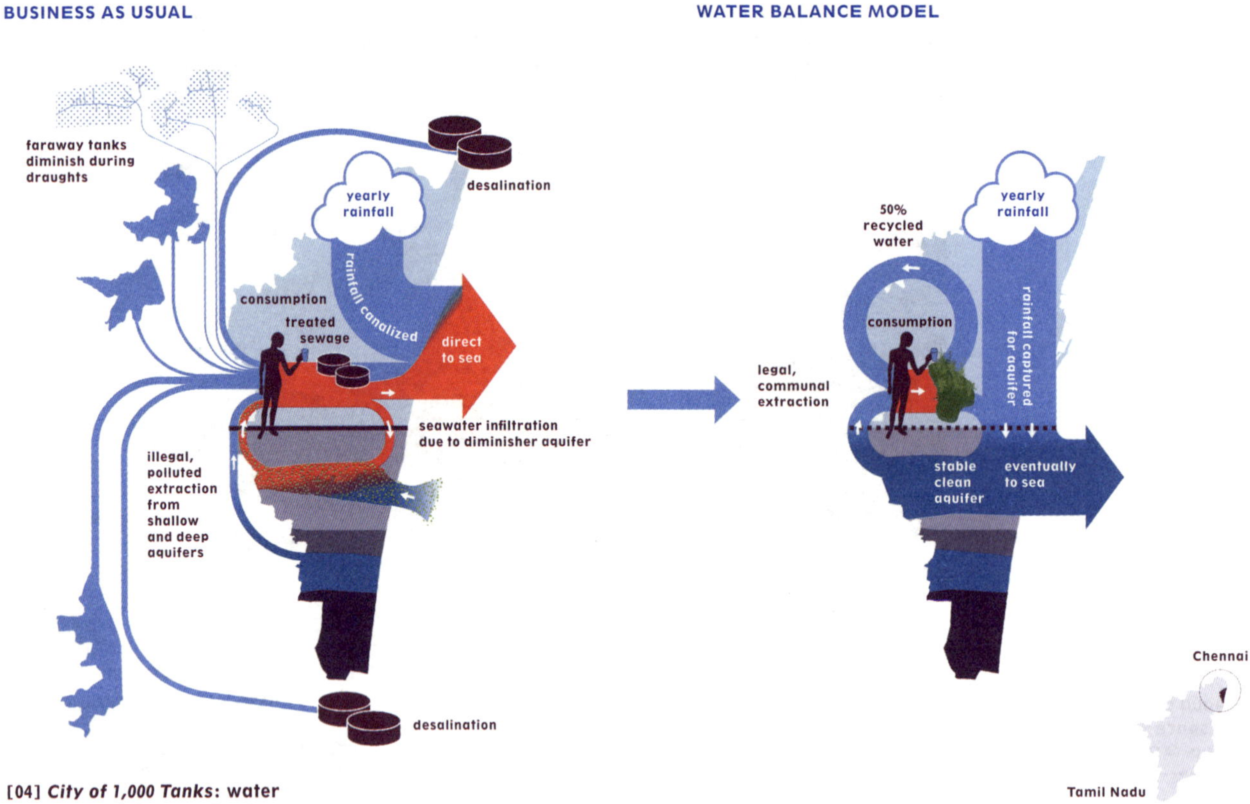

[04] ***City of 1,000 Tanks*****: water balance model versus business as usual. © OOZE, 2018**

citizens understand where their water goes. This model is akin to a human body with umbilical organs placed far outside its own remit. It would be much more efficient to bring the organs—the mechanisms that process this material—back inside. While the existing model is linear and produces waste, what is needed is a circular model wherein water is treated and reused locally.

Given Rio de Janeiro's climate, domestic wastewater could be treated with only 1.2 square meters of constructed wetland per person. Beds of gravel, helophyte plants, and septic tanks can be easily squeezed into existing open spaces—even, and especially, within informal settlements which currently have no existing sewerage system. Instead of many kilometers of sunken pipework, water treatment becomes an enjoyable green space. The research resulted in a series of proposals at different scales, from the building to the community to the city. The idea was tested in a pilot project in the Sítio Roberto Burle Marx, making visible and understandable how an amazing soup of microorganisms and plants are able to treat wastewater, returning it to an almost pristine state [03].

CITY OF 1,000 TANKS

For another project in India, we took a further step: connecting nature not only to urban systems, but to financial systems by considering how nature performs economically. The project was created as part of the Dutch Government's "Water as Leverage" initiative, which invests upfront to find innovative and bankable solutions for climate-related problems in several global cities. Chennai, in southeast India, has a monsoon climate characterized by alternating periods of extreme rainfall and extreme droughts. Residents find themselves "floating in floods and fighting for drops." This seasonal disparity is being exacerbated by climate change, but also by recent patterns of urbanization. Traditionally, Chennai was a smart city: relying not on artificial intelligence, but on an intelligent system of lakes and open temple tanks that collected monsoon rains, slowly dispersing the water to the soil during the remaining eight months of the year. But now, two thirds of the city are sealed with concrete and asphalt. The technological solution to excessive flooding was to build stormwater drains to expel the water into the ocean as quickly as possible. Yet this deprives the city of its water resources, and saline water from the rising sea levels penetrates the dry aquifer. In the meantime, much like in Rio, untreated wastewater pollutes the city's natural waterbodies.

We developed a "water balance model" which compares the flows of water, money, and carbon within different scenarios. We found that there are many hidden costs in the existing system, ranging from the money and carbon resources expended on transporting water across long distances, to the methane emissions from exposed sewage. Speaking to women in one neighborhood of around 10,000 inhabitants, we found that they spend four hours each day sourcing water—draining the economy of productivity and depriving women of social and professional advancement [04].

By contrast, there are many benefits to harnessing the potential of natural processes in managing water flows. Rather than ignoring these methods—as is the tendency within Cartesian thinking—we integrated them into our economic calculations. Solutions such as constructed wetlands, parks, and forests are not only cheaper than the usual solutions, but they improve urban health, prevent damage from floods, cool the environment, sequester carbon, and increase biodiversity. There is enough rainfall in Chennai to accommodate the city's needs were it to capture, treat, and store this rainwater in the sandy aquifer over the course of the year. The challenge remains that even when these benefits can be integrated into economic models, they represent *savings* rather than new revenues, which are typically deemed less interesting for financial institutions. The challenge then is to build support among development banks *and* among beneficiaries on the ground, working not only from the top down but also from the bottom up.

Here as well, we built a pilot as a stepping stone to demonstrate the effectiveness of nature-based solutions. Within the garden of a school for visual- and hearing-impaired children, the pilot replenishes the aquifer with clean rainwater and treated wastewater. Making these ideas and systems visible is paramount because people often only come to appreciate something once it is actually performing and actively improving their lives. In many ways, the pilot was a microcosm of Chennai: frequently flooding, polluted, and with failing infrastructure. Its transformation into a functioning green space suggests how nature can transform the city, through scalable nature-based solutions [05] [06] [07].

The pilot does more than just use nature to solve a problem. It reveals how, in the context of the city, nature is always coproduced with humans and how ecosystems can be designed for particular interactions. For example, the plants in the pilot require human waste in order

[05] ***City of 1,000 Tanks*****: Water Balance Pilot in the Little Flower Convent. © OOZE, 2023**

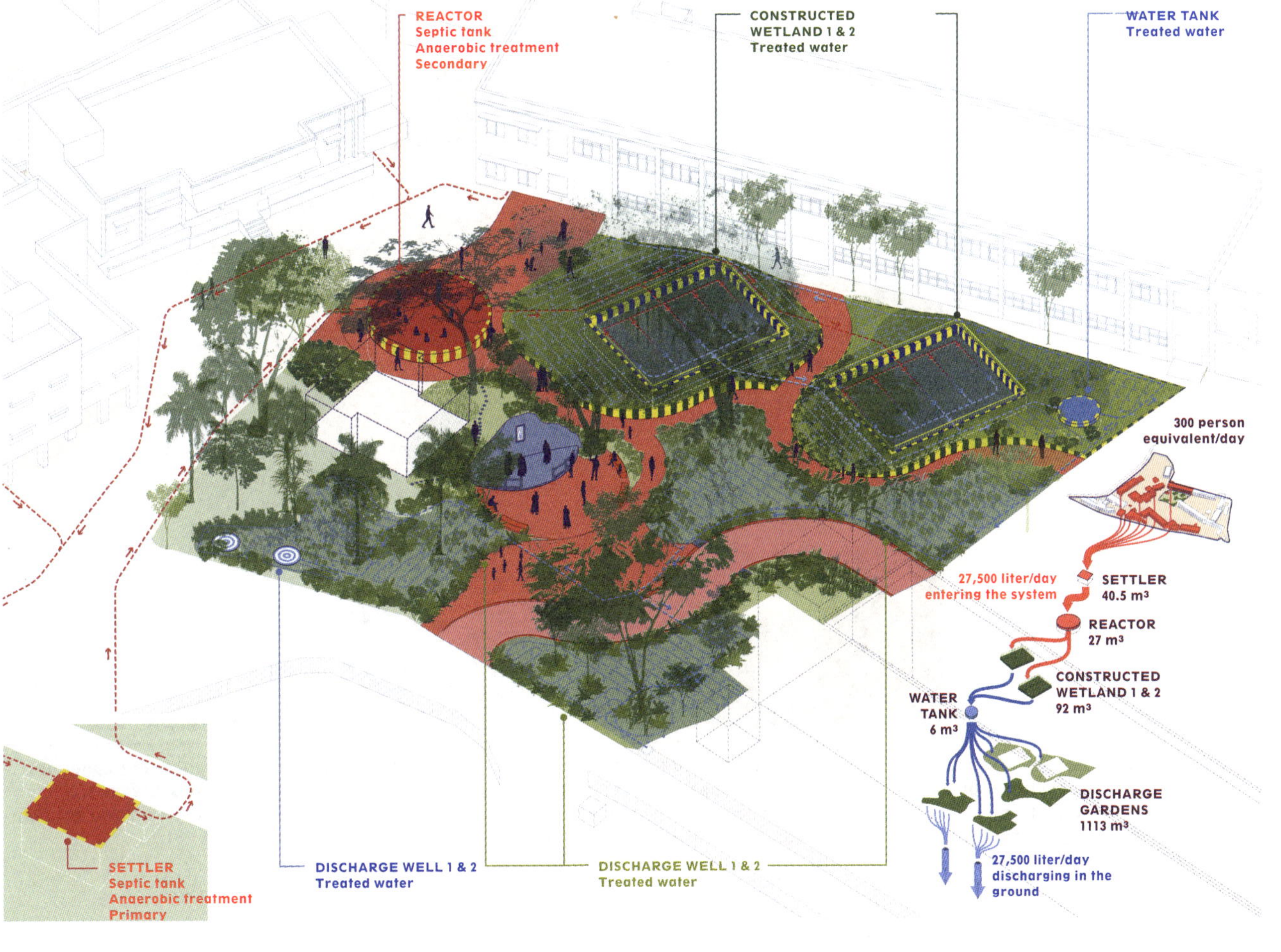

to thrive—and they would have to adapt if the school were to stop flushing its toilets. There is no singular, inherent "nature" of the plants, the people, or the pilot; rather their nature is created when connected to one another. Nature does the job if we see ourselves as an integral part of it, with all the consequences that this implies. Instead of embracing endless GDP growth which can only lead to burn-out, we can embrace the growth of nature as a long-term objective.

[06] *City of 1,000 Tanks*: Water Balance Pilot, path in a filtering garden. © Cynthia van Elk, 2023

[07] *City of 1,000 Tanks*: Water Balance Pilot, anaerobic reactor. © Cynthia van Elk, 2023

DESCARTES, R. (1985) *Philosophical Writings of Descartes*. Translated by J. Cottingham, R. Stroothoff and D. Murdoch. Cambridge: Cambridge University Press. Vol I.

DUCARME, F. and COUVET, D. (2020) 'What does "nature" mean?', *Palgrave Communications*, 6(14).

PATEL, R. and MOORE, J. W. (2017) *A History of the World in Seven Cheap Things*. Berkeley: University of California Press.

RAWORTH, K. (2017) *Doughnut Economics: Seven Ways to Think Like a 21st-Century Economist*. New York: Random House.

Making Urbanism Greener is not Enough!

Eva Schwab

[01] "People must also want the transformation," Ulrich Brand claims. This is more likely to happen with agreeable spaces that become part of people's everyday lives. © Martin Grabner

"The world is on fire" are the opening words of this book. They establish the framework for looking at the different contributions, they convey a position of urgency, they call on us to question the routines of urban planning and design, demanding as well that we confront the profession's complicity in (and responsibility for) an Anthropocene urbanism that is the main driver of resource consumption and biodiversity depletion around the world. What, then, can a territorial approach to urbanism do to improve this situation [01]?

TERRITORIAL URBANISM

Territorial Urbanism describes the essential change in fundamental framework conditions and values in urbanism. It stands for a holistic, cross-sectoral, and networked understanding of space, as well as a close connection between the built environment and living systems. It is a practice that is specifically focused on just, ecological, and collaborative urbanism. As such, it fits into a series of attempts (**e.g. Mostafavi and Doherty, 2016; Mostafavi, 2017; Hagan, 2015; Fitz and Krasny, 2019; Latour, 2017**) to address the current situation and to locate social and ecological interrelationship and interdependency at the center of the discipline's wider efforts. Both interrelationship and interdependency are at the heart of a robustly ecological, ecosystemic understanding of our settlement spaces, which highlights "the structure and function of levels of organization beyond that of the individual and species" (**Odum and Barrett, 2005, p. 3**) and has been foundational in thinking the city as a system (**Odum, 1994**).

Such an ecosystemic understanding drives an urbanism in which cities ideally reach "the same interdependent efficiencies and life-preserving redundancies as natural ecosystems" (**Hagan, 2015, p. 4**). In turn, the realization of this interconnectedness and interdependency brings forth an ethical framework encompassing both human and more-than-human actors.

Looking back at the history of the profession, ideas for an improved (human) life in the city have logically tended to revolve around positioning architectural development in relation to nature. Certain of these concepts remain in active use today, finding expression in models that continue to shape contemporary settlement spaces. Sadly though, the interpretation of these ideas is often wildly *un*imaginative; by failing to tap into their potential to offer new meaning and pertinence through an expanded integration of socio-ecological demands, they also fail to react to the existential challenge of the 21st century.

Ebenezer Howard's 1898 model of the *Garden City*—with its "belt of country" around the urban metropolis and green infrastructure reaching into it—can serve as a loose inspiration for thinking about how to integrate energy and food, mobility, recreational, and ecological needs to serve both the city *and* its borderlands, e.g. through the application of biodiversity corridors, thus dissolving the urban–rural dichotomy. Howard's original idea for the social organization of the *Garden City* was that of a cooperative, reminding us of the importance of collective forms of organization and—on a metalevel—of the different actors and their relationships, which form part of building the contemporary city. While overall planning and legislation is needed for such a structural approach, public and private actors can also contribute their part to the network.

Le Corbusier's *Ville Contemporaine* of 1922 serves as an inspiration for density, not in its original social or functional zoning intentions, but through the reminder that high densities need high design quality. It also deftly illustrates the idea that compactness limits ecological impact on the surrounding environment. Ideally then, density would be a function of a self-sustaining site where new or retrofitted developments could support themselves with renewable energy for heating, cooling, hot water, and electricity through water harvesting and recycling, which are only feasible if the strict boundary of the original idea is overcome by the integration of the city into the wider region. For Susannah Hagan, metabolic environmental analysis provides an ethical and material guideline for questions about how much density and compactness are desirable: too much density shows "when the regional metabolism can't sustain [the city]. When we export poisonous wastes to developing countries. When we import energy from oppressive regimes" (2015, p. 52).

While, at first glance, Frank Lloyd Wright's *Broadacre City* of 1932 epitomizes a large number of today's challenges (e.g. car-dependent mobility, sprawl, segregation) it also serves as an inspiration for how to conceptualize an urban–rural continuum wherein urban–rural dichotomies can be dissolved and thus all forms of settlement—urban, peri-, or suburban and rural—can receive respective appreciation as individual parts of this continuum. As a result, a cultural de-centering can take place.

Through the dissolution of these dichotomies emerges the contiguous possibility of breaking down the dichotomy between built and unbuilt land. The implication of this dissolution would be a redefinition of our settlement spaces beyond the notion that building leaves some areas empty: namely, recognizing that land *not* built on isn't vacant, empty, or fallow, but is already full of something else that is equally productive and valuable—a performative landscape. To understand this performativity requires sensitivity to (and knowledge of) its initial condition and, furthermore, an awareness of the "simple regulations which ensure that society protects the values of natural processes and is itself protected" (McHarg, 1995, p. 55). Speaking of natural systems in this context, then, makes clear that peripheral areas can become potential sites for fertile hybrids, areas in which built and performative landscapes can be viewed inclusively (Meyer, 1997; Kahn and Burns, 2021).

In this sense, urbanistic practice is the scale of choice to incorporate landscape as an in frastructure (Doherty/Waldheim, 2015) to deal with resources and energy supply, with waste recycling as well as food production, climate regulation and biodiversity restoration. Moreover, it integrates into these requirements the spatial qualities that ensure socially inclusive access to the benefits these measures yield across all scales, from the local to the global.

Actual urbanistic practice, however, is currently falling short of its huge potential, compromising not only the future of our cities but also, as Hagan pointedly puts it, the future of the profession:

"The longer architects and architecture schools ignore the politics, economics and science of meaningful change in the built environment, the closer they will come to being what they profess to despise: stylists to the rich and famous. If the worthy can't design, and designers are unequipped, architecture is finished as a profession with any influence on the improved future of cities." (2015, p. 31)

In all the contributions to this book, however, one sees reflected both exciting and feasible positions that demonstrate innovative approaches towards rethinking architectural and urbanistic practice in the face of present social and ecological challenges. With such a broad spectrum of topics, each one convincingly argued and illustrated, one can't help but ask why we are yet to see more change unfolding in the world around us. Evidently, good practices and approaches guide the way, and knowledge abounds on what to do and how to do it—but still, not enough is currently happening.

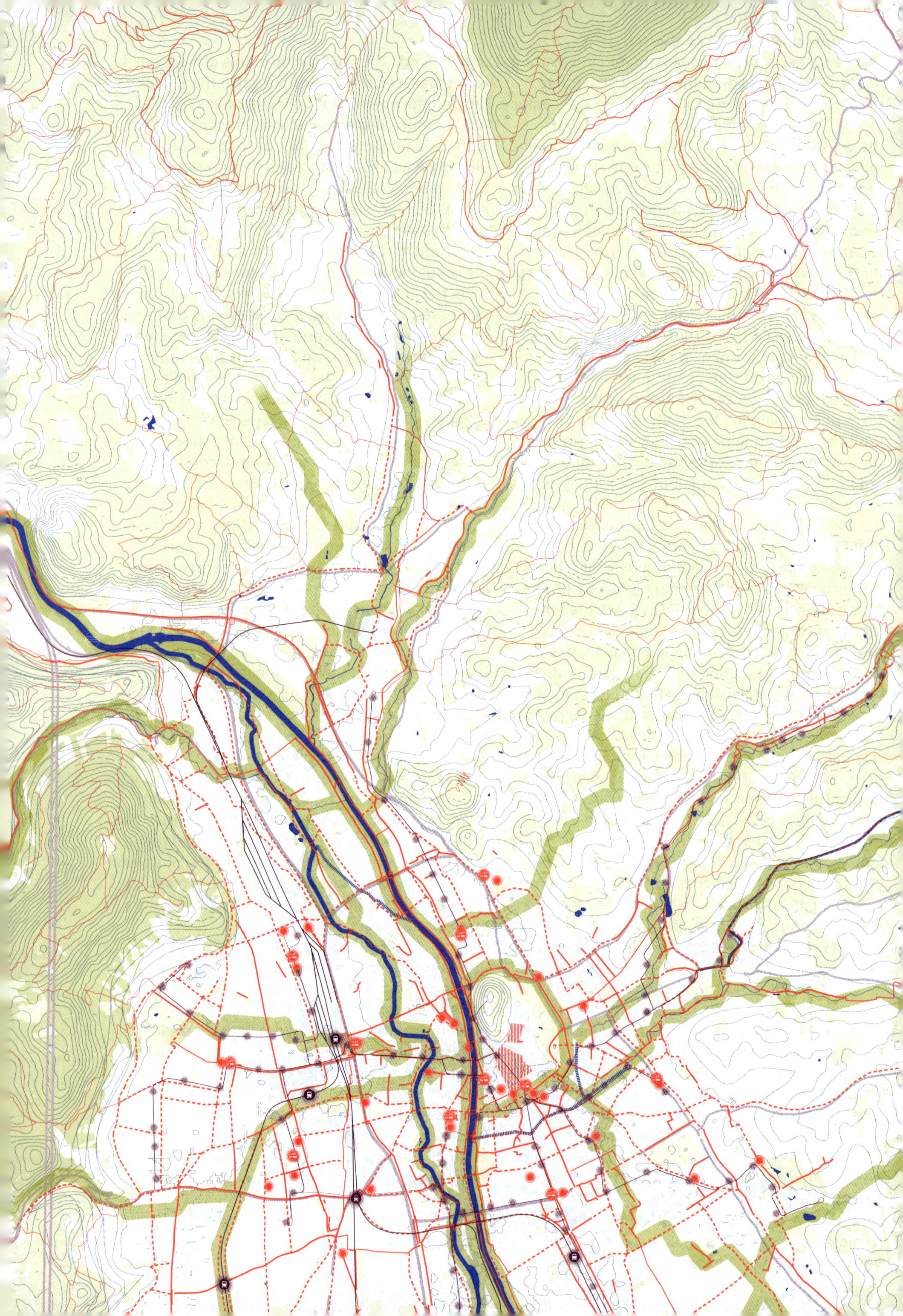

IT'S A STRUGGLE

According to the International Energy Agency, over $850,000,000,000 was funneled into fossil fuel production in 2022 to turn profits and increase wealth (not to mention fill state coffers). This is more than double the investment in renewable energy. Equally, the building industry is still doing well enough for itself that "[s]ystemic change happens at a snail's pace because vested interests and lobby groups rule... ."[1] **(Misselwitz 2022).**

Critical urban studies research investigates class, gender, and nationality biases that influence decision taking and points to the fact that decision-makers (who can either be recognized politicians or influential lobbyists working behind the scenes) are often those that profit most from the processes[2] that destroy our biosphere as well as our global sociosphere. These same parties thus tend to have the least interest in mobilizing change, frequently using their power to oppose it and perpetuate the domination of non-human nature, as well as Indigenous peoples and cultures. It also points to how rational hubris and anthropocentrism foster illusions of invincibility that blinker us from understanding the actual dangers we face—despite informative research from bodies like the IPCC and the IPBES,[3] and the growing severity of weather events.

Not just powerful interest groups, but also common people—who make up the majority of the electorate—take decisions based on their values, which often put personal before public interest. Unfortunately, to many peoples' minds, issues of sustainability and social equality are connected to public rather than personal interest—they are therefore seen as being somehow less important or in downright opposition to personal interests **(Herd and Jonkman, 2023).** As Ulrich Brand puts it: "The people must also want the transformation![4]"

Clearly, new tools and approaches are not enough. Urban designers, architects, and planners are confronted with an almost absurd

[02] Territorial Urbanism describes the essential change in fundamental framework conditions and values in urbanism. It stands for a holistic, cross-sectoral, and networked understanding of space, as well as for a close connection between the built environment and living systems. It is an urbanism in reverse, prioritizing what has been neglected for too long: our interrelationship and interdependency with the Earth's live-giving systems. © Institute of Urbanism, TU Graz

GRAND GRAZ
- Existing cycle paths
- Existing main cycle routes
- Planned cycling infrastructure
- Walking and hiking trails
- Train tracks
- Existing tramway tracks
- Planned tramway tracks
- Tramway stations
- Train stations
- Roads
- Park & ride
- Multimodal hubs
- Car-sharing locations
- Selected shared space and pedestrian zones
- Expansion of green corridors
- Water area
- Built-up water area

1 Original: "Systemische Veränderungen passieren im Schneckentempo, weil Besitzstandswahrer und Lobbygruppen walten. Aber auch in weniger stark regulierten Ländern ist es kompliziert, weil wirtschaftliche Interessen dominieren. Die Bauwirtschaft ist von den eigenen Interessen enorm korrumpiert."

2 According to a recent study, the bottom 50% of the world's population (measured by income and wealth) has emitted 16% of global emissions since 1990, while the top 1% accounts for 23% of global emissions. See: Chancel, L. (2022) 'Global carbon inequality over 1990–2019,' *Nature Sustainability*, 5, pp. 931–938.

3 https://www.ipbes.net/news/Gulbenkian_Award

4 Orig. "Die Menschen müssen die Transformation auch wollen!" https://www.derstandard.at/story/3000000189072/es-wird-sp252rbar-ungem252tlich

situation, in which they must work within existing power relations, with established instruments, towards a disruptive, transformative transition process (Armengaud, 2023). And so, business as usual continues in many areas and the current ecological crises—global warming, acidification of the oceans, loss of biodiversity, plastic pollution, and deforestation—are becoming ever more threatening and un-graspable at the same time.

DE-COLONIZING NATURE

As a proxy for these multiple, intersecting crises—each one threatening not only our immediate comfort zone, but our actual survival—we often talk about a broader crisis of "ecology," which suggests a crisis or failing of nature. There are good arguments, however, for conceiving of it differently: "The 'ecological' crisis is a crisis or failing of reason and culture, a crisis of monological forms of both that are unable to adapt themselves to the earth and to the limits of other kinds of life" (Plumwood, 2002, p. 15). The ecological crisis, thus, is an expression of a crisis of understanding, valuing, and adapting to our embeddedness in the Earth's life-giving systems, which are truncated by the imaginary separation of humans from nature that is the founding narrative of Western culture (Brennan, 1993; Plumwood, 2002; Vicent, 2023). In turn, this narrative finds expression in long established professional dichotomies, such as culture–nature, mind–body, subject–object, urban–rural, center–periphery,[5] etcetera.

It is therefore crucial to not only reposition urbanism *vis-à-vis* ecology, but to arrive at an understanding of our embeddedness in the environment around us that signals a fundamental cultural change.

"Nature is the unpaid housewife of culture, without which our lives would grind to a halt." This brief quotation by Susannah Hagan (2015, p. 66) beautifully and pointedly sums up the West's relationship with nature. Changing this relationship and realizing that urbanism and architecture can be bounded by an environmental framework and its laws—while remaining unlimited in terms of creativity and intellectual innovation (Benton, 1993)—is one of the central tasks that lies ahead for the profession. The challenge is not simply to come up with new technologies that might be less energy consuming or more able to sequester CO2. Rather, we must develop an environmental culture that values and fully acknowledges the non-human sphere and our dependency on it and, further, is able to make good decisions about how we live and impact on the non-human world. There are some advances in this direction within urbanism, at least. Books are being written, competitions are being held (Armengaud and Degros, 2023) that try to navigate the uncertainty of the situation by expanding the professional repertoire to include processual thinking and transitional dynamics as well as multiplicity and plurality, to name only a few.

Full acknowledgment of the more-than-human sphere, then, also suggests a shift away from the traditional binary view of nature as either pristine wilderness or human-dominated urban areas. Instead, it requires recognizing a more dynamic and interconnected relationship between humans and their surroundings. Anthropocentrism is put to the test by the supposition that more-than-human entities, such as animals, plants, and even ecosystems, exhibit forms of intentionality or agency in their actions or interactions with the environment (Davies, 2022; Bennett, 2009; Lowenhaupt Tsing, 2017; Plumwood, 2002; Haraway, 2016). It is this idea, together with the acceptance that the well-being (and survival) of humans depends on the functioning of natural processes, that necessitates ecological thinking. The profession must now turn to questions of ethics and decide how we want to live together so that both spheres thrive.

Claims have been made, for instance, that "our failure to situate dominant forms of human society ecologically is matched by our failure to situate non-humans ethically, as the plight of the non-human species continues to worsen" (Plumwood, 2002, p. 2). This implies advocating for a cultural and societal transformation that extends beyond the Western rationalist framework and the concept of humans being separate from—and superior to—nature, relegating nature to a position of inferiority and manipulation. It also entails challenging the notion of human superiority, which is rooted in the idea that humans possess active minds and reason, while non-human entities are reduced to passive, commodifiable bodies.

The term "culture" here emphasizes the profound, extensive, and multi-dimensional transformation required for our system to better connect us—both materially and in terms of our mindset and beliefs—with the ecological world we all-too-unwittingly inhabit. Western rationalist thought has developed hegemonic

5 The dichotomy itself, of course, is not problematic per se. However, it limits our understanding of nuances and hybrid forms by looking at phenomena in their "purest" form only. Especially problematic, however, is the inferiorization that comes with it: one part being the norm, the other part its "lacking" counterpart.

power,[6] seeing the biosphere as a passive, inferior, limitless resource and thus plays a major role in reinforcing an exaggerated sense of human autonomy. It legitimizes and normalizes the dominance of a privileged class associated with reason, justifying their control and disproportionate rewards. This powerful system of ideas is so deeply ingrained culturally that it can secure a form of tacit "consent" even from those disadvantaged by it.

GLIMPSES OF A POSSIBLE FUTURE

Such deeply colonial thinking and the "imperial way of life" (**Brand and Wissen, 2017**) that goes with it, however, is being challenged. Philosophers like Eva von Redecker, as well as legal scholars like Margaret Davies and political scientists like Ulrich Brand, among others, bring forth new ideas of how to implement better co-operation with nature for the benefit of both partners, serving as inspiration for a socially and ecologically relevant urbanism. Their ideas are wide-ranging: while Redecker argues for the importance of collective action and taking a critical position towards traditional liberal conceptions of freedom which prioritize individual autonomy, Davies proposes new ethical and legal imaginaries concerning human/non-human relationships. Elsewhere, Brand takes a firm stance against current consumption practices as well as those political-economic framework conditions that prevent us from exercising care and living in ecologically embedded, responsible ways. As diverse as these standpoints may be, they converge in the conviction that the cultural horizon of Anthropocentrism and Eurocentrism that condition our current understanding of our position in the world needs to be changed in favor of cultivating an attitude that listens to and engages imaginatively and openly with non-Western ontologies, such as Indigenous, First Nations and Andean worldviews. Doing so includes a broader set of human relationships with nature by referring, for example, to "gifts of nature" instead of the ubiquitous "ecosystem services," a term which has become mainstream in discourses around what value nature holds for humans (**Berghöfer et al., 2022**).

These concepts speak to ideas of "'living with' rather than 'living over'" (**Hagan, 2015, p. 11**) nature and populations who are marginalized by its destruction. Although this position has been finding its way into urbanistic and architectural practice recently, it is far from becoming mainstream (**Krasny and Fitz, 2019; Mostafavi, 2017**). Most recently, Lesley Lokko's 2023 Venice Architecture Biennale invited people to rethink dominant narratives through a wide array of projects which aimed at decolonizing nature and humans alike, creating possible futures of cooperation and togetherness as well as freedom. Many of the contributions to the Biennale took their strength from a synergy between architectural expertise and activist drive, thus showing one way forward for architectural practice:

"Architects don't always understand the potential they have in doing more activist-charged work. We thought we could convince architects that they can't go at it alone—that they need other people to work with. [...] We've found that the architects can diagram things in a way that is really clear to a wider audience. While the advocates and activists know the issues, the architects can translate them into diagrams (Sarah Stevens of AAHA! in an interview[7])".

Today, such projects combining activism and design work are singular enough to be remarkable, often finding their way into books and exhibitions that allow them to extend beyond their initial local reach. They might, however, be glimpses of the future: of a future in which more and more human actors acknowledge their embeddedness in both ecological laws and social responsibilities. This shift creates a basis for a Territorial Urbanism that is ecosystemic in the essential sense of providing an organization of space in which both human and more-than-human spheres can thrive. Only through such a fundamental cultural change will we be able to face the profession's complicity in and responsibility for an urbanism that has for too long poured oil on the fire. Greener, better quality settlements are good, but they are not enough [02]!

6 The term hegemony denotes the predominance of an institution, organization, or social group within a socio-political order. The term was primarily coined by the Marxist theorist Antonio Gramsci. Gramsci understands hegemony as the "ability of the ruling groups and classes to assert their interests in such a way that they are regarded by the groups and classes to be dominated as their own or as the general social interest. [...] The existing conditions are largely accepted and thus consolidated."

7 https://www.cbc.ca/arts/venice-biennale-architects-against-housing-alienation-1.6900479#:~:text=%22Architects%20don't%20always%20understand,other%20people%20to%20work%20with.%22

ARMENGAUD, M. (2023) 'Who wants to start a revolution? Note on the profession of transition planner,' in: A. Degros, M. Armengaud and R. Radulova-Stahmer (eds.) *Towards Territorial Transition*. Zurich: Park Books.

BENNETT, J. (2009) *Vibrant Matter: A Political Ecology of Things*. Durham, London: Duke University Press.

BENTON, T. (1993) *Natural Relations: Ecology, Animal Rights and Social Justice*. London: Verso.

BERGHÖFER, U., RODE, J., JAX, K., FÖRSTER, J., BERGHÖFER, A. and WITTMER, H. (2022): 'Societal Relationships with Nature: A framework for understanding nature-related conflicts and multiple values', *People and Nature*, 4, pp. 534–548.

BRAND, U. and WISSEN, M. (2017) *Imperiale Lebensweise: Zur Ausbeutung von Mensch und Natur im globalen Kapitalismus*. Munich: Oekom Verlag.

BRENNAN, T (1993) *History after Lacan*. London, New York: Routledge.

DAVIES, M. (2002) *EcoLaw: Legality, Life, and the Normativity of Nature*. London, New York: Routledge.

DOHERTY, G. and WALDHEIM, C. (2015) *Is Landscape...? Essays on the Identity of Landscape*. London, New York: Routledge.

HAGAN, S. (2015) *Ecological Urbanism: The Nature of the City*. London, New York: Routledge.

HARAWAY, D. (2016) *Staying with the Trouble: Making Kin in the Chthulucene. Experimental Futures*. Durham, London: Duke University Press.

HERDT, T. and JONKMAN, A. (2023) 'The acceptance of density: Conflicts of public and private interests in public debate on urban densification', *Cities*, 140, p. 104451.

KAHN, A. and BURNS, C. (2021) *Site Matters: Strategies for Uncertainty Through Planning and Design*. 2nd ed. London, New York: Routledge.

KRASNY, E., FRITZ, A., and ARCHITEKTURZENTRUM WIEN (2019) *Critical Care: Architecture and Urbanism for a broken Planet*. Cambridge, MA: The MIT Press.

LATOUR, B. (2017) *Où atterrir? Comment s'orienter en politique*. Paris: La Découverte.

LOWENHAUPT TSING, A. (2017) *The Mushroom at the End of the World: On the Possibility of Life in Capitalist Ruins*. Princeton, NJ: Princeton University Press.

MCHARG, I. (1995) *Design with Nature*. Chichester: Wiley.

MEYER, E. (1997) 'The Expanded Field of Landscape Architecture', in G. Thompson and F. R. Steiner (eds.) *Ecological Design and Planning*. New York: Wiley.

MISSELWITZ, P. (2022) 'Roadmap für das Bauhaus Erde', *Bauwelt*, 13. Available at: https://www.bauwelt.de/rubriken/interview/Roadmap-fuer-das-Bauhaus-Erde-3788724.html

MOSTAFAVI, M. (2017) *Ethics of the Urban: The City and the Spaces of the Political*. Harvard, Zurich: Lars Müller Publishers and Harvard University Graduate School of Design.

MOSTAFAVI, M. and Doherty, G. (2016) *Ecological Urbanism*. Harvard, Zurich: Lars Müller Publishers and Harvard University Graduate School of Design.

ODUM, H. (1994) *Ecological and General Systems: An Introduction to Systems Ecology*. Niwot: Colorado University Press.

ODUM, E. and BARRETT, G. (2005) *Fundamentals of Ecology*. 5th ed. Andover, Hampshire: Thomson Brooks/Cole.

PLUMWOOD, V. (2002) *Environmental Culture: The Ecological Crisis of Reason*. London, New York: Routledge.

VINCENT, C. (2023) 'Aux origines du désastre écologique', *Le Monde*, 23 July. Available at: https://www.lemonde.fr/series-d-ete/article/2020/07/23/aux-origines-du-desastre-ecologique_6047013_3451060.html

Appendix

ACKNOWLEDGMENTS

This book stands as the result of extensive engagement spanning several years, delving into the essential question of how to envision our future built environment in terms of its ability to effectively confront forthcoming challenges. The foundations for this publication were laid out in the book *Basics of Urbanism*, published in September 2021. Early dialogue regarding the publication began with an online symposium and continued with an exhibition: the online symposium titled "Where City and Territory Meet..." was held on September 16 and 17 2021 and the exhibition, titled *Territorial Turn* was hosted at Haus der Architektur Graz from February until April 2022.

Building on these pivotal events, the subsequent symposium, "Territorial Turn!", took place on September 15 and 16 2022, at TU Graz. Notably, previous contributors, including Elena Andonova (UKIM in Skopje), Tommaso Pietropolli (EPFL), Johannes Bernsteiner (TU Graz), Beatrice Galimberti (Politecnico di Milano), Julio de la Fuente and Natalia Gutiérrez (Gutiérrez-delaFuente Arquitectos), Ward Verbakel (KU Leuven), Stefan Devoldere (Hasselt University), as well as Lilli Lička and Hannes Gröblacher (BOKU and Westbahnpark), were invited to refine and present their initial submissions. Distinguished experts within the discipline, including Susanne Eliasson (GRAU), Stefan Rettich (University of Kassel), Eva Pfannes (OOZE), and Paola Viganò (EPFL Lausanne, IUAV Venice), were also engaged as keynote speakers, sharing their knowledge. Our sincere thanks go to them. Further thanks go to testimonies given by Ali Madanipour (University of Newcastle), Christian Schmid (ETH Zürich), Maarten Van Acker (University of Antwerpen), Erik Wieërs (Flemish Government), Judith Schwentner (City of Graz), and Chris Younès (École spéciale d'architecture and École nationale supérieure d'architecture de Paris La Villette).

Great gratitude goes to Han Meyer (Em.prof. TU Delft) and Marcel Smets (Em.prof. KU Leuven) who accompanied both symposiums with great expertise and plenty of dedication, as well to all the other participants: Petra Petersson (Dean of the Faculty of Architecture), Andrea Jany (University of Graz), Klaus K. Loenhart (TU Graz), Philipp Misselwitz (BAUHAUS EARTH), Alexandra Würz-Stalder (FH Joanneum Graz), Julia Fröhlich (Wohnlabor), Anselm Wagner (TU Graz), Anna-Maria Jäger (Wohnlabor), Andreas Lichtblau (TU Graz), Isabel Stumfol (LandLuft Association), Günter Getzinger (TU Graz), Judith Schwentner (Vicemayor City of Graz), Christine Braunersreuther (Councillor of Graz), Bertram Werle (City Planning Director Graz), Günter Riegler (Councillor for Culture Graz), Sophia Walk (TU Graz), and Socrates Stratis (University of Cyprus).

Subsequently, during the academic term September 2022 to January 2023, Professors Aglaée Degros and Stefan Bendiks furthered the exploration of the discussed theories and findings. As visiting professors at Harvard GSD, they navigated the course "Towards Territorial Transition – Decarb Luxe," deciphering how to craft transitions on a territorial scale, adeptly addressing current ecological, economic, social, and spatial challenges. The results of the students' investigations find expression within the pages of this book. Sincere appreciation is extended to Jialei Tang, Pavin Banternghansa, Abhishek Desai, Magic Sun, and Rongqing Liu as well as all the other course participants: M.C. Abbott, Giovanna Baffico, Gerardo Corona, Matt Khinda, Matthew Lee, Shuyue Li, and Zhou Zhuohan for their invaluable cooperation. At this point we also want to thank all the contributors to the course: Anita Berrizbeitia, Claudia Dobles Camargo, Jungyoon Kim, Alex Wall, Gary Hilderbrand, Carlos Guedes, Carole Schmit, Christa Reicher, Didier Rebois, Dirk Sijmons, Florian Hertweck, Matthias Armengaud, Panos Mantziaras, and Philipp Misselwitz.

Crucially, we express our gratitude to our esteemed sponsors, Stadt Graz, Holding Graz, Land Steiermark, Haus der Architektur, Ziviltechniker:innen Kammer, New European Bauhaus, Stiftung Lebendige Stadt, Baunetz Campus, Flanders State of the Art, Embassy of the Kingdom of the Netherlands in Austria, Embassy of Spain in Austria, Embassy of Switzerland in Austria, whose support was instrumental in realizing both these pivotal events.

Lastly, immense gratitude extends to the diligent team at the Institute of Urbanism: Sandra Guinand, Karina Brünner, Ingo Candussi, Markus Monsberger, Simone Feigl, Dalila Bilbani, Carina Fechter, Philipp Flachhuber, Angelika Haar, Carola Hilgert, Barbara Holler, Johanna Kremser, Barbara Langmann, Carina Mazelle, Barbara Russo, Johannes Sauer, Lukas Schneider, and Michaela Haselbacher-Berner, whose unwavering dedication and efforts facilitated these impactful events and this publication.

To Rieke, Tom, Lou, Vito, Lina, Tilo, and Koba

BIOGRAPHIES

Editors

AGLAÉE DEGROS is professor and head of the Institute of Urbanism at Graz University of Technology (TU Graz) and honorary science fellow at the Vrije Universiteit in Brussels (VUB). In 2001, together with Stefan Bendiks, she founded the Urbanism and Architecture office Artgineering. Degros has held various teaching positions and visiting professorships: at Delft University of Technology (TU Delft), Rotterdam Academy of Architecture and Urban Design (RAvB), VUB, the Academy of Fine Arts Vienna, TU Wien, the Politecnico di Milano (Polimi), and the Harvard Graduate School of Design (GSD), among others. She is co-author of books such as the Routledge publication *Public Space and the Challenges of Urban Transformation in Europe, Traffic Space is Public Space, Territorial Justice, Basics of Urbanism* and *Towards Territorial Transition*. She is a regular jury member for international urban planning and design competitions. Since 2021 she is one of four experts in the team of the Bouwmeester of the Flemish Region, the Antwerp Ring, and the Brussels-Zaventem Airport.

EVA SCHWAB has been deputy head of the Institute of Urbanism at TU Graz since 2018 and is responsible for devising the Institute's research agenda. She trained as a landscape architect in Vienna and Barcelona. After some years in practice, she developed a career in research—focusing on the politics of public space production and use, spatial justice, and urban development, especially at the urban periphery. Her doctorate won both the Landscape Research Dissertation Prize and the Talent Award of the City of Vienna in 2016. Since then, she has been teaching and researching in interdisciplinary and international teams at TU Wien, University of Natural Resources and Life Sciences (BOKU) in Vienna, University of Kassel, and FH Nürtingen. Recently, she co-edited the books *Basics of Urbanism* and *Territorial Justice*.

RADOSTINA RADULOVA-STAHMER is an architect with a focus on urbanism. She studied Architecture at Karlsruhe Institute of Technology (KIT) and received her Diploma with honors in 2010. She is currently a postdoc at the Institute of Urbanism at TU Graz. Her research focuses on climate-oriented urbanism and transition. In her PhD she researched the spatial effects of digital change (*summa cum laude*) at KIT. In 2010 she co-founded the office STUDIOD3R with Deniza Horländer, which received several international awards, such as First Prize at EUROPAN Graz, First Prize at the Young Architects Program at MAXXI (Rome) in collaboration with MoMA (New York), and Constructo Association of Santiago de Chile. She is part of the scientific advisory board of the Wüstenrot Stiftung and sits on the international jury of EUROPAN Austria. From 2024 she will be full professor for urbanism at Jade University of Applied Sciences in Oldenburg.

ANNA MARIA BAGARIĆ has been a university assistant at the Institute of Urbanism at TU Graz since 2019. She studied Architecture at TU Graz and graduated from the Institute of Urbanism. From 2018 to 2019, she worked at Team M in Linz and has also previously completed several internships, e.g., at Nickl Architekten Lambach and Wallack Architekten Graz. At the Institute of Urbanism, she works as a teacher for students on bachelor's and master's courses and is responsible for the overall organization of teaching at the institute. Currently she also conducts research on the ecological and social revitalization of Styrian town centers and formed part of the research team on enhancement of pedestrian mobility in Styria.

SABINE BAUER has been a university assistant and PhD candidate at the Institute of Urbanism at TU Graz since 2019. She studied Architecture at Graz University of Technology and during her master's focused on planning for bicycle mobility, transit-oriented development as well as strategic planning and networking of peri-urban infrastructures. During her studies she worked at the traffic planning office verkehrplus in Graz and as a freelancer at Sisyphus publishing house. Her current research concerns the design of public spaces, particularly those facilitating public mobility and promoting active, multimodal transportation. She also conducts research on development planning in peri-urban areas and teaches bachelor's and master's courses.

JENNIFER FAUSTER has been a university and research project assistant at the Institute of Urbanism, TU Graz since 2020. Jennifer's academic background includes studies in architecture, landscape architecture, and urbanism at several institutions, including the University of Edinburgh, the Academy of Architecture at Amsterdam University of the Arts, and ETH Zurich. She has gained practical experience through work at various international firms, including Vogt Landscape Architects, Bureau B+B, CNTXT, PLACE, and Studio Boden. Currently, she is engaged in research as a university assistant at the Institute of Landscape Architecture at BOKU in Vienna. Her primary research interest revolves around investigating research methods and strategies applicable to peri-urban areas. In addition, Jennifer is involved in teaching and conducts research that lies at the intersection of spatial planning, landscape architecture, and urban design.

MARIO STEFAN has been a university assistant and PhD candidate at the Institute of Urbanism, TU Graz since 2023, where he works as a teacher for bachelor's and master's students. Before he joined the Institute of Urbanism, he worked at Nussmüller Architekten in Graz and the Architecture and Urbanism Office DeZwarteHond in Rotterdam. He studied Architecture at TU Graz and graduated from the Institute of Urbanism. His research focuses on improving potential hydrological retention areas and flood capacities along peri-urban transport infrastructures through well-designed, multifunctional, and multi-coded open spaces.

ALICE STEINER has been a university assistant and PhD candidate at the Institute of Urbanism, TU Graz since 2023. She studied Architecture at TU Graz and graduated from the Institute of Integral Architecture by Anne Femmer and Florian Summa where she dealt with the dualism between nature and culture and its effects on our built environment. Before she joined the Institute of Urbanism, she gained practical experience at architecture and landscape architecture offices in Graz and Vienna. Her research focuses on strengthening and improving local centers in peri-urban areas.

RACHEL GYŐRFFY has been a research scholar of the New National Excellence Initiative (ÚNKP), examining the possibilities of the digital reuse of cultural heritage. She is also a research and teaching assistant at the Institute of Architectural Theory, History of Art, and Cultural Studies at TU Graz. Rachel is currently a lecturer at Moholy-Nagy University of Art and Design, Budapest (MOME). She studied Architecture at the Technical University of Munich (TUM) and at the Arts University Bournemouth. After close to ten years of professional experience in Germany and Hungary, she started her PhD at MOME in 2019. Her doctoral research focuses on the spatial practices of identity construction and the layers of urban memory within the context of current paradigms of architectural reconstructivism.

Essays

PAOLA VIGANÒ is a professor in Urban Theory and Urban Design at the École Polytechnique Fédérale de Lausanne (EPFL), where she leads the Habitat Research Center, and professor at IUAV Venice. She is also the head of the urban planning agency StudioPaolaViganò (formerly Studio Bernardo Secchi Paola Viganò) in Milan. She received the Grand Prix de l'Urbanisme 2013 in France, the title of Doctor *Honoris Causa* in 2016 from the UCLouvain, the Flemish Culture Award for Architecture 2017, and the Gold Medal for her career at the Milan Triennale in 2018. Her research develops a reflection on the new territories of the project, framing the project itself as a knowledge device.

CLAUDIA BODE is a senior researcher and project coordinator at Bauhaus Earth. A registered architect with a background in international urbanism, she has worked at the intersection of research, writing, and design in a variety of academic and nonprofit contexts in the United States, Peru, Tanzania, and Germany. At Bauhaus Earth she leads the experimental demonstration project "ProtoPotsdam," which explores architecture as a tool for research and communication in the context of the climate crisis. She holds an MA in Architecture from the Massachusetts Institute of Technology (MIT).

PHILIPP MISSELWITZ is an architect, urban researcher and professor at the Department of Design and International Urban Studies (Habitat Unit) at the Technical University of Berlin (TU Berlin). In various research, teaching and consulting projects, he deals with the interaction of migration and urban development. His current research focuses on actor-based urban development processes and co-production in housing in Europe and the Global South, rural urbanization processes, trans-local production of space, as well as transdisciplinary teaching methods in the field of urban design. He is a network partner at Urban Catalyst studio, a planning design consultancy group based in Berlin, and has curated several exhibition projects such as Grenzgeografien (Berlin, Zurich, Istanbul, 2007) and Refuge (Rotterdam Architecture Biennale, 2009). Since September 2021, he is the managing director of Bauhaus Earth, whose goal is to develop a new future narrative for the design and construction of buildings and human settlements in which nature and civilization are re-entangled.

ERIC LUITEN is a registered landscape architect and planner. He is a self-employed advisor and part-time professor on the chair of Landscape Architecture at TU Delft. Luiten was co-founder of the Dutch landscape architecture journal *Blauwe Kamer*, the biannual magazine *'scape, the international magazine for landscape architecture and urbanism*, and of *Landscape Architecture Europe's Annual Review*. He was curator for *A WIDER VIEW on Cultural Landscape Challenges* during the summer of 2008. In 2009 Luiten was appointed Special Advisor on Spatial Quality to the Board of Governors of the Province of South Holland. Between 2012 and 2016 he was appointed State Advisor on Landscape and Water, and between 2018 and 2022 he was Chief Architect for National Rail.

STEFAN RETTICH is an architect and professor of Urban Planning at the University of Kassel. From 2011 to 2016 he was a professor for Theory and Design at the Bremen University of Applied Sciences. Before that he taught for four years at the Bauhaus Kolleg in Dessau. Rettich is a founding partner and co-owner of KARO* architekten. Among other things, he is a member of the Urban Resilience Expert Advisory Board as well as the IBA Expert Council of the German Federal Ministry of Housing, Urban Development and Building. His work focuses on basic questions of space and politics, land issues, as well as strategies for sustainable urban development.

SUSANNE ELIASSON is an architect and urban planner based in Paris. In 2010, together with Anthony Jammes, she founded the architecture and planning office GRAU. With work spanning France and Europe, GRAU works in the space between architecture and urbanism, developing urban visions that are necessary to transform our common environment. Through numerous urban renewal projects, strategic studies on densification, master planning of new districts, and ongoing research on horizontal urbanism the office has developed a strong expertise on issues regarding housing and the urban environment. In 2022, GRAU won the international competition for the redesign of the public spaces around Notre-Dame cathedral in Paris. GRAU received the Young Planners Award from the French Ministry of Housing and Sustainable Habitat in 2016. In 2021, Eliasson was appointed Chief Architect of the city of Bordeaux.

ANSELM WAGNER is professor of Architectural Theory and head of the Institute of Architectural Theory, Art History, and Cultural Studies at TU Graz. He was born in 1965, and studied Art History, Philosophy, and Classical Archaeology at the universities of Salzburg and Munich before going on to work as a gallery director, art critic, and editor. He has held visiting professorships at TU Wien, TU Graz, and the University of Minnesota in Minneapolis. He is also head of several FWF (Austrian Science Fund) research projects and is the editor of the *architektur + analyse* series (jovis, Berlin). Between 2011 and 2020 he was a member of the Graz Old Town Expert Commission. He is the founder of the "ArchitekturTheorieTage" symposium and co-founder of the Architectural Archive Styria (ASt). His current publications include *Architekturführer Graz* (together with Sophia Walk, DOM Publishers, 2019, 2nd ed. and English version 2024), *SOS Grazer Schule* (together with Sophia Walk, TU Graz-Verlag, 2021, 2nd ed. 2022), and *Ein Pavillon für die Kunst im Salzburger Mirabellgarten und sein Architekt Karl Mayr* (Müry Salzmann, 2023).

SANDRA GUINAND is an urban planner and geographer. She holds a doctorate in Geosciences and the Environment from the University of Lausanne, in Geography from the University of Paris 1-Sorbonne, and is an associate researcher at EIREST Paris 1-Sorbonne University. She was a Swiss National Science Foundation visiting scholar (2014–2016) at the Center for Place, Culture, and Politics at the Graduate Center, City University of New York and Johns Hopkins University, as well as in the Department of Geography and Regional Research, University of Vienna (2017–2019). Since May 2022, she is a researcher at the Institute for Urban and Regional Research (ISR) and teaches at the Institute of Urbanism, TU Graz. Her research interests are centered on urban regeneration projects, and socioeconomical transformations of urban landscapes, with a specific focus on heritage processes, public-private partnerships, and tourism.

EVA PFANNES is an architect and urban designer working in Europe, India, and Brazil. She is co-founder of OOZE architects and urbanists. Her expertise covers urban, participatory, and climate resilience strategies including nature-based solutions. She received the 2017 Landscape Institute Award UK for Best Design for Temporary Landscape and the 2017 LafargeHolcim Bronze Award for Latin America. From 2020–2021, she was co-curator of the International Architecture Biennial Rotterdam (IABR) and has served as a jury member for several international architectural awards.

JESSE HONSA is a US-born architect based in Brussels, with a research focus on housing economy and construction. He is currently a postdoctoral researcher for the "ImpaC3t" project at the Faculty of Engineering Science in KU Leuven, focusing on the collective circular renovation of neighborhoods in Flanders. He frequently collaborates with OOZE Architects in Rotterdam and has also worked with DB Mimarlik in Istanbul, Rutz Architekten and AGPS architecture in Zurich, and Aardvarchitecture in New York City. Jesse holds degrees from the Rhode Island School of Design (RISD), The Berlage Center at TU Delft, and a PhD in Architecture from KU Leuven. His doctoral dissertation was supervised by Martino Tattara and explores the concept of economies of scale within housing, using three historic case studies in London.

Papers

TOMMASO PIETROPOLLI is an architect, postdoctoral researcher, and lecturer at EPFL in Lausanne. He completed his PhD on the figure of horizontality and the project of contemporary city-territories at EPFL, where he coordinates the Habitat Research Center (HRC) and the postgraduate master's program in Urban and Territorial Design (ETHZ and EPFL). He has been participant, coordinator, or co-director in several academic research projects, focusing on socio-ecological transition and the future of contemporary urbanized territories. Since 2015, he has collaborated with StudioPaolaViganò, focusing on projects at different scales—from territorial design to urban design and public spaces.

ELENA ANDONOVA is a PhD student at the Department of Urban and Regional Planning at the Technical University of Madrid (UPM), Spain. Elena currently works as a teaching and research assistant at the Institute of Urbanism at the University of S. Cyril and Methodius (UKIM) in Skopje. She has worked on numerous projects both in the private sector as well as on several international competition entries, mostly focusing on public spaces. Her interests are oriented towards understanding the relationships between social processes, cultural values, and urban forms through exploring urban planning and its ties to social and environmental sciences in different socioeconomic systems, focusing on spatial justice.

JULIO DE LA FUENTE is together with Natalia Gutiérrez cofounder of Gutiérrez-delaFuente Arquitectos, an architecture, urbanism, landscape, and research office with international scope founded in 2006. At present, the office is developing urban design plans and building several projects in Spain, Germany, and Belgium. Their completed works have received international awards, including the Bauwelt Preis 2013, the COAM Award 2013, and the COAM Award 2023. De la Fuente has also been a guest lecturer at universities in Germany, Sweden, and Spain. Currently, he is a member of the Europan Europe Technical Committee (2013–onwards).

NATALIA GUTIÉRREZ is together with Julio de la Fuente co-founder of Gutiérrez-delaFuente Arquitectos. At present, the office is developing urban design plans and has realized several projects in Spain, Germany, and Belgium. Their completed works have received international awards, including the Bauwelt Preis 2013, the COAM Award 2013, and the COAM Award 2023. Since 2012, Gutiérrez has been the Head of Planning of a town in the Madrid Metropolitan Area as well as Member of the Association of City Planners of Madrid. She is a member of the COAM Ethics Committee and the COAM Young Architects Committee. In collaboration with Julio de la Fuente, she curated the Madrid Pavilion at the 2019 Seoul Biennale.

WARD VERBAKEL is an architect and urban designer who founded plusoffice in 2006. His practice combines architecture and urbanism, with various projects ranging from transitional urbanism and master planning to public buildings and collective housing projects. Over the last few years, the research conducted by plusoffice architects has focused on the productive city and village urbanism. Currently, Verbakel coordinates the master urban design studios as a guest professor at KU Leuven, and has started his PhD research on "Small Town Urbanism." He previously taught at GSAPP Columbia University, New York. He is also president of the artistic board of the magazine *A+ Architecture* in Belgium.

BEATRICE GALIMBERTI is an architect and PhD student in urban planning, design, and policy at the Department of Architecture and Urban Studies, Polimi. Her interests focus mainly on public space design and the role of uncertainty in design processes.

HANNES GRÖBLACHER is a landscape architect and artist based in Vienna and Carinthia. He works on projects and competitions exploring art in public space, landscape architecture, as well as urban renewal and installation exhibitions. He teaches Landscape Architecture and Design at BOKU in Vienna, TU Wien, and FH Campus Vienna.

LILLI LIČKA is professor and head of the Institute of Landscape Architecture at BOKU in Vienna, the Archive of Austrian Landscape Architecture (LArchiv), and LL-Landscape Architecture as well as founder of Lilli Lička Landschaftsarchitektur, Ingenieurbüro. She studied Landscape Ecology and Design. Her research, teaching, and design focus on parks, squares, streets, historic sites, gardens, and green space justice. She is internationally active in juries and scientific selection committees and is committed to urban quality of life.

JOHANNES BERNSTEINER is a PhD candidate at the Institute of Urbanism, where he is investigating the effects of obsolescence in urban planning through the lens of transport infrastructure. He studied architecture at TU Graz, Polimi, and ENSA Paris-Belleville, graduating with a proposal for the transformation of the Paris ring road for the 2024 Olympic Games. He has been a visiting researcher at the Laboratoire LIAT at ENSA Paris-Malaquais and the department of Integral Design and Management at TU Delft. Recently, he has joined the Behavior in Networks Studies Unit at the University of Tokyo.

STEFAN DEVOLDERE is a professor and dean of the Faculty of Architecture and Art at the University of Hasselt. From 2004 till 2010 he was the editor of the Belgian architectural review *A+*. From 2011 till 2016 he safeguarded and stimulated the quality of the built environment in Flanders as deputy and acting Vlaams Bouwmeester (Flemish Government Architect). As chairman of the Stadsatelier Oostende—an expert platform that develops a framework for strategic building projects and a long-term vision for urban development in Ostend (Belgium)—he has been exploring the potential of research by design as an instrument for policymaking.

Photoessay

DAVIDE CURATOLA SOPRANA is an Italian photographer. He graduated from La Sapienza School of Architecture in Rome after attending classes in Seville and Madrid. He extended his professional profile by studying Photography at the Institute of Cinematography R. Rossellini. In 2015 he co-founded Urban Reports in Madrid, a European documentary photography collective, focusing his research on the visual study of the landscape, the city, and the territory. He exhibited at the 16th Venice Biennale of Architecture in 2018 and at the Seoul Biennale of Architecture and Urbanism SBAU in 2019. In 2019, the work exhibited in the Italian Pavilion by the project Arcipelago Italia became the book *L'altra Italia: Racconto per immagini delle aree interne del Paese*, edited by Johan & Levi of Milan. In 2021, Davide was the finalist and winner of the Photography Prize at the 15th BEAU Bienal Española de Arquitectura y Urbanismo. Currently, his work is reflecting on photography and art installation as participatory art practices supporting communities.

Harvard GSD

STEFAN BENDIKS is an architect and urban designer. In 2001, he founded Artgineering together with Aglaée Degros. He devises and implements design strategies for complex inter-urban conditions with a great interest in mobility and, in particular, in the potential of cycling to create a better city. In various research and design projects, he reinterprets the relation between mobility, landscape, and urban development. With Artgineering he works on the transformation of public spaces, such as the Park Belle-Vue in Leuven, which was awarded the Vlaamse Infrastructuurprijs 2021 for the best cycle infrastructure in Flanders, or the refurbishment of the Grote Markt Sint Niklaas. He advises cities in Europe and further afield on mobility and urban planning. Stefan has taught and lectured on architecture, urban planning, and design at various institutions, such as TU Delft, TU Graz, the Academy of Fine Arts Vienna, the Polimi, and GSD. He is the author of the publications *Cycle Infrastructure* and *Traffic Space is Public Space*, the study "Fietsland" for the Dutch Ministry of Infrastructure, "Leefbuurten" for Fietsberaad Flanders, and the new Flemish "Vademecum fietsvoorzieningen" for AWV. Stefan is a member of the Dutch Cycling Embassy and the German Academy for Urban and Regional Planning (DASL).

ABHISHEK DESAI holds a master's in Architecture from the University of Michigan, Ann Arbor, and a master's in Landscape Architecture from GSD. He co-founded "Saltech," a startup dedicated to manufacturing plant-based fabrics that aim to decarbonize the architecture and fashion industries, for which he received the Harvard President Innovation Challenge Ingenuity Award in 2023. While at Harvard, he worked as a research assistant to Martha Schwartz for the Urban Linear Forest Project, which is supported by the Harvard Climate Solutions Fund. Currently, he is actively engaged in projects addressing urban challenges related to decarbonizing urban mobility, tree equity, soil restoration, and carbon sequestration in cities.

RONGQING LIU is a student in the master's program of Landscape Architecture at GSD. Born in Tianjin, China, Rongqing has also studied and lived in mainland China, Hong Kong, Taiwan, Bangkok, and the US. He has worked as a landscape architect in seven different international companies, including Snøhetta, TLS, HOK, and Mcgregor Coxall. With rich experience in wide-ranging projects and awards in international urban design competitions, he believes that the space formed by technical methods should meet the diversity and needs of human beings, animals, and plants.

JIALEI TANG is a multi-hyphenate professional based in Hong Kong and New York. She has worked in architecture, finance, fashion merchandising, pharmaceuticals, hospitality, and real estate. Since 2018, she has been the director of Haiyi Holdings, a private investment office, and is currently also a board director at Cromwell Property Group and TauRx Pharmaceuticals. Previously, Jialei has worked at UBS AG, Tange Associates, ANTHOM, Parsons School of Design, and GSD. She received her BFA in Architectural Design from the Parsons School of Design and her BA in Liberal Arts for Epistemology and Language from the Eugene Lang College of Liberal Arts at The New School. Jialei graduated with a master's in urban planning from GSD.

MAGIC SUN is a dedicated landscape designer with a focus on sustainable strategy and environmental planning. She believes sustainability is the balance of social, environmental, and economic needs, and seeks to make changes towards a low-carbon society on both strategic and implementable levels. Magic earned her bachelor's degree from Cornell University, with a minor in Environmental Science and Sustainability. She also holds a master's degree in Landscape Architecture from GSD.

PAVIN BANTERNGHANSA graduated with distinction in 2023 from the GSD Master in Landscape Architecture I AP program. Banternghansa is currently establishing a design-research firm that concentrates on landscape infrastructure in Thailand. Prior to the GSD, Pavin worked as a Senior Landscape Designer at Landscape Collaboration in Thailand where he had over six years of experience. There, he specialized in designing landscapes for comfortable microclimates as part of the shopping mall's transition from big boxes to outdoor commercial spaces. Currently, he is deeply interested in landscape architecture's function as an infrastructure for reparation, since he believes this focus plays an essential role in reshaping the damaged socio-ecological relationships between humans and non-humans.

Interviews

ERIK WIEËRS took position as Flemish Government Architect on August 17, 2020. He is an architect and co-founder of the Antwerp-based office Collectief Noord architecten. Erik graduated in 1987 as an architect at the University of Antwerp (UA) and gained his master's in Philosophy at VUB in 1991. He is attached to the Faculty of Design Sciences at UA as associate professor. From 2004 till 2006 he was guest lecturer at TU Delft. He was a founding member of Huiswerk architecten. In 2011 he co-founded Collectief Noord architecten, established in the Seefhoek in Antwerp. Wieërs is interested in the societal dimensions of architecture. During his career he built up notable expertise in collective housing. The core mission of the Flemish Government Architect is to promote the architectural quality of the built environment. The Flemish Government Architect and his team advise public patrons in the design and realization of buildings, public space, landscape, and infrastructure. In addition, the Flemish Government Architect stimulates the development of visions and reflection, with an emphasis on interdisciplinary and cross-sectoral initiatives. The Flemish Government Architect acts as an advisor to the entire Flemish Government.

CHRIS YOUNÈS is a psychosociologist, doctor honoris causa and HDR (habilitated to supervise research) in Philosophy. She is a professor at Ecole Spéciale d'Architecture, Paris (ESA), founder and member of the GERPHAU laboratory (EA 7486, ENSA Paris-la-Villette), of the PhilAU Thematic Scientific Network (Ministry of Culture, ENSA Clermont-Ferrand), and co-founder and member of the Architectural Research European Network (ARENA), as well as a member of Europan Scientific Committee. Younès is also a member of numerous architecture and urban planning competitions, and author of several book prefaces. She regularly gives conferences in France and Europe, the Middle East, China, Canada, and South America, among others. Her work and research develop the question of inhabited spaces at the crossroads of nature and artifacts, ethics, aesthetics, and politics. She has edited more than twenty collective publications, and authored numerous articles and books, including *Architectures of Existence* (Hermann, 2018/Routledge, 2023).

MAARTEN VAN ACKER serves as full professor of Urban Design within the Faculty of Design Sciences at UA. He is recognized for his role as the spokesperson of the Research Group for Urban Development and the Design Sciences Hub at UA. With a focus on healthy urban design and robust infrastructure projects, Van Acker contributes his expertise to the master's programs in Architecture and Urban Design & Spatial Planning. He is also noted as an expert in infrastructure design and urban project development, indicating a comprehensive grasp of the multifaceted challenges in developing sustainable and livable urban environments. Additionally, he holds the position of expert in several urban design review panels and quality teams.

ALI MADANIPOUR (MArch, PhD) is professor of Urban Design, and a founding member and former director of the Global Urban Research Unit (GURU) at the School of Architecture, Planning and Landscape, Newcastle University, UK. His research has engaged with urban transformation processes and their social and environmental implications, with particular emphasis on public space, urban neighborhoods, social exclusion, and urban governance. His work has been translated into French, German, Italian, Japanese, Mandarin, Persian, and Spanish. He has been the City of Vienna's senior visiting professor at TU Wien, the Wits-Claude Leon Distinguished Scholar at the University of Witwatersrand, Johannesburg, and visiting professor at Polimi. His books in the field of urbanism include *Design of Urban Space* (Wiley, 1996), *Public and Private Spaces of the City* (Routledge, 2003), *Urban Design, Space and Society* (Palgrave Macmillan 2014), *Cities in Time* (Bloomsbury, 2017), and *Rethinking Public Space* (Elgar, 2023).

CHRISTIAN SCHMID is sociologist, geographer und urban researcher. He is professor at the Department of Architecture, ETH Zurich. His scientific work focuses on planetary urbanization, comparative urban analysis, and theories of urbanization and space. He is a founding member of the International Network for Urban Research and Action (INURA). In 2022, he published an encompassing overview of Henri Lefebvre's *Theory of the Production of Space* (Verso). He is also co-editor of two books recently published by Birkhäuser (2023): *Vocabularies for an Urbanising Planet: Theory Building through Comparison* (together with Monika Streule), and *Extended Urbanisation: Tracing Planetary Struggles* (together with Milica Topalović).

IMPRINT

An imprint of Walter de Gruyter GmbH, Berlin/Boston
Texts by kind permission of the authors.
Pictures by kind permission of the photographers/holders of the picture rights.

Editors: Aglaée Degros, Eva Schwab, Anna Bagarić, Sabine Bauer, Jennifer Fauster, Radostina Radulova-Stahmer, Mario Stefan, Alice Steiner
Overall editing: Mario Stefan, Alice Steiner
Project coordination jovis Verlag: Franziska Schüffler
Copy editing and proofreading: Cecilia Tricker
Design and setting: Liza Borovskaya-Brodskaya, Jakob Mayr
Graphics editing: Carina Fechter, Lukas Schneider, Angelika Haar
Printing and binding: Medienfabrik Graz GmbH

Bibliographic information published by the Deutsche Nationalbibliothek
The Deutsche Nationalbibliothek lists this publication in the Deutsche Nationalbibliografie; detailed bibliographic data are available on the Internet at http://dnb.d-nb.de

jovis Verlag
Genthiner Straße 13
10785 Berlin

www.jovis.de

jovis books are available worldwide in select bookstores. Please contact your nearest bookseller or visit www.jovis.de for information concerning your local distribution.

ISBN 978-3-98612-063-4 (softcover)
ISBN 978-3-98612-064-1 (e-book)

TU Graz

Institute of Urbanism Graz